I Can't Be the Only One Hearing This:
A Lifetime of Music through Eclectic Ears

By

Cedric Hendrix

Foreword by Mike Keneally

Track Listing

SIDE ONE
1 – Introduction: It Can't Be Just Me
2 – "Ground Control to Major Tom …"
3 – Radio, Radio
4 – The Record Store: Profit and Loss
5 – "Black" Music
6 – Jazz Day
7 – *Seconds Out*

SIDE TWO
8 – Entering the Court of King Crimson
9 – The Left Side of the Dial
10 – Frank
11 – Miles
12 – Nobody's Talkin' 'Bout *My* Pop Music
13 – The Alternative Approach

SIDE THREE
14 – Coffee House Sirens
15 – T.J. DuPree and the Return of the Crimson King
16 – The Unsung Heroes of J. Gravity Strings
17 – Up Close and Personal
18 – DIY via the Sheltering Sky
19 – My Guru Belew

SIDE FOUR
20 – (Near) Death by Download
21 – Ced Music: Indefinable
22 – Well of Course He Listens to *That!*
23 – It's about the Music
24 – I'm Not Really Alone
25 – Going Forward by Looking Back
26 – Bonus Track: What's Next?

Written, performed and produced by Cedric Hendrix
Recorded (written) in houses, apartments, police stations, and cars in
and around St. Louis, Missouri between November, 2014 and
November, 2016
Engineered (edited) by Edward L. Wehrenberg and Cedric Hendrix

Guest Performers

Musicians: *Adrian Belew, Vernon Reid, Rob Fetters, Deborah Holland, Mike Keneally, Julie Slick, Billy Barnett, Jimmy Griffin, David Smith, Mike Newman, Tory Z Starbuck*
Radio Personality: *Randy Raley*
Record Store Specialists: *Al Karniski, Jim Sullivan*
Web Designer: *Rob Murphree*
Journalists: *Anil Prasad, Sid Smith*
Fans: *Abbi Telander, Rhea Frankel*
Guitar Shop Owner: *Jimmy Gravity*
In-person interviews recorded in clubs, restaurants, coffee shops, guitar stores, a church, and homes throughout St. Louis, Missouri.
Skype interviews recorded from Nashville, Tennessee; Cincinnati, Ohio; San Francisco, California; San Diego, California; Vancouver, British Columbia; and Whitley Bay, England
Mastered in Sacramento, California

Thanks are due to my interview participants, whose insight made my words sound much more legitimate; my friends and family for listening to me prattle on during the writing phase; Ed Wehrenberg for taking on the challenge of editing page after page with candor and good humor; Howard Emerson, who taught me "If it's worth doing, then it's worth doing well," and "Good enough is NOT good enough!"; my "Beta" testers, for helping assure the narrative was flowing properly; the college radio stations of the 1980s who opened countless musical doors; Every cool record store employee I ever spoke to and helped me expand my musical palate; Trey Adams for being the ultimate guitar foil; my Facebook followers for their support and encouragement; and every member of every band I mention in these pages for being there and giving me something to get excited about day in and day out.

Extra special thanks are due to Brian the Surfer Guy from California. How I regret forgetting your last name. Without you, there is no discovery of King Crimson. Without that, this work does not exist. I hope you're still out there, and I hope this book finds you.

The musical experience does not end here. Follow me on Facebook, on the page entitled, **I Can't Be the Only One Hearing This***, and on my WordPress blog at* ***cirdecsongs.com***

If you've ever gone into a record store and taken a chance, this book is dedicated to you.

Photo courtesy of Mike Keneally

Foreword

By Mike Keneally

Those of us who love music, *really* love it to an obsessive degree...we who still remember quotes from album liner notes we read over 40 years ago...we who added up the lengths of songs on album sides to determine the value of our investment...we who had *very serious* discussions about the ideal drummer for Yes, or the peak periods of Miles Davis' career, or which Zappa album was "best"...we, geeks, you know. We LOVE talking about music.

If we happen to lock in with a kindred soul, we can go on for days, likely exasperating the patience of anyone within earshot who isn't on the same wavelength at that moment. If you love music to that degree, you will recognize Cedric Hendrix as a kindred soul.

Reading this book makes me feel that I'm sitting in a bar with him, digging deep into mutual obsessions. Fortunately, and unlike many loquacious bar denizens, he can really communicate. He taps readily into his formative musical experiences and translates them into something we can feel and relate to. His desire to share his love for below-the-radar musicians is a blessing, and on behalf of all such musicians, I must express my deep gratitude for his passion and energy.

While I share many of Cedric's concerns about the state of modern music, radio, and the pitfalls of instant accessibility, I feel hopeful reading his words, knowing that someone who is at the beginning of their own journey through the endless, boundless world of music will pick up this book and feel what he feels, and a new love affair with music will begin.

One of my favorite writers about music was Paul Williams, the creator of *Crawdaddy!* and the author of essential works on Dylan, Neil Young, Brian Wilson and others. What I love about Paul's writing is the lack of any pretense, the unashamed acceptance of itself as solely the expression of one person's love affair with music. I get precisely that same feeling from reading Cedric's words, although he is his own writer, beholden to no forerunner. It gladdens me to think of Cedric continuing his journey through music and sharing his findings with us.

Here is a document of several such findings. Get on board and join the journey.

(Mike Keneally is a musician known for his guitar/keyboard/vocal work with Frank Zappa, Steve Vai, and Joe Satriani. He has also enjoyed a successful solo career, and has a great band called Beer for Dolphins.)

*Mike Keneally and Cedric Hendrix at Progtoberfest 2017 in Chicago **(Photo by Kevin Pollack, provided by Cedric Hendrix)***

SIDE ONE

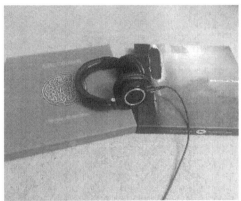

It almost always starts with quality music and a good set of headphones.

Track 1
Introduction: It Can't Be Just Me

Through it all, there has always been music.

Regardless of age, marital or family status, place of employment, or location, instrumental and vocal sounds combined to create melody and harmony have always accompanied me on the journey. I can remember becoming aware of the effect music had on me around age six. Nothing has changed as I enter middle age. But according to conventional wisdom, I have not been hearing the music meant for me.

According to modern American demographics, I should have a media shelf full of rhythm and blues, jazz (traditional and smooth), hip-hop, and perhaps a little gospel. Yet as I type these words, I have played CDs from the likes of John Wesley, Steven Wilson, Living Colour, Animals as Leaders, Joe Satriani, and David Bowie. Mine is a musical life lived against "type."

I've known for quite some time my ears receive music much differently than other people. This does not bother me. What *does* bother me is why there aren't more people like me out there. At least, that's how it seems. The music scene in general, and in America in particular, seems to have become hopelessly regimented and segregated. Music lovers straying from their assigned demographics are sometimes looked upon with befuddlement or even scorn. I actually know people afraid to admit publicly they enjoy music against type. This makes no sense to me. Why is it so odd to admit I enjoy Nine Inch Nails,

Johnny Cash, and Peter Gabriel as much as I love Stevie Wonder, Miles Davis, and B.B. King?

Europeans, Latin Americans, South Americans, and Asians seem more open-minded about music. To them, it is not a question of black or white, American or British, or any other divisive category. Rather, it seems to be a question of good or bad. Why are so many Americans unable to grasp music the same way? Why does it need to be spoon fed to them via radio's rigid formats?

Speaking of which, when and why did radio become so utterly impotent when it came to the exposure of new music? When and why did the formats become so narrow and stilted? Whatever happened to record stores? Why did they take their focus off of music and put it onto merchandising? Why has the modern music industry de-emphasized the album? Has the mp3 ruined the music industry as we know it? How did my ears manage to attune themselves to so many musical frequencies? Why is it so difficult for others to do the same?

These questions form the groundwork of this book. But the path to those answers is no short walk.

My musical education has been a perfect storm of timing and circumstance. Through no design of my own, I just found myself in the right place at the right time for the right sounds. Parents, peers, radio, television, movies, knowledgeable people, and technology crossed my path precisely when they needed to. The previous musical experience left me open to the next sound to caress my eardrums and added a new layer to what I already knew and enjoyed.

The result is a personal library of more than 30,000 songs on CD, LP, and mp3, with the knowledge of at least 10,000 more. While I haven't done the math, I am willing to bet nearly 70 percent of my music comes from outside the traditional musical norm. I didn't hear about it on the radio, I didn't read about it in a commercial trade magazine, and I didn't see it on a chart. Again, this does not bother me. I'm just floored by the small size of the club enjoying this music with me.

Does this make me a musical "expert?" Am I a voice of authority in the world of harmony and melody? I, for one, don't see it that way. I hold no degrees. I have received no certificates. I'm just a fan of music, and I've been listening for a very, very long time.

My ears have become, in my opinion, more sophisticated with age. This is far from unusual. But based on the many musical conversations I've had with peers, I'm one of the few people to embrace that maturity, constantly challenging myself to find more sophisticated sounds. It would seem most others are content to find that good beat they can dance to, and little more.

This is the story of my journey through music, and the people and artists who came with me. I can't talk about this music without talking about myself. But I also want to talk about the artists, fans, journalists, record store owners and web designers (among others) who played a pivotal role in exposing me to this world.

Make no mistake: what follows is a true labor of love. This is not a hard-hitting expose on the ills of the music industry. If that's what was expected, best you put this book down and move on.

This is a book written by a music fan for music fans. It will be positively inundated with my opinions and will annoy members of the "mainstream" music industry from time to time. I will unabashedly gush over some of the artists I mention, because I am a fan and I adore what these people do musically. Sorry, but that's the way it goes. It's my book, and those are my rules.

You have been warned.

At some point, one of you is going to read these words, and realize your favorite artist or band was never mentioned. You are going to declare this work somehow incomplete or lacking, because I didn't share your discovery. To that, I can only say this:

The discovery of music is personal and varies from person to person. So, I may not have gotten into the same music as you. You know what? That's ok. Feel free to write your own book of musical discovery. I would love to read it.

King Crimson founder Robert Fripp once said, "Music is for anyone brave enough to give it ears." I wonder why more people don't seem willing to try?

Because I refuse to be the only one hearing this.

About half of my CD collection.
The rest is in the next room.

David Bowie made his name in the '70s, but his 21st century output is nearest to my heart.

Track 2
"Ground Control to Major Tom ..."

If someone must be blamed for my musical eccentricity, I blame David Bowie.

His is the first memory I have of music from outside what would be considered my "norm." I was born in November of 1966, the first child of John and Bobbie Hendrix, natives of the state of Arkansas. We settled in St. Louis, Missouri, when I was 10 months old. As African-Americans, it should come as little surprise my parents filled the house with music from the Motown, Stax, and Philly International music labels. They were the sounds of Rhythm and Blues, soul, and funk.

I remember hearing Gladys Knight and the Pips, James Brown, Al Green, Stevie Wonder, The Jackson 5, Billy Preston, Ray Charles, the Temptations, and Aretha Franklin among countless others. Dad also had a passion for jazz, while Mom could be heard enjoying classical and gospel music from time to time.

I would not consider my parents to be musical trendsetters, or people who went out of their way to go against the grain. They listened to the radio and bought copies of what they liked. Dad's biggest musical stretches probably came from Miles Davis, as I recall seeing copies of *Bitches Brew* and *On the Corner* in his LP collection in the '70s. I also noticed he didn't play those records very often. He would later admit to simply not "getting" them and chose to stick with the acoustic Miles Davis bands he had come to know and love.

By age five, I had a small record player in my room. Mostly, I played the records accompanying picture books my parents bought me. Through a single tinny-sounding speaker, I read along with the narrator and heard the tales of *Rumpelstiltskin, Jack and the Beanstalk,* or whatever else was popular then. By '72, I had begun to find music more entertaining than storybooks, so my mother loaned me singles of the Jackson 5, the O'Jays, and Roberta Flack.

I have no idea how David Bowie got into that stack of singles. Something tells me it was Mom's doing. Unfortunately, she passed away before I could ask. Whatever the reason, it found its way onto my record player. While I didn't know it at the time, I was about to experience "Space Oddity" for the very first time.

A six-year-old may not know a lot about music, but I knew I was experiencing something very different from what I was used to. The slow opening swell of the acoustic guitar, the English accent in the vocal, the otherworldly sounds following the first verse … something very, very unusual was happening here. And I *loved* it!

I remember playing the record again and again, almost to the point of distraction. I was smitten with the sound. There was no turning away from it. Equally compelling was the B-side, "The Man Who Sold the World." I loved it as much as "Space Oddity." They remain among my favorite songs to this day.

This was not Motown, or Stax, or Philly International. This was … something else. Miles Davis often spoke of how music he loved would "get up into (his) body." Music he didn't like would be rejected in the opposite fashion. On that fateful day in 1972, David Bowie got up into my body, and opened my mind to what else was possible in the world of music. I didn't know it at the time, but a powerful seed had been planted. And I would spend my lifetime reaping its benefits.

* * *

In '73, my family moved to a section of unincorporated St. Louis County, where my dad built a house for us. I was entering first grade. I had no idea mine was a pioneer family of sorts. I would later learn we were one of only three black families in our subdivision.

My parents were not, by definition, "race people." They saw to it my younger sister and I knew who we were and where we came from, but we did not use our Blackness as a form of rebellion or a way to lash out. We were a middle-class family like those around us. We took care of our home and made friends with those who would be friends with us.

To my new white friends, I was something of a novelty. While I don't recall experiencing a great deal of overt discrimination, I do recall being protected by the Molden family whenever trouble arose. David, who was my age, and his older brother Harry saw to it that I wasn't picked on or called names by any kids with "integration issues." And they were ready to fight anybody who tried.

I remember spending a lot of time at the Molden home, playing football, basketball, baseball, and street hockey. When the weather was bad, we went into the basement (where Harry had his own room) and listened to records. I was invited to bring over my 45s, but more often than not, I was exposed to their music. It was here I was introduced to the music of the '50s. I heard the Everly Brothers, Bill Haley, and the Platters, among others. It was far from revelatory, but those sounds added another layer to a growing musical palate.

It was around this time the radio also began to have an influence on my listening habits. Mom and Dad had the local soul and R&B station, which also introduced me to the rise of Disco. Saturday nights were a cool time in my house. My parents would invite friends over, and the children were shooed away to play in my room or the basement. Meanwhile, the sounds Al Green, the Ohio Players, Kool & the Gang, and Sly and the Family Stone would reverberate through the house. I may not have been invited to the party proper, but the sounds of those parties became part of me nonetheless.

My new friends helped me to locate the local rock and Top 40 radio stations. I became heavily influenced by whatever was popular at the time. It may not have been the best music, but at least I was finding some kind of musical direction.

I had found other sources of musical amusement as well. I'm not sure which movie started it, but I soon found myself captivated by motion picture scores. The menacing music behind *Jaws* was certainly an influence. But it was most likely the music behind *Star Wars* (which became a sensation in the summer of '77, just before I turned 11) that caught and held my attention. The music for both of these films was written by John Williams and performed by the London Symphony Orchestra. I would soon discover other remarkable music in scores written by the likes of Jerry Goldsmith and Lalo Schiffrin. These composers are credited with opening my mind to instrumental music.

I found incredible music in the most unlikely of places. As a football fan, I enjoyed watching highlight reels produced by NFL Films. While watching footage of bone-crunching hits, acrobatic catches, and remarkable runs, I noticed the music in the background. It was majestic and beautifully orchestrated. Before I knew it, I was in the library looking for music from these highlight reels. Eventually, I found it. I can't count the number of hours I spent listening to those music scores, often playing with my own electric football game as I did. My game may have only featured molded plastic men on a vibrating metal board, but in my mind they were doing everything the players were doing in NFL Films presentations.

Music was all around me, and I wanted to hear every note. The radio provided my foundation as I switched from station to station. Then came the records. Even television had an influence on me, while still a few years away from the beginnings of MTV. Most kids were getting their kicks from shows like *Soul Train* and *American Bandstand*. I took things a step farther by enjoying late-night weekend shows like *The Midnight Special*, featuring the popular syndicated disc jockey Wolfman Jack, and *Don Kirshner's Rock Concert*. Thanks to these shows, I was able to see musical acts from across the musical spectrum. I've always enjoyed shows like that, which is probably what has made me such a big fan of modern day shows like the BBC's *Later with Jools Holland*. The more eclectic the music, the happier I was.

And through it all, there was David Bowie.

The Thin White Duke was finding his way onto the local soul station with singles like "Fame" and "Young Americans." I seem to remember my parents really liking those tunes for a while. I know I did. Through shows like *Rock Concert*, I was also able to see Bowie perform tunes like "Suffragette City" and "Boys Keep Swinging." The latter freaked young me out, since I was hardly ready to absorb the image of David Bowie in drag. But there he was. Before long, I was just focused on the music, yet another trait I've maintained over the years.

David Bowie's singing voice ranks among my favorite things in music. It positively drips with soul. Plus, it maintains an English quality I've always been fascinated by. No doubt, this helped plant the seeds of fascination I have for musicians from Great Britain.

I would come to obsess over many musical acts in my lifetime. Oddly, Bowie was never one of those obsessions. My friend and musician Tory Z Starbuck can cite anything about Bowie's Ziggy Stardust period, the Thin White Duke era, or any other part of Bowie's musical timeline. I can't do that, even though I can with more than a few other acts. For me, Bowie has always just been *there*. He was omnipresent. I would listen to tons of other bands and styles. But sooner or later, I would need a little Bowie.

The early '70s era would always hold a place in my heart, since that's where "Space Oddity" and "Ziggy Stardust" came from. In the mid- to late-'70s, there were the soulful sounds of "Fame" and "Young Americans." The late '70s brought more experimental sounds from albums like *Heroes* and *Lodger*. I even enjoyed the more pop-oriented material from the early '80s, like *Let's Dance*.

Bowie and I parted ways for a while after I discovered progressive rock and jazz in the mid-'80s. I stayed with those styles for quite some time, pushing Bowie aside for a while. But even that time wasn't completely Bowie-free. Looking to re-ignite a flagging career, Bowie teamed up with guitarist Reeves Gabrels and the rhythm section of Hunt and Tony Sales (drums and bass, respectively) and formed a band called Tin Machine in '88. They released two albums worth of hard-charging rock and roll that still get occasional "air time" on my CD player. The music was much different than the experimental sounds Bowie had been putting into his music before then. It was a lot of fun to hear him sing in a more straightforward style. I wish I could have seen that band live.

In '95, Bowie managed to recapture my attention in a big way. That year, he released *Outside*, a concept album produced by Brian Eno. The two collaborated successfully in the past, and this record struck me as having a great deal of potential. While there were some people who didn't like it, I thought the album was incredible. "Hearts Filthy Lesson" was the high point for me, with its stark, stabbing, percussion-fueled soundscape. The rest of the album followed suit. There can be no doubting it: *Outside* made me a born-again Bowie fan.

I was even more excited by his '97 release called *Earthling*. I developed a liking of the DJ-inspired "drum and bass" style, featuring hyperkinetic electronic beats, samples, and deep bass grooves. The sound was all the rage in nightclubs, but that was one place I had no desire to be. I believed such a sonic backdrop would make for an interesting place to add some guitar pyrotechnics. Bowie and I were on the same wavelength, as he hired Reeves Gabrels to provide the six-string fireworks to his electronic rhythms. Not only were the guitar parts cool, but Bowie managed to layer melody and harmony on top of rhythms that seemed too frantic to be able to support them. "Little Wonder" and "I'm Afraid of Americans" are the album's highlights for me.

I never really thought much one way or the other for Bowie's multiple personalities and image makeovers. From the earliest days of my music fandom, anything on my stereo had to pass the Headphone Test: If I could enjoy the music in a dark room while wearing headphones and doing nothing else, then the music was worthy of my time. Perhaps this is why I enjoy the music Bowie made since the turn of the century most. He discarded the alter egos and just *sang*. That decision paid huge dividends.

The definitive David Bowie live album, taken from his 2003 tour.

Heathen, released in 2002, is a positively stunning album. "Sunday," the album's opener, ranks among my favorite songs from any artist, any time, ever. It starts with an electronic loop created by guitarist David Torn. Almost immediately, Bowie's soulful voice lands on top of the mix, with the singer baring the depths of his soul. The song builds and builds to a crashing crescendo, with Bowie's rising voice augmented with a bass guitar and drum groove until the song fades out. Not since "Space Oddity" have I ever been so deeply moved by Bowie's voice. A music critic described *Heathen* as, "21st Century Thin

White Duke." I just know it is remarkable music from a remarkable musician.

Bowie's subsequent releases, *Reality* and *The Next Day*, also stand up nicely. But as time went on, the artist became more and more reclusive. It was said that Bowie was finished with touring. I thought that a shame, particularly considering how incredible his live DVD, *A Reality Tour*, released in '03, was. But if he *was* finished, he left an incredible legacy.

***

As I've said, I've never really obsessed over David Bowie's musical output. Yet he has a knack for being a primary influence in my music listening. This is particularly true where his taste in guitar players is concerned. However unwittingly (from my point of view), Bowie has managed to employ four of my favorite guitarists.

The most recent is Reeves Gabrels. From the first notes I heard him play with Tin Machine, I knew I was hearing an axe-slinger with a completely different mindset from the guitar players I had been enjoying. Gabrels eschews traditional blues-based rock guitar in favor of dive-bombs, shrieks, and extended wails. He was even known to use a vibrator to help achieve his single-note sustains! (1) Gabrels solo album output is wildly eclectic, incorporating traditional western, middle-eastern, and other tones. I have to be in the right mindset to listen to him. But once I'm there, the sound is plenty exciting.

For his '83 release *Let's Dance*, Bowie hired a young Texan named Stevie Ray Vaughan to handle his guitar needs. There can be no mistaking the bluesy power of Vaughan's sound, which steals the show on many of the album's tracks, particularly the title track and "China Girl." Bowie invited Vaughan to handle the guitar duties on the album's subsequent world tour. But Vaughan turned him down, opting to return home and focus on his own career with his band, Double Trouble. The rest, as they say, is history. Vaughan's decision would lead to a new American blues renaissance, breathing new life into an art form considered long dead. Within a couple of years, I would be introduced to the Vaughan's music, and would become smitten (and yes, obsessed) with his guitar playing. While I don't blame Vaughan for his choice, I wonder what he would have done within the confines of Bowie's band.

In 1977, Bowie released *Heroes* and *Low*, both featuring the guitar of Robert Fripp. I was more than familiar with "Heroes," which had earned a prominent spot on FM radio at the time of its release. However, I didn't know Robert Fripp from a hole in the ground. All of that would change eight years later, when a surfer from California named Brian would introduce me to the band that changed the way I viewed music forever. That band was King Crimson. While Bowie was the seed of my musical eclecticism, Crimson was the root branching out in multiple directions and introducing me to a plethora of musicians and styles, reaching across genres as diverse as classical, world beat, and jazz. Without King Crimson, I am never inspired to write a book about my musical adventures.

When Fripp left Bowie's side in '78, the singer needed a guitarist to replace him for an upcoming world tour. Bowie found him while watching Frank Zappa perform in Germany. The guitarist's name was Adrian Belew. Not only did Belew establish himself as a "go-to" musician while playing for Bowie, Belew's connection to Bowie and Brian Eno led him (by way of Talking Heads) to Robert Fripp and King Crimson! Belew and Fripp connected in '80, leading to a three-decade plus musical partnership ranking among the most important in my collection.

If not for an accidental discovery at age six, my musical world might be very, very different. To say the least, I believe it would be a lot less adventurous. The Chinese philosopher Lao Tzu once said a journey of a thousand miles begins with a single step. David Bowie provided the first step on my musical journey.

It's safe to say I owe him one.

***

The early morning hours of January 11, 2016, unfolded like any other when I'm scheduled to work at 6:50 a.m. I rose at 5:30, made my way through my early morning routine, and checked my iPad for the day's headlines, just in case something happened overnight. It turned out something *had* happened.

David Bowie died.

I've been duped by misleading headlines before. The social media era has made such things a cottage industry. So, I was instantly skeptical. But the headline I read came from the New York *Times*. I saw the same headline come from the Associated Press, CNN, and my local paper, the St. Louis *Post-Dispatch*. There may be something to this after all, I thought. I could feel my heart sinking.

I made my way to Facebook, where I follow more than a few musicians. The outpouring of grief and personal tributes flowed like water. This was really happening. One of my earliest musical influences was really gone. I had become "cyber-buddies" with Julie Slick, who plays bass in Adrian Belew's Power Trio. Adrian and David were friends, so if anyone could cut through it all, Julie could by way of Ade. I sent a brief note, expressing my sadness and hoping I would learn it was an elaborate hoax. Instead, I received a reply consisting of a crying emoji and a single sentence: "I'm still in shock." That sealed it.

Three days before, I picked up Bowie's latest release, *Blackstar*. It was nothing short of remarkable. I would learn Bowie recorded the album not long after being diagnosed with terminal cancer. In fact, the term "blackstar" originated from the way cancerous tumors look on a PET scan. Bowie *knew* he was going to die. Evidence lay within the lyrics of songs like the title track and "Lazarus." Bowie wasn't just making a record. He was saying goodbye.

David Bowie wasn't an artist I followed religiously. I couldn't tell you about his movements from one day to the next. I couldn't tell you the last time he came to St. Louis to perform. Still, I took comfort in knowing every few years, a new record would come forth, and I would experience the joy of "re-discovering" Bowie's music. I will never enjoy that experience again.

I don't cry often, but tears streamed down my face that day.

(1)   Once I decided that my guitar playing needed some extended single notes, I opted for the commercially available "e-bow." The presence of that device is much easier to explain to one's significant other.

Track 3
Radio, Radio ...

"Radio is a sound salvation
Radio is cleaning up the nation
They say you better listen to the voice of reason
But they don't give you any choice
'cause they think that it's treason
So you had better do as you are told
You better listen to the radio"
Elvis Costello, "Radio Radio" (a)

There was a time when I couldn't live without the radio. It was the center of my universe.

I was a radio geek from an early age. I listened to the morning talk shows on news radio. I enjoyed the old morning variety shows, the classified ads read by people looking to buy and trade all sorts of things, and my day wasn't complete without either a ball game or some form of Radio Theater in the evening. And in between, there was music. There was a *lot* of music.

It seemed like there was always a radio on somewhere in my house. I remember having a small, portable AM-FM radio atop my chest of drawers. This was just before the portable cassette decks (aka "boom boxes") that dominated the '80s landscape. I can still hear the sound of static as I changed from one station to the next, wandering from format to format without a care in the world. If I was lucky, I could take my musical exploration to the living room, where Mom and Dad's stereo component set was stationed. Not only could I hear the latest happenings in music, I could hear them through the wonder that was 12 by 18-inch stereo speakers. I didn't know a woofer from a tweeter, but I did know the music sounded a lot better here than it did in my room. At bedtime, things got more elemental, as I dozed off to the voices carried on the AM transistor radio tucked under my pillow, since I was supposed to be asleep. I don't know how many 9-volt batteries I drained listening to "Radio Mystery Theater," the St. Louis Blues, or the St. Louis Cardinals on KMOX 1120, which boasted one of the strongest signals in the Midwest. So powerful was that station's signal, I could listen to Jack Buck and Mike Shannon call Cardinals games from my grandmother's bedroom in Fort Smith, Arkansas, a good 400 miles from Busch Stadium.

My weekend wasn't complete until I heard Casey Kasem's nationally syndicated radio show, *American Top 40*. I couldn't possibly be expected to get through the '70s without knowing what was at the top of the Billboard magazine Pop chart, even if it was something like Debbie Boone's "You Light Up My Life." Yeah … the radio pretty much led me through my existence. At the time, this wasn't necessarily a bad thing. But there was a change blowing in the wind. The breeze just hadn't reached me yet.

But for the glorious period that ran – for me – through the late '70s and early '80s, radio could do almost no wrong. I was warmly swaddled in its embrace, heeding the words of Elvis Costello, and doing what the music box told me to do. I wondered if I was the only person who felt that way. As it turns out, I wasn't. "Radio was *hugely* important to me!" exclaimed singer/songwriter Deborah Holland. "I was addicted to AM Top 40. I would hear songs I liked, and then go buy the 45s."

For multi-instrumentalist/composer/singer Tory Z Starbuck – a man who clearly marches to the beat of his own drummer -- the effect was even more profound. "Radio had a VERY important effect on me with music the same way PBS television did in that they both helped me to discover the strange stuff that makes me the way I am," he said. "And I was very selective about these things."

For others, the impact was a bit subtler. "Early on, (radio) forced me to listen to stuff I never would have otherwise, because at home, all I heard was vinyl," said singer/songwriter Rob Fetters. "I heard the light jazz and classical records my parents listened to, and the Beatles, Beach Boys, and Barbara Streisand records my older sisters had." But the radio pushed his mind in a different direction. "I remember hearing a song about a purple people eater that had me pretty worried about the world when I was four or five years old," Fetters reflected with a chuckle.

"Radio was hugely influential for me, and still such a memorable part of my childhood," said singer/songwriter Mike Keneally. "I can still remember standing in my bedroom at age six, looking at the glowing dial of my radio at 2 a.m., while the ending of 'My Green Tambourine' (a 1967 song by the Lemon Pipers) churned on. AM radio provided my life with a varied, wonderful soundtrack until 1971, when I discovered FM radio for the first time, and was introduced to Emerson, Lake & Palmer and King Crimson for (a full album side at a time!)."

As it happens, a former King Crimson member was also influenced early on by the airwaves. "As a child, radio had a big impact on me. I loved all kinds of songs and learned to emulate a variety of singers," said Adrian Belew. "I'm sure it inspired my interest in being musical, but I was too young to know what to do about it."

For each of us, radio was the key opening the door to a vast world of musical possibility. Today's formats make the musical world resemble an interstate highway divided by solid lines. Those lines are put in place to ensure traffic remains in that particular section of the road. Those lines were dotted in the '70s, and the musical acts were free to cross over those lines whenever they saw fit.

I was certain I was part of the best days of radio. As it turns out, I had already missed it.

"I grew up in the Golden Age of Radio, as far as I'm concerned," said Randy Raley, who was a disc jockey from 1976 to 2009, where he achieved his greatest notoriety as the top-rated afternoon jock at KSHE-FM in St. Louis, a legendary classic rock station. "It ran from the time I was in the 8th grade, in 1968, until I graduated from high school in '74. I could turn on the radio and hear Paul Mauriat doing 'Love is Blue,' followed by the Temptations 'Ball of Confusion,' followed by Sly and the Family Stone, then James Taylor, followed by Three Dog Night, the Beatles, Harold Melvin and the Blue Notes, the O'Jays, the Eagles, and Sammy Davis Jr. singing 'Candy Man.' It was a different time."

Disc Jockey Randy Raley

Like me, Raley grew up in a world inundated with music. His earliest memories are of his mother singing to him at age four or five, when he was growing up on a farm in southern Missouri. In addition to his mother, the radio had a profound effect on the future DJ. His biggest early influence was an AM radio station originating in Little Rock, Arkansas. "It was a 50,000-watt AM station that played Top 40 during the day," he said. "But at night, it switched over to a program called *Bleeker Street*. It was there, on a stormy night, with the airwaves cracking through the Phillips AM radio I had sitting on my window sill, that I heard (King Crimson's) 'Epitaph' for the first time. It scared the bejesus out of me, man! What a monstrosity of a song!" What sounded like criticism was actually high praise, as Raley had turned a corner and found his way down a new musical road. "I ordered *In the Court of the Crimson King* (from a small department store in town), and got it two weeks later. Just like that, I was a (guitarist) Robert Fripp fan forever. I was a (vocalist and bassist) Greg Lake fan forever." King Crimson opened Raley's mind to similar music from the likes of bands like Ten Years After, Savoy Brown, and Yes. In the mid '80s, I would undergo a very similar transformation.

While his early years were rural, his world would expand even more during his teenage years, when he relocated to the Quad Cities, eventually going to high school in East Moline, Illinois. It was quite the culture shock to a young man who stood out because of his southern accent. "I went to a high school that was 17 percent Latino, and 22 percent black," Raley said with a laugh. "You learned to get along (with everyone), because you got your ass kicked every day."

Raley found his inroad to acceptance by way of music. "On Fridays, if you got your work done, our teacher would let you bring records in to play for the rest of the class," he said. "You could play two songs, and I would do my best to play things that would impress people." His efforts paid off, as he soon made friends in both the Hispanic and African-American communities. They were quick to share their music with an impressionable Raley, who soaked it up like a sponge. "From my Latino brothers, I learned about Santana and El Chicano," said Raley. "My black brothers taught me so much about funk and soul."

His musical mind would be expanded even further on the weekends, when he and his new friends took things to the next level. "A great way to find new music was to go to a 'head' shop on Saturday afternoons," Raley reminisced. "We would get high and listen to music from the Mahavishnu Orchestra, Billy

Cobham, Gong, and Steve Hillage. It was such a cacophony of music!" The memory brings a huge smile to his face.

But there was another constant that aided in Raley's musical development, and that was the radio. And in those days, a great deal of the music he was discovering was played on the same radio stations, with little thought to a primary target audience. "Radio back then provided the word of mouth it took for great albums to find their way through our neighborhoods," he said. "But then, in the mid '70s, money came into it."

I'm not sure what's sadder: the fact Raley made that statement; or the fact it didn't surprise me in the least. Raley saw the look of recognition in my face. His expression became a bit grimmer. "You had non-radio guys running radio companies," he said. "When I first got into (listening to) radio, there was a lot more freedom. When I first started (working) in radio, there was a lot less freedom. It ceased to be an art form, and turned into a business. The thing about radio, and what it morphed into the in the mid-'70s, is that there was a lot less experimentation because there was a lot more research being done by consultants. They were like the sabermetrics guys in baseball."

So it would seem "Moneyball" was being played in radio long before the concept was brought to my favorite sport. But rather than look for players who frequently got on base, radio consultants were looking for the songs they could play frequently.

"(Consultants) wanted to make sure we played the exact best song that appealed to the most people," Raley said. "As radio moved from AM to FM, the stations found a way to make a lot of money. How did they do it? By playing the hits!"

People like me tend to think of KSHE-FM as the place to go for cutting edge music when we were growing up, particularly in the '80s. But that wasn't quite true. The cutting-edge station was becoming continuously more mainstream right under our very noses. "KSHE was a cool and hip station in the early '80s," Raley said. "Sometimes, it was too cool and hip for its own good! The station did well, but it was still coming in fifth or sixth in the ratings. Stations like KSLQ and KWK did better, because they played the hits." I listened to all of those radio stations, and I knew Raley was right. In fact, I remember turning away from those stations at times, because I was tired of hearing the same song over and over again!

"When Emmis Communications bought KSHE (in the mid-'80s), the station went from playing Emerson, Lake &

Palmer's 'Fanfare for the Common Man' to Phil Collins's 'Sussudio,'" Raley lamented. "And KSHE's ratings went through the roof! By the time I joined KSHE in '85 from KY102 in Kansas City, KSHE's entire dynamic had changed. They were no longer playing bands like Mama's Pride, the J. Geils Band, and longer cuts from the Allman Brothers. Instead, they were playing Steve Winwood and ZZ Top. They had gone from being underground to being the mainstream."

I've always known I don't listen to music the same way most people do. I didn't realize how different, though, until Raley explained how radio was actually designed. "Radio is for the *masses*, not the musicologists," he told me. "The consultants knew people listened to the radio while they were driving to work, on their way home, and a little at night. It usually came out to about 90 minutes a day, tops. People don't get to hear their favorite songs that often in that short a period of time, so those songs get played over and over to remind them of those favorites."

And just like that, a very tarnished penny dropped.

When I'm on patrol, I listen to the radio for five to seven hours a day. And yes, I would be the first one to complain about hearing the same songs over and over again. As it turns out, I was never meant to hear those songs so frequently, because I should have turned the radio off hours before!

Raley and other disc jockeys also felt the pain of repetition, but the consultants and station managers were firm about the lack of musical exploration from the on-air personalities. "We were told, 'Look, we spent a lot of money researching these songs,'" Raley said. "'This is NOT your thousand-watt record player! *Nobody* gives a shit *what* you think!' KSHE became a monster because no matter what time it was, you were either hearing something you liked or something you knew. And in between, you heard a guy or gal (personality) you liked or knew."

Of course, there were moments here and there when the program managers would allow their jocks to explore. But even then, they weren't to stray very far from the station's format. When Raley would play KSHE's "Daily Dose of Led Zeppelin" at 5 p.m. every day, he knew there were certain songs within the band's catalog that were off limits. "Even with that freedom, I knew better than to play the 26-minute drum solo from 'Moby Dick,'" Raley said with a laugh. Battles in radio, it seemed, had to be picked carefully.

Keneally, whose pop music deserves – but has never received – mass appeal, is even more pragmatic about his lack of airplay. "A lot of good music has failed to reach multiple ears because there wasn't a working mechanism that even had a chance of placing it in front of those ears," he said. "Radio was unlikely to ever seek out music that didn't slot comfortably with things that were already on the playlist. It was happy to accept acts that were promoted aggressively by major labels and sounded somewhat similar to things they'd already played."

Something you liked, or something you knew. The jock and the musician were very much on the same page, even if they were reading the book from different angles. Jeez.

I wanted to believe there was room on radio for artists like Keneally, Belew, and XTC, who have created some of my favorite pop music since the '80s. Keneally shot that notion down almost as quickly as I verbalized it. "XTC was aggressively and unapologetically smart, with a LOT of lyrics that required some concentration to deal with, and delivered in a somewhat hectoring, barking tone, which probably proved annoying for a large portion of listeners who prefer not to be challenged," he said. "Adrian has been a part of so many fantastic projects, but he has never benefitted in his solo work from a support system that would make it impossible for mainstream media to resist him. That's my story as well."

All of this information was bad. But as time went on, things were only going to get worse.

***

In 1996, President Bill Clinton signed the Telecommunications Act, which replaced the last version of the act, signed in '34. To the uninitiated, the bill didn't amount to much, other than including the fledgling Internet into the realm of broadcasting, along with radio and television. But Title 3 of the act proved devastating to the owners of smaller media companies, as major communications conglomerates were now allowed to compete in any market against anyone. This may not sound like a big deal, but it was the first step in the quick sprint that became making most radio stations sound the same, regardless of where they were located.

Media companies like Clear Channel and Emmis Communications began buying up smaller stations left and right. Once that was done, the consultants moved in and determined which 50 or so songs should get the most air time on any given station. Individual radio stations began to lose their personalities, as the music setting them apart began to disappear, and similar playlists cropped up. Before long, it became more and more difficult to tell one radio station from another.

I was brought back to commercial radio by KPNT (the Point), located at 105.7 on the FM dial. The station embraced the "alternative" musical movement, which included grunge, alt-pop, new wave, industrial, and a little world music as well. When the station first aired, it was nothing to spend a day hearing songs by Pearl Jam, Ned's Atomic Dustbin, Suzanne Vega, Nine Inch Nails, and Peter Gabriel. There was so much music available, it was nearly impossible to repeat songs *ad nauseum*. I was in hog heaven. But over time, things began to change.

I'm not even sure I noticed at first. But over time, a lot of the artists I was digging -- like Toad the Wet Sprocket, Liz Phair, Fishbone, and Midnight Oil – were vanishing from the airwaves. While I appreciated the likes of Nirvana, Pearl Jam, Alice in Chains, and Soundgarden, I realized I was not just hearing those core bands with increasing regularity, but most of the other bands the Point was playing sounded a lot like those bands. It was like driving a race car, but never taking it out of second gear. Once again, consultants and specialists found a way to make my music listening experience intolerable. And they weren't finished yet.

"(The conglomerates) began to take the localness out of the radio stations," Raley said with a sigh. "Clear Channel figured out a way – called NexGen – to sync up radio personalities to stations all over the country." Here's how it worked: Raley was hired to broadcast not only his show, but to track his voice onto other radio stations around the country. In other words, a St. Louis-based disc jockey would be broadcasting the exact same program during the same time slot in Seattle. The only change would be in the announcements geared toward a specific community. This was in addition to radio stations relying on nationally syndicated shows like Bob & Tom and Howard Stern in the mornings, meaning there was no-one local for listeners to connect to on a daily basis.

Raley was well paid for his efforts, but even he began to get bad vibes about what he was doing. He figured it was only a matter of time before he was exposed. "I didn't know anything about those other towns," he said. "Have you ever seen the street names in Seattle? They're all long, old Indian names! You had to figure, one mispronunciation, and everyone would know I wasn't from around there." But NexGen became the wave of the future, and hundreds of disc jockeys around the country found themselves out of a job, because their shift was now being covered by a radio personality based hundreds of miles away.

"Radio is half about the music, and half about what goes on between the songs," Raley continued. "I never wanted to be bigger than the music. I wanted to be a part of the music. To me, it was 'say what you gotta say, and then shut the hell up.' Let the music do the talking instead." These changes signaled the beginning of the end of Raley's disc jockey career.

The internet era ushered in a new way of listening to music, via digital playlists and mp3 players like the iPod. To Raley's dismay, radio stations chose not to fight these changes. Instead, they rolled over and let themselves be dominated by the Next Big Thing. "Radio just up and decided not to compete," Raley said with disgust. "I remember hearing a consultant say, 'We're not going to compete with iPods, because we are entertainers, and iPods are machines!' But instead, the radio stations just gutted their marketing departments, and cut everything else to the bone. We were no longer the conduit of information we could've been. People were finding other avenues for that."

In 2000, Raley found himself back in Kansas City, where he once again hosted a morning show, which consisted mostly of him playing music. The time slot had been rated 13th in the region among 25-54 year olds before Raley took over, and his efforts managed to get it as high as fifth. He and his crew maintained a rating between fifth and seventh, and everything seemed to be headed in the right direction. But as it happens in so many other lines of work, a new general manager took over the station. That general manager wanted to bring in his own people. That meant some established people had to go. "I remember having a meeting with the new GM on a Tuesday," Raley said, doing his best to mask the bitterness. "I remember him saying how much he loved the show, how things were really coming together. And that Friday, we were fired! I was told they were 'going in a different direction.' I said, 'I thought you were happy with the way things were.' But the truth is, he wanted to bring in his own people. So, that new direction didn't include me."

Raley soon found himself on the sales end of the radio business, where he made the most out of a new opportunity. He also found his way to the internet airwaves via a web site called

Planet Radio. Since then, Raley has gradually removed himself from disc jockey-oriented work. But he has done so without regret. "I tell people all the time, good Lord, don't cry for me. I've had a wonderful life," he told me with a smile. He's even working on a book on his adventures in radio. I, for one, can't wait to read it.

***

For me, radio has gone down a path of darkness and despair that seems unrecoverable. Yet it would seem the musicians I admire have accepted this fate and are taking it all in stride. Asked what it would take to bring radio back to its past glory, Deborah Holland would only say, "That ship sailed long ago." Mike Keneally doesn't seem to think radio airplay would be the be-all, end-all I thought it might be. "There are zero guarantees that (his music) would have found favor with a mass audience, no matter how 'good' the music was," he said. "People respond to a sound, it either resonates with them or it doesn't. And in the majority of those cases, that resonance is a result of the sound reminding the listener of something they heard before, which provides them with familiarity, and therefore comfort."

For sonic reasons, Keneally doesn't even listen to the radio any more. "I noticed about ten years ago that radio seemed to be adding increasing amounts of compression to make their signal pop more, and it was making the sound of the music harsh and unlistenable to me," he said. "I still listen to CDs in the car. That's how far behind the times I am!"

Adrian Belew takes it one step further, eliminating what I call "passive listening" altogether, out of fear of mimicking what he hears when he works on his own music. "In my twenties, records took the place of radio," he told me. "And by my thirties – when I was finally making my own records – I stopped listening to the radio entirely."

The ever-affable Rob Fetters has also accepted his non-commercial radio fate. "Public and college radio stations have always been the avenue for me and my ilk," he said. "Certain large urban areas sometimes support commercial stations that are more open to progressive/diverse playlists." And while some of the artists achieving commercial fame may not be his cup of tea, Fetters has come to grips with it. "I don't begrudge anyone success in the music world," he said. "People have been complaining about the cookie cutter approach to pop music from the beginning of rock and roll."

Radio has brought forth wondrous things over the years, but its time as a major musical influence has essentially come to an end. The internet offers up a multitude of choices, making it possible for anyone to hear just about anything at the click of a mouse. The glory days of being exposed to what's new and exciting in the world of music via radio are pretty much an exercise in nostalgia. I can only imagine what could or would have happened had the powers-that-be in radio decided to maintain equal footing with the internet. I also wonder what might have happened had the Clear Channels of the world not taken over the airwaves, and radio stations had been allowed to maintain their individuality. But this seems to be little more than an exercise in mental futility. "I'm sorry to see what has happened to commercial radio," Randy Raley told me with finality. "But they brought it on themselves."

Perhaps Mike Keneally summed it up best. "If radio had, early on, decided to champion unusual and provocative entertainment as a matter of course, the public's tastes would have been changed," he said. "More parents would have passed on their unconventional musical tastes to their children, and everything would be different now.

"Maybe."

Inside my new home away from home,
Planet Score Records.

Track 4
The Record Store: Profit and Loss

The revelation hit me during one of my regular chats with Jim Sullivan, a friend of mine and employee of F.Y.E. (For Your Entertainment) Music and Movies, located at 3801 Hampton in south St. Louis. Having a record store on my patrol beat certainly has its advantages, and I usually found myself sharing a chat and a laugh or three with Jim at least a couple of times a week, usually while he was stocking the store's browser bins.

While I like the people who work there, F.Y.E. is not exactly the perfect place for an obscure music junkie. Still, there was an above average chance I could score something from the "edgier" side of the charts, provided I got there early enough. My friends were willing to special order an item for me (if possible) or hold something special behind the counter until I had the cash to pay for it. So why not spend a hard-earned buck or two there?

Every Tuesday, the new CD releases are placed on a multi-tiered shelf near the store's front, next to the cash registers. There's rarely anything I want on these shelves (which were normally packed with Billboard Top 40 fodder), but I always look anyway. One particular Tuesday, I looked for the new releases, only to discover the shelf wasn't in its usual place. New movie releases were there, but the music was gone. I took my befuddlement to Jim, who was dutifully putting his products in their proper place elsewhere in the store. "What, no new releases this week?" I asked. "That seems odd."

"Oh, they're out there," he replied, his face changing slightly from its usually jovial self. "We moved them back a bit to the racks next to the other CDs. He pointed some six or seven feet behind where the new release rack used to be. There before me sat the collection of new releases for the week. "We're reconfiguring the store soon and moving different product out front."

I was befuddled. "Different product?" I asked. "Like what?"

Jim's face darkened more as he walked past me and picked up a pair of socks festooned with one of Marvel Comics "Avengers" characters on them. "Stuff like this," Jim said. "We're putting more emphasis on things like this."

I think Jim was expecting me to blow my stack. I think I was anticipating it, too. But I couldn't do it. Instead, I simply looked around. Jim's news was, in the grand scheme, far from shocking. The store where I went for music was littered with DVDs, stereo accessories, posters, t-shirts, and more movie tie-in toys and souvenirs than I could count. The shelves actually storing music took up far less space than I realized.

What was the revelation? Record stores aren't what they used to be.

* * *

It would have been impossible to learn about the most of the artists in my collection without the aid of the amazing people I met in record stores. Walking into these shops was like going to a really cool school, where I was an eager student and the employees were the experienced professors.

My first trips to the record store were taken with my dad, starting around 1977. Dad had a vast appetite for music, which caused him to find his way to a shop at least twice a month. Taking those trips with him became one of the ways we bonded, even if our musical choices were vastly different.

Most times, we found ourselves at Peaches Records and Tapes, a nationwide chain store. While there were at least three stores in the St. Louis area, ours was located at the intersection of West Florissant and Chambers in north St. Louis County, some twenty minutes from where we lived. The store was massive (at least in the eyes of an 11-year-old), with browser bins full of records from all genres. Perhaps that was the biggest difference between records stores back then and now: record stores back then were dedicated first and foremost to the sale of … wait for it … *music*. There was a very small section where one could buy a t-shirt, a poster, or perhaps a button representing their favorite bands.

Invariably, Dad would head off to the R&B and jazz sections, while my focus was on rock. There never seemed to be enough time to explore everything I wanted to. It would also take me forever to get to where I was trying to go, as I was almost always distracted by the cover art of a record by a band I knew little or nothing about. Nevertheless, I had to know what the album was all about. Sooner or later, I would wind up where I intended. A trip to the record store was about the journey, not the destination.

At some point, I would notice one of the store's employees wandering close by. They would be casually and unobtrusively monitoring my choices. I would come to find I was being monitored in a good way, for the records I picked would get me placed in the hands of one of the store's specialists. While smaller record stores might have only one or two people working there (both of whom had extensive knowledge of the store's inventory), Peaches – and large stores like it – would have seven or eight people working, each with intimate knowledge of a certain musical style.

My first employee encounter was with Rock Guy. He could tell me just about anything about what was in the AOR section. Rock guy was usually white, between eighteen and twenty-five, wore his hair a little longer, and sported a concert t-shirt from Led Zeppelin, the Who, or one of the other major arena acts of the time. His jeans always had a "bell" bottom, and they were usually accented with a pair of hiking boots. In junior high school, I would learn his type was usually referred to as a "burnout." He could be located in the school's smoking area between classes. No matter, Rock Guy was a great deal of help when it came time to choose between Styx and REO Speedwagon.

Meanwhile, Dad would find himself in deep conversation with Soul Brother. This dude was almost always black, in his twenties or thirties, and sporting a freshly blown-out

Afro. A dashiki was not necessary, but it was sometimes worn. Soul Brother could tell you anything you wanted to know about Stevie Wonder, Marvin Gaye, Al Green, or anything on Motown, Stax, or the Philly International labels. I remember watching Soul Brother and Dad have more than a few animated conversations. These almost always left Dad in a good mood, which worked out nicely for me, because my limited budget would suddenly go into surplus. *I can have two albums today, instead of one? Thanks, Dad!*

Dad would also spend a great deal of time with the Jazz Man. He was usually a little older, say in his late twenties or early thirties. Jazz still had a beatnik vibe to it in the '70s, so Jazz Man might sport a beret or a pork pie hat. He most certainly had some kind of beard. Since jazz musicians tended to dress up for gigs, Jazz Man might wear something close to a suit. At the minimum, his pants would come with some form of collared shirt, with the tips of those collars seeming to touch his shoulder blades. Jazz Guy could walk you through the various periods of Miles Davis, talk at length about John Coltrane, or introduce you to some of the fusion acts like Return to Forever or the Mahavishnu Orchestra. He also had a thing for some of the upcoming young guns, like David Sanborn. Jazz Guy always seemed to make Dad more introspective about his musical choices. Soon, he would have the same effect on me.

Dad and I had little use for Pop Girl, who spent most of her late teen to early twenties time trying to get the guys to play the Top 40 songs she loved. She wore whatever it was that trendy teenagers wore in the late '70s and early '80s. And she always seemed to be chewing gum. And I mean *always*. My little sister and Pop Girl would become fast friends once she started making trips to the record store with Dad and me.

On the very rare occasions that Mom would come with us, she always sought out Professor Classical. He had the receding hairline, beard, and tweed jacket you came to expect. He and his ascots spent most of their time in a section of the store that was closed off from everything else. After all, one could not sully the sounds of Beethoven, Bach, and Mozart with the musical swill being played outside the Professor's doors. I don't think I made more than two trips into this section. I could talk about liking Bach and Wagner all I wanted, but Professor Classical didn't want any teenagers anywhere near his product, period.

Punk Guy stuck earnestly to his section; seeming to give out suggestions with the speed and intensity of the music he loved. He looked a lot like Rock Guy, except for the "Mohawk" haircuts, studded bracelets, and tattoos. Metal Dude was the grungier version of Rock Guy. He also smelled more of marijuana. I rarely crossed paths with these guys, even though they tended to be the coolest clerks in the store.

I did cross paths and get along with New Wave Man. He looked like a perfect impression of Devo, Gary Newman, or Wendy O. Williams. His hair was not only spiked, but it was decorated in more colors than my young teenage mind could comprehend. Once in a while, he was a she. I won't lie: New Wave Gal could be more than a little hot to my newly hormonal mind. It must have been the spandex or the ultra-tight blue jeans she wore.

Eventually, my best friend in the record store would eventually become Prog Guy. He was usually small in stature, in his twenties, and wore a pair of bookish glasses, making him seem even more intelligent than he already was. His jeans were neatly pressed, and his t-shirts declared love for Frank Zappa, Emerson, Lake and Palmer, or King Crimson. To get Prog Guy's attention, you had to be able to pry him away from the philosophy book he was reading. You also had to ask him the right question. You were one stupid remark from being shipped off to Rock Guy. But if his attention could be gained and maintained, the customer was in for a musical adventure.

I got my musical Bachelors Degree from Rock Guy and Soul Brother. But my post-graduate certificates came from Prog Guy and Jazz Man.

***

Peaches Records was my primary choice when it came time to go to the record store. As time wore on, other shops got my attention. My other favorite chain store was Streetside Records. Between the early '80s and the turn of the century, I spent more than a little time in three different Streetside Records stores, each containing a version of the clerks I knew.

Now and then, I found myself in specialty stores. Each of these places was relatively small, and usually occupied by only the owner and one or two employees. These cats seem to have a much larger musical vocabulary, and couldn't wait to share it with you.

Sometimes, Dad and I made our way to Joe's Music (specializing in soul and jazz), or Euclid Records. But the best musical treat came about four times a year. That's when Dad and I would head to the University City Loop (a haven for the '70s and '80s equivalent of the hipster) and Vintage Vinyl, the hippest record shop in St. Louis.

To my pre-teen senses, Vintage Vinyl was everything Peaches was, only cooler. The corporate sheen was absent from the moment I walked in, and the store's vibe became nearly omnipresent. The entire store didn't seem much larger than the family room and kitchen at my house, combined. And nearly every square inch was covered with LPs. "The original store had its own funky little vibe," Jim told me. "The first time I went there, I went with friends. They told me how this place was so frickin' *cool*! From the time you walked in, you were tripping over records, because the place was so small and there weren't that many bins."

Even the music pumping through the store's speakers was hip. The chain record stores churned out the latest Top 40 or AOR nuggets for immediate consumption, but Vintage Vinyl went out of its way to play records from off the beaten path. It was nothing to hear punk, jazz, vintage soul, and metal played back-to-back, depending on who was in charge of the record player. "I distinctly remember hearing the Clash the first time I walked in," Jim said. All of the standard characters worked at this store, as well. But their personalities seemed a bit more ... intensified.

It was here I learned about the deeper sides of my favorite music and musicians. I remember bringing a Genesis import single (I believe it was "Spot the Pigeon," which was only released in Europe) to the checkout counter, where I met Vintage Vinyl's version of Prog Guy. He smiled at my choice and said, "Did you know Phil Collins is in another band besides Genesis?" I shook my head. "Well, before you buy this, why don't you wander over to the 'B' section and look for a band called Brand X. Something tells me you'll like them." I did as I was told, and a copy of *Product* followed me home. Prog Guy was right. I loved it. That album was infinitely jazzier than anything Genesis had to offer. It remains a favorite.

For a long time, Vintage Vinyl was precisely about what the store was named for: records. The harder the album was to find, the more likely Vintage Vinyl had it. If they didn't have it, they didn't hesitate to order it. Vintage Vinyl had a firm hold on jazz, blues, punk, and soul. The store's employees thrived on the customer's attempts to stump or baffle them with musical choices. Not only could the employee track down the record in question, he would brought three or four alternatives back with him, so the customer had more to choose from. When the jazz bug bit, this came in handy.

***

It took Dad at least two attempts to get me outside to mow the lawn. It took at least three tries to get me motivated to go to the barbershop. But here's something he only had to say once: "What do you say we head over to Peaches for a while?" The last word of that question would still be floating in the air while I leaned on the car horn, trying to get Dad to hurry up so we could *go!*

I don't know why Dad bothered giving me an allowance between '78 and '82. He *knew* where it was going. He may as well have budgeted it into the monthly bills. "Records for Ced: $20. Check!"

I can still see the first seven-inch single I bought with my own money. It was from a Canadian band called Trooper. The song was called "Raise a Little Hell." Dad's eyebrows rose a little as he read the title, which was followed by a look saying, "Really?" without any words being spoken. My hopeful, pathetic, look in reply sealed the deal. The record came home with me.

Not long after, I remember putting up the $6.98 plus tax for my very first self-purchased LP: *Pieces of Eight*, from FM-rock stalwarts Styx. Once again, Dad was baffled by his son's musical tastes. (1) But he saw no reason to nix the deal. Before long, my bedroom shook to the refrains of "Blue Collar Man" and "Renegade." My AOR-oriented period had begun.

***

There was so much to like about Peaches. The store measured some 1,700 square feet inside. A stereo speaker was hung up in each corner. This was both cool and annoying. It was cool because, hey, *there was a speaker hanging from the ceiling in each corner of the store!* Who wouldn't want to do that in his own house? That being said, stereo sound placement was also a major "thing" during the late '60s and '70s. Whoever mixed the albums in those days wanted it known this album was in *stereo!* That meant most instruments only occupied one speaker or the other. So it was nothing to hear only half of Jimi Hendrix's "Purple Haze" or "Come Together" by the Beatles, depending on where I was standing in the store. (2)

Peaches had a limited supply of t-shirts in those days. Every other visit, I would find myself in that far away corner, looking at all the rock and jazz acts displayed on a cotton shirt. Images of Led Zeppelin, Miles Davis, and the Rolling Stones were prominently displayed on black, white, and tie-dye colored fabrics. The shirts were fun to look at, but I don't remember ever really wanting one.

There were a few posters on display as well. Since I was still a few years away from the full-on frontal assault of MTV, posters were the best way to get to know a band aside from any photos on the LPs. I remember lingering over images of the Jackson 5, David Bowie, Donna Summer (yep), and others. I don't recall pining for a poster, either. They were just interesting to look at.

My personal favorite feature was the gigantic album cover recreations decorating the store's walls. I can still see the reproduction of Supertramp's album *Paris* staring me in the face the instant I walked into the store. I was captivated and ready to buy the album without knowing anything about the band. Luckily, Rock Guy was there to point me toward the album the concert was promoting, *Breakfast in America*. How I would have loved to take one of those paintings home with me. But even in the late '70s, it would cost me at least $500. Somehow, I didn't see Dad going for that.

* * *

If there was a downside to record shopping with my dad, it was time. He was a *very* efficient shopper. He may have taken a few minutes to chat with Jazz Man or Soul Brother, but most times, Dad knew exactly what he wanted. That meant finding the record, paying for it, and leaving. (3) There just wasn't a lot of time for dilly-dallying.

I liked to linger, and not rush into any particular selection. After all, if I hurry up and buy *this*, I might miss out on *that*, which could have been waiting for me in another bin.

Dad saw record shopping like a game with a clock, which was counting down from the moment we walked in. As soon as the clock hit 0:00, it was time to go. I moved through record shops more like I was playing baseball. There was no clock, and each section I visited might take me a couple of innings. I knew it was the bottom of the ninth when I began to wander aimlessly, not really looking at anything. The final out, as it were, was recorded once I looked in my hands and found I was satisfied with my selections. Then it was time to make my way to the register.

There is no freedom like having your own car. I always suspected being able to go wherever I wanted for as long as I liked would have its upside. Where record stores were concerned, the value of being my own Chauffer cannot be underestimated. As much as I cherished my outings with Dad, heading to the record store with friends – or even alone – was every bit as good, if not better.

Within days of taking ownership of my first car – a 1963 Plymouth Belvedere – I was off on my first solo trip to Vintage Vinyl. I don't remember if I bought anything. I do recall taking full advantage of "baseball time" as I wandered casually from bin to bin, scanning album covers, reading liner notes, and sampling records through the store's ceiling-mounted speakers.

The best part of record shopping with friends was being able to speak a common musical language with them. Dad and I were still a few years from our shared adventures, so I found it immensely satisfying to go to the store with certain friends on certain days, depending on my musical mood. I had rock friends, jazz friends, and soul friends. I even knew a couple of people who would wander to the more adventurous side of music, like prog. We could compare notes, talk about the records we had and the ones we wanted, and introduce one another to the sounds we hadn't heard yet. There was always something new, even if the record itself had been out for some time. The conversations and sampling went on for hours. If there is one conversation I will never tire of, it will revolve around music.

***

We all have an image that comes to mind when we hear the phrase "record store." Most people picture a place like Sam Goody or some other corporate store. It's large, brightly lit, and loud. The speakers pump out whatever is in the Top 40 that week. Exchanges between customer and clerk are brief and to the point. ("Do you have the latest by so-and-so?" "Over there, in rock.") For these people, a trip to the record store is little more than means to an end. For music junkies like me, it is something different altogether.

The movie wasn't released until 2000, but most true music fanatics in the '80s and '90s wanted to hang out in a store like Championship Vinyl, which was featured in the movie *High Fidelity*. The store is smaller, darker, and the music playing is so obscure, you're forced to engage the clerks about it. There is next to no Top 40 to be found, even though there are records stacked all over creation. You might be able to find a couple of buttons or a t-shirt, but extraneous merchandise is kept to an absolute minimum. It's the kind of store where the clerks store their personal records autobiographically, like John Cusack.

The employees in those stores were truly dedicated to their craft, even if they only worked there part-time. They simply could *not* be stumped. No matter how obscure my request, they knew about it. And they knew about three or four related albums I was clueless about. "Dude! How can you be into King Crimson and not own anything from Allan Holdsworth or Jeff Berlin? Are you *kidding* me? Come on, let me fix you up!"

In stores like these, it's almost a given the customer will be chided and chastised for one of his musical choices. The key is to have thick skin and understand the store's employees are only looking out for your musical best interest. Anyone not wanting to be ripped on might be safer shopping for music in a mall. It can be argued that there is no small amount of snobbery coming forth from the Championship Vinyl-like record store. But for the consumer looking for more than mere background noise or something to dance to, these stores were the best places to learn from. Jim Sullivan admits to being one of those "tough" clerks. He has solid knowledge of what's popular, and the will to steer the customer clear of it. "I put stuff in your hands because I thought it was cool," Jim confessed. "Some people might come in to buy Bon Jovi, and I'd steer them away from the Top 40. With other people, I'd guide them toward something I liked. Put that down! *This* is what you need."

Jim's abilities as a professional musician helped to guide his choices. He has played keyboards since he was six, becoming serious about it in his teens. He has a solid sense of quality pop music, leading him to admire Brian Wilson, Steely Dan, Michael McDonald, Todd Rundgren, Squeeze, and XTC. By the time he started working at Warehouse music in the late '80s (in addition to playing in top-tier wedding bands on weekends), Jim had the pulse of the pop music fan. And he could play what he was recommending, which had a most positive effect on his social life. Girls *love* a musician.

Jim's record store adventures started at Peaches, too. His store was in south St. Louis, precisely where his F.Y.E. stands. He and his mother (an avid music collector) started exploring the store in '76. Before long, Jim went home with a copy of his first album, Peter Frampton's *Frampton Comes Alive*.

Like me, Jim dug specialty stores. His favorite was the Record Bar, located in west St. Louis County. Like me, Jim loved the way the place was focused solely on music. "There wasn't any of that other jive, man. This was a *record* store!" he said. "The people in there were so cool. They were really nice. They tried to engage you. They wanted you to go home with something really good. I remember thinking *all* record stores should be like this. But they're not!"

For me, that store was Record Reunion. It was tucked away in the back of a shopping center called Village Square, located in Hazelwood, Missouri. I found it by accident, while trying to escape the trinket, ceramic, and pottery stores littering the rest of the shopping center. My mother and sister loved these places. I would rather take a sharp needle to the eye than spend more than two minutes there.

I wandered into the store for the first time in the fall of '84. My plan was to duck out of the pottery place and make my way to the sporting goods store at the far end of the plaza. Somehow, I got turned around, and I found myself wandering through a leather store. The rear exit to led me through a small corridor, followed by a doorway draped in translucent plastic. I could hear music playing. It was something odd, not normally found on the popular music stations. I was intrigued.

As I got closer, I could see the bins full of LPs. The entire store didn't seem much bigger than a broom closet, but I had to see what this was about. In I went. I walked out some 40 minutes later, feeling dizzy from the smell of LPs, cheap cologne and clove cigarettes. In my hands was a record by a German band called Triumvirat. Plus, I had a new record store to add to my rotation.

Record Reunion had all kinds of music, but of the two or three guys who worked there, each seemed to be some variation of Prog Guy. Over the years, it was them I turned to for King Crimson and its vast number of offshoots, Frank Zappa, and assorted fusion bands. It was the kind of place where I could go to just talk music for a couple of hours without feeling the pressure to buy anything. These guys were just happy to have a knowledgeable customer eager to absorb any sounds they saw fit to pump through the store's speakers.

Without a doubt, the '80s were my Golden Age of record store exploration.

***

For a brief period in '87, I actually worked in a record store. I don't know if my employment would have been deemed "official," since I was never paid. Not in cash, anyway. I was already working for a temporary service during the day. But a couple of nights a week, I found myself in Sound Revolution, also in Hazelwood, stocking shelves, ringing purchases, and talking music with anybody who walked in.

I'd become friends with Warren, the store's owner, not long after my first visit. Our conversations were endless, and often continued while I went with him to a record warehouse, where he prepared his next shipments. While Warren held serious conversations with the warehouse manager, I was the proverbial kid in a candy store, reading hundreds of album spines and wishing I could set up a small apartment inside the warehouse, since this was clearly the place to meet my musical needs.

I went to the warehouse so often, I learned how to read the Universal Product Codes on the records. I was delighted to learn that the Yes album title *90215* actually came from the UPC code. I've long since forgotten how to read those codes. But it was little things like this that helped me to appreciate Warren's friendship.

One day, I remember telling Warren there was no way I could ever afford all of the records I wanted. Plus, now I had a car, so I couldn't spend the money from my day job on music and little else. That's when my friend made me an offer I couldn't refuse. "Come in after five and hang around for three or four hours," he told me. "After that, I'll let you pick up a couple of records at cost, based on what I would have paid you." I couldn't shake his hand fast enough.

Which record store character was I? That's hard to say. My musical tastes were all over the place, so I could usually have at least a competent discussion about almost anything. I suppose I would call myself the Demographic Destroyer. I doubt anyone else did.

I don't know how happy my mother was to know I was spending eight hours a week in a record store, working strictly for product. But there I was, laboring away. And after the eighth hour was complete, and before the store's lights were turned off for the night, I spent a few minutes wandering through the browser racks, looking for seven or eight LPs to sustain me until the next "work week." Warren was probably "paying" me the equivalent of about five dollars an hour back then, which wasn't bad considering the minimum wage was $3.35. Albums usually sold for between $6.99 and $9.99. So "cost" on an LP was around four bucks. So eight hours work would usually net me a nice handful of records. Warren was even cool enough to throw in the occasional promotional copy of an LP I had been excited about. Working at Sound Revolution was, without a doubt, the best "volunteer" job I ever had.

***

I joined the United States Air Force in the spring of '88. This was my chance to see the world. And to explore record stores wherever I went. Over the next four-plus years, I wandered in and out of shops in South Carolina, Florida, North Carolina, Virginia, Maryland, Washington, D.C., Texas, California, Puerto Rico, and Japan.

Most of the stores I saw were relatively corporate, containing the same things I saw in the shops at home. Still, it was fun meeting Prog Guy with a southern accent, Hispanic Metal Dude, and California Jazz Man (who always seemed to be very, *very* mellow). The accents might have changed, but one thing was certain: the language of music is universal.

One of my favorite shops was called Papa Jazz, located in the Five Points section of Columbia, South Carolina. It was the ultimate "college town" record shop. Believing myself to be of "The Big City," I wandered into that store expecting very little from the people that worked there. After all, I had already been given strange looks in grocery stores when I asked about the availability of bratwurst. What could these hicks possibly teach me, I wondered? Within ten minutes, I learned the value of not judging a book by its cover.

If there is a bright southeastern center to the obscure musical universe, I found it. The employees, mostly college-aged, were hip to just about anything I told them about. They were an absolute joy to talk to. Columbia was about 45 miles from Shaw Air Force Base, where I was stationed, and I didn't have a car. So, I didn't get into Papa Jazz as often as I would have liked. This also put me at the whim of my friend's timetables, much like my shopping trips with Dad. Needless to say, I cherished any time I got to spend at that little shop in Columbia. For many years, I kept a bright yellow Papa Jazz bumper sticker on my cassette tape case. It's the only thing I really miss about that case.

The record shops I visited in and around Tokyo overwhelmed me. Even the commercial shops, like Tower

Records and the Virgin megastores, had a cool vibe to them. Sure, they had more than their share of the pop music I despised, but they also had title after title of the music I loved. Many of these items weren't even available in America. It's a crying shame my salary as an airman was so low, and the Japanese yen exchange rate was so high. I would have come home with a *lot* more CDs.

By the time I returned to the states in late '92, my priorities had shifted. I was under the impression I was getting married soon, so the time for record stores was minimized. I still wandered into Record Reunion (which had changed its name to CD Reunion) now and then, even though they had moved into a larger location. Warren opened a second Sound Revolution store, some 30 miles from the place where I worked. Eventually, "my" store closed down and became a pawnshop.

Vintage Vinyl also moved and expanded. While that was certainly good for the store, I could feel the vibe changing. Maybe I was just getting older, but the place didn't seem to exude the same joy it had for me in my teens. The people were still cool, but there was a distance to them I didn't care for. For every two cool cats I could talk music with, there was another wanting little or nothing to do with me.

In the fall of '94, I moved out of the suburbs and into the city of St. Louis. I didn't want to, but it was a requirement if I was to become a city police officer. I found a small apartment just west of the Anheuser-Busch brewery. My neighborhood was, like many others in the city, spotty where crime was concerned. It was a case of good block, bad block. I was fortunate enough to live on a good block. My landlord lived above me, and an elderly lady lived next door. Still, I didn't do a lot of exploring outside of my immediate surroundings.

By May of '95, I was a commissioned police officer, assigned to patrol one of the rougher areas of north St. Louis. I lived on the south side, and my beat made my spotty block look like Shangri-La. This is probably what spurred me to explore my surroundings a bit more. My apartment was located just a couple of hundred feet from a street called Arsenal. To get to work, I went east on Arsenal to Interstate 55 north. One particular off day, I decided to head west on Arsenal, just to see what was there. Within about 12 blocks, I found a new purpose for being. I located Streetside Records.

Streetside was a chain store. There was one just east of Vintage Vinyl in the University City Loop. I only went there a few times. My impressions were that the product was usually more expensive, and Professor Classical pretty much ran the place, so the vibe was a bit snooty. I didn't spend a lot of time there. There was another in a strip mall called Grandview Plaza, some 15 or 20 minutes from where we lived in North County. It was a pretty cool place. I spent more than a little time there in the early '80s. I distinctly remember buying copies of *Synchronicity* by the Police and *Abacab* by Genesis at this store.

The City store was located at the corner of Arsenal and South Grand. Even though it was a chain store, this Streetside had a cool vibe to it, which I felt from the minute I walked in. It was clear the people working there came from all walks of life, even if it wasn't a snap to determine who Prog Guy, New Wave Man, and Pop Girl were. Maybe that's what was so cool about the place. The people working there seemed able and willing to overlap when it came to musical knowledge.

It was at this store where I met some people who remain friends to this day. One of them is Al Karniski, the store's manager. Al is a record store "lifer," having been around the business since 1980. He spent his first six months with the company working as a clerk. His efforts got him promoted to assistant manager. Six months after that, he was made manager and transferred to the store at Grandview Plaza. Al and I are quite certain we crossed paths during his time at the Grandview store. We just failed to realize it until nearly 15 years after the fact.

Al returned to the Delmar store in the mid '80s, and remained there until '93, when he was named district manager. This is how he wound up at the South Grand store, where our paths crossed again. I lost track of Al shortly after he transferred to another store in the suburbs. A New Jersey company called CD World owned Streetside Records. The owner of CD World hatched a plan to merge his company with another group, called Trans World Entertainment, known in St. Louis as F.Y.E. Al continued to manage stores for F.Y.E., first under the Streetside banner, and then under the name of the parent company. But his stores were repeatedly swallowed up by the parent company, and he ultimately found himself back where he started, working as a sales Clerk at the F.Y.E. on Hampton. It was here Al and I crossed paths for the *third* time.

Al's entry into the record store world came via his knowledge of Jazz, coupled with his knack for organization. It was a different world back then. There were no computers to track inventory. The store employees would keep track of what they sold via cards and notebooks. They reported what was sold, and kept track of their inventory for future orders. This is part of what created the store specialists like Jazz Man and Prog Guy. As a manager, Al couldn't care less about what his prospective employee looked like. He wanted someone knowledgeable about music. "I wasn't concerned about what was on your head," he told me. "I wanted to know what was *in* your head. I told the people who worked for me that music specialists were like fingers on a hand. A finger alone can't carry what an entire hand can. So, we needed those specialists." It was Al who hired my friend Tory Z Starbuck – who distinguished himself by dressing in Glam Rock outfits and makeup – to work in his Delmar store. Some people may have found Tory's look off-putting, but there could be no doubting the man's musical knowledge.

Working in a record store was a completely different job when Al started there. The only focus was music, and the stores and their employees did everything they could to maintain that focus. 'The record labels loved people that worked in record stores," Al said. "Your job to go to concerts and go to parties and things like that to promote what the labels were selling. Every label had a representative, no matter how small. They came to the store, told you about the product, gave you samples … it was fun. It was a *lot* of fun. That's why I stuck with it for so long." Al told me about meeting artists like Prince, Michael Jackson, and Barry White at different company functions. Unfortunately, the business model didn't last.

The change came about for a couple of reasons. One was because of the way Trans World Entertainment (who bought out most of the record chains) did business. According to Al, "They were known as the Evil Empire. They were pretty much the death of record stores as we know it." The other came from the elimination of Minimum Advertised Pricing in the year 2000.

MAP pricing, as it was known in the record stores, was an agreement between suppliers and retailers. It stipulated the lowest advertised price for an item being sold in a store. This is key, because it meant record stores could no longer offer better-advertised deals than a major chain store, like Wal-Mart. For musicologists and collectors, this didn't have a major impact. They still went to their local record stores. For the average consumer – who made up a large portion of the record store's business – it was a *very* different story. If Wal-Mart could offer a CD for the same price as Streetside, and the consumer could get all his other shopping done at Wal-Mart as well, then why bother going to Streetside or any other record store. The impact was immediate and brutal. "At that point, the record labels wanted to get rid of record stores," Al said. "They thought they could make a bigger profit by selling their product online. That didn't fly at the time, because it was too early, (and people weren't using the internet to shop that much). It works better now."

There is no doubt in Al's mind the elimination of MAP pricing destroyed record stores. "That's when everything fell apart," he said. "The manufacturers charged us more, so we had to charge more. The manufacturers would charge less to a Wal-Mart because they would buy more volume. So the record stores would actually go to the box stores and buy their product, then mark it up and sell it at their stores in order to make a profit. We couldn't control our pricing. That killed us."

Modern day record stores have a different set of priorities. "They don't really care about music at F.Y.E.," Al said with a grimace. "They care about selling those magazines. They care about selling discount cards." Music, it would seem, has become an afterthought. Thinking of F.Y.E., and how little of its interior space is used to sell music, really drove the point home.

One of the worst days of my record shopping life came when I was looking for a particular new CD, and the F.Y.E. employee could tell me nothing about where it might be. After spending a couple of minutes telling her about the artist in question, she basically waved me off, saying, "You know, I don't even like music that much." It was quite some time before I got past my shock.

To be certain, Al would *never* hire anyone like that. "I had to know how you were going to fit into my store," he said. "I wanted you to be part of that hand. If you came into my store looking for a job, the first thing I would want to know is why you wanted to work in a record store. Then I would give you a product quiz to see where you fit in. You've got to be able to gel with everyone else. Otherwise, it just screws everything up."

When I apply Al's principles to the Streetside on Grand, it all makes perfect sense. He had a specialist for just about everything. But even so, there were times when I felt like I was teaching just as much as I was learning. The record store landscape was changing, and I didn't like where it was heading.

***

Major change doesn't take place overnight, and record stores are no exception. While I didn't make a habit out of shopping for music at stores like Best Buy, there could be no arguing with their massive CD selection and lower-than-average prices. To my shame, I confess I may have contributed to at least a small portion of the decline of record stores.

I can't point to the exact day record stores hit the skids, but I do remember what made me notice.

I digitized my music collection in 2006. It took time, but I began to regret that choice more and more every day. There was something thrilling about looking at a media shelf loaded with more than 1,000 CDs. Now I was looking at less than 100. To some, this collection would be more than sufficient, coupled with an iPod library. To a true music junkie, this was travesty. It was time, I decided, to replenish my collection.

The few new CDs I was buying I got from the artist's web sites. I spent very little time in record stores. I was looking forward to going back. But it didn't take long to see how things had changed, and not for the better.

My plan was to recollect a lot of what I sold off via the "Used" CD section of assorted stores. The majority of what I sold was released on major labels, so I figured it would be easy enough to reacquire these items in the same stores I sold them.

I had no idea how wrong I was.

Record stores changed a great deal in the scant few years I was away. The effect of downloading and streaming, along with an increase in internet sales, had begun to render some record stores rather … quaint. Inventories shrank, and artists once common in the browser racks were becoming harder and harder to find. Label representatives were a thing of the past, and distribution deals were laughable, at best. Special orders that used to take three to seven days now took a month, and the asking prices were getting ridiculous. There was a time when trading in unused CDs could net between three and five dollars a disc for common releases. Rarities could net 10 bucks or more. Now, every day discs rarely rated more than two or three dollars. At times, it was a miracle to get more than a buck. Not exactly the best motivation to seek out a deal.

Record stores weren't nearly as much fun anymore. One of the best things about shopping in a good record store is the never-ending series of happy accidents. I would go to the store with one artist in mind and wind up coming home with half a dozen discs having nothing to do with the artist I was thinking about! More than once, I forgot about the original artist altogether. Looking for an artist whose name started with "C" could lead in any number of directions. Maybe I was in the jazz section, looking for Chick Corea. Instead came home with Larry Carlton or Stanley Clarke. I wasn't thinking about them when I walked into the store. But there they were in the browser bins, and my fingers happened upon their work. This meant I had to take the time to examine the accidental CD by looking at the song titles and seeing who else was in the band. "I wasn't looking for this guy," I would say to myself. "But he's got a killer rhythm section! I need to check this out!" And just like that, I had a new purchase.

There aren't nearly as many happy accidents these days, because there aren't nearly as many CDs to stumble over. I was far more likely to think of an artist I wanted to reacquire, head to his section of the store, and find an empty space behind his title card, assuming he had a title card to begin with. Inquiries as to the whereabouts of said artist would be met with a shrug or a reply along the lines of, "Corporate doesn't think that music is worth keeping in stock." All I could do was walk away grumbling and shaking my head.

The situation was no better at the retail outlets. In fact, it was much worse. I live near a Target store. I don't go there to shop for music, but the CDs are located next to the movies, where I almost always make at least a cursory stop. There was a time when Target stocked quite a few CDs, some of which were quite reasonably priced. Sure, their emphasis was on the Top 40 artists, but I got lucky every once in a great while. Some artists, like Prince, even had version of their music distributed exclusively to stores like Target, with bonus tracks included on the disc. But that appears to be a thing of the past. The store still stocks a few Top 40 artists, but precious little else. It's not worth my time to leaf through their browser bins.

Best Buy had a CD section rivaling most quality record stores. Now they have next to nothing. It's as though the CDs flowed through this gigantic faucet, and it was suddenly and violently turned off. There was a time when I could count on Best Buy to carry a title or two F.Y.E. wouldn't. I never understood why this was so. It just was. But that day is long gone. And if I know anything for certain, I know those days are never coming back.

And as it turned out, the worst was yet to come.

***

Just after Thanksgiving of 2016, I wandered into F.Y.E. during my work shift, just to say hello to the gang. As I walked in, Jim and a couple of his cohorts were watching a man through their large plate glass windows. Being the vigilant cop I am, I looked outside with them, thinking something might be wrong, and I might be needed in an official capacity. (4) They were watching a man in his 40s, wearing a plaid shirt and jeans with a blue construction hat. Hardly the suspicious character I would normally have to deal with. He was carrying a staff or some sort, and he appeared to be taking measurements. I was mildly perplexed, and looked to Jim to see what was going on.

"He's a surveyor," my friend told me. "He was inside the store a little while ago. We weren't told of anybody like that coming by today. We think something might be up."

F.Y.E. is not a place I go for deep, philosophical conversations. So I kept my tone light. "Ah, something foul may be afoot, methinks," I said, expecting at least a grin from Jim, one of the more jovial people I know. But his face remained grim.

"Yeah, something's going on," he repeated.

Jim should've been a damned detective.

A couple of days later, I was skimming St. Louis *Post-Dispatch* headlines on my iPad. I happened across a headline declaring a Chick-Fil-A restaurant would be opening soon, the first inside the City limits. I gave up eating meat three years ago, including chicken. So the opening of such a place meant little or nothing to me. But something told me to read the article, anyway. Maybe my daughter would like to eat there sometime. It took less than two paragraphs to learn the new restaurant would open at 3801 Hampton, in south St. Louis. It's about five minutes from where I live. And there was something familiar about that address. It didn't take long to hit me.

It's the same location as F.Y.E.

Well, shit.

I reached out to Jim, who confirmed my fears. Corporate sold the location to Chick-Fil-A. While the exact dates were still up in the air, the store – already long on life support – would be no more within a few short months.

I suppose I should've seen it coming. The store's vast interior space was becoming more and more cluttered with non-musical trinkets. F.Y.E. was receiving shipment after shipment of t-shirts, action figures, bobble-heads, lanyards, key chains, and pretty much anything else that could hold the name of a movie or band. But there was next to no music coming in. There was an air of desperation to the store's overall inventory. In its heyday, a record store was about 90 percent records and tapes, with the rest saved for the odd trinket or two. I remarked to the store's manager a few months before it looked like the musical inventory took up less than a third of the store. He told me it was more like a quarter. And that number had been shrinking steadily. I guess the company rode the merchandising pony as far as they could and were finally bucked. But instead of re-evaluating and getting back on the musical horse, the company decided to put the nag out of its misery.

I hate to see the store go, for obvious reasons. But more importantly, I hate it for the people who work there, many of whom I consider friends. I will have to get through my day and evening watches without sharing a laugh with Jim, Ross, Scott, Joe, and the rest of the crew. What's worse, these fine people are now out of a job. I'm sure there are retail gigs out there, but will any of them be as fun as this one?

All things end, the wise man says. It's too bad this one had to end this way. But given the nature of the modern music industry, there really wasn't any other way for it to end.

***

Now that F.Y.E. has left St. Louis, I'd say my days of shopping in chain record stores are over.

In all likelihood, F.Y.E. is the last chain record store I will ever shop in. St. Louis has never had a Tower Records (now defunct) or a Virgin Superstore (all but gone as well). Chances are, I will be buying my major label releases from Amazon, since I need more than a mere download to satisfy me. For the rest, I will have to rely on Bandcamp and boutique record shops. This is not the worst thing in the world.

I can't begin to express the excitement Bandcamp brings me. Thousands of bands, hundreds of thousands of records, and genres inside of genres will keep me busy until Kingdom Come. Even now, there are some 400 albums waiting for preview in my wish list. Checking out two albums a day would sustain me for seven months or so. But the list will never run dry, because I'm always adding new records, based on what I'm reading in *Prog* and other magazines. There will always be something out there to explore.

I still take the odd trip to Vintage Vinyl. It's not the same, but it's not completely horrible, either. I come across a few more empty spots behind title cards than I would like, but I'll take what I can get. Once in a great while, I go out of my way to make it to Euclid Records. I just wish they weren't so damned expensive! The guys at Music Record Store in the Grove section of St. Louis offer a fairly cool (but also somewhat pricey) record shopping experience. There is another record store a mile or so south of F.Y.E. It's stacked from top to bottom with CDs and LPs. I could absolutely lose my mind there. But I rarely visit. I've never felt welcome there. The people there put off an air like they're doing me a favor by allowing me to spend my money there. That's an attitude I can do without. I'll pay someone else 10 or 20 percent more for the same music if they offer better customer service. That particular store is a last resort for me.

I'm sure it wasn't planned, but the guys at F.Y.E. gave me another place to go. I was in the store one day, lamenting the loss of great record stores. (5) I was talking about how I went to CD Reunion – one of my original hangouts – one day recently, only to find the store had been closed. I had no idea it was gone! My visits to that part of town are rare these days, particularly since my mother (who lived nearby) passed away and I have no real reason to go. Well, I said, I guess I'm out another record store.

"Oh, they're still around," Ross told me. "They just moved." It was then I was told about Planet Score Records, located at 7421 Manchester Road in Maplewood, just west of the City limits. It's about a 15-minute drive from my home. A month or so after being told about it, I made my way there. As it turned out, the previous owner of CD Reunion decided to retire.

He sold the place to Joe Stulce and Tim Lohmann, the two guys I met the day I walked in. Within seconds, I knew I'd found a pair of kindred spirits. These were record shop owners who actually like to talk about music. How about that? The store itself looks like a record store should. The browser bins and walls are full of CDs, LPs, and concert DVDs. No bobble-heads. No action figures. Just music. Among my first purchases were two CDs from Brand X. This store speaks my musical language! It's perfect! One visit was supposed to be a five-minute trip to pick up a couple of Aretha Franklin CDs being held for me. It turned into a 60-minute venture where I not only got the CDs, but I talked Miles Davis and other musicians with Joe over a beer.

I was home.

As I write these words, I've made several visits to Planet Score. If I have my way, those are the first of many trips. Record stores may not be what they used to, but Planet Score has managed to capture some of that prior glory. The modern music market will make it difficult for Joe and Tim to sustain their business model. I, for one, will do all I can to keep them around. Believe me when I say all profit from that store's existence.

Watching my daughter explore Vintage Vinyl
for the first time. It's a wonderful right of passage.

(1)   It's poetic justice that I now raise my eyebrows to the musical tastes of my teenage daughter. Trying to get her into my "decent" music is an exercise in futility. So, I let her walk her own musical path, hoping better music will eventually take hold. She recently professed a love for

Pink Floyd in general, and *Dark Side of the Moon* in particular. There is hope.

(2)   Thank God there were no 5.1 surround mixes back then. That would have been too much for my brain to take!

(3)   Dad didn't even waste time parking the car. He pulled in to the first spot he found, regardless of whether or not there was something closer. This was especially true when we had to visit the local shopping center. ("Dad, there's another spot right up there, near the front," I would plead. "Son, by the time I get up there and park, we could be in and out of the store. Let's go!") To this day, I refer to this as the John Hendrix Mall Parking Principle. And yes, I use it myself.

(4)   I have been able to add to my arrest statistics on more than one occasion thanks to the guys at F.Y.E. They are forced to endure their share of shady characters. Luckily, they have a cop who likes to hang out there and ask questions.

(5)   The folks at F.Y.E. know I love them, and in no way do I blame them for their store's inventory issues. They are doing their jobs and doing their best to sell what they've been told to sell. They can no more rebel and do what they want at work than I can.

*One of the best genre-defying bands going, Living Colour,
came to my town in 2014. I was fortunate enough to
meet them, and spend some time talking to guitarist
Vernon Reid (seen here photo-bombing his own band).*

Track 5
"Black" Music

Throughout the '70s, music was a river flowing endlessly, and I was a sponge. The sounds I was absorbing came from all over the place. Where they came from made no difference. All that mattered was whether or not the music went into my body, as Miles Davis once said.

The year 1978 found me in the sixth grade and enjoying my musical growth. With this newfound maturity came an overwhelming urge to share this musical knowledge with others. So, when the Music teacher in my school gave students a chance to share their records with the rest of the class, I jumped at the chance.

The first record I brought to class was Boston's *Don't Look Back*. It was the second record I had ever purchased with my own allowance. There was a marvelous 90-second instrumental on the first side called "The Journey" that really had me transfixed. I was anxious to share these sounds with the rest of my class.

The presentation itself went without incident. I don't even remember whether or not my classmates found the tune interesting (a theme that would continue on to the present day, it seems). It's what happened after class that disturbs me.

After class ended, I was accosted by one of three African-American students in my class, a kid named Tony McFarlane. "Hey," he said, more than a little aggressively, "Why didn't you bring any *black* music?"

The question baffled me. Black music? What did *that* mean? I wanted to ask Tony, but he walked away. He never raised the issue with me again. Nobody else offered an opinion on my musical choice. But the question has never left me. To be honest, I am wounded by it.

So, again I ask myself, what is "Black" music?

***

In retrospect, I understand the nature of Tony's question. What I didn't understand is its necessity.

My classmate wanted to know why I hadn't brought in a record that was made by predominately African-American musicians. Had he hung around, I probably would have told him it never occurred to me to worry about whether the musicians were black or white. In my mind, there are only two kinds of music: the kind I like, and the kind I don't like.

I understand the basis of Tony's mindset. After all, I was a student of St. Louis radio. The ethnic makeup of radio stations of the time seemed to fall into three categories: Top 40, where an ethnic crossover was possible, even likely; Rock, which was dominated by white artists with little to no crossover from black artists; and R&B or Soul, which was dominated by black artists with little crossover from white artists. It was far from unusual for a music fan to get fixated on a single radio station, therefore making it highly unlikely he would experience music from outside his comfort zone. Commercial radio formats have not deviated much from this way of presenting music.

The St. Louis metropolitan area is not known for being the most ethnically open-minded. Sadly, this has not changed for more than a few people in the second decade of the 21st century. I didn't realize how culturally backward my hometown could be until I spent nearly five years away from it, splitting time between Air Force bases near Sumter, South Carolina and Tokyo, Japan.

I remember how freaked out I was in '88 by having to spend two years "in the South." I was certain that I would see at least one Ku Klux Klan rally or get threatened with a lynching at least once during my time in South Carolina. Not only did that not happen, I met some of the friendliest, most open-minded people imaginable in South Carolina, Virginia, North Carolina, Georgia, and Florida. I'm not saying things were perfect, but they were a damned sight better than the social attitudes I deal with today in my beloved St. Louis. It's really sad, when I think about it. It's also no real surprise I would have to deal with such a question from my classmate a full decade before my first military assignment.

Like social closed-mindedness, the inability to absorb music from outside the "norm" is a learned behavior. My parents didn't teach me to hate music dominated by white people. They may not have been big fans of it, but they never prevented me from exploring it. So, it was nothing for me to switch, footloose and fancy-free, from one radio format to the next. What set my dialing hand in motion was little more than the desire to avoid hearing a metric ton of commercials. The rock station played 30 minutes of music, and then started airing ads. That meant it was time for a little soul music. When the commercials started there, it was time for a little Top 40, and so on. It never dawned on me to remain on one station for the entire day. If I did, it meant I was busy doing something else, and the radio was little more than background noise at the time.

Apparently, it was different in many of my friends' homes. They could go on and on about the music on the rock station, or the soul station, or the Top 40 station, but they couldn't speak intelligently on anything outside of those arenas. They found it highly unusual – weird, even – that I would go to the library and check out soundtracks from movies like *Star Wars* or *Close Encounters of the Third Kind*, or the music from NFL Films. Those same friends would have thought I was out of my mind if they knew I was also listening to classical music from Beethoven, Bach, and Brahms.

Not every friend's home was like that. I remember going to my friend Danny's house and hearing his mother play Scott Joplin on her piano. She was playing "The Entertainer," and she was good. I don't know if this very blonde woman ever pointed out to her very blonde son that the composer was black. I'm guessing it didn't matter. Nor should it.

Yet for some, ethnicity (I hate using the word "race") mattered a great deal where music was concerned.

I may be part of the last generation to really spend time worrying about the ethnic makeup of a musician or band. My daughter is the same age now I was when Tony asked me about "black" music. Whether an artist is black or white is a non-starter for my little girl. All she cares about is whether the music is good. I wish I could say the same for my generation.

***

For some reason, the vast majority of the black people I grew up with held on to the staunch belief that people like us had no business playing or listening to rock and roll. That was a musical realm for white people, period. Of course, that is preposterous. African-Americans helped *invent* rock and roll.

Part of rock's foundation was the blues, which meant being influenced by B.B. King, Howlin' Wolf, Muddy Waters, Bo Diddley, and Buddy Guy, among others. Bands like Led Zeppelin and the Rolling Stones couldn't pay enough homage to the blues acts they worshipped and credited them at every turn.

The Beatles are the most influential musical act of the 20th century. Yet John, Paul, George and Ringo would not have been who they were without Little Richard and Chuck Berry, and they have said as much.

Legendary guitarists from Eric Clapton to Jimmy Page, Jeff Beck to Eddie Van Halen, and countless others point in the same direction when it comes to major influence. They all point to Jimi Hendrix. Even if they don't emulate his style directly, rock and roll guitarists the world over cite Jimi as a major source of inspiration. Nothing makes me crazier than hearing some kid declare Jimi "overrated" in the grand scheme of modern music. Idiots! They simply don't grasp that before Jimi came on the scene, *there was no scene*. Everything built needs a foundation. And Jimi Hendrix makes up at least a small portion of every rock guitarists foundation after 1967, whether they realize it or not. Period.

My black friends were not hearing this. "Black folks don't play rock and roll," they said. "We have our own music." They were referring to R&B, or soul. Well let's look at that for a minute.

Take, for example, the Isley Brother's recording of "Summer Breeze," released in '73. Not only was the Seals and Croft song taken to the next level by the Brothers's vocals, Ernie Isley's guitar solo is among the heaviest, *rock*-oriented solos you will hear on record during this era. Did it straddle musical borders? You're damned right! And the song is classic because of it.

George Clinton is known as one of the godfathers of funk. His band Parliament never failed to get the party started with tunes like "Up for the Downstroke" and "Flashlight." But there was another aspect to this band that actually came before Parliament, called Funkadelic. And they could flat-out *rock*! "Maggot Brain," a ten-minute guitar solo played by Eddie Hazel, is considered one of the seminal moments in rock guitar, essential listening for any guitarist learning how to play with raw emotion, and the deepest feeling.

Maggot Brain was released in the summer of '71. Around that same time, the foundation for punk and death metal was being laid in Detroit, Michigan. The band consisted of three siblings named Bobby, David, and Dennis Hackney. These brothers were also "brothas," in the soulful sense of the world, and their band was called Death. The trio became the stuff of legend in the punk and metal circles, in spite of the fact only one of their singles was released commercially, in a run of 500 copies. Like many others, I only heard about the band in 2012, when the documentary film *A Band Called Death* was released. I'm not a huge fan of punk music, to be honest. But that didn't stop me from beaming with pride when I see a trio of black men was at the forefront of the movement that gave me bands like Fugazi and Dinosaur Jr.

Black people don't play rock? Ridiculous. They do. And they do it well.

***

In the summer of '88, I was settling into life as an airman in South Carolina. One day, my friend Dennis McDaniel came running up to me, excited as all get-out. He was aware of my passion for music and had something to show me. "Dude, you've got to check these guys out! They're the most awesome rock band I've ever heard!"

Hyperbole aside, my friend had my attention. "Okay," I said. "Who are they?"

"They're called Living Colour," he told me. "They have this awesome song called 'Cult of Personality.' It's serious hard rock! But here's the thing ... they're black!" While I silently agreed with Dennis that a black rock band was indeed a rare thing in music at the time, I didn't quite see it as the musical unicorn he did. Still, I decided this band deserved a bit of my time.

Dennis was on to something.

Living Colour was fantastic! "Cult of Personality" showcased the vocal talents of Corey Glover (1) and the unreal guitar pyrotechnics of Vernon Reid, and the rock-solid rhythm section of bassist Muzz Skilings and drummer Will Calhoun. The album was called *Vivid*, and it told me that there might be some hope for commercial music after all.

How to describe the guitar playing of Vernon Reid? This is no easy task. Though I could probably start with the word *tsunami*, and branch out from there. Vernon's guitar approach can be an all-out assault on the senses, featuring lightning-fast picking and fingerboard dexterity that eludes mere mortals. He comes from a free-form jazz background, making things even more interesting, since he rarely plays his solos the same way twice. (2)

I don't know if Corey Glover sings so much as he reaches into the well of his soul and channels. There are plenty of singers doing amazing things with their voices. But there can be no doubt that Corey is trying to put a message across. Taking time to listen to what Glover is singing reveals quite the additional layer of depth to Living Colour's music. A common complaint in rock music is that the lyrics of the vocalist cannot be clearly understood. With this band, that is not a problem.

Living Colour's rhythm section is equally awesome. The bass skills of Muzz Skilings are never up for debate. He brought a great sense of groove and low-end thump nearly unrivaled in rock music. This is particularly evident in tunes like "Funny Vibe," where Skilings appears in touch with his inner Stanley Clarke. Drummer Will Calhoun possesses the drive to propel the band forward brilliantly. He has the right levels of aggression and touch that makes his presence known without overwhelming the rest of the band.

It's a good thing they can be clearly understood, because Living Colour has a *lot* to say. In addition to having a killer hook and a scorching guitar solo, "Cult of Personality" warns of the dangers of idolizing celebrities, reminding the listener, "Only you can set you free." Vivid contains other, equally powerful songs like "Open Letter (to a Landlord)," about the people who live in the run-down neighborhoods disdained by others; and "Funny Vibe," the song I relate to best, as it speaks to the way non-black people have looked at (and continue to look at) me from the opposite side of the ethnic fence. Based solely on what I look like, people have moved to the opposite side of the street, protected their purses in elevators, and followed me around nice stores while I shopped for suits. And I carry a badge for a living. Go figure.

The album closes with "Which Way to America," an aggressive, heartfelt anthem asking why skin color continues to equal inequality. I want to believe in the quarter century since *Vivid*'s release, tunes like this one would be dated, and largely irrelevant. But if recent events are any indication, "Which Way to America" still holds weight, and swings a heavy bat.

***

Living Colour was not the only "black rock" act to emerge from the late '80s and early '90s, even if they were the most well- known. (3) While Vernon and company started their band in Brooklyn, New York, Fishbone – a band of equal power and rock influence – was emerging from Los Angeles, California. Not only did Fishbone draw from punk, rock and metal influences, they added an element of reggae and ska, thanks in part to the fact they had a horn section.

Fishbone was raw and aggressive. Their live shows are the stuff of legend. After achieving a solid underground reputation, the band broke out with a cover of Curtis Mayfield's "Freddie's Dead" on their second album, *Truth and Soul,* CD released in '88. Fishbone possessed a level of comic silliness Living Colour did not, which brought forth tunes like "Bonin' in the Boneyard." But they, too, had a level of social consciousness, which helped usher forth songs like "Change," which closes the album.

While I like the *Truth and Soul* album, Fishbone really hooked me with the follow-up, *The Reality of My Surroundings*, which came out in '91. I would never have known about this record, if not for the limited viewing options of Far East Network Television.

I had about seven channels on my dorm room TV while I was stationed in Japan. Five of them were exclusively in Japanese. (4) The Far East Network, a television and radio signal run by the U.S. military, offered up a few of the shows being aired on the networks in the States, along with a few old sitcoms and the occasional stale old movie. Needless to say, I didn't watch a great deal of television during my two years overseas. But I never missed *Saturday Night Live*.

I can't tell you what I had for breakfast this morning, but I do recall that day in the spring of '91, when Jeremy Irons was the guest host of the long-running sketch comedy show. And the musical guest was Fishbone. The band came out and tore into "Sunless Saturday," the first single from *Reality* .... Thank God my VCR was running that day, because that performance ripped the top of my head off. (5) I couldn't believe these cats were actually on *SNL*. Neither could my roommate, Steve. I distinctly remember him looking at me and asking, "What just happened?" All I could do was shake my head and shrug with a big smile on my face.

By the end of Fishbone's second song, "Everyday Sunshine," I had my shoes on, and was headed out the door. "Where are you going?" Steve asked, as I appeared to be in a hurry.

"To the base exchange," I replied, referring to our military shopping center. "I've got to find that album!" As luck would have it, the exchange had one copy of *Reality* ... (in the miscellaneous "F" section) and it came home with me, along with a couple of other long-forgotten titles. I wasted no time putting it on my CD player. And Fishbone wasted no time blowing my mind.

The Reality of My Surroundings is an eclectic mix of metal, funk, jazz, hip-hop, and ska. The album comes out smoking with "Fight the Youth," a steaming slice of metal with funk undertones. Another personal favorite was "So Many Millions," which managed to be heavy while being carried by the horn section. Fishbone had a vibe unlike any other band I knew.

Tunes like "Housework" veered toward the sublime. But Fishbone never forgot to bring the social awareness with tunes like "Behavior Control Technician" and "Pray to the Junkiemaker." This was a band that allowed you to have fun while teaching you something. I couldn't find any fault in that.

The whole record seems like a buildup to "Sunless Saturday," which closes things out. Maybe that's where I've developed the mindset that the best albums put their singles on the end of the record, rather than the beginning. All too often these days, bands offer up their best song first on a CD, only to have the rest of the material fail to measure up to the single. Leave it to Fishbone to save the best for last.

***

Prior to grabbing hold of Fishbone, I was introduced to a quintet of African-American gents from Atlanta called Follow For Now. They released their self-titled debut in '91. While not quite as powerful as Living Colour or Fishbone, FFN was a solid rock band with a debut album that seemed to be laying the foundation for future greatness. They recorded a killer cover of Public Enemy's "She Watch Channel Zero," one of the album's highlights. "Fire 'N' Snakes" offered up a funk/rock bit of '70s nostalgia, while "Holy Moses" and "Milkbone" got heads rocking.

Naturally, FFN was also socially aware. "White Hood" addressed the issue of racism felt by the band throughout their lives. And "Trust" chronicles difficulties with interacting with the police, once again sounding like it could have been recorded yesterday, rather than more than 20 years ago.

I was eagerly looking forward to hearing more from Follow for Now, but things didn't work out, and the band dropped out of sight after just one record. They have been known to perform in the Atlanta area in the recent past, but no new recordings have surfaced.

***

My brief foray with rap brought me into musical contact with Ice T. His album *O.G.: Original Gangster* remains one of my favorite hip-hop albums of all time. It paints a vivid picture of the life of street hustlers, drug dealers, pimps, and gang bangers in South Central Los Angeles during the early '90s. I don't know how much of this stuff Ice T actually lived, but he was able to put me in the middle of the action better than anything CNN was broadcasting. These songs also served as the backdrop for the mayhem ensuing from the Rodney King verdict, and the subsequent riots, in '92. Ice T appeared to have his finger on the pulse.

More importantly, *O.G.* featured a song by Ice T's new metal band, Body Count. That band subsequently released an album called *Cop Killer.* The title track stirred up an enormous amount of controversy, due to Ice T's perceived endorsement of targeting police officers. The uproar reached the point where Ice T ultimately pulled the song from the album.

I have been a police officer for two decades. It may surprise more than one person to learn "Cop Killer" does not particularly offend me. To me, it is a statement of social outrage, based on a problem that *does* exist between the police department and some of the citizens we are sworn to protect. Whether I agree with it or not, the outrage is real, and I have seen it first hand on more occasions than I care to count. (6)

***

Meanwhile, 1990 saw the return of Living Colour, as they released what I consider their best album, song for song, called *Time's Up.* It took everything they had been doing to the next level.

The album opens with the title track, a wicked piece of thrash metal that morphs into a heavy metal stomp. The band allows the audience a brief moment to catch its breath with an interlude called "History Lesson." Then it's time for the social commentary with a wonderful tune called "Pride." In it, Corey sings about the social dilemma that comes with being in a popular rock band, yet being unable to do simple things like interact with white people away from the concert venue, or hail a cab on a New York City street. Vernon, Corey, and the guys keep the messages coming in tunes like "New Jack Theme," "Someone Like You," and "Fight the Fight."

The band also reveals a little more of the sense of humor they alluded to on "Glamour Boys," a tune from *Vivid*. This time, the tongue is planted firmly in the cheek for tunes like "Love Rears its Ugly Head" and "Elvis is Dead." The latter tune features spot-on cameos from Little Richard and saxophonist Maceo Parker, who made his name playing with James Brown.

"Type," the first single off *Time's Up*, is a great tune about society's attempt to place labels on people, however improperly. It has a different vibe from "Cult of Personality," a move made intentionally by the band. I could almost feel them growing and maturing before my eyes. They were changing, and it was for the better.

The album ends with a powerful tune called "This is the Life," which reminds us to take advantage of the world we live in, as opposed to the world we want to live in. To me, the song's message is, "Don't wait for things to be ideal. You may not get another shot." On more than one occasion, *Time's Up* has left me emotionally drained once the last strains of this final song have faded.

The band released *Stain in '93*. It is a dark, complex album, putting the tougher side of Living Colour on display. Perhaps their new sound was inspired by the change at bass, where Doug Wimbish replaced Muzz Skillings. Where Muzz was all about groove and thump, Wimbish brought forth a fierce, effects-driven attitude to his playing that took the band in new directions. Why this didn't seem to catch on like *Vivid* remains a mystery to me.

Maybe it was the song titles, which didn't exactly conjure up images of sunshine and rainbows. The album opens with a killer tune called "Go Away," in which Corey Glover appears to be at war with his conscious. Three of the next four tunes are even less inviting, sporting the titles "Ignorance is

Bliss," "Leave it Alone," and "Mind Your Own Business." The album's saddest lyrics come from a tune called "Nothingness," during which Corey sings that all he has to feel is his loneliness, and all there is in his (mental?) attic is an empty chest. And nothing, he says, lasts forever. Yikes.

Things get positively grim on the next track, called "Postman." The song's meaning is not hidden. A postal worker has had enough, and it's time to take that anger out by … well, going postal. A brief instrumental break called "WTFF," which I learned stood for "What the Fuck Factor" (an inside joke amongst the band and crew during recording) gives way to "This Little Pig," which I can assure you has nothing to do with the nursery rhyme. It is a blistering piece of metal, infused with dark industrial sounds. This is not a tune to be used for finding the bright side of life.

Still, Living Colour appears to have purged its collective demons by albums end. With "Wall," Corey seems to declare he is ready to re-engage with the world around him, as his personal wall of cover has fallen, despite what has been going on around him. He wants us to drop our walls as well. It seems easier said than done, but Living Colour seems to believe anything is possible.

Despite the dark overtones, I really enjoy *Stain*. Perhaps because I have spent more than a little time isolating myself from the world, while battling my own personal demons. In the end, I am willing to step into the light and engage my fellow man, if only for a little while.

I figured Living Colour was headed toward even bigger and better things. But the dreaded "creative differences" between band members reared its ugly head and Living Colour called it quits in '95. (7) Even the best music can be overshadowed by conflicting personalities.

***

Vernon Reid onstage in the Duck Room, 2014.

I wonder what Tony McFarlane would make of Living Colour. What I wouldn't give to have a conversation with him about this band. Here are four brothers from New York City, bringing it with the best of them. They just happen to be doing it in a rock context. Are you going to tell me this isn't "Black" music? Seriously, Tony, what the hell is "Black" music? What about Fishbone, Funkadelic, or Follow for Now, Tony?

I may never get a chance to ask my 6th grade classmate that question. But I did get to ask Vernon Reid.

The guys in Living Colour managed to work out their differences and returned to service in the early 2000s. Their first release was *Collideoscope*, which came out in '03. The album is solid, but could have done with a little trimming, as it feels about three songs too long. A strong opening gives way to a slightly muddy middle. The record picks up steam again toward the end.

The highlight is a touching 9/11 tribute song called "Flying," which offers a dramatized first-hand account of a man working in the World Trade Center on that fateful day. Prior to seeing the hijacked plane heading for his building, the protagonist's biggest concern was working up the nerve to ask one of his co-workers out on a date. In the end, he does get to hold her hand, as they jump out of their office building together in an attempt to escape the flames caused by the crash. It was a long time before I could pick my jaw off the floor after hearing that song. It stirs up a tear or two.

In '09, Living Colour released *The Chair in the Doorway*. I would call this the weak entry in the band's catalog. There are some decent moments, but nothing that absolutely grabs me and demands that I come back for more. It is the sound of a band full of ideas, but those ideas do not gel the way *Time's Up* did. Nevertheless, it still makes its way to my CD player now and again. Sometimes, it takes a while for a record to grow on me.

In 2014, Living Colour hit the road once again, in support of a new album called *Shade*. One of their stops was in my hometown, where they played in Blueberry Hill's Duck Room, one of my favorite venues. Intimate and full of energy, the room was a great place to check out one of my favorite bands. Living Colour did not disappoint. About 200 of us had our ear hairs torn out and stomped flat, as Robert Fripp would say. (9) The band played for about two hours, and then came out to mingle with fans after the show.

Prior to Vernon, I got to spend a few minutes chitchatting with Corey. And then the three of us (and two of Vernon's friends) spent 20 or so minutes talking about science fiction and comic book movies. It was a surreal moment for me, but it also grounded the band members in a very helpful way. It humanized them, making it infinitely easier to ask what I thought was going to be a very difficult question.

My time with Vernon finally came. I told him the Tony McFarlane story. I can't begin to express my relief and amusement when he appeared to be as baffled as I was about the reference to "Black" music. I asked Vernon for his take on the subject. After a deliberate but thoughtful pause, Vernon Reid answered my question. "Black music is whatever a black person conceptualizes," he said. "When people talk about 'black' music, they're speaking in a very narrow conception. It's music that's identified with black people, mainly African-Americans. It's very disturbing to me, because so much of popular music – jazz, blues, rock – was originated by black people.

"Music is not a color. Music is a sound," Reid continued. "If it resonates for a particular person, who is to say that person should not play that music? The notion that by playing rock you don't identify or you can't identify with black cultural things … that's the thing I find objectionable. My love for James Brown was not lessened by my appreciation for Led Zeppelin.

"To have a wide (musical) aesthetic is a challenge," Vernon Reid said. "A lot of people are challenged by music they can't identify. It's a kind of parochialism. There's a way to be. There's a way to express yourself with certain things. Anything outside of a certain narrow set of parameters is challenging to identity. And when it challenges identity, it's a threat."

Like me, Vernon understood where Tony and his ilk were coming from. And like me, he doesn't condone it. "Certain social pecking orders have to be established. So to (people like Tony), you have to be white because you like rock music. The thing is, you have to be able to say, 'No, man. No. I'm not singing that song.' That's *your* problem. That's *your* issue.

"The idea that black is this, this, or *this* ... no! Black is expansive. Black is jazz. Black is blues. Black is metal. Black is jungle. Black is classical music. Black is minimalism. Black is *all* of it, to embrace all the colors. Every other problem (with other music) is *their* problem."

Vernon looked me dead in the eye before firmly reminding me of the ultimate truth. "It's not your problem."

Take *that*, Tony. (10)

(1)   I didn't realize I had already been introduced to the talents of Corey Glover, only as an actor. He had a small role in Oliver Stone's Vietnam opus *Platoon* in 1986. Corey plays Francis, the guy sharing a foxhole with Charlie Sheen's character during the big battle sequence near the end. When I met Corey in 2014, it was all I could do not to ask him, "Manny, where are you *at*?" It was one of his *Platoon* lines. Luckily, common sense prevailed.

(2)   I sold off my copy of *Stain*, Living Colour's third release, after downloading it to my iPod. Realizing my mistake, it was one of the CDs I re-acquired when I strode to make my collection whole again. Imagine my surprise when my new CD contained different guitar solos from Vernon Reid on at least three songs. "It was a gag pulled off by me, the producer, and our A&R man," Vernon told me. "Two masters, two plants, opposite coasts. To see if anyone was paying attention." I was, Vernon. I was.

(3)   Living Colour's profile was raised significantly, courtesy of Mick Jagger. Vernon Reid played on a Jagger's *Primitive Cool* in '87, and Jagger helped

produce a couple of Living Colour's demo recordings. Jagger also opened the door for Living Colour at Columbia Records, who gave the band their first deal. Best of all, Living Colour opened a series of stadium shows for the Rolling Stones in '88, giving the new band a great deal of exposure before an audience who might otherwise never have known them, or what they were about.

(4)   I never felt dumber than the day I attempted to watch a movie on Japanese television. The movie was German, which is what the actors were speaking. The subtitles were in Japanese. Needless to say, I never got the full gist of what was going on.

(5)   Even back then, I tried to get the best possible sound from my audio/video system. So, I had my VCR's audio output running into a pair of 280-watt Cerwin-Vega stereo speakers. We were getting Fishbone at full throttle. Or as close as I could get at the time.

(6)   This is a heavy subject and will be covered in a book I have planned for a few years from now. I'm calling it *A Two-Legged Tripod: How Policemen, Politicians and the Public Compromise and Complicate Public Safety.*

(7)   Vernon Reid stayed very busy, releasing a string of outstanding solo records in between bouts with Living Colour. *Mistaken Identity* (1996), his first album, is probably my favorite. Although *Other True Self* (2006) is rock solid as well. *Known Unknown* (2004) also has some enjoyable moments. Reid also played in a band called Yohimbe Brothers, where he connected with his hip hop and drum 'n' bass personas, and Free Form Funky Freqs, where he returned to a progressive, free jazz element.

(8)   *Shade* was finally released in September of 2017, and it is fantastic!

(9)   This was actually the second time I saw Living Colour in concert. The first time, they were opening for King Crimson in November of 2003. One of the highlights of their set was looking to the left of where I was standing to see Crimson guitarist Robert Fripp leaning against a post, loudly cheering on the band in his clipped British accent.

(10)   While Tony McFarlane is a real person, he is far from the only one I've had the "Black music" conversation

with. I haven't seen this guy in more than 35 years. He could have evolved musically just as much as I have. But there are plenty of other Tonys out there, and I'm talking to them just as much as I am to the original.

*The album that started it all was Jean-Luc Ponty's
Cosmic Messenger. My dad knew exactly which bug to
plant in my ear, and did it ever take hold!*

Track 6
Jazz Day

My father was a clever man.

Throughout my life, I remember him doing his best to pass his passions along to me. Dad taught me the joy of football and baseball, showed me the tranquility of fishing, and gave me the taste for many of his favorite foods (particularly the spicy ones). If not for my father, I would not appreciate the look and feel of a good suit. I'm quite certain he gave me the desire to drive a European sedan, as opposed to a sports car. And, of course, Dad did his best to pass along his love of jazz.

As a general rule, children tend to avoid listening to the music of their parents. For the most part, I was no different. Sure, some leaked through, whether I wanted it to or not. And thank goodness for that. Otherwise, I may never have come to appreciate Marvin Gaye, Stevie Wonder, and Aretha Franklin, among countless others. But my friends were in to rock and roll, so that's where my personal musical compass directed me as well.

I was among the first of my peers to have my own stereo system. While most of my friends made do with a portable record player or played records on their parent's home systems, my dad pulled out all the stops and got me my own Realistic (from Radio Shack) stereo components. I had an AM/FM receiver, a turntable, and a pair of 18-inch speakers destined for volumes that would drive my mother absolutely bonkers. Yes, 1978 was a good year indeed. I was well on my way to a lifetime of musical exploration.

We didn't see much of Dad during the week. He spent more than three decades working as an insurance agent for New York Life. (1) His clients were at home during the evening, so that's when he did the vast majority of his work. On the rare occasions we saw him at home during the day, he was almost always on the phone, setting up appointments for the next few evenings. By the time Dad got home from work, my sister and I were in bed, since we had school the next day. While we were getting ready for school in the morning, Dad was asleep, having been up until one or two in the morning. The entire family could be found in the same place at the same time on the weekends.

Saturday was for errand running, chores and family outings. Overall, that was probably the best day of the week. I might not have liked the way the day started, since it usually involved me mowing the lawn, cleaning the garage, or undertaking some other Dad-mandated arduous task. But it was almost always worth it, since the day ended with the family going out for dinner, catching a movie, or heading to the record store.

Sunday was a day of rest for pretty much everyone, particularly Dad. The afternoon was usually about a football or baseball game. During the spring and summer, there was a good chance he would barbecue on the deck. But before any of that took place, Sunday was about jazz.

My mother, sister, and I were almost always up before Dad was on Sunday morning. Even though he was a pretty sound sleeper, the three of us moved about the house relatively quietly for the day's first couple of hours. Dad usually woke up at around 10. We knew for certain he was up when we heard his stereo come on. Dad would make his way to the kitchen for a cup of coffee. Mug in hand, he would go from there to the family room, where he would fire up his components. (2) Within 60 seconds of that familiar hum, the day's first strains of music would waft through the house. Jazz Day had begun.

***

Dad would have been in his early 30s by the time I started noticing what was coming out of his speakers every Sunday. I'm not going to pretend for one second that I understood what he was playing. All I knew was it made him very happy. The music was almost always instrumental, and full of horns and pianos playing things that sounded nothing like the rock and roll I enjoyed, or the soul records Dad and Mom played for friends on the occasional Saturday evening.

While the music didn't make a ton of sense, I remember looking at the album covers. I started to see the same names over and over again. Names like John Coltrane, Ahmad Jamal, Keith Jarrett, Herbie Hancock, Dizzy Gillespie, and Miles Davis started to stick in my mind, even if I had no idea what it was they were doing. When Dad saw me linger over an album cover, he would invariably say something along the lines of, "See, son? *That's* what a musician sounds like!" Apparently, Dad was under the impression that Styx, Supertramp, and other corporate rockers I loved just weren't getting the job done.

Still, my resistance held for quite some time. To my pre-teen mind, jazz was a never-ending series of notes played at random. The music was all over the place, and there was little to nothing catchy about it. It certainly didn't rock, by any stretch of the imagination. But all that changed sometime around 1979.

There was no getting to the kitchen without going through the family room. This meant I had no choice but to hear what Dad was playing on the turntable that day. Normally, the notes rattled around in my head like so much noise before being rejected by my mind as quickly as they entered. I was one of those kids Mark Knopfler talked about in the song "Sultans of Swing." I didn't give a damn about any trumpet-playing band. It wasn't what I called rock and roll. So normally, I just dismissed what I heard. But on this particular Sunday, I realized something was different.

Most of the jazz Dad enjoyed was traditional, or "straight ahead," meaning there were no electric instruments to be found. On this day, however, my chest vibrated to the sound of electric instruments. The bass was definitely electric, as were the guitars. The keyboards were synthesizers, rather than the usual piano. I recognized these sounds from my own music. Plus, there was an additional element. It was an instrument I couldn't quite identify, a sound I couldn't put my finger on. I had no choice but to ask Dad what was going on.

"What's that sound?" I asked.

"What sound?" he replied, aware he very nearly had me on the hook.

"That instrument. It's not a guitar. It's something else. What is it?"

"That's an electric violin," Dad told me as he handed me the album cover. "It's being played by a guy named Jean-Luc Ponty. What do you think?"

I was intrigued. "This is pretty cool," I said. Dad began to smile, because now he had me. Nevertheless, he reeled me in slowly.

"These guys use the same instruments you've been listening to," he told me. "They just use them a little differently. And the music they play is a little more complicated. Listen to the way they're playing. Isn't that something?"

It's funny how things fall into place when you least expect it. Because just like *that,* the incredible jumble of notes had a distinct sense of flow. I was able to count the time signature and pick out the actions of each instrument. Everything was making sense!

I didn't even realize I had taken a seat next to Dad until long after it happened. The trap was sprung. The mentor had his protégée.

I spent the next couple of hours on the couch, listening to album after album from Jean-Luc Ponty. Dad was smart enough not to overwhelm me with multiple artists on my "first day." When all was said and done, I had taken his copies of *Cosmic Messenger* (released in '78) and *Enigmatic Ocean* ('77) back to my room for more intense study. Thus, began my first jazz-oriented musical obsession. And, for the life of me, I can't remember why I was going through the living room in the first place.

***

Dad's perception of jazz was not a narrow one. There are more than a few people out there who are real purists where jazz is concerned. Only certain styles are deemed "worthy" or "acceptable." I won't lie: even I have become a little guilty of this tendency. But I'll get back to that.

Because of Dad's musical open-mindedness, I was able to hear many different forms of jazz, often from the same artists. Dad exposed me to the early styles of Louis Armstrong and Duke Ellington; I heard the frantic be-bop of Charlie Parker and Dizzy Gillespie; I listened to the cool of Miles Davis, Wayne Shorter, and Charles Mingus; I heard the heat behind John

McLaughlin, Weather Report, and Herbie Hancock; I was even introduced to the "smooth" sounds of Earl Klugh, the Jazz Crusaders, Larry Carlton, and Bob James. Like any other form of music I was being exposed to, I held on to the sounds I liked, and pushed aside those I didn't. But not very much was pushed aside.

If not for the jazz/rock hybrid called fusion, I may never have gotten into jazz. Dad figured the best way to get me into the music he loved was by way of the music I loved. Rather put down the music I enjoyed, he showed me how elements of rock were being used in another form to help create an entirely different sound. I have no doubt this is why I enjoy listening to bands like Tortoise, because they incorporate so many different styles into their music to create the sound they're looking for.

In Jean-Luc Ponty, I found a musician who could be heavy and precise at the same time. The music appealed to the portion of my brain usually reserved for soundtracks and orchestral music. Since Ponty's music was instrumental, there was no lyrical hook. So each time I played his music, I picked an instrument, and focused on what it did throughout the song. It was a fascinating approach for a 13-year-old kid. Not surprisingly, my friends didn't get it. Even at age 50, many of my friends *still* don't understand. But this rarely discouraged me. As a kid, I actually reveled in it. I understood something they couldn't grasp. And I had something I could share with my dad.

I spent the early- to mid-'80s absorbing as much fusion as I could. Most of that exposure came from sitting next to Dad on Sundays. Not everything he tried worked. But when it did, there was no stopping my obsessing over what I was hearing.

***

There was no questioning my dad's love of jazz. More importantly, he loved sharing his musical finds with friends. I remember watching him talk to his friends, bubbling over with excitement as he put another record on the turntable. I never knew Dad to be an excitable man, so it was always amusing to watch the look on his friend's faces as they took in what he was saying about this amazing new record.

*I came for the artwork on the cover of Return to Forever's
The Romantic Warrior. I stayed for the incredible music!*

Of course, Dad continued to work on his youngest listener. Now that I was well versed in Jean-Luc Ponty, it was on to the next artists. My attraction to the art on LP covers served me well one particular Sunday, as I was marveling over an ornate piece of art serving as the album cover for a band called Return to Forever. The album was called *Romantic Warrior*. The cover art came straight out of the tale of King Arthur and his Knights of the Round Table. A fully armored knight in shining armor, lance resting in his lap, sat atop a noble, similarly armored steed. A pair of doves fluttered over his left shoulder. The knight appeared to be posing in the meadow, with his castle situated in the background. On CD, the album's artwork is enjoyable. But in its full LP glory, the Romantic Warrior (assuming that was the knight's moniker) was a sight to behold.

I was still marveling over the cover art – and the four interesting looking musicians on the back – when Dad strode into the room. He was instantly amused by my discovery. "You think the cover is impressive," he said, "Wait until you hear the music." I handed over the album and allowed Dad to go through his routine of properly removing the album from its sleeve. It's a ritual I repeat to this day.

The LP's sleeve is held gently – but firmly – in the left hand, as the LP is removed with the right. The vinyl is never, *ever*, to be touched. So the record is removed gently with the middle and ring fingers of the right hand. The edge of the LP is cradled carefully in the crook between the thumb and forefinger. Once the LP is removed, the cover is placed aside and the record is gripped with the palms of both hands along its edges. The fingers are to float well away from the vinyl, so as not to smudge, scrape, scratch, or deface it in any way. Once this task is completed, the LP is placed gently on the turntable, and wiped clean with a wood and felt device known as a Discwasher. Careful execution of this ritual ensures years of enjoyable playback without the annoying pops and scratches many albums pick up over time. (3)

I was intrigued from the opening notes of keyboardist Chick Corea's synthesizer. The song was called "Medieval Overture," and sounded like it could indeed have come straight out of those times. That changed when the rest of the band joined him seconds later. Al DiMeola (guitar), Stanley Clarke (bass), and Lenny White (drums) dropped the musical hammer, establishing a theme of pure fusion, straddling the line perfectly between jazz and rock. White took things to the next level with a drum break that sounded more like Neil Peart than Tony Williams. The band was off and running. I could feel the hair from my short "Afro" being blown back by the sound. Dad recognized the look and smiled broadly. He had me, and he knew it.

The next 40 minutes passed in a blur, as I was mesmerized by the skills of these four supremely talented musicians. Corea moved deftly from one keyboard to the next, mixing modern synthesizer sounds with classical piano. Sometimes, he did both at the same time! DiMeola, who had joined the band in '74 as a precocious 19-year-old prodigy, ran his fingers up and down his Les Paul's fretboard with skills far beyond his years. Clarke redefined how the bass guitar was played, combining blistering runs of rock, subtle touches of jazz, and the pure thump of funk. White held it all together, propelling the beat forward with his drum kit. I would learn in time that RTF was regarded as the Led Zeppelin of fusion, blowing minds and selling out arenas wherever they went in the mid '70s. I would also become enamored with the solo efforts of each of the band members. For quite some time, it was difficult to slip a Chick Corea, Stanley Clarke, or Al DiMeola record past me.

Romantic Warrior established itself as one of the most important records in my collection (Dad ultimately gave me his copy, and then went and got another one for himself), and Return to Forever became one of my favorite bands. Two of their earlier recordings, *Hymn of the Seventh Galaxy* and *Where Have I Known You Before*, became equally crucial to my development as a fusion fan. There can be no underestimating this band's influence toward my own musical ambitions.

***

In the grand scheme, the worldwide fraternity of musicians seems large. Within the context of my personal collection, it's funny to see just how small and intertwined that world really is. Connections can be made from one musician to the next, over a vast array of genres, often without my initially realizing it.

I was still a good five or six years from discovering Miles Davis. Once I did, I would learn that both Chick Corea and Lenny White spent time in his band. For his '82 solo album *Scenario*, Al DiMeola hired the rhythm section of bassist Tony Levin and drummer Bill Bruford to play on a couple of tracks. That rhythm section is half of the '80s version of King Crimson, who changed the way I looked at music forever. Stanley Clarke's favorite solo bands featured a guitarist named Jeff Beck, who would ultimately become one of my heroes. Jean-Luc Ponty rose to prominence by playing in a band with Frank Zappa. I wouldn't make that connection for six years between the time I first heard *Cosmic Messenger* and when I was introduced to *Shut Up 'n' Play Yer Guitar*, one of Zappa's best releases.

The musicians fraternity is a game of "Six Degrees" that goes on and on.

***

Not everything Dad introduced me to stuck. Some of the "smoother" material, like the Crusaders, Earl Klugh, and Larry Carlton held my attention briefly, but eventually faded into the background. The sound of "smooth jazz," as it is known, was a bit too soft for my personal tastes. As time goes on, I have a hard time referring to it as "jazz" at all. To me, "instrumental R&B" makes a lot more sense.

Still, quality moments could be found in the smoothest of jazz moments. I've always enjoyed the alto saxophone sound of David Sanborn, even if most of his records get very little personal airtime these days. Of course, once I became familiar with his sound, it was easy to recognize Sanborn's sax on none other than David Bowie's "Young Americans." Like I said, the fraternity of musicians is smaller than one thinks.

One of Dad's favorites was a pianist named Bob James. His music is relatively innocuous. Dad's favorite Bob James album was called *Touchdown*, which caught my attention because of its cover art, a full-sized NFL football spreading across the width of the gatefold cover. The opening track on the album is called "Angela," a pleasant enough piece of light jazz fare. It also happened to be the theme song from *Taxi,* which was one of my favorite TV shows. Dad had never seen an episode. He just loved the music.

I remember being fascinated for a brief time with trumpet player Herb Alpert, particularly on an album called *Rise* (released in '79). It would be a stretch to call anything on that album jazz. If anything, it smacked more of pop and disco, performed without vocals. But the album's opener, called "1980" lent just enough virtuoso pomp to the proceedings to allow the record to be filed in the jazz section, I suppose. I haven't played that album in at least 25 years, but I would imagine there might be a tune or two on there I still enjoy. Alpert released another record in '86, called *Keep Your Eye on Me.* I remember playing it a lot for a brief period. But shortly after that, I discovered trumpeter Wynton Marsalis and Alpert's music lost just about all its meaning.

The discovery of Marsalis (who actually hails from an entire family of jazz musicians) put me on the cusp of the "Young Lions" jazz movement, which began in the early '80s. Now that many legends of straight ahead jazz (Miles, John Coltrane, Dizzy Gilespie, et al) were aging or had passed on, a new generation of musicians was making its way to the forefront. Pianist Marcus Roberts, drummer Jeff "Tain" Watts, and bassist Christian McBride were among many garnering attention and acclaim on the local jazz stations, in the clubs, and at the awards shows.

Now that Dad knew he had my attention, he found other ways to introduce me to music. We couldn't always sit together on Sundays (I *was* a teenager after all), so from time to time I would find a record sitting on the stereo speaker in my room. There was never a note. I would just notice a record that didn't belong in my collection sitting there, seeming oddly out of place. That was all I needed. Most of the time, I dug what Dad was trying to share with me. Sometimes I didn't. But I always listened. And sooner or later, we wound up talking about it.

Before long, I started returning the favor. The Young Lions were putting out some remarkable work, and by the mid

'80s, I was leaving LPs on Dad's speakers, eagerly awaiting feedback. We'd find ourselves discussing the records while doing the yard work, or on a long drive. It was during this time I introduced him to the drumming of Bill Bruford, which completely blew Dad's mind. He didn't always dig what I left him, either. But our discussions were always constructive, and never dull.

In the spring of '88, I left home for my first assignment in the U.S. Air Force. But my musical exchanges with Dad continued. Our phone conversations invariably turned to music and what we had discovered recently. Birthdays, Christmas, and Father's Day were all about buying one another new music. In between those times, I would compile various tunes and create mix tapes for him (hey ... it *was* the '80s). Dad would have taken a lot longer to discover the compact disc had I not bought him a player for Christmas and included a couple of jazz discs. I don't think my mother ever forgave me for opening that particular Pandora's box. By the time I came home for the first time, I saw Dad had built up quite a collection.

Jazz Day also found a new home in my dormitory room.

My desire to spend every waking moment hitting tennis balls was pushed aside nearly every Sunday morning, as I fired up the stereo system (which made the trip from my childhood home) and played a record or two before heading out the door. While my South Carolina roommates didn't always get the music, at least they indulged me for a couple of hours while I played it. (4) When I transferred to Japan in '90, I had no idea I was about to create a resident jazz maniac. But that's precisely what my roommate Steve became. The Boston native I met was all about classic rock when he first moved in. I had no problem indulging him. But Sundays were all about jazz, which led to him asking me tons of questions. "What instrument is that?" "What the difference between a tenor and a soprano saxophone?" "Do they really make up the solos as they go?"

One day, I came home from tennis practice to the sound of my stereo blaring. This was nothing new, since Steve was free to borrow my CDs if he liked. What caught me off guard was the music being blared. I was hearing a sizzling trumpet solo from Wynton Marsalis. That wasn't the disc I'd left in the player the night before. I swung the door open to the sight of Steve sitting on the floor, some six feet from the speakers. He was perfectly centered between them. His head was bobbing up and down rhythmically, a common sight at jazz clubs full of like-minded listeners. My roommate was fully engaged in the sound he was absorbing. I probably stood there, staring at him, for two minutes. Only when the solo ended did he turn toward me. Chances are, that's the first time he realized I was in the room.

He must have seen the bemused look on my face, because it made him laugh. "What?" he asked. "I love this stuff, man!" All I could do was laugh and offer my friend a high five.

***

I can't say with any kind of assuredness whether any of the women in my life have enjoyed Jazz Day. (5) But as it is quite literally part of my DNA, they have indulged me. I must admit, very little of my music is geared toward attracting the admiration of women. I don't find that particularly important. Music is an intensely personal statement. Jazz takes that concept to the highest level.

I've been fortunate enough to surround myself with women who, for the most part, understand my need to express myself musically, even if they don't fully understand it. Over the years, more than a few ladies have browsed through my LP, CD, and mp3 collections. More often than not, their trip through the titles offers up the same question: "Who *are* these people?" Naturally, this cues my mild rant about the difference between rock stars and musicians, and why I prefer the latter. Over the first couple of dates, this diatribe is politely absorbed via nods and smiles. But after a month or so (usually after being triggered by something we hear on the radio), my rants are cut off with an abrupt, "I know. I *know*! Just let me enjoy the song! Not everyone listens to music the same way you do!" And just like that, the boundary is set.

I love my daughter like nothing else in this world. I would really enjoy passing along my love of this music to her, primarily by showing her how our music tastes aren't as diametrically opposed, as she may believe. I could find the elements of her favorite music and show her how they are used in the music I enjoy. Before she knew it, we might be sitting on the couch, listening and talking, just like I did with my dad.

He really was a clever man.

(1)   I made the mistake of referring to Dad as insurance "salesman" once. I was soundly corrected. "Salesmen go door-to-door and aim for one sale," Dad told me. "I'm an agent. Agents have clients, and we keep them for life."

(2)   With the benefit of hindsight, I now believe Dad never had his turntable grounded properly. That hum used to drive me crazy on my own system until I discovered the ground wire, which ran from the turntable to the receiver. Once the two were linked, there was no more hum. Eventually, I crawled behind Dad's system and made the same fix. I seem to recall earning many "Good Son" points that day.

(3)   I remember having a "Record Day" with a friend when I was in my early 20s. He watched with complete and utter bemusement as I went through the record care routine when I put a new record on the turntable. Naturally, I was unaware of why he was so amused, since it was habit for me. I finally had to ask him just what he was staring at. "You do the same thing every time," he told me, laughing. "I mean every. Single. Time." He was right. He still would be.

(4)   I was actually pretty lucky, where roommates were concerned. I rarely saw my first one, since he lived off base for nearly a year. My second, a native of Puerto Rico (by way of the Bronx) gave me a love for Salsa music. My hips move to it almost automatically to this day.

(5)   Well, I can say without reservation my daughter *hates* it. Then again, she hates 95 percent of my music. But what does she know? She's a teenager!

Without a doubt, Seconds Out is my favorite live album of
all time. The music of Genesis opened the door to a much
wider musical world I was only just coming to know in the '80s.

Track 7
Seconds Out

For the first half of the '80's, no band meant more to me than Genesis. This was not a common statement made by black male teens. Come to think of it, not a lot of my white male teen friends were into them, either. Nevertheless, I absorbed every note played by the talented outfit from England. And while I have obsessed over other bands since, any mention of Genesis gets my attention.

When Genesis was inducted into the Rock and Roll Hall of Fame in 2010, I was happy for them. I remember thinking, "It's about damned time." Genesis, to me, was one of the bands who should automatically be there. The music they made was too influential to ignore. It was nice of the music industry to finally catch up.

I cannot overstate how integral Genesis was to my musical growth. They laid the foundation for the music I would absorb in the future and influenced on my own compositions. Bands like Led Zeppelin and Supertramp introduced me to longer-than-normal rock songs, but Genesis (and shortly afterward, Yes) taught me about progressive rock. Without Genesis, there is no understanding King Crimson later. The set-length pieces, odd time signatures, and virtuoso performances paved the way for the sounds I have heard and loved since then. I have no doubt I am a better music fan for the discovery.

Admittedly, I arrived late the Genesis party. I'm reasonably sure my first album was *Abacab* (released in 1981). I bought *Duke* (their previous release) shortly after. This automatically – though unintentionally – put me in a position of ignorance.

As far as I knew, Genesis was and always had been Phil Collins (drums and vocals), Tony Banks (keyboards), and Mike Rutherford (guitar and bass). And while I was familiar with Peter Gabriel's "Solsbury Hill," I had no idea he was in fact the original lead vocalist of Genesis. That education would come later.

While I enjoyed the albums I had, the Genesis tide truly turned when I bought a scratchy used copy of *Seconds Out* at Vintage Vinyl. I found it in the dollar bin, which still amazes me. Released in '77, *Seconds Out* is a live album covering the band's first six albums, which I was completely clueless about (1). But after hearing the songs performed live, I went out and bought those early records. I was treated to a level of musicality I had rarely heard before and haven't heard much since.

Seconds Out propelled me from casual Genesis admirer to a full-on fanatic. Not only was the music positively incredible to my neophyte ears, I kept reminding myself the band was carrying out these complex pieces live, on stage. There was no safety net. A misplaced note or chord would destroy the song. And yet there stood Genesis, pulling it off without a hitch.

Seconds Out listeners can find something to hang on to throughout the show. Steve Hackett's guitar was an instrument of wonder, weaving in and out of complex time signatures, tickling the eardrums one minute, and stomping them flat the next. The keyboard playing of Tony Banks could be used as a master class on the subject. The man's hands never stopped moving, and they rarely play the same keyboard at the same time. Mike Rutherford was rock-solid on bass and guitar. He also introduced me to the glorious sound of the bass pedal synthesizer, a sound I would also hear on records by Rush, the Police, and others. The bass frequencies from those pedals could punch a hole through the listener's chest. Drummers got more than their fill – pardon the pun – from Phil Collins and Chester Thompson (and on "Cinema Show," Bill Bruford), who could make two drummers sound like one, two, or four, depending on the needs of the song. I have no doubt that *Seconds Out* is the jumping off point for my infatuation with drums.

The lyrics were smart as hell, too. I'm still deciphering many of them, 30-plus years after hearing them for the first time. Collins doesn't get nearly enough credit for being able to handle the songs originally sung by Gabriel. Some fans say Collins's efforts did not reach the same level as Gabriel. In some areas, they have a point. But this was not easy material, and Collins got better over time. There is a reason Genesis tried out dozens of potential singers after Gabriel left, only to offer Collins the gig. For what it's worth, Collins didn't want to be the front man. He was perfectly happy behind the drum kit. One can only imagine how his career would have gone had he insisted on staying there.

Abacab may have given me a new band to admire. But *Seconds Out* showed me the Genesis I loved actually came together a decade earlier.

***

For most, Genesis is divided into two distinct eras: with Peter Gabriel (1970-'75) and after him ('75-'92). I believe that's too general. My eras are the Gabriel Years ('70-'75) the Post-Gabriel Prog Period ('75-'78); the Post-Steve Hackett Prog to Pop Transition ('78-'82); and the Pop Period ('83-'92). Of course, any Genesis fan will tell you there are prog elements in the music all the way to the end, and they would be correct. But clearly, the emphasis veered toward making hits starting in the early '80s, to the delight of Banks, who loved making hit records.

Seconds Out became my map to the '71-'76 period, and made it my favorite. I could hear Peter Gabriel's vocal take via the studio albums, and marvel even further at the virtuosity of the band's musicians. I could also further appreciate the efforts of Collins as the new lead vocalist, since songs from the first two post-Gabriel records are covered on the live album.

I can still see the sly grin on the record store clerk's face as I presented him with my copies of *Nursery Cryme*, *Foxtrot*, and *Selling England by the Pound*. To be certain, Prog Guy was handling my purchase. "You, my friend, are in for a treat," he told me. "But you forgot an album. You can't buy all of these and ignore *The Lamb Lies Down on Broadway*. That's their best album!"

I had seen a copy of *The Lamb* ... in the browser bins, and I wanted it. But it would have to wait until the next time I got my next allowance. I explained my dilemma to Prog Guy, and asked if I should trade in one of the records I had for the double-album I also wanted. He laughed and pointed to the section of where the album was. "Just go get it," he said. When I came back, he rang up my purchase. Amazingly, it came to right at what I had to spend. "Anyone with musical tastes this good is entitled to an employee discount," Prog Guy told me. "But you have to come back and tell me what you like about the records." I extended a hand for shaking, thanked him, and assured him I would return.

The next several days were glorious. I can't begin to describe the sense of awe and wonder going through my mind as I absorbed some of the most remarkable music I ever heard. Much of which wasn't even included on *Seconds Out*. I decided that it was best to listen to the albums in order.

Nursery Cryme, released in '71, came first. I knew I was in for something different when Genesis opted to open the record with the 10-minute opus called "The Musical Box." Who does that? Shortly after, I heard "The Return of the Giant Hogweed," which opens with Hackett employing a two-handed tapping method Eddie Van Halen would make famous seven years later. Of course, I hadn't put those two elements together. I was just awed by the sound Hackett made, along with the rest of the band. The album closed with another epic, the nearly eight-minute "The Fountain of Salmacis." This song provided my first real foray into the mythological lyrics used by many progressive rock bands.

Foxtrot, released in '72, came next. This album features two of my favorite Genesis moments ever. The album opens with a mellotron-based string section introducing the listener to "Watcher of the Skies." But the front of this bookend nearly pales in comparison for what closes the record. Side two begins with a beautiful guitar solo from Hackett, called "Horizon's." I was disappointed the song was just over 90 seconds long. But my disappointment was short-lived, because for the next 23 minutes, I was enthralled by the wonder of "Supper's Ready."

I was already familiar with this tune, as it makes up side three of *Seconds Out*. When I heard the live version, I had no idea where the tune originated. I only knew I loved every note. The tune opens with beautiful guitar arpeggios (essentially chords played one note at a time), and continues to build from there. "Seconds Out" is prim, proper, stylish, goofy, and majestic all at once. The "Apocalypse in 9/8" section of the song makes life worth living. I remember being near tears toward the end of the song, which is a staggering musical crescendo awash in bass pedals, drums, and soaring keyboards. I have never gone out of my way to declare any one Genesis song my absolute favorite. But if I did, "Supper's Ready" would be in the top three.

Foxtrot is such a sonic revelation, *Selling England by the Pound* (released in '73) almost seems like a step back. With the benefit of objectivity, the record is more like a breath of fresh air. Lyrically, songs like "I Know What I Like," "Firth of Fifth," and "Cinema Show" are not as dark as the songs on *Foxtrot*. But there can be no doubting the musicianship of these songs (which wound up on *Seconds Out*) and the others included on this set. It was as though Genesis was preparing us for what was to come. For what came next was epic.

In '74, Genesis released *The Lamb Lies Down on Broadway*, a double album and "concept record" every bit on par with the Who's rock opera *Tommy*. On *Lamb ...*, Gabriel tells the story of Rael, a Puerto Rican man searching for his brother in New York City (which was *very* different from the tourist-friendly NYC of today). The story captures the grittiness and depravity of New York through titles like "Fly On a Windshield," "In the Cage," "The Carpet Crawlers," and "The Colony of Slippermen." Banks said he had a great deal of personal difficulty with this album, since Gabriel seized command of the lion's share of the lyric writing. Banks and Gabriel were the two strongest personalities in Genesis, and frequently clashed over the musical direction of the band. Now, they clashed even harder. By the time Genesis completed its tour to support *Lamb ...*, Gabriel was done. He quit the band and started on what would ultimately prove to be a very successful solo career.

It was time to unleash Phil Collins.

***

As promised, I went back to the record store, where I couldn't wait to talk to Prog Guy. I found him dutifully restocking the browser bins. After a little small talk, I talked his ear off for the next 15 or 20 minutes. I kept waiting for him to shut me up, but all he did was smile and nod.

I recognize it now as a moment of understanding between two people who grasp something many others do not. I have since given that look to a few others. It is one of the best feelings a music fan can experience.

When I finally stopped talking, Prog Guy motioned for me to follow him. We went back to the front counter, where he sauntered around to his side and reached under the cash register. In his hand were two more records. "I've been waiting for you to come back," he said. "It's time for you to hear what Genesis sounded like right after Peter left."

The albums he handed me were *A Trick of the Tail* (released in '76) and *Wind and Wuthering* ('77). These were the albums Genesis was supporting when they recorded *Seconds Out*. Once again, my allowance remained in my hands for a scant few hours. Once again, it was worth it.

A Trick of the Tail's opening track, "Dance on a Volcano," put me directly into *Seconds Out* mode. The feel of the song in the studio was nearly identical to on stage. But I could feel the band's sound changing. While they had not veered directly toward pop music, there was definitely a lighter touch at work. The epic songs weren't quite as long, and the lyrics (save for "Robbery, Assault and Battery") had taken on a friendlier, not so sci-fi tone. The trend continued into the next album, *Wind and Wuthering*, even if it was a little more adventurous, musically. It was becoming clear (especially with the benefit of hindsight) things were definitely changing in the Genesis camp. Perhaps that's what Steve Hackett felt when, during the mixing of *Seconds Out*, he decided to leave the group.

Hackett's departure cleared the path for the change in musical direction in Genesis. 1978's ... *and Then There Were Three* introduced love songs to the band's repertoire. "Follow You Follow Me" was the band's first hit single. This ushered in a new element, previously foreign to the band and its audience: girls. Hardcore prog fans slowly peeled away as women expresssed their love for the band. The band must have loved what was happening, because more of the same came forth on *Duke* (released in '80) and *Abacab*. There were prog elements to these albums, to be sure. But the songs were shorter, and the lyrics got sweeter. Since I knew there were different eras to explore, I found myself listening primarily to *Seconds Out* and the records before it.

***

Apparently, my obsession with Genesis meant I had to start dressing like Phil Collins. For the better part of '84 and '85, I could be found sporting a short-sleeved shirt, skinny tie (I particularly remember a hot pink number I really liked), and wristbands. If I had been thinking, I would've added a pair of drumsticks to my ensemble. Did I play the drums? No. But that was hardly the point.

My friends would ride me about songs like "Illegal Alien," "Misunderstanding," and "Me and Sarah Jane," which ran toward the sappy. I would begrudgingly acknowledge those songs didn't exactly rock, but there were still tunes from those albums that did. Besides, I would almost always point them back to *Seconds Out*. Trouble was, my friends had no interest in 10-minute prog songs, either. And they certainly couldn't understand how I could endure a 23-minute song like "Supper's Ready." They had things to do. Why couldn't the band just get to the point, already? Telling them that the song in and of itself *was* the point fell on deaf ears. I was alone on an island in a sea of sonic brilliance.

My obsession with Genesis began to fade by the time '86's *Invisible Touch* was released. I found the album decent, but it did nothing to make me forget the music I loved from the '70s. I couldn't even bring myself to flout *Invisible Touch's* success to my friends, because I didn't like it as much as the *Seconds Out* material. The worldwide success of one of my favorite bands was, at best, a hollow victory. Not long after, I moved on to other artists and styles. I bought *We Can't Dance* in '92 more out of a sense of loyalty than genuine excitement. I was rewarded by a couple of attempts at epic prog in "Driving the Last Spike" and "Fading Lights." But the silliness of "Jesus, He Knows Me" and the sappiness of "Hold On My Heart" once again won the day. The Genesis I knew and loved was no more. No matter: I had plenty of other music to listen to, including a CD copy of *Seconds Out*.

***

In '14, Genesis released a three-CD set called *R-Kive*, chronicling the band's catalog along with some of each member's solo material. As a companion, the Showtime cable network aired a documentary called *Genesis: Sum of the Parts*. I found it hard to believe I would learn anything new, given my level of fanaticism. For the most part, I was right. Still, there were some interesting moments, and I was able to make a few observations I probably wouldn't have noticed 20-plus years before. For example:

90 MINUTES IS NOT ENOUGH. For all intents and purposes, Genesis was active for a little more than twenty years. They went through more than a few trials and tribulations. To try and cram all of that information into a mere 90 minutes was an unrealistic goal.

By contrast, *The History of the Eagles* (which aired on the same network) ran about three hours. Between '71 and '07, the Eagles released seven albums, including a live LP. During the same time period, Genesis released 14 albums, four of which were recorded live. The Eagles got *twice* as much documentary for *half* as much music. I'm not saying Genesis needed a three-hour documentary, but two hours would have helped fill a few gaps.

Because of the time constraint, I don't feel like I got a real insight into Genesis's music making process. This is something I am *very* interested in. They could have done twenty minutes on "Supper's Ready" alone! The film completely blew past *Wind & Wuthering*, which is an album I enjoy very much. I also would like to have seen a more comprehensive look at *A Trick of the Tail.*

Sum of the Parts offered up a good chunk of information, but didn't want to do anything with it. There wasn't enough depth for me. My approach would have been different. But then again, nobody asked me to film a Genesis documentary.

THE TONY BANKS FACTOR. To look at Tony Banks, one would think he did little other than show up, sit behind his keyboards, and play his ass off. The man appears to be deeply introspective, and very soft-spoken. Or so I thought.

I always figured that Collins was the dominant personality in the band. I was very, very wrong! Not only is Banks a very imposing force behind the scenes (particularly where musical direction was concerned), he could also be a bit of a jerk.

As a policeman, I've interviewed enough people to recognize in Banks's eyes how he saw himself as Quality Control for Genesis. And if the other members of the band were fine with it, what do I care? The problem is I don't think all of the other band members were fine with it. Rutherford and Collins went along with the Banks program. Gabriel and Hackett were another story. Gabriel admitted he and Banks clashed constantly during his time with Genesis. I can see where this would erode band chemistry, and eventually force one party to go in a different direction.

While it was never verbalized precisely, I have no doubt Banks is a major reason behind the departure of both Gabriel and Hackett. Speaking of which …

HACKETT IS RIGHT TO BE PISSED. Steve Hackett slammed *Sum of the Parts* on Facebook, saying it was "biased" toward the other band members, and his impact and subsequent solo work is largely ignored. I tend to agree. One need look no further than the interview with the "Prime Five" to see there is still more than a little friction, even after all these years.

The body language displayed by Banks, Rutherford, Collins, and Gabriel when Hackett spoke said it all. Those four appeared to view Hackett as their talented guitarist, and little else. I can almost hear them ordering him to show up, shut up, and play during his time in the band. When Hackett attempted to explain why he needed to record a solo album, the rest of the group (particularly Banks) greeted his words with stony silence. Music journalist Anil Prasad pointed out the documentary's editors could have played a role in the perceived tone. But I watched the band's faces while Hackett spoke, and everyone was in the same frame. I stand by my observation.

Still, Hackett insisted he had no desire to foster ill will or air dirty laundry about the band or his time with them. It was equally clear he had a lot to say about the matter. Perhaps he will one day address it all in a book of his own. I, for one, would love to read it. I was really sad for Hackett, and I don't blame him for leaving.

THE INVERSE POPULARITY FORMULA. The more popular Genesis became, the less I dug them. My musical secret had been pulled into the light and corrupted. So while Genesis moved toward mega-stardom in the mid-'80s, I moved on. By then, I had been introduced to the likes of King Crimson, Miles Davis, and Frank Zappa. The music I found there was, to me, infinitely more adventurous than what Genesis was churning out. And there was one other thing bugging me …

PHIL PHATIGUE. After Collins released his first solo record, *Face Value*, in '81, he became virtually inescapable. The man was EVERYWHERE. By the time *No Jacket Required* arrived in '85, I had pretty much had enough of Phil. Banks expressed what I think most Genesis fans were thinking at the time when he said, "We wanted him to be successful (as a solo artist), but we didn't want him to be *that* successful." There was more than a touch of jealousy in Banks's face when he said it (there's that jerk again), but I understood his point. I remember hearing David Letterman say during one of his *Late Night* monologues, "Ya know, I'm just not hearing enough from Phil Collins lately." If that wasn't a sign that he was over-exposed, I don't know what is.

I don't blame Collins. He was in demand, and he took advantage of the situation. Good for him. In *Sum of the Parts*, Collins remarked he was being asked to do things he never thought he would be asked to do, and he didn't know if he would ever be asked again. So, who can blame him for jumping on any and every opportunity to be a guest musician, record songs for a movie soundtrack, or produce other artists?

Let's face it: a little Phil Collins goes a long way.

THE REUNION TOUR. When the last strains of *We Can't Dance* faded from my speakers in '92, I remember thinking, "That's it. Genesis is done." I was partially right. Collins officially left the band in 1996. It's just as well, where I was concerned. I was pretty much done listening. Banks and Rutherford made one more attempt to carry on, releasing *Calling All Stations* in '97 with Ray Wilson handling the lead vocals. I had no interest in this record. Nobody else did, either. Sales were tepid, at best. Plans for a North American tour were cancelled due to slow ticket sales. As a result, Banks and Rutherford put Genesis on extended hiatus. So that was that.

Sort of.

I'm glad Gabriel passed on the Genesis reunion tour in '07. There were rumors he would come back into the fold, and the band would tour, performing the whole of *The Lamb Lies Down on Broadway*. The rest of the band worked hard to recruit Gabriel, and he came close to coming back. I was dubious about it from the get-go, because it smacked of a money grab. Nevertheless, I was on board for *When In Rome,* a live release complete with a "making of" documentary. Collins (whom I put on strict personal musical probation) found a way to anger me when it seemed that he turned up for rehearsals without practicing. One scene showed him throwing his drumsticks in frustration when he couldn't grasp one of the difficult sections of a classic '70s song. I yelled at the TV, "You've got to practice, you idiot! What did you *think* was gonna happen?" Of course, everything worked out, and the tour went on to be a big success. I found it an underwhelming experience.

The songs were now being played at lower octaves, because Collins couldn't hit the high notes any more. The schmaltzy pop and love songs became essential. The epic pieces were now being abbreviated and relegated into medleys. This was not the Genesis I knew and loved. At least the drum duet between Collins and Chester Thompson was still cool.

There's been clamoring for the band to come back again. I hope they don't. I want to remember the Genesis as I heard as a teenager. That band inspired me to become a musician. That band still sends me into fits of air-drumming, often in public. That band plays "Supper's Ready" so well, I am in tears by the end.

That's the band I want to remember.

(1)   The first two Genesis albums, ... *From Genesis to Revelations* and *Trespass* have largely been marginalized and were recorded before the more famous Gabriel/Banks/Rutherford/Hackett/Collins lineup was in place. And while I did eventually collect them, they never achieved the level of impact that the next six albums did.

SIDE TWO

*My musical world was changed forever when I
was introduced to King Crimson and their landmark
album, Discipline. To this day, I refer to this record
as my musical ground zero.*

Track 8
Entering the Court of King Crimson

By the summer of '85, I had a firm grip on my musical
identity. My choices were still mostly rock-based, but I had a
feel for R&B as well. I was absorbing so much music, I could
identify most of what I was hearing by the sound (and
sometimes the feel) of the bass line. I upgraded my personal
sound system from cheap off-brand portable cassette player to a
genuine Sony Walkman, complete with the foam headphones
enabling everyone around to hear what was being played. No
matter. I had a collection of homemade cassettes, and life was
good.

The day after graduating high school, I shipped off to
Fort Lee, Virginia, for Advanced Individual Training with the
U.S. Army. The specialty they taught me became useless within
a year or two. But where my musical growth was concerned, this
particular assignment proved pivotal.

While the training I underwent was still rigorous,
soldiers were given more free time than we had in basic training
the summer before. This meant I would either find myself
pumping quarters into the Spy Hunter video game at the arcade
near my barracks, or (more likely) I would walk and play

cassettes on my Walkman, which made the trip to Virginia with me.

One Saturday morning in July, I found myself strolling through the barracks dayroom, where we had a television and a pool table at our disposal. Those items were going unused at the time, however, and only one person was in the room. I can only remember him as Brian, a tall, blonde surfer-type from southern California. He was sitting in one of the padded chairs, polishing his combat boots.

Sitting on the floor next to Brian was the quintessential eighties "boom box," a portable stereo with a dual cassette deck. My headphones were on as I walked past Brian, but it was clear there was music playing. But I couldn't feel or recognize the bass line. There was no way I could let this go unchecked.

I took off my headphones, but still couldn't recognize the music. "What are you listening to?" I asked Brian, who had barely noticed I was in the room.

Brian grinned at me. "It's a band called Roxy Music," he replied, his brush still making its way over his boots. "Ever heard of them?" I shook my head. "Do you like it?" I took a few moments to listen closely and nodded. His smile widened a bit, and he took the tape out of the player. "Why don't you check it out for the day? If you like it, I'll make you a copy."

Always eager to hear something new, I took the tape. The album Brian had loaned me was called *Avalon*, and it sounded unlike anything I had ever heard. The vocals, sung by Bryan Ferry, seemed to have more "air" in them than I was used to. The instruments weren't as heavy-handed as Bruce Springsteen (who's instruments seemed to be in the listeners face) by comparison. It reminded me of some of the British pop acts I was seeing and hearing on MTV. Except this was different. It was more sophisticated. I loved it, and I wasn't going to wait a whole day to get my own copy. I raced back to my room, grabbed a blank cassette, and went back to the dayroom, where Brian was packing up his shoeshine gear.

Brian listened to me go on and on about what I heard, his smile getting bigger by the second. He had found a musical kindred spirit, which was not the easiest thing to do. I know this because I smiled like that a few times.

Brian nodded his approval. "You have a really open mind for music," he said. It's a compliment I still cherish.

"Sure," I replied sheepishly. "I'll listen to anything once."

"Well let's see how you handle this." Brian fished around in the black canvass bag containing cassette tapes. After a moment, he produced one and tossed it to me. I asked who the artist was. "It's a British guitarist named of Robert Fripp and his band, King Crimson." The names meant nothing to me. I looked at him blankly. His omnipresent grin was warm and understanding. "Yeah, I figured you didn't know them. Well, check it out anyway. I think you'll dig it. Some of the music is a little complicated, so play it at least twice before you bring it back. Enjoy!" With that, Brian left the dayroom, boots and cassette bag in hand.

***

Having had experience with Genesis, I was far from fearful of what I was about to hear. How hard can it be, I wondered? A check of my watch told me that it was a little after noon. I decided to take a walk to the arcade, where I could also have lunch. I'd play this King Crimson stuff as I strolled there and back.

It was a cloudless summer day just outside of Richmond, Virginia. Temperatures were in the low 90s, and it was a bit humid. I left the dorm, walked across the street, through the small grassy field, up a slight hill, and onto the blacktop lot which served as our parade ground, where we worked on Drill and Ceremony (marching and facing movements) far more than I care to remember. As I made my way up the hill, I plugged the tape into my Walkman.

Anyone who has walked across blacktop on a hot summer day knows the surface doesn't get cooler in the sun. When I began my walk, my objective was to get across the asphalt as quickly as possible, and into the air-conditioned arcade. With that in mind, I pressed the "play" button on the Walkman.

What I heard literally stopped me in my tracks.

The first King Crimson song I am consciously aware of hearing is called "Three of a Perfect Pair." It is the title track of their 1983 release. How to describe what I heard? It was unlike anything I had experienced to date and have rarely experienced since. The harmony of three or more voices swelled, followed immediately by some of the craziest guitar playing I ever heard. An interlocking 6/8 figure was scrambling my brain (not that I knew what an interlocking 6/8 figure was at the time). The guitar lines weaved between one another. They were accompanied by a bassist playing a line that went with, yet also against, the guitar lines. (The bass, I would learn later, came from a Chapman Stick.) And the drummer ... *good Lord*! He seemed to be going out of his way to play against the other three musicians, shoving his snare drum in between the beats left by the other players. For the next four-and-a-half minutes, I repeatedly asked myself the same question:

What the hell is THIS?

The lyrics were far more sophisticated than anything I knew. What the hell does "cyclothymic" mean, I wondered. The guitar solo I heard defied description. The song had a pop feel, but it was far from any pop music I could fathom.

I was completely baffled, and totally infatuated. When the song ended, I rewound it and played it again. And then I rewound it and played it again. And then I did it again. Just for good measure, I did it twice more. It was after half an hour I realized I was still standing on the same spot, on a 100–degree asphalt parade ground. The realization came only after a drop of sweat nestled into my eye, stinging me back to reality.

I shook off the sweat and resumed walking. The next song was called "Elephant Talk," and it was every bit as incredible as the first tune. Then came "Frame By Frame" and "Neal and Jack and Me." These guys were beyond incredible. How is it that I never heard of them?

Oh, yeah ... the sound I was hearing was not even remotely commercial. No way this gets on the radio. Absolutely *no way*!

For the remainder of the day, that hour-long cassette tape became my mission in life. I don't know how many times I played it, but it was a *lot*! And I still didn't grasp everything I heard. No matter. This was the kind of music I wanted to experience. I had found my new favorite band in Robert Fripp (guitar), Adrian Belew (guitar and vocal), Tony Levin (bass and Stick), and Bill Bruford (drums). They established themselves – in one day – as my new musical Ground Zero.

***

I found Brian later that evening, bringing him another blank cassette. I ranted and raved, starting with telling him what happened on the parade ground. If I didn't know any better, I would swear I saw tears of pride come from his eyes. He was witnessing a musical conversion. I became a King Crimson disciple.

While I continued to play some of my other cassettes during my summer in Virginia, there could be no denying King

Crimson had a hold on me. When I returned home, I wasted no time making my way to the record store. I had a new musical mission in life, and a new genre to explore to the fullest. First objective: buy every King Crimson record I could get my hands on. What I didn't know was my musical education was truly about to begin.

The first thing I learned was the Crimson I fell in love with that summer made only three records: *Discipline, Beat,* and *Three of a Perfect Pair.* That was a disappointment to me. And then the record store clerk really rocked my world: the band I "discovered" in the summer of '85 no longer existed! They broke up after their '84 tour. (1)

I was crushed. No more records from these guys? How could that be? They're the greatest things to happen to me musically in the history of, well, *ever!* I had not yet entered the musical mind of Robert Fripp, which would not happen for more than a decade. Once I did, I understood a lot more. One of the most crucial things I learned from Fripp was this: he did not view King Crimson as a band, *per se.* King Crimson, to its founder, was "a way of doing things." The band is more than the sum of its personnel. The right people must be in the right place at the right time to make the music Fripp envisions a reality. As such, the personnel on a particular project were subject to change. This is a musical philosophy I came to adopt as one of my own.

Throughout the history of King Crimson, band founder and leader Robert Fripp is the only constant member. The '80s band was the first one to record consecutive albums using the same personnel. This didn't happen again until 1999-2003, when the same Crimson lineup made two straight records (and a couple of official bootleg recordings).

But all was not lost. King Crimson made quite a few records between 1969 and 1974. In addition to the '80s albums, I left the record store with *Red, Starless and Bible Black*, and the seminal *In the Court of the Crimson King*, the debut album many believe laid the groundwork for the Prog genre. They were good records, but it would take time for them to achieve "classic" status in my book. Not because they were bad records, but because they sounded little or nothing like the '80s Crimson I was completely in love with.

For me, the best way to describe Crimson's early records boils down to one word: *British*. The music was stolid. It was proper. From an instrumental standpoint, everything was precisely where it needed to be.

But it could also rock. Hard. My knowledge of progressive rock was limited, so I didn't fully grasp how many future artists used *In the Court of the Crimson King* (released in 1969) as their musical bible.

The songs on *ITCOTKC* were adventurous. They pushed boundaries, defying the laws of rock and roll as they were known at the time. Mellotrons ran into saxophones, which were intercut by Fripp's searing guitar lines. Michael Giles' drums rumbled and tumbled, making the rest of the band seem, at times, as though they were racing to keep up. The music could also take on an ethereal quality, giving the listener an opportunity to breathe before it took off again.

The album's title track is a masterwork in stoic beauty. It achieves its emotional impact by initially seeming free of emotion, compared to many other rock acts of the time. There was no need for screaming or over-the-top grandeur. Still, vocalist and bassist Greg Lake was able to make his point perfectly. And when his vocals reached their crescendo (precisely when they were supposed to and not an instant before), the listener could not help but be moved.

***

King Crimson's debut album is a classic, but it sounds dated. I can picture the tie-dye, round-framed glasses, bell-bottom jeans, and locks of lengthy hair being worn by the band and its fans. This is not necessarily a bad thing, but it does explain (to me, at least) why Fripp was hesitant to re-visit this material during subsequent King Crimson tours. While Fripp has been willing to dip his toes into the waters of his band's back catalogue in concert, he has done so while continuing to move Crimson forward sonically. The new technology Fripp and his band mates embraced may not have been able to capture the sounds he may have been looking for in satisfactory fashion. Maybe he just didn't want to play those songs any more.

While I enjoyed *ITCOTKC*, *Red*, released in '74, solidified my love of the British King Crimson. By then, Crimson was stripped down to a remarkable power trio consisting of Fripp (guitar), John Wetton (bass and vocals), and Bruford (drums). This band was as close to heavy metal as King Crimson would get prior to 2003. The title track, which opens the album, blisters the eardrums. I have heard more than a couple of hard rock albums from bands like of Led Zeppelin and Black Sabbath. "Red" was something else altogether.

I love Led Zeppelin. I always will. But I feel there is a certain degree of sloppiness in their playing. I call it the "Blooze Effect." Zeppelin's roots were in the American blues, which meant their playing was rooted in the moment, and based on the emotions during said moment. American journalists took to giving Zeppelin's British take on the art form a slightly different spelling, which was forever linked to Jimmy Page and company. Their playing, while certainly heavy, was often far from precise. Crimson, on the other hand, knew exactly what it was doing at all times. (2)

Unlike *ITCOTCK*, *Red* holds up after all these years. Yes, King Crimson still sounds very British, but one can hear the musicians stretching beyond those musical barriers. I would soon discover this particular stretch had begun a couple of years before *Red* was released. As I've said, it takes the right musicians to arrive at the right place at the right time. To my ears, those musicians had not arrived when *In the Wake of Poseidon, Lizard,* and *Islands* were released between '70 and '72. They are decent albums, but rate at the bottom of my playlist favorites.

On these albums, King Crimson is heard attempting to move away from its original sound and closer to jazz, featuring some improvisational aspects. The results, to my ears, are mixed. The revolving door of musicians going in and out of the band did not help things. One of the most important aspects of improvisation is the musician's faith in his bandmates. This trust is rooted in chemistry, and that chemistry comes from time spent together in the studio or on stage. The '70-'72 Crimson lacked that chemistry.

But some of Crimson's most popular material came from this era. At shows, I heard fans clamoring for "Cat Food," "The Devil's Triangle," "Pictures of a City," "Cirkus," "Sailor's Tale," and "Ladies of the Road." Some of the early material was revisited during King Crimson's 2014-'16 tours, which featured band members from various eras, and two new members helping make up the triple-drum lineup. This band has received rave reviews during their travels throughout North America, Japan, and Europe.

***

Had I been exposed to '69-'72 King Crimson first, I cannot say with certainty I would have become a lifelong fan. In fact, I may have relegated them to the same status I give to Emerson, Lake, and Palmer: Interesting music, but not something I need to spend a lifetime absorbing. Luckily, I met the '80s Crimson first.

When drummer Bill Bruford left Yes to join King Crimson, I believe Crimson's music got a lot more interesting. Bruford's approach to drums (once described by a music journalist as "making a series of skittering adjustments to the backbeat") gave Fripp a new musical foil, opening up new avenues of musical possibility. When bassist and vocalist John Wetton came on board, Crimson had the powerful voice its music needed. Crude as it may sound, the music of King Crimson found its balls. Wetton's approach to the bass was far more powerful than his predecessor, Boz Burrell. The tandem of Wetton and Bruford made for one of the most powerful rhythm sections in rock, based on sheer volume alone. One couldn't help but feel for David Cross, who joined the '72-'74 band as the violin player. How in God's name was Cross going to make himself heard over the din of the rhythm section, which now included percussionist Jaime Muir? But if King Crimson has done one thing well in it's nearly 50 years of existence, it's to see each band member is heard. And so, a classic quintet was created. Variations of this quintet created the three best King Crimson studio records of the '70s: *Lark's Tongues in Aspic*, *Starless and Bible Black*, and *Red*. (3)

When I'm in the mood for "vintage" King Crimson, the Fripp, Wetton, Cross, Muir, Bruford quintet is where I wind up. Their sound is as powerful 40 years after the fact as it was at the time.

***

One can never accuse Robert Fripp of staying at the fair for too long. He has never been one to work a band past its expiration date. The incredible '70s incarnation of King Crimson were no exception. In September of '74, shortly before *Red* was released, Fripp announced his band had "ceased to exist." This was a kick in the gut not only to fans, but to Bruford and Wetton, who believed the band would continue for some time.

But according to Sid Smith, author of the outstanding King Crimson biography *In the Court of King Crimson*, Fripp was having a difficult time working with Bruford. The two possess very strong personalities, so it is easy to imagine extraordinary clashes. Ironically, this dynamic seemed to bring out the best in both Fripp and Bruford, creating a symbiotic musical relationship. The two realized hey needed each other to thrive, which no doubt drove both of them bananas.

Fripp was not completely certain Wetton was going to hang around if Crimson didn't rise in stature. Wetton was an anachronism in the Prog community, as he thrived on his ambition to be a star. This is funny to prog fans, because if one thing is certain, a Prog musician will *never* become a mainstream star. He will become legendary within this musical niche. He will probably even be able to carve out a living. But mainstream musical stardom? Forget about it!

I have no proof of this, but I believe Robert Fripp has a hidden talent more than a few musicians could use: he knows when his band and its sound have run their course. There have been eight versions of King Crimson. So far, none of them has lasted longer than it was supposed to. Each version did what it needed to do, and then faded into the ether. Sometimes, the band would only make one album. Other versions only toured briefly. But Fripp is the head of King Crimson's Quality Control Department for a reason. I, for one, have learned to trust his judgment, even when it pisses me off.

And so, it seemed King Crimson was no more. Fripp moved from England to New York City, playing with David Bowie, Blondie, and Talking Heads over the next few years. He also started on a spiritual and educational path that had a profound impact on his musical output for years to come.

Meanwhile, Wetton and Bruford became half of prog supergroup U.K. The rhythm section was augmented with legendary guitarist Allan Holdsworth and the violin of Eddie Jobson. The quartet created one of the more popular prog records of the '70s. "In the Dead of Night," the opening track of their self-titled debut LP, sums up everything that was great about U.K. in seven minutes: thunderous bass riffs, powerful drums that played on and off-beat, and an angular guitar solo that many amateurs are still trying to learn. While I heard the record well after the fact, something tells me that U.K. made it possible (though not easy) for me to forget about King Crimson for a while.

But as it turns out, the King was far from dead.

***

As the '80s dawned, Fripp was ready to form a new band. His first call was to Bruford, who was just coming off the road with the critically successful band which just happened to share his last name. Fripp also recruited a dynamic young guitarist named Adrian Belew, who was playing with Talking Heads. In the past, it seemed unfathomable Fripp would need a second guitar player to bring his musical vision forth. But times changed, and Fripp's new approach required a second six-stringed voice. Belew's was a perfect fit, if only because it seemed to come from the opposite end of the musical spectrum. Fripp and Belew formed a Yin and Yang within the band, initially named Discipline. Belew's dissonant riffing, tremolo-arm induced dive-bombs, and animal noises provided a sense of near-comic relief from Fripp's mathematical methods.

The two Englishmen and Belew found themselves in New York, auditioning bass players. The search lasted three days before high-caliber session musician Tony Levin walked in. Fripp first met Levin while the two of them were working for Peter Gabriel. The bassist's talents were such that he was constantly in demand, and Fripp assumed Levin would not be available to join a band. Fortunately, this assumption was in error. The audition could not be deemed safe for the faint-of-heart. "Mostly, Bill played the rhythm to 'Discipline,'" Belew said. "The bass player was expected to play the correct bass line, in 15/8!" Levin was up to the task.

Tony Levin is a big reason why I love the '80s King Crimson. He is an absolute master of his instrument, and he carries that mastery with a presence exuding quiet confidence. Admittedly, when I look to introduce people to the bass sound of Tony Levin, I don't point to King Crimson. Rather, I direct them to the incredible bass sound of Peter Gabriel's "Sledgehammer." This almost always elicits a brightening of the eyes and a knowing expression from the casual music fan. *Then* I can tell them about Levin's playing in King Crimson.

When listening to music, it is customary to follow the drummer in order to find the beat and maintain the groove. This was not the best idea in the '80s Crimson. Imagine watching the band on stage and being told, "Whatever you do, do NOT follow the drummer for the beat. See that bass player over there? Follow him. He'll get you where you need to go." Levin understood his role in the band, and that is what made him and Bruford a positively remarkable rhythm section. The drummer was free to play around and invert the beat, while the bassist remained the rock that held down the rhythmic fort.

This is not to say Levin's bass playing is simplistic. Some of the most complex bass lines in the King Crimson catalog come courtesy of Tony Levin. But even with all of those notes cascading about, the music's groove is never lost. This is not the easiest thing on Earth to do. Yet Levin pulls it off like he is taking a Sunday stroll.

Belew gave King Crimson a much-needed personality boost. His easygoing smile and showmanship helped the band break free of their '70s-era stodginess. Belew's pink suits were a nice touch as well. Levin seemed to feed off this, and he passed Belew's infectious joy to Bruford. This new quartet was sending a subconscious message: playing in King Crimson was not just a rare musical honor. It was *fun*!

That musical joy manifested itself in the form of the '81 album, *Discipline*. Original King Crimson fans may have been alarmed by the band's new sound, which incorporated not only the interlocking guitar methods, but a new wave influence as well. To say the least, it sounded nothing like *Red*. Critics of the new album complained songs like "Elephant Talk" (the album's opening track) sounded more like an extension of Talking Heads than the prog group they knew and loved. But the Talking Heads influence was almost unavoidable, as Fripp played with the band on *Fear of Music*, and Belew recorded AND toured with them. (4) King Crimson is not known for making "sing-along" songs, but I find I can't help but spout out the lyrics to this gem every time I hear them, if only because of how clever they are.

"Elephant Talk" is a prime example. I don't know how long I was singing with Belew before I realized he was spouting out a semi-alphabetical list of synonyms for talking:

"Talk, it's only talk
Arguments, agreements, answers, advice, articulate announcements
It's only talk
Talk, it's only talk
Babble, burble, banter, bicker bicker bicker, brouhaha, bolderdash, ballyhoo
It's only talk." (a)

I'd be lying if I said I made the King Crimson/Talking Heads connection immediately. I only knew I loved the music this Crimson made. "Elephant Talk" veered directly into "Frame By Frame," one of my favorite songs in the band's catalog. Swirling and churning guitar riffs give way to an astounding interlocking 7/8 guitar pattern critics want to dismiss as creative use of a delay effects pedal. Only after seeing the band live does the critic see both his mistake and the virtuosity of Fripp and Belew. Equally impressive is the ability of Belew to sing while playing these difficult guitar parts. One of the proudest moments of my life as a musician came when I learned to play this song. But it never occurred to me to sing while playing. That's too damned hard.

"Elephant Talk" and "Frame By Frame" introduced me to a new instrument: the Chapman Stick, wielded by Levin. It's a wooden plank with 10 or 12 strings, with which the musician was able to elicit both bass and guitar tones by tapping on its fretboard. The mentality needed to play the Stick was similar to that of a pianist, as both single notes and chords could be struck while playing. The Chapman Stick (which can also be heard in Levin's work with Peter Gabriel) added a remarkable dimension to the Crimson sound. It was light-years away from John Wetton's '70s sound, but still very King Crimson.

Not to be left behind, Bruford added weapons to his percussion arsenal, including roto-toms, boo-bams, slit drums, and splashy cymbals. The biggest development, however, was the addition of Simmons electronic drum pads. These drums were used on a multitude of recordings throughout the '80s. Played alone, they put forth a plastic sound that instantly dates the recordings they are played on. Bruford, however, used them in conjunction with the rest of his drum kit. Rather than being the primary percussion sound, they augmented Bruford's kit, giving him the opportunity to expand his sound palate while still making the signature Bruford snare drum sound.

Fripp and Belew also embraced new technology by incorporating Roland guitar synthesizers into their rigs. The guitars provided traditional tones and simulated the sounds of exotic instruments as well. In "The Sheltering Sky," Fripp induces the sound of Turkish trumpets, the last thing one might expect to hear coming from a King Crimson song. But there they are, and it works!

Sid Smith's *In the Court of King Crimson* documents the making of *Discipline* as the ultimate honeymoon record. No doubt this is the reason it rates as one of a few perfect albums I have heard. Eager to maintain that momentum, Fripp rushed the band back into the recording studio, where they found they lacked sufficient new ideas. If *Discipline* was the honeymoon, then King Crimson's next album, *Beat* (released in '82), could have been grounds for a messy divorce.

My lack of band context proved to be a blessing rather than a curse. Brian, who introduced me to this band, included every song from *Beat* on his mix tape. As part of a larger collective, the songs struck me as remarkable. Had I obtained *Beat* individually, I might have found myself asking, "Is that all there is?" The album was just over 36 minutes long, hardly the effort of a prog rock band who had written epic-length pieces in the past. Also, compared to the songs on *Discipline,* there was a noticeable drop-off in the strength of the songs. They were still stronger than the efforts of the average '80s pop band, but with King Crimson come high standards, and this album was falling short.

Belew has admitted he wished he had not given a couple of his songs to King Crimson for *Beat*, as they would have been better served on a solo album. That speaks to the lack of material the band had on hand when they started recording. Smith documents the recording process well in his book. And unlike the other '80s albums, there is no bonus material to be found from the *Beat* sessions. The band got what they needed for a record, and then they got the hell out of there.

Things were looking up again for King Crimson with the release of *Three of a Perfect Pair* in '83. Bruford refers to it as the most difficult of the three '80s albums to complete. But he says that more as a point of pride than a source of contention. Bruford told Smith, "Crimson is a band that scuffles for its music." The effort (built over recording sessions in three locations) reveals itself here.

In addition to the pop-like efforts of the title track, "Model Man," and "Sleepless," Crimson also churns out period-specific tunes like "Nuages (That Which Passes, Passes Like Clouds)" and "Industry." Both make the most of the '80s electronic percussion and synthesizers. While they both sound like the '80s, they are only a little dated when heard today. One doesn't cringe from the sounds so much as grin from amusement.

King Crimson also managed one more epic in "Larks Tongues in Aspic, part III," which closes the album. I didn't have to be in the studio to know that the band was having a good time with this one. The piece manages to blister, smolder, and groove. Toward the end of the track, Bruford can be heard yelling, "Whoo! Yeah!" And then he laughs.

That sums things up pretty nicely.

***

Shortly before I joined the Air Force in April of '88, I found myself at a friend's house. I was transferring copies of my favorite records to cassette and putting together a few mixes.

We were having a good time reminiscing about some of the older songs, while I introduced him to a few things he had never heard.

Inevitably, I began my transfer of King Crimson material. I was still happy as a clam. But my friend's face had darkened a bit. "What is it with you and this band?" he asked, sounding a bit irritated. "I don't get it. I know you love it, but I think it sucks."

I remember feeling physically wounded by his remarks. I felt them in the pit of my stomach. I can handle constructive criticism. But this seemed a little more … personal. Still, I buried the hot flash of anger that was rising in me and attempted to explain. "These are musicians. REAL musicians," I said. "Their talent level goes so far beyond anything that's on the radio, it defies belief." I continued my argument, but it was clear I was getting nowhere. His belief in the talent of a musician lay in a couple of simple, overrated factors.

"Then why don't they have any gold records?" he asked flatly. "Why isn't their music on the charts?" He decided it was the perfect time to pick up the pizza and beer we were having for dinner. He could leave me to my own devices and go enjoy the music he liked. So be it. He did me a favor.

While I would never go so far as to call my friend (and the many who think like him) dumb, there is a certain level of ignorance among music fans. Songs which stretch beyond the basic confines of commercial radio ("It's got a great beat, and I can dance to it!") are not deemed worthy of Mr. and Ms. Causal's time. They take too much effort to understand. King Crimson is definitely not music for the casual fan. It is not danceable. But it is highly rewarding for those willing to give it time and effort. Alas, it doesn't seem to be a priority for many listeners.

The older I get, the less I feel the need to explain the brilliance of King Crimson and bands of their ilk. Perhaps because explaining the music doesn't make it sound any better. Music and musicians of this level and mindset must be absorbed into the listener's mind and body. Only then can it truly be grasped.

Still, if I can't find a way to defend my band verbally, then are they really worthy of a defense?

So, then … why King Crimson? What makes this band so special? Why have they remained an integral part of my musical consciousness for more than three decades? Why do they, along with Miles Davis and Frank Zappa, deserve to be a third of my Musical Holy Trinity? My answer is this:

King Crimson is one of the first bands to ever teach me music is about endless possibility. Their approach went against nearly everything I learned before (save, perhaps, for Genesis and a couple of related bands). Few guitarists played with the precision of Robert Fripp. Even fewer took the approach of Adrian Belew, who remains on the cutting edge today. Tony Levin showed me playing bass is about much more than landing the root note and maintaining a simple groove. What Bill Bruford taught (and continues to teach) me from behind the drum kit would probably fill another book. These four men taught me what it means to be an artist, because they took what they knew and then melded it with what they didn't. The result was, as Fripp often liked to view it, a re-invention of the wheel. And with each successive record, King Crimson continues to try to re-invent their wheel.

Like Miles Davis, Crimson has never been content to rest on its laurels. The next challenge is out there, and they continue to pursue it. Like Frank Zappa, Crimson's sound transcended multiple styles of music, even as they put their own touch on every new musical direction. It is impossible to get bored with King Crimson, because there was and is always a new avenue to explore.

It would have been nice to be able to take my friend to a King Crimson concert and let him experience the power of the music first hand. But even I hadn't seen Crimson live, because they disbanded a year before I learned about them. Fripp's sense of timing struck again. Another band ran its musical course.

I had the albums. Still, something was missing from my experience. Seeing this band on stage would have filled the gap. But it would not come to pass. Not yet, anyway.

I believed I was going to be deprived of amazing music from four amazing musicians. How would I be able to hear more from Adrian Belew, Robert Fripp, Tony Levin, and Bill Bruford? It was time to head back to the record store, and have another talk with Prog Guy. I was soon to find out I was only at the root of a very fruitful musical family tree.

***

To be a fan of progressive rock makes one a fan of King Crimson, directly or indirectly. Founder Robert Fripp is the only constant in each of the band's many lineups. Other band members found musical glory not only in Crimson, but with others as well.

Consider my favorite '80s band alone. Adrian Belew got his first major notoriety playing for Frank Zappa (a major nurturer of young musical talent in his own right) and played for both David Bowie and Talking Heads before making his way into King Crimson (5). He is also the front man for Intelli-Pop band the Bears and has an extensive solo catalog. And then there are the sessions. Belew has found his way onto albums as diverse as Paul Simon's *Graceland* and Nine Inch Nails' *The Downward Spiral*. He has worked with Herbie Hancock, Stewart Copeland (known best as the drummer for The Police), Laurie Anderson, Bela Fleck, Porcupine Tree, and countless others

Tony Levin's bass career took off while working for the likes of Buddy Rich and John Lennon in the '70s. He is also the primary source of low frequencies for Peter Gabriel, who considers Levin a virtual right-hand man. One would be hard pressed to find a signature Gabriel hit that doesn't revolve around the thunder of Levin's bass. In addition to those venues, Levin can be found on the recordings of David Bowie, David Torn, Pink Floyd, Robbie Robertson, Al DiMeola, prog supergroup Liquid Tension Experiment (which features members of King Crimson-influenced Dream Theater), and many more.

Bill Bruford's major breakthrough was with legendary band Yes, whom he left to join King Crimson. After Crimson's first breakup in '74, Bruford found himself (among other places) playing for the traveling version of Genesis, as well as U.K., and his own band, Bruford, which made four records in the late '70s and early '80s. He also cut two keyboard/drum duo albums with Moody Blues alum Patrick Moraz. After Crimson's '80s breakup, Bruford found his way back to his first love, jazz, by forming Earthworks. That band was active in various incarnations until Bruford's retirement in 2006.

Robert Fripp's impact is felt not only in his playing, but as a teacher. In addition to his ambient works with Brian Eno, his production efforts with Peter Gabriel and Daryl Hall, and guest efforts with the likes of Blondie, Led Zeppelin's John Paul Jones, Talking Heads, and Porcupine Tree. Fripp formed a school based around his meticulous method of playing, called Guitar Craft. Fripp has set up and run classes in Europe, North and South America, teaching all comers.

Going back to King Crimson's '69 origin produces a family tree of bands and musicians defying belief. This tree was published in '92 as part of a box set called *The Compact King Crimson: Frame by Frame*. The tree branches out even more since the band's reformation in '94.

Because of this, was easy for me to walk away from commercial radio for nearly eight years, beginning in the fall of '85. There was just too much good music to explore. And amazingly, I found a radio format willing to play it.

(1) In 1997, King Crimson released *Absent Lovers*, a live recording of the last show from the 1984 tour. Recorded in Montreal, Crimson put forth one of the most blistering sets of live music I have ever heard, taking everything the band had recorded into the studio to an entirely new level. *Absent Lovers* is a must for any King Crimson fan.

(2) I am well aware of King Crimson's love for live improvisation during that era, particularly between '72 and '74. The music Crimson seemed to pull out of the sky could be positively stunning. Quality examples of this work can be found on *The Great Deceiver* and *The Night Watch*, live box sets documenting the '73-'74 Crimson, released more than 20 years after they were recorded. "Providence," which takes up half of *Red*'s second side, is an improvisation from the band's second show at the Palace Theater in Providence, Rhode Island, recorded on June 30, 1974.

(3) Muir is absent from *Starless and Bible Black*. The entire quintet is present for *Lark's Tongues in Aspic*. Only Fripp, Wetton, and Bruford remain for *Red*, with guest appearances made by other musicians, including Cross.

(4) Adrian Belew very nearly declined the offer to join King Crimson. Talking Heads made him a solid offer to join them full-time, as it appeared David Byrne was heading for the exit. Belew was also a part of Tom Tom Club, the Chris Franz/Tina Weymouth offshoot from Talking Heads that scored a hit single with "Genius of Love." (The tune was reworked into a mega-hit for Mariah Carey, called "Fantasy.") To top it all off, Belew had just signed a record deal as a solo artist. It took more than a little solid negotiating from Fripp and his

management to get Belew into the fold. I thank the musical gods they were able to do so.

(5)   Like Miles Davis, Frank Zappa had a remarkable eye for young musical talent. In addition to Belew, incredible musicians like drummers Terry Bozzio, Chester Thompson, and Chad Wackerman, guitarists Mike Kenneally, Steve Vai, and Warren Cucurillo, bassists Scott Thunes and Patrick O'Hearn, violinist Jean-Luc Ponty, keyboardists George Duke and Alan Zavod, and many others cut their professional teeth on stage with Zappa. Each young musician took Zappa's perfectionist mindset with them to their own or other bands, often to critical and popular acclaim.

(a)   "Elephant Talk," written by Adrian Belew, Robert Fripp, Tony Levin, and Bill Bruford. Lyrics by Belew. Published by UMG Publishing, Ltd.

*A few of the many "underground" artists I heard
on college radio in the late '80s. More than a few
went on to superstardom, but all had their roots in cult status.*

Track 9
The Left Side of the Dial

I would love to tell you I discovered most of the music I love by precise, scientific means. The truth is, a great deal of my collection was discovered purely by chance. My music library is a never-ending series of happy accidents, usually connected by a common artist, sideman, or producer.

Some musical discoveries actually came by way of a radio format. But even that discovery was not intentional. In the fall of 1985, I was just looking for a radio station playing my latest musical obsessions. Thus, began a three-year love affair with college radio. The sounds I heard created a fundamental shift in the way I heard music.

The summer of '85 was about the discovery of King Crimson and the bands flowing from that musical artery. I returned home from Fort Lee, Virginia, with little idea of what I wanted to do with my life. My parents expected me to go to college. Supposedly, that's why I joined the Army in the first place. So I found myself enrolled in junior college, primarily because I hadn't taken the time or put forth the effort to pursue a major university. What the hell … at least my parents couldn't bust my chops about abandoning my education.

I found my way into the office of the campus newspaper, where I found a home. Before long, I was named

114

sports editor. I spent a great deal more time there than I did most of my classes. It wasn't long before I learned the school had a radio station. I had a new reason to appreciate school.

College radio is vastly different from its more traditional counterparts. The stations are independent, kept afloat by university budgets and individual donations, and run by students, as opposed to sponsorship, commercial advertising sales, and professional disc jockeys. Because of this, college stations are able to free themselves of the traditional radio "formats" which had become more and more prevalent. Rather than focus solely on one style of music, college radio stations often divided the air day into two- to four-hour blocks featuring a wide variety of music, talk, and sports. On any given day, any given thing could come pouring out of my stereo speakers. I absolutely *loved* this concept!

There was also a downside. Since there was no commercial sponsorship, college radio stations were relegated to the weaker end of the FM frequencies. In those days, radio stations were located by turning the large dial on the FM receiver hard to the left, toward frequencies starting around 87.1 megahertz. The signals were leaden with static, and sometimes one station would overlap with another from a nearby campus. What poured forth from the speakers often depended on exactly where the radio was situated. In the car, it was very possible the reggae tune I was enjoying would end up sounding like jazz or bluegrass, depending on the time of day.

I can't remember how many stations from the left side of the dial I was playing in the mid- to late '80s. There was a jazz station out of Edwardsville, Illinois, holding my interest for hours at a time, even when its format switched to "New Age" late in the evenings. I found one or two stations flirting with the occasional King Crimson tune, much to my delight. But they also expanded on that ideal, introducing me to related acts that soon became part of in my collection.

The King Crimson family tree contains many, many branches. So, while I might not hear a lot of KC's music, I did hear a lot from Bill Bruford (who played drums with Crimson), Allan Holdsworth and Jeff Berlin (who played guitar and bass, respectively, in Bruford), Peter Gabriel (who had not quite broken commercially yet in America), Brand X (Phil Collins's other band besides Genesis), and Emerson, Lake, and Palmer. But prog was far from the dominant sound on college radio stations. That sound came from somewhere else entirely.

***

Punk rock and I rarely crossed paths in the late '70s and '80s. Let's face it: punk was the living, breathing antithesis of the progressive and jazz sounds I loved. Punk rockers hated the music I adored. They thought my music was showy and self-indulgent. I heard the term "musical masturbation" more than once from my spiky-haired, leather-clad musical nemeses. What punks called "three chords and the truth," my camp called "an overwhelming lack of musical ability." So, there was no logic in believing punk would help spawn a musical movement I would come to embrace. Yet that is precisely what happened.

A musical movement is often spawned out of rebellion of what came before it. Therefore, the "post-punk" movement came forth as a counter to the punk movement, while still maintaining some of its core elements. The relatively simplistic sound of punk's guitar, bass, and drums was soon augmented with keyboards, electronics, dance beats, and other exotic instrumentation. The Ramones and the Sex Pistols gave way to Public Image Limited, Siouxsie and the Banshees, Devo, and Talking Heads. But rather than label these groups post-punk, they were called precisely what they were: the new wave.

At last, it was musically possible to have both musical chops and a punk attitude. Bands like the Police could spike their hair, sneer at the audience, and play their asses off using jazz chords and alternate time signatures. And thanks to the creation of MTV, many of these bands were seeing airplay driving them to commercial success. And the sounds continued to fluctuate. A new musical door had been opened, and artists from everywhere were walking through.

The artists in college rock hit me in much the same way Motown or Stax record artists did. I can't point to the day I heard artists like R.E.M., U2, the B-52s, and 10,000 Maniacs for the first time any more than I can point out the day I first heard the Temptations, Stevie Wonder, Isaac Hayes, and Marvin Gaye. The radio was on, and I heard them all at pretty much the same time. I'd still be absorbing songs like "Radio Free Europe," "I Will Follow," "Rock Lobster," and "What's the Matter Here," when the next wave of artists would flood over me via static-laced college radio stations.

As much as I hate labeling music, I realized college rock seemed to come from one of four distinct places. Many of the bands I enjoyed came from pure attitude, and that 'tude came from punk. The music made by Husker Du, the Pixies, and the

Red Hot Chili Peppers came from the grimiest clubs, battered instruments and shredded vocal cords, enthusiastically pushed to the max in front of 100 people, or less, at a time. I didn't always understand what was being said, but I never doubted the band's sincerity.

There were bands playing music coming from the deepest, darkest corners of the soul. Kids clad in black leather and/or nylon, heavily made up in bright red lipstick, black nail polish, spiked or buzzed haircuts, and white face paint in various degrees of completion sang (wailed?) and danced along with the synthesizers, electronic beats, and minor chords created by the likes of the Smiths, Love and Rockets, Psychedelic Furs, the Sisters of Mercy, and New Order. Back when I created mix tapes, I put artists like these on a cassette I called "The Masters of Mope Rock." It was music for a rainy, depressing day.

Some college bands seemed to be all about a cause. The '80s were rife with social and political injustice, depending on one's point of view. Apartheid, the English occupation of Northern Ireland, the treatment of Australian Aborigines, the Church … there was always something to protest, and always a band around to lead the charge. This decade saw the rise of the human rights organization Amnesty International. Artists like U2, Midnight Oil, 10,000 Maniacs, and Sinead O'Connor made me more conscious of social evils taking place throughout the world. I would be lying if I said these groups didn't rub off on me more than a little. (1)

A lot of college rock was little more than quirky pop music. I don't mean that in a derogatory way. In fact, the quirk makes the music more appealing. The songs contained intelligent lyrics, unusual instrumentation, or just approached the song in an unusual fashion. Over time, some of these bands broke through to the mainstream, ultimately becoming part of the "alternative" movement of the '90s. One or two found their way to television shows like *Saturday Night Live*. Artists like Simple Minds, the BoDeans, the Sundays, and Edie Brickell & New Bohemians came from this particular vein.

Each "category" of college rock contained a band that really got its hooks in to me. My favorite band with attitude was the Red Hot Chili Peppers. Most casual music fans believed they were hearing something brand new in '91 when *BloodSugarSexMagik* took the airwaves by storm. Others thought they were in the know because they were familiar with *Mother's Milk*, which the Chili Peppers released two years before (and included a decent cover of Stevie Wonder's "Higher Ground"). But I remember hearing the band's *Freaky Styley* (released in '85), and *The Uplift Mofo Party Plan* ('87) all over college radio. Even I was a little late to the party, because the Chili Peppers released their self-titled debut in '84. Theirs was a delicious combination of punk, funk, ska, and rock that delighted and shocked audiences in clubs like Columbia, Missouri's Blue Note. By the release of *BloodSugarSexMagik*, the band perfected its craft and taken things to the next level. It's as though the band had no choice but to become international superstars.

My favorite "mope rock" bands were the Cure and Depeche Mode. Coincidentally, a fellow airman who heard me listening to some music from off the beaten path while we worked together at Tyndall Air Force Base, Florida, introduced them to me on the same day. My musical choice of that day in the fall of '88 (damned if I remember what it was) led to a lengthy conversation about music from off the beaten path. Before our conversation ended, my new friend slid me a couple of cassette tapes. "I think you'll like these," he said. One tape was Depeche Mode's *Black Celebration*. The other was the Cure's *Kiss Me, Kiss Me, Kiss Me*. I played the latter first. Within seconds, I felt my brain beginning to melt, in a good way.

A jagged chord was played twice, augmented with a bass drum. On the "off" beat, a snare drum (most likely electronic) found its way into the mix. The jagged pattern continued for several bars before a guitar solo took over, blazing away over the odd rhythmic pattern. This went on for three minutes or so. I was still digesting this unusual sound when the earnest wail of lead vocalist Robert Smith entered the picture. His voice ran counter to just about anything I had heard to date. It sounded desperate, earnest, and longing. It was the sound of a man enamored with someone he wanted no part of. "Your tongue's like poison," he sang. "It turns my guts all inside out." Apparently, it was not a relationship he cared to relish. "Get your fucking voice out of my head," he demanded, finishing the song with, "I wish you were dead. I wish you were dead." (a)

Wow. Not exactly Pat Boone.

The album is full of songs of love, loss, lament, and revenge. It was far from the cheeriest music I'd ever heard, but its sincerity sank its hooks into me, and I became a fan. I could picture Smith pining away on verse after verse, pounding his forehead with the microphone during instrumental portions. How anyone could sing from those depths consistently night after night was beyond me. But that was Robert Smith, and it's what he did song after song, album after album. And I was buying, be it previous albums like *Head on the Door*, or future releases like *Disintegration*. I remember using the song "Fascination Street" to fire myself up for tennis matches for nearly a year. Why that song lit me up is anyone's guess. But it worked.

A musician has to be careful when trying to draw fans into his cause. There's a fine line between being a genuine voice of reason and being an egocentric know-it-all. U2's dynamic frontman, Bono, has seen that line blur on him in the eyes of both fans and detractors. I've been listening to U2 since the days of *War*, which was released in '83. I picked up on *Boy* ('80) and *October* ('81) retroactively. Even then Bono, guitarist the Edge, bassist Adam Clayton, and drummer Larry Mullen, Jr., were earnestly pushing toward something bigger than themselves. U2 found firm footing with the release of *The Unforgettable Fire* in '84, and then took "cause music" to its apex in '87 with *The Joshua Tree*. Like so many others, I loved those records. I could also see the potential for runaway egotism within the band. And that is pretty much what happened, even if the music was still pretty good. As it turns out, there was another band out there fighting for causes, even if they were a little more low-key about it.

Hailing from Sydney, Australia, Midnight Oil had a musical career running nearly parallel to U2's, though they didn't reach the same level of fame. Like the Irish rockers, they rose to international prominence in the mid '80s. While U2 was attaining fame in '87 with *The Joshua Tree*, the Oils (as they were affectionately known) broke through at nearly the same time with *Diesel and Dust*. I remember seeing the video for the album's hit single, "Beds Are Burning," on MTV … and completely blowing it off. If any moment sums up my problem with promotional music videos, this was it.

I was too busy looking at the video's harsh imagery of the Australian outback and trying to figure out just what the deal was with Peter Garrett – Midnight Oil's 6'6" lead singer, in all his bald glory – to actually pay any attention to the song. It went right over my head. Several months later, while driving a minivan around Panama City, Florida (near Tyndall AFB), I heard – really *heard* – the song on the radio. Garrett's unique vocal growl, the *Peter Gunn*-ish guitar line, augmented with a driving bass groove, and drummer Rob Hirst's battering snare got its hooks into me, and it stuck. Within an hour, I was at a record store, tracking down this band and its album.

Over the years, I've learned to be wary of any album that leads off with its hit single. Sure enough, "Beds are Burning" is the opening track on *Diesel and Dust*. But there are exceptions to every rule, and where this album was concerned, I needn't have worried. The album was fantastic, from beginning to end. The Oils were an airtight band. Five musicians had no doubt become one unit. Hell, "Beds are Burning" wasn't even my favorite song on the album! That pleasure belonged to "The Dead Heart," which opens side two. It is a powerful piece of music.

The song opens with a relatively simple acoustic guitar lick, driven, as usual, by Hirst's drums. It doesn't take long before the harmonic background vocals give way to Garrett's in your face lead, which in this case covers the plight of embattled Aborigines. "We don't serve your country, don't serve your king. Know your custom, don't speak your tongue. White man came, took everyone." (b)

Say *what*, now?

But Garrett wasn't finished. "We don't serve your country, don't serve your king. White man, listen to the song we sing. White man came took everything."

Whoa! Hearing these words come from a white musician made the words all the more powerful. And then I heard the chorus, which never fails to move me. "We carry in our heart the true country, and that cannot be stolen. We follow in the steps of our ancestry, and that cannot be broken." Now, I'm not Australian. I've never been to Australia. But it was hard to ignore the power and the passion of Midnight Oil and its causes. Perhaps that's why they remain one of my favorite bands. Whether it was human rights, the environment, nuclear disarmament, or the dangers of strip mining, the Oils always had just the right song for the occasion. The band mastered the art of being down for the cause without being too in your face about it. That is essentially what separated them from U2. And their music got stronger as time went on.

The follow-up to *Diesel and Dust*, called *Blue Sky Mining*, was released in '90. Its songs were every bit as powerful as it predecessor. The Oils followed that up with the live album *Scream in Blue*, which taught me the Aussie quintet was twice as powerful on the stage as they were in the studio! In the liner notes, it was mentioned the environmentally friendly band would play in parks, attaching their PA speakers to trees with straps instead of nails. The straps were secured as tightly as humanly possible. When a passer-by asked the roadie why he was securing the speakers so tightly, the roadie is said to have replied, "Because the Oils are coming." It takes exactly one song on the live release to understand this. That song is the record's blistering opener, "Read About It," taken from the album *10, 9, 8, 7, 6, 5, 4, 3, 2, 1*. I was not familiar with Midnight Oil's pre-*Diesel* releases. That tune sent me running back to the archives.

Midnight Oil never achieved the worldwide superstardom of U2, but that didn't seem to matter. The band continued to evolve, modernizing its sound while remaining true to themselves. The last thing I ever expected to hear from this straightforward rock and roll band was an element of electronic, "drum & bass" groove. But there it was in '98, augmenting the title track to their album "Redneck Wonderland." The guitar groove behind that electronic lick will shake valuables off the shelves. The Oils could never be accused of not bringing the rock. And they were forever down with the cause.

By the turn of the century, Garrett left the band to pursue a career in politics. But now and again, Midnight Oil would surface for a charity gig or festival. But even if they never play another note in the studio or on the stage, their legacy is secure in my personal archives.

***

College rock spawned a remarkable amount of pop music. Some of it made its way to commercial radio. Most of it didn't. To my ears, a lot of it was too intelligent for Top 40 radio. And since the "Alternative" format had not yet taken hold, there was nowhere but the left side of the dial for this music to go.

A party anthem from a band like the B-52s (who had been slugging it out since '76) might have snuck out now and then in the mid- to late '80s. For a minute or two, I might see a teenager bopping along to "Planet Claire" or "Your Own Private Idaho." But things didn't really break for the Athens, Georgia band until '89, when they released *Cosmic Thing*. The album featured the single "Love Shack," which hit the airwaves like a tidal wave. There was no going back. Bands like the Smithereens, the Sundays, and the BoDeans released perfectly palatable pop/rock, but they couldn't seem to break through. That's a real shame. The commercial world had no idea what it was missing.

Another Athens band, R.E.M., managed to break through and achieve superstardom while writing highly intelligent music. While I heard many things about this band on my college rock stations, I may have missed out on them had I not been old enough to legally go into a bar.

Working musicians playing in bar bands will often speak with fondness or lament about playing covers. Bar owners want their patrons dancing and/or drinking, musicians say. And the way to get that done is *not* by offering up unfamiliar music. So bar bands have a nice stockpile of other artist's music at the ready, doled out over two or three sets in three or four hours. In '87, R.E.M. released *Document*, the album that brought them into the mainstream. It featured the single, "The One I Love," which was burning up the left side of the dial.

I turned 21 in '87, which made it possible for me to explore the sounds on Laclede's Landing, once a hotbed for live music in St. Louis. Situated just west of the Mississippi river, the Landing was home to some of the hottest music clubs in town, including Mississippi Nights (the go-to spot for bands on the rise), the Trainwreck Saloon, Kennedy's, and others. Music fans in the know found themselves on the Landing at some point on the weekends, and I was no exception.

I found myself in the Trainwreck one particular evening, doing what I did best: soaking up live music and nursing a soda. (2) As I made my way to the men's room, I heard the band (don't ask me who they were) playing a familiar song. It actually caused me to stop in place. As near as I could tell, the song only had one verse. The chorus was a desperate cry, as opposed to actual words. Still, there was no doubting the song's power and vibe. When the band finished, the 50 or so of us in the audience went wild. "Thank you," the band's frontman said graciously. "That one's from R.E.M." It wasn't long before I found myself in the record store, hunting that song down. It didn't take long to find a copy of *Document*, emblazoned with one of those gold stickers on the LP's plastic shrinkwrap, declaring, "Contains the hit, 'The One I Love.'" A new obsession was born.

The band got bigger and bigger as time went on. But every time I listen to R.E.M., I think of the Trainwreck Saloon, and imagine myself connecting to the band for the very first time, in that tiny room, even if it wasn't really them. (3)

***

By the spring of '88, I was in South Carolina, at the dawn of my professional life. I made new friends from all over the United States, and wasted little time introducing them to my favorite music. Naturally, they returned the favor. One Saturday evening, after exhausting myself on the tennis court (as usual), I was enjoying a pleasant evening of lying on my dorm room floor and listening to records. I was startled out of my music-induced stupor by urgent knocking on my dorm room door. I opened it to find my friend Dave from Buffalo (once again, a last name eludes me), sporting a look of mild shock. "Dude, you've gotta hear this!" he exclaimed without waiting for an invitation inside.

No doubt he had a hunch I'd be sucked in by his excitement. He was right. "What is it?" I asked. Dave wasted no time thrusting a CD into my hands. My transition from LPs to CDs was in its infancy. I had recently bought a player, but had less than a dozen discs to play on it, compared to the 500 or so LPs that followed me from St. Louis. Dave also knew of my penchant for music nobody else knew about. I took a minute to glance at the green and gold artwork encased inside the jewel box. If I was reading the titles correctly, the band Dave was all worked up about was called XTC. The name of the album was *Skylarking*. I looked at Dave and shrugged. "Never heard of them," I said.

Dave took the jewel box in order to remove the disc. "Just you wait," he said, racing to my player. There was no stopping him. He loaded the disc into my player, switched my receiver's input to "CD," and started to push the "play" button. But suddenly, he stopped. He gave me a sober look. "You're not real religious, are you?" he asked.

That seemed like a very odd question. But now I was really intrigued. "Well, both of my grandfathers were Baptist ministers," I said. I saw Dave's face start to contort. "But that spirit never really reached me," I concluded, inducing an audible sigh. "Why do you ask?"

"You'll understand in about 20 seconds," Dave said. And then he started the disc. Actually, he skipped all the way to track 12, but I hadn't realized it. Dave, still planning ahead, took out the CD booklet and turned it to the appropriate page, where I was able to see the song's lyrics. I had just enough time to see he was pointing to a song called "Dear God."

The song started out with a solo acoustic guitar. Shortly afterward, it was accompanied by the voice of a child. "Dear God, hope you got the letter and, I pray you can make it better down here," the child sang. "I don't mean a big reduction in the price of beer. But all the people that you made in your image,

See them starving on their feet, 'Cause they don't get enough to eat from God. I can't believe in you." (C

I was floored. "WHAT did he say?" I asked, my mouth remaining agape. Dave started to laugh and help up an index finger that said I hadn't heard nothin' yet. And he was right.

The child's voice was replaced by the adult voice of singer/songwriter Andy Partridge, who had only begun his scolding of the Almighty. "Dear God, sorry to disturb you but ... I feel that I should be heard loud and clear. We all need a big reduction in amount of tears. And all the people that you made in your image, see them fighting in the street, because they can't make opinions meet about God. I can't believe in you." (a)

I sat on my bed, hard. I had never been so mentally divided in my life. On one hand, this young Englishman was cutting to the heart of my agnostic beliefs, voicing his rationale and displeasure in ways I couldn't even fathom. On the other hand, I could hear my very religious mother yelling at me from some 900 miles away, demanding that I turn that heathen crap off! But there was no turning back.

It was three-and-a-half minutes of sheer musical brilliance. And it was pop music! It was far too intelligent (and controversial) for commercial radio, I figured. Though I was sure there were college radio stations playing the daylights out of this. I just didn't know where they were. When the song ended, all I stared at Dave for a moment. Finally, I found the thought I was looking for. "I have to hear the rest of this," I said.

Dave grinned. "I thought you might say something like that."

And that was the night I met XTC.

***

As it turned out, the band had been around since the '70s. *Skylarking* was the album that got them the most attention. I assumed it was because of "Dear God." And while that was partially true, there was another reason. Legendary singer/songwriter Todd Rundgren produced the album, and according to word around the campfire, the sessions had been less than amicable between the producer and Partridge, the primary songwriter.

If the stories relayed by both Partridge and Rundgren are even close to true, it's a miracle the recording sessions resulted in a completed album instead of a homicide. These two gentlemen (and their respective egos) were not even close to being on the same page during the recording sessions. I'm sure someone will discuss the positive results of friction or opposites attracting during the creative process. In the end, Partridge conceded Rundgren's judgment was the right one more often than not. The stars aligned, and from it came forth one of the best albums of the '80s, according to critics. And as it happened, the view of music critics in those days was very important to me.

Since I no longer cared for commercial radio, I needed alternative sources to find the music I was looking for. The Internet was still a full decade from becoming a Thing, so I relied on other sources of information. These came in the form of college/independent radio, record store clerks, watching album credits (4), word of mouth, and music critics.

While *Rolling Stone* magazine and I were slowly but steadily going our separate ways, we could almost always come together where record reviews were concerned. If David Fricke dug what was being played, I figured it was worth at least a cursory listen. The same went for reviews in magazines like *Spin* or *Musician*, which I recall seeing once in a great while back then. *Rolling Stone* charted the sales of not only pop records and albums, but of college rock as well. That was the only chart of interest to me. If one of the magazines happened to review one of those college records, so much the better.

A critically acclaimed band had staying power, because critics are more focused on the band's music than its image. Pop stars and their fans are very of the moment, and one could measure the relevance of most pop stars and their music with an egg timer. Of course, over time I came to see that certain bands could do no wrong in the eyes of *Rolling Stone*, like Bob Dylan and Bruce Springsteen; while other bands, like Rush or Genesis, could do no right. But we saw eye to eye on bands like R.E.M. and XTC. So I felt my latest musical hunch had been validated.

Skylarking was followed three years later by *Oranges and Lemons.* Once again, my mind was blown by the superior songwriting and bouncy pop tempos on tunes like "The Mayor of Simpleton," "Across this Antheap," and "Poor Skeleton Steps Out." I was particularly enthralled with the propulsion coming from behind the drum kit. XTC's original drummer left, so they hired an ace. That drummer happened to be Pat Mastelotto, who was still riding the semi-fame wave from his regular band, Mr. Mister. (5) While I appreciated his drumming in XTC, I gave little thought to Pat's name, until I saw it again five years later, when he took the throne beside Bill Bruford in the "double trio" incarnation of King Crimson.

In '92, XTC released *Nonesuch*, which I consider to be pound-for-pound their best album. The lessons learned during *Skylarking* were taken to the next level, as the band not only continued to sharpen its songwriting, but overall sound quality as well. XTC used the studio as an instrument in much the same way the Beatles used Abbey Road.

The album opens with one of my favorite songs, "The Ballad of Peter Pumpkinhead," the story of a mysterious, Christ-like stranger who reinvigorates the thinking of those he meets, to the chagrin of the establishment. This ultimately leads to the equivalent of his crucifixion. The irony of such a song coming from the same man who penned "Dear God" is not lost on me.

Nonesuch is a 17-course master program in the fine art of writing intelligent, timeless pop music. That being said, I am unaware of any form of Top 40 success for the album or any of its songs, which says much more about Top 40 than it does XTC. By the time the stellar guitar solo at the end of "Books are Burning" fades out, I could only sit back and marvel and the superior talents of the band and wonder just what in bloody hell a radio programmer would deem superior to this level of songcraft. But then I remember songcraft has absolutely *nothing* to do with Top 40 radio.

I was stationed in Japan by the time *Nonesuch* was released. College radio and I were forced to part ways, and I was now subject to the whims of the Armed Forces Radio Network. Needless to say, there was not a lot of Midnight Oil, the Cure, or XTC being played over those airwaves. I was discharged from the Air Force in October of '92 and returned home to St. Louis in early November. Almost immediately, I sought out many of the college radio stations I'd enjoyed nearly five years earlier. But it wasn't the same. I can't put my finger on what it was, but the music being played didn't reach me. The vibe had changed. The jazz stations were still cool, even though they trimmed off what little fusion they were playing. But I was unable to re-engage with the sound of the bands I'd loved when I first discovered the left side of the dial. There was a reason for that.

The secret was out. My college rock was going mainstream.

(1)   As I've said in other places, this book is not about my personal politics. I believe in treating everyone in a humane fashion, until they prove they are not deserving of such treatment. That's all I really need to say about it.

(2)   I'd be lying if I said I waited until I turned 21 to start
        drinking. Let's just say I got a couple of years "head
        start." That's part of the fun of college: pushing
        boundaries. By the time it was legal for me to buy a beer
        in a bar, the thrill was pretty much gone, since I wasn't
        pushing the envelope any more, I was more than content
        to be the designated driver.

(3)   One of my many regrets in life: I never saw R.E.M. live.

(4)   One of the great things about preferring musicians to
        rock stars is musicians are always seeking out another
        session, as opposed to waiting for their band to complete
        another album. Therefore, a fan of someone like bassist
        Tony Levin is liable to find him on any number of
        albums. Naturally, an exploration of the artist Tony is
        playing for is in order, which leads to the discovery of
        more musicians and their projects. And so on, and so on.

(5)   That's right: one of my favorite drummers was front and
        center for two '80s hits I was ambivalent about, at best,
        in "Broken Wings" and "Kyrie Eleison." A gig is a gig,
        and some of them make you famous. Recently, I've
        become a huge fan of Steven Wilson, who hired an ace
        bassist named Nick Beggs, whose playing I can't get
        enough of. In the early '80s, the English group
        Kajagoogoo had a huge hit called "Too Shy." I *detested*
        that song. Guess who the bass player was?

(a)   "The Kiss," written by Smith/Gallup/Thompson/
        Williams/Tolhurst. (c) 1987 APB Music

Who could imagine a collection of guitar solos triggering
a lifelong obsession with one man's music? Yet that's exactly
what happened, and I became a Frank Zappa fan for life.

Track 10
Frank

In the spring of '86, I was in the early stages of my "No Commercial Radio" phase. Any new music I heard came via articles in music magazines, college radio stations, or word of mouth. I never lacked for information. I was surrounding myself with the kind of people who got me the information I needed. So it was no accident I happened across Brad Nelson.

I met Brad in college, where I spent more time hanging in the school newspaper office than I did going to class. The man had an air about him. I couldn't put my finger on it at the time, but Brad had a sense of cool I would come to recognize in others later in life. It was a cool shared by only one type of person in every case. It was the cool of a musician.

Brad and I bonded because he loved music as much as I did. He knew who King Crimson was. He dug Genesis the same way I did. (1) He thought the vast majority of music being played commercially was crap. Best of all, Brad was a guitar player.

It wasn't long before I was spending a great deal of my free time at Brad's house, where he wasted no time introducing me to the two great objects of his affection. He was the proud owner of a tomato soup red Fender Stratocaster and a pink paisley Fender Telecaster. They were beautiful instruments, and Brad was a more than capable player. Alas, his attempts to teach

128

me a chord or two were largely futile efforts. The guitar bug wouldn't bite for another decade (2).

Brad had a thing for the blues, which he was happy to share with me. My friend introduced me to Muddy Waters, Albert Collins, Johnny Copeland, Lonnie Mack, and Robert Cray. Most importantly, Brad taught me about Stevie Ray Vaughan. I remember Brad laughing with glee at my face when I heard "Change It" for the first time. The sound of Vaughan's band came out of the speakers in waves. Had my hair been long and stringy, it would have flown backward. Instead, my jaw went slack and my head listed slightly to one side, a la the RCA Victor dog. I was so smitten, I left Brad's house and drove straight to the record store, where I purchased all three of SRV's studio albums.

Brad saved the best for last. We were enjoying another of our "study sessions" at his house (that is to say, we were listening to records), when he gave me a quizzical look. I didn't know what his face was about, but it was throwing off my musical groove. "What?" I asked, checking to see if something was stuck between my teeth.

The quizzical look turned into a nod of approval. "You're ready," he said.

"Ready for what?"

"Hang on." With that, he left the room and went across the hall, where a large chunk of his LP collection was stored. When he came back, he had an LP. More accurately, an album-sized box I could only assume contained multiple LPs. He pulled one of the records out of the box and handed the package to me.

On the cover was a man sitting at a piano bench with his back to the keyboard. He was a white man with dark features (possibly Italian) and a prominent nose. His face was accentuated with an incredibly thick black mustache and accompanying "flavor saver" under his bottom lip. A straw fedora sat on top of a bushel of black hair like it had been placed there as an afterthought. He wore a simple blue t-shirt. On his lap sat a guitar, which I would learn was a cherry burst Gibson Les Paul. In the upper right-hand corner sat the album's title: *Shut Up 'n' Play Yer Guitar*. "Who's this?" I asked.

"That, my friend, is Frank Zappa," Brad announced with a reverence making me think I should genuflect. "He's one of the most important musicians of our lifetime. Ever heard of him?"

The name rang a very vague bell in my mind. Our classic rock station, KSHE, took it upon itself to play a "riskier" tune now and then. This was their chance to spin a tune from Arlo Guthrie, or King Crimson, or this Zappa guy. "Did he do a song about yellow snow?" I asked hesitantly.

Brad nodded. "Yeah, 'Don't Eat the Yellow Snow' is one of his. A lot of people know that one. That and 'Titties and Beer.'"

I couldn't help but chuckle. "Wait a minute. 'Titties and Beer?'"

Brad blew right past my bemusement. "What they don't talk about is what an amazing guitar player Zappa is. You've got to check this out. It's a compilation of guitar solos." He turned toward his turntable, but hesitated, and turned back toward me. "I should warn you," he said, "this is unlike pretty much anything you've ever heard before."

I snorted. "Dude, I'm a King Crimson fan," I said. "How bad can it be?"

Brad smiled. "Don't say I didn't warn you." And with that, he turned and dropped the needle onto the vinyl. And for the second time in less than a year, my musical world was torn asunder.

The sound poured out of the speakers like an avalanche. I thought I might fly right out of my chair. I grabbed its arms, thinking it would protect me from the sonic onslaught. I took about twenty seconds to realize Brad was right: I had never heard anything like this before.

The opening track of *Shut Up 'n' Play Yer Guitar* is called "five-five-FIVE." It begins with Zappa's nasal-ish guitar firing off a high-speed staccato riff that defies description. Just as the ears adjust, everything changes, and Zappa launches into his guitar solo, his band seeming to struggle beautifully in an attempt to keep up. It was as though Zappa was going out of his way to play against his band's established backing.

The guitar solos I was accustomed to were mostly blues based. They used the pentatonic scale. Granted, I had recently been exposed to Adrian Belew and King Crimson, and those solos were far from pentatonic. But Frank Zappa was introducing my ears to something altogether different.

Brad could see me trying to process the information being fed to my brain. But he said nothing, and waited for me to speak. Eventually, I did. "This shit is *WILD!*" I declared in a far louder voice than necessary. Brad laughed. He had me, and he knew it.

The format of *Shut Up* ... makes for a tough entry point into the musical world of Frank Zappa. Fortunately, I was too ignorant to know that. When Brad told me the album was a collection of solos, he wasn't kidding. That's *exactly* what I was hearing: a solo, an abrupt segue, and then another altogether separate solo. The song titles – "Hog Heaven," "While You Were Out," and Treacherous Cretins" – did nothing to help me understand what was happening. This went on for 18 minutes or so. Then Brad flipped the record over, and we started again. There were three LPs in this particular collection, which were actually three individual releases: *Shut Up 'n' Play Yer Guitar, Shut Up 'n' Play Yer Guitar Some More,* and *The Return of the Son of Shut Up 'n' Play Yer Guitar.* Frank Zappa was a funny guy.

By the time side two ended, my head was spinning. Brad could see that, and calmly put the LP back into its protective sleeve before returning it to the box. Then he handed the box to me. "Want to take a couple of days and get to know this guy?" he asked.

All I could do was nod.

"Cool. Enjoy it. Let me know what you think. I don't have to tell you to take care of these, do I?"

I shook my head. Brad knew I was meticulous about caring for my LPs. With that, he sent me home, where I spent the next several days absorbing the amazing, unconventional, out-of-this-world guitar sound of Frank Zappa. These were the first steps of an amazing musical odyssey.

***

My entry into Frank Zappa's musical world came via his guitar. So it took a while before I could appreciate his abilities as a composer. At first, I was only interested in what he made happen with his primary instrument. My first two purchases were the *Shut Up* ... box set, which contained solos recorded between '77 and '80, and a second set of solos, mostly from '87and '88, called simply *Guitar*. My desire to hear Zappa play solos took precedence over everything else. Nevertheless, it didn't take long to figure out I had entered a new musical stratosphere.

I can't recall the first non-guitar-oriented Zappa album I bought. Regardless, I'm sure I had the following thought upon hearing Frank's compositions:

This shit is *WEIRD!*

I use that word in the most positive possible sense. Here I was, a music lover steeped in Soul, R & B, AOR Rock, and Progressive Rock. I was also walking toward jazz, and had a small Classical vocabulary. Still, with all of that musical experience under my belt, I had to absorb a completely new musical language.

The key to appreciating Zappa's music is to understand it should not be categorized in any way, shape or form. Frank's music might be found in the "Rock" section of the record store, but what pours forth from the speakers is far from "rock" music.

The first thing to strike me about Frank's compositions is the positively *staggering* amount of musical information they contain. There was so much coming out of the speakers; it was impossible to capture it all in a single sitting. I've often told people that I have to be in the right frame of mind to listen to Frank's music, because it requires intense focus and study to understand it all. This is not how the casual music fan wants to listen to music. And this is why not everyone got what Frank tried to put across.

The title track from *The Grand Wazoo*, released in '72, serves as a good case in point. While there are certainly rock elements to this tune, it is not a rock song. There are also jazz elements, but I wouldn't venture to call this tune jazz. There's even a portion of the tune that sounds like Classical music. But "The Grand Wazoo" is not a Classical piece. There is a reason Frank referred to himself as an American composer, as opposed to some regimented conventional label.

The track opens with a funky vamp from the guitar, bass, and drums. A nice groove is established, and then the horn section steps in to state the theme. For the next 12 minutes, the tune shakes, shimmies, moves and grooves precisely and intelligently. Each musician has a chance to shine. Frank wrote every note, and "The Grand Wazoo" comes off not so much as a conventional rock tune, but as something Mozart might have written had he been given the same instrumentation.

One of the most difficult things in the world to do is describe Frank Zappa's music. It defies description. I have no doubt he wanted it that way. To obtain the full effect, the music must not be merely heard. It must be experienced. In the end, I find myself saying the same thing, time and again:

This shit is *GENIUS!*

***

Frank Zappa released his debut album, *Freak Out*, in '66 (the year I was born). He continued to write, record, and release records until his death in '93 (his final album, *The Yellow Shark*, was released that year). He released 61 albums during his lifetime. And I did my best to acquire every one of them. (3)

There were many elements to Zappa's musical personality. There was the guy who loved doo-wop, R&B, and the blues. There was the guy who dug jazz and big band orchestration. There was the hard rock guy, the guitar virtuoso, the *musique concrete* specialist, the comedian, the social satirist, and the modern classical composer. Most times, these styles were heard independent of one another. Sometimes, two or more of these styles collided violently, yet beautifully, within the same song.

As a lyricist, Zappa had a knack for biting social commentary, earnest sincerity, or outright buffoonery. Nobody was safe from his caustic wit. Frank was quite the intellectual, and did not suffer fools gladly, regardless of social status, level of celebrity, or political affiliation.

A great place to learn about Zappa is with his posthumous release, *Läther*. The three CD set was originally conceived by Zappa in '77 as a four-LP box set. His record company balked at the idea, however, and the music ultimately became part of four individual releases: *Live in New York, Studio Tan, Sleep Dirt,* and *Orchestral Favorites.* Each of Zappa's musical personalities is represented within the confines of this release. The album's opener, "Re-gyptian Strut" showcases Zappa's abilities as a Big Band composer. "The Purple Lagoon" allows his band to show off its jazz chops. "Filthy Habits" contains a positively *blistering* guitar solo from Zappa, easily amongst my favorites. (4) His sense of humor comes to the fore in tunes like "The Illinois Enema Bandit," "Punky's Whips," and yes, "Titties 'N Beer." Doubters of Zappa's abilities as a composer need look no further than "The Black Page #1." The song received its name because of how the music's notation looks on staff paper. The notes practically blot out the page with their density. The tune was written as a drum solo for Terry Bozzio, who pulls every complex beat, fill, start and stop with deft precision. As a drum solo, "The Black Page" is insane enough. But then Zappa decided that he had to write a piece for his band to accompany Bozzio. No matter how many times I play it, I still can't help but be amazed.

***

It takes a special skill set to play in Frank Zappa's band. So it can't be a coincidence that some of my favorite musicians are Zappa alums. Adrian Belew got his first big break playing for him in the late '70s. Mike Keneally, Steve Vai, Ike Willis, and Warren Cuccurullo are also alums. All of them cut their teeth playing Frank's complex compositions.

Zappa alums have left their mark throughout music. Players like George Duke, Chester Thompson, Chad Wackerman, Jean-Luc Ponty, Eddie Jobson, Allan Zavod, Lou Marini, and Tom Malone have impacted my record collection on multiple occasions. Their skills can be heard in a variety of contexts, from jazz to R&B to rock. Tenure in Frank Zappa's band opened the door to countless musical possibilities.

But becoming a member of Zappa's band was no small undertaking. Being a genius equates to zero tolerance of mediocrity, so there are no doubt far more tales of failure to attain membership in Zappa's band than there are stories of triumph. Zappa wanted his music played correctly and consistently, and only musicians of the highest caliber were brought into the fold to achieve this aim.

Zappa once described what it is like to try out for his band. Rehearsals took place in a warehouse near Zappa's home in Los Angeles. "Come into the room and sit in a metal folding chair," he said. "There will be sheet music in front of you. Start playing. Now imagine me standing over you, smoking a cigarette, and slowly shaking my head."

The thought of such a tryout sends shivers down my spine. The material is intimidating enough while being played on CD. On more than one occasion, I have caught myself sitting down with my guitar, attempting to duplicate what I was hearing. The results were rarely what Zappa would have considered fruitful.

Adrian Belew gave a vivid account of his audition to *Guitar Player* magazine in '94. "Frank gave me a list of difficult songs from several different records," he said, "and his instructions were, 'Figure out how to play and sing this the best you can, however you can.' The music was pretty complicated for a guy who was just playing in a bar band. I had never played in odd time signatures, and I didn't read music, whereas the rest of the Frank's band did. And I was so poor at the time (this was 1977) that I didn't even buy the records. I borrowed them from my friends, because I didn't know if it was going to work out anyway.

"The audition was pretty brutal, and I didn't do very well. It was like the chaos of a movie set with people moving pianos around and so on. And there's little me standing in the middle of a room with a Pignose amplifier and a Stratocaster trying to sing and play lots of Frank Zappa songs. I was so nervous. I remember doing 'Andy,' and 'Wind Up Working in a Gas Station.' I thought I did poorly, and I had nowhere to go. I had just flown in, and was driven to his house, so I sat there all day watching everyone else. I watched some really tough auditions, especially for keyboard players and percussionists. I didn't see any other guitar players, but I was later told that he auditioned 50 guitar players.

"At the end of the day, when it all calmed down and people were finally leaving, I finally got my time to speak to Frank again. I said simply this: 'Frank, I don't think I did so well. I imagined this would have happened differently. I thought you and I would sit somewhere quiet, and I would play and sing the songs for you. And he said, 'OK, then let's do that.'

"We went upstairs to his living room, and we sat on his purple couch. I placed my Pignose amplifier face down on the couch so I could get a little bit of sustain, and I auditioned all over again. At the end of it, he reached out his hand and said, 'You got the job.' We shook hands, and that was an absolute turning point in my life."

Musicians like Vai and Keneally have described the tortuous nature of a Zappa tryout. It wasn't enough to merely know the song, they reported. Frank would want his musicians to be able to play variations on material that was already dense and complex. Time signatures frequently defied the traditional 4/4. A song that sounded great played straight would now need to be played with a reggae feel, or with a disco vamp. A drum riff might need to be executed by the non-drummers with the feet. One simply never knew where Zappa might go. But it was the musician's job to keep up, and be accurate. Frank Zappa was not for the faint of heart.

Terry Bozzio found his own way to get Zappa's attention. "The one thing I'd noticed was a lot of the drummers were sort of flaunting their chops," he said in a '92 interview. "I thought the least I could do was go up there and listen and try and play with the guy. So I did the best I could; sight-reading a very difficult piece, memorizing a very difficult piece, jamming with a very odd time signature – like 19 – and then playing a blues shuffle. At the end of that, Frank said, 'You sound great,

I'd like to hear you – after I hear the rest of these guys – again.'
And I turned to his road manager. (The) road manager turns to
the twenty or so guys that were hanging around, and they're all
shaking their heads. The road manager turns around and says,
'That's it. Nobody else wants to play after Terry.' So, Frank
turns to me and says 'Looks like you've got the gig if you want
it.' So, I was completely blown away."

Attaining membership in a Frank Zappa band required
more than mere competence as a musician. Perhaps that is why,
to a man, Zappa band alums seem to consider tenure in this
group a true high-water mark of their professional careers.

***

My favorite era of Zappa music, which I call The Roxy Era.
It's difficult to imagine a greater collective musical skillset.

I can find something to love in any part of Frank
Zappa's discography. I didn't hear the records sequentially. But
it's telling that my favorite Zappa albums were released during a
relatively brief period between mid-1972 and '75. This time
frame saw the release, in order, of *Waka Jawaka, The Grand
Wazoo, Over-Nite Sensation, Apostrophe ('), Roxy and
Elsewhere,* and *One Size Fits All.* If forced to choose, the last
record in this run would probably be considered my favorite of
all. It can't be a coincidence my favorite volume of the *You
Can't Do That on Stage Anymore* series, released between '88
and '92, is *Volume 2, The Helsinki Concert.* It was recorded on
September 22 of '74.

What was it about this era? Like picking a favorite
anything, the answer is highly subjective. The music Frank
wrote during this time appealed to me the most, probably
because it had the most jazz-like qualities, with funky
undertones. There were comic moments, like always, but

Zappa's compositions contained some *serious* music. And his guitar playing was unparalleled. The Gibson SG has never been my favorite guitar. I always preferred the Fender Stratocaster. But in Zappa's hands, the SG took on a quality that made me long for one of my own.

My favorite Zappa band members made the most appearances during this time. I made an effort to follow many of their solo careers, often before I knew they had been in Frank's band. Between '72 and '75, Zappa shared the stage or studio with the likes of Jean-Luc Ponty (violin), George Duke (keyboards and vocals), Chester Thompson (drums), Ruth Underwood (percussion), Tom Fowler (bass), Napoleon Murphy Brock (saxophone and vocals), and Walt Fowler (trumpet). These players took Frank's already intricate and complex music to another level.

What's particularly remarkable about *The Helsinki Concert* is the level of comfort coming from the band. They had been playing the material on hand for a year or two by then, and had really settled into it. This would be no big thing had the music been your basic, everyday rock and roll. But this was highly complex, mind-melting music. Not only was the Helsinki band playing the music precisely, they were playing it *faster!* (5) My jaw never fails to hit the floor any time I listen to this gig. It's like watching a high-wire act at the circus. The band's actions thrill and amaze, because one wrong step would spell certain disaster.

It is clear Zappa's musicians respected and revered the music they were hired to play. This reverence is on display in an episode of the documentary series *Classic Albums* featuring *Apostrophe(')* and *Over-Nite Sensation.* "It's the music I would have written for myself, if I'd had that talent," said Ruth Underwood of the percussion parts Zappa wrote for her. "Frank knew how to do that for me. I think he knew how to do that for everybody."

As an example, Underwood points to a solo Frank wrote as part of "St. Alphonso's Pancake Breakfast," called "Rollo Interior." Underwood shows the interviewer the notated lead sheet, a music staff that simply defies description. There are notes *everywhere!* The sheet itself looks like a work of art. It looks like it was printed off by machine. But Underwood insists Zappa not only wrote the sheet out by hand, but he did so as fast as he could. The man was gifted on many levels.

Underwood plays the section, which she has not had to do regularly in more than 30 years. By the time she finishes, I am on my feet, applauding wildly. Underwood is less enthusiastic, grousing that she made three mistakes, "One for every decade I've been away from the music and the instrument." Upon repeated listens, I believe I can hear two of the errors. Maybe. But they are so minor, the only reason I know they exist is because Underwood told me so.

It would seem Frank was not the only driven perfectionist, where his music was concerned.

***

I have to prepare myself mentally before playing Zappa's music. This is no exaggeration: there is simply too much going on to approach it with an unfocused mind. It's also best for me to play the music while wearing headphones to minimize distractions. There is nothing quite so annoying as being immersed in an intricate run of Zappa brilliance, only to have my mental groove thrown off by a ringing phone or barking dog. Of all the music in my collection, Zappa's compositions have required the most "rewinds." No matter how many times I play certain songs, I always feel I've missed something.

This speaks to one of my favorite aspects of Frank's music: no matter how often I play it, I am *always* amazed by what I'm hearing. My other Musical Holy Trinity favorites – Miles Davis and King Crimson – never fail to amuse or satisfy me. But Zappa's music is an entirely different animal. His ear for detail and gift of sonic nuance are nearly unrivaled. It's one of the main reasons I view him as one of the greatest composers of the 20th century.

There is plenty of great music in my collection. Yet it pales in comparison to Zappa on a compositional and arrangement level. After immersing myself in almost nothing but Zappa's music for three days, I decided to cleanse my musical palate with a little Gov't Mule, a band rooted in the blues and the sounds of the Allman Brothers. As much as I loved the deep groove and remarkable guitar work of Warren Haynes, I was shocked by the simplicity of his arrangements. With no real effort, I had taken the song apart in my mind, and given each instrument a spot in the stereo spectrum. There was so much room to spare! I can only wonder what Frank would have done with the extra space. (6)

Frank had a knack for arrangement defying belief. His music comes out of the speakers in densely layered waves.

138

Zappa music would work just fine in the traditional rock format of two guitars, bass, and drums (along with the occasional keyboard). But Frank added trumpets, trombones, saxophones, vibraphones, finger cymbals, and anything else he deemed necessary to make the music not flow, but resonate.

Frank's singing voice was far from operatic, but he knew how to make the most of its nasally, baritone sound. He also knew how to get out of the way and let one of his band members sing when the tune called for it. George Duke, Napoleon Murphy Brock, Terry Bozzio, Adrian Belew, and others have carried the vocal load when needed. Zappa never let his well-developed sense of self become a detriment to the music.

***

Not everything Zappa did struck a personal chord. His satire could ring of misogyny, and his political rants could be off-putting, distracting me from the brilliance of the music, whether I agreed with what he was saying or not. Sometimes, I just wanted Frank to take the advice of his own album and shut up and play his guitar.

Frank had a knack for thumbing his nose at authority. In September of '85, shortly before I was introduced to his music, Zappa went to Washington, D.C., to speak to the U.S. Senate Commerce Committee on behalf of musicians against the Parents Music Resource Center, an organization led by then Senator (and future Vice President) Al Gore's wife, Tipper. (7) The PMRC believed music – rock and roll in particular – was corrupting the youth of America by way of its lyrical content. To combat this, Tipper's group wanted to put warning labels on albums they deemed potentially dangerous to children. To artists like Zappa, this smacked of censorship. And he was *not* having it.

Frank dropped the hammer on the PMRC, who were probably expecting some dim-witted testimony from a drug-addled smut merchant. His testimony is available in its entirety on YouTube. Watching him verbally smack down a room of stodgy, out of touch politicians is worth the price of admission. Zappa's genius extended beyond his music, and his mind was drug-free. (8) He spoke eloquently and passionately, and while the warning stickers did eventually come to pass, musicians the world over knew they had a champion in Frank Zappa.

***

Frank's catalog is so vast, it is impossible for me to choose a favorite record (even though *One Size Fits All* satisfies my Zappa needs the quickest). In order to truly appreciate the catalog, I have to view it in segments.

Of the material released between 1966 and '72, I prefer to enjoy *Freak Out, We're Only in it For the Money, Lumpy Gravy,* and *Hot Rats.* The music from this era at times sounds almost quaint compared to what Zappa would eventually unleash. Still, this early material serves as a great foundation for what was about to come.

My love for the '72 to '75 period has been documented. Between '75 and '80, I enjoy *Bongo Fury, Zoot Allures,* and *Joe's Garage.* There are other enjoyable records from this period, but those albums stand out. Once again, it's subjective.

Album for album, I listen to the albums Zappa released after '80 the least, even though some of my favorite musicians (like Steve Vai, Mike Keneally, Scott Thunes, Allan Zavod, and Chad Wackerman) play on these albums. Frank seemed to spend more of his time focusing on comedy and satire. This is right in the wheelhouse of some of my friends who love Zappa, and they can't get enough of it. Well, to each his own. It just doesn't work as well for me. Still, I'm a great fan of *Ship Arriving Too Late to Save a Drowning Witch, Make a Jazz Noise Here, The Best Band You Never Heard in Your Life, Guitar,* and *The Yellow Shark.*

One of my all-time favorite Zappa albums emerged from this period. In '86, Frank released *Jazz From Hell.* The songs were performed on the Synclavier, which was one of the earliest digital synthesizers to feature sampling technology. Once again, Zappa was ahead of his time. And the music was positively mind-blowing! The album won a Grammy award for "Best Rock Instrumental Performace" in '87. (9)

Zappa's catalog is so vast, I am not ashamed to say I haven't heard it all. But I am working on it. The 60 or so records I have heard give me more than enough material to establish Frank as one of the most influential artists in my life.

***

Frank Zappa's music continues to find fresh ears, thanks in large part to his son, Dweezil. An accomplished guitarist and composer in his own right, Dweezil formed Zappa Plays Zappa, a touring band playing Frank's catalog, and helping it breathe again on stage. Rather than hire alums from Frank's band, Dweezil hired musicians his age and younger. They have not only shown a love and appreciation for Frank's music, they have proven to be more than capable players, executing those difficult passages of music as though it had been written for them. The CD/DVD compilation *Zappa Plays Zappa* and *Return of the Son of ...* are valuable parts of my music collection.

I have no doubt Dweezil is playing this music out of love, respect, and admiration for his father. I also believe there is another, unspoken reason that Zappa Plays Zappa tours. Dweezil and fans of Frank alike know: it will be a long, long time before we see and hear another artist like Frank Zappa.

(1)   In fact, Brad's mother was from England. Given my love of British bands and accents, talking to her was one of the coolest things in the world. I relished every opportunity to do so.

(2)   It wasn't just Brad. A woman I dated briefly also tried to teach me how to play. No such luck. I also hung out with another friend who played. His guitar was also little more than a wooden plank with wires in my hands. I don't know what took me so long to catch on. Eventually, I did.

(3)   Frank was savant-like with his creativity, and never stopped working. Since his passing, the Zappa family trust has released nearly 40 additional recordings, culled from Frank's vaults.

(4)   My all-time favorite version of this song is found on *You Can't Do That on Stage Any More, Volume 5*. Words defy the intensity behind Zappa's playing on this solo. And how he found a band to play the opening theme with that level of precision leaves me shaking my head in awe and wonder.

(5)   No band is perfect, and Zappa's was no exception. Frank's perfectionism extended to the bandstand, even mid-performance. During *The Helsinki Concert*, the band flubs the beginning of "Approximate," yet another complicated piece. Rather than plow through, Zappa stops the band in its tracks. After chastising them gently, he starts the number again. Naturally, the band nails it.

(6)   This is not to imply that Zappa looked down upon artists like the Allman Brothers. Quite the contrary. "Whipping Post," an Allman Brothers staple, was a part of Zappa's set list during more than one incarnation of his band.

(7)   Also testifying with Zappa were Dee Snider, lead vocalist of hair metal band Twisted Sister, and John

Denver. Snider's appearance made perfect sense to me. But to this day, I continue to ask myself just what on God's green Earth was John Denver doing there? I never sensed a great deal of evil in "Country Roads" or "Thank God I'm a Country Boy." But what do I know?

(8)   On at least a dozen occasions, I have baffled friends by telling them Frank did not do drugs and kicked people out of his band for doing them. My friends would look at photos of Zappa and draw their own conclusions. "Have you listened to his music?" I would ask them. "It's *impossible* to play that stuff loaded! It's too difficult!" If Frank had a drug problem, it was nicotine. He smoked constantly, which probably contributed to the prostate cancer that ultimately killed him.

(9)   There was a time when my favorite artists winning a Grammy meant a great deal. That feeling has long since faded. I don't remember the last time I went out of my way to pay attention to the Grammy Awards. They are little more than label-driven popularity contests.

Thanks to Columbia House, my Miles Davis collection begin here, with Tutu. This was also one of the few albums to survive Hurricane Hugo in 1989, as the damage along the bottom shows.

Track 11
Miles

I heard the name a hundred times. It just never sunk in. When my dad talked music with his friends, it was only a matter of time before they heard the name Miles Davis. This almost always triggered a lengthy sidebar from the original conversation. Miles Davis got tongues wagging. In time, I would understand why.

By 1987, my radio was rooted to the left side of the FM dial. College rock was having a profound influence on me. Some of those bands – like R.E.M., U2, The Cure, and 10,000 Maniacs – were making their way above ground, and into the commercial mainstream. I was staying put and enjoying the next generation of bands that found their way onto my radio station. Plus, I was looking to branch into new territories, like jazz.

My quest brought me to WSIE, out of Edwardsville, Illinois. It was there I started learning about contemporary jazz and artists like saxophonist David Sanborn, guitarists Earl Klugh and Larry Carlton, keyboardist Bob James, and bands like Spyro Gyra, Pieces of a Dream, and the Yellowjackets. (1) Dad and I shared our musical finds. I thought I earned full membership into his musical stratosphere. But Dad told me I hadn't even scratched the surface. Until I grasped Miles Davis, I was still going to be lost. Once again, my staggering ignorance was about to pay a huge dividend.

***

Who could have predicted a shipment of records from Columbia House would ignite the fire of a lifelong musical obsession? Yet that is precisely what happened. Does anyone even *remember* Columbia House?

I recall seeing their ads in *Parade* magazine, which is found in the Sunday newspaper. (2) The Columbia Record and Tape Club was a mail-order group based in Terre Haute, Indiana. They offered music fans a chance to add to their music collections for what seemed like a rock bottom price.

For a mere penny (plus shipping and handling) you could purchase something like 15 LPs. This made you a member of the club. After that, all you had to do was purchase one album a month at "regular club prices." (3) Why wouldn't I jump at that kind of opportunity? In the blink of an eye, my card was filled out. A few weeks later, my records arrived.

I can't recall a single record from my initial shipment, save one. It was the latest release from Miles Davis, called *Tutu*. The record's cover, a stark black and white close-up of the trumpeter's face, was a little intimidating. The photo *demanded* your attention. I could only assume the music was of equal importance.

For me, the album's producer, Marcus Miller, gave the record credibility. Miller made his name as a virtuoso bassist and was a big part of Miles's "comeback" bands of the early '80s. He played on the David Sanborn records I enjoyed during that period. I had one more reason to be excited about *Tutu*.

On the whole, I found the album … decent. I liked it, but it didn't blow me away. The title track was a plodding, deliberate piece that lurched its way forward, driven primarily by Miller's Fender Jazz bass. My favorite track, "Splatch," was more rooted in funk than jazz. Truth be told, *Tutu* is really more of a Marcus Miller album than a Miles Davis album, since Miller played nearly all the instruments. Miles was not so much a bandleader in these sessions as he was merely reacting to pre-recorded tracks being piped through his studio headphones.

But the foundation had been laid, and Miles Davis was on my musical radar.

***

The first jazz I enjoyed always featured at least one electric instrument. This music was classified as either contemporary jazz or fusion. Traditional, or "straight ahead" jazz was my next avenue of musical exploration. I saved the best for last.

My first straight ahead jazz album did not come from Miles Davis. That moment came courtesy of another trumpet player named Wynton Marsalis. I heard my dad go on and on about him, saying he was the next Miles. Marsalis was a prodigy from New Orleans, and part of an immensely talented family. Father Ellis was a well-respected pianist. Brother Branford was making a serious splash as a saxophone player. There were also two younger brothers, trombone player Delfeayo and drummer Jason, a few years away from making names for themselves. (4)

Whenever Dad talked about jazz, he inevitably brought up Miles and Wynton. So when I saw Columbia House had Wynton Marsalis in its catalog, I wasted no time ordering it. Before long, *Marsalis Standard Time, Volume 1* was a part of my collection.

There was a brief period when I preferred the sound of Wynton's trumpet to Miles. I believed Wynton had a fuller sound. His tone shook the room with its intensity. It cut through any and everything standing in its way. Miles's sound struck me as weaker, because he frequently used a mute. His tone seemed tighter and more constricted. You could hear it, but it didn't rattle my cage.

Yep. Staggering ignorance rears its ugly head once again.

I learned the tone of Miles Davis was revered not only in jazz, but nearly all musical circles. This was particularly true when he played with the mute. Fans would say that the tighter sound gave the trumpet a vocal quality. Clark Terry, a trumpet legend whom Miles idolized, said Miles Davis was a singer. But rather than use his vocal cords, Miles used the trumpet to get his lyrics across. I can't think of a better description.

***

The part-time and temporary jobs I was working didn't pay well. What little money I was making was going toward gas for my '63 Plymouth Belvedere, a little food, and my record collection. The next order from Columbia House was from Miles. It was a big one, and it was a game-changer.

When *The Columbia Years, 1955-1985* arrived on my doorstep, I had no idea what I was in for. Selections from 30 years of music Miles made for Columbia Records was jam-packed into five LPs. The records were divided into the key musical aspects of Miles's career (jazz standards, blues, moods, originals, and electric). This collection served as a crash course in all things Miles Davis. Like the '80s King Crimson, this music opened more musical doors than I can count.

The deal was sealed by the second cut of side one on the first album. The song was "All Blues," a cut from the legendary 1959 album *Kind of Blue*. (5) I had never heard anything so hauntingly beautiful. I was moved to tears. I remember calling my dad to tell him about the experience. I could hear him smiling on the other end of the line. All he said to me was, "I told you." That's all he *had* to say.

Of all the albums in the collection, the electric material was hardest to grasp. I had experience with fusion, but nothing could prepare me for tunes like "Miles Runs the Voodoo Down" from the legendary – and to many infamous – 1970 release *Bitches Brew*. My brain was being scrambled in unimaginable ways. It's funny: music melting my mind 15 or more years after it was recorded must have done no less than tear the music world asunder when it was released. I thought I was confused? What the hell were people thinking about the music *then*?

"All Blues" told me Miles's straight-ahead material was essential listening and would soon be a part of my collection. When I heard "Star on Cicely," I knew the electric period had to be part of my life as well. The song came from his '83 recording, *Star People*. This was some of the funkiest shit I ever heard. Were they sure this was the same artist playing both tunes? A serpentine trumpet/soprano saxophone riff opens the tune, and then the bass, percussion, and drums provide the anchor that drive the next four minutes, 36 seconds. The muted trumpet of Miles cuts through the dense funk, with quick hits from the sax of Bill Evans and the guitar of John Scofield. Without warning, the tune jumps back to the "head," re-stating the theme before Miles grooves for a while more. For my money, the tune fades out far too quickly. If I knew nothing at all after absorbing *The Columbia Years*, I knew *Kind of Blue* and *Star People* were now top priorities for addition to my record collection.

Kind of Blue was an easy find, since it is probably the most popular record in the Miles Davis catalog. It wasn't a question of whether or not the record store had it. The question was simply which format did I prefer? *Star People*, on the other hand, was a different story.

Record store after record store told me the same thing when : it was out of print. The electric Miles simply did not go over as well with fans, so pressings were limited, even though the record had been released just four years before. And since Miles left Columbia for Warner Brothers (no doubt the primary cause for the release of the Columbia box set), there was little chance the album would find its way back to store shelves any time soon. Keep your eyes open, record store employees told me. You never know when it might pop up.

I only had to wait five years.

***

Kind of Blue served as the entryway to my Miles Davis obsession. The only thing better than the complete enjoyment of a musician is the complete enjoyment of a musician with a vast back catalog. Nothing made me happier than spending time in the "Miles Davis" section of the record store. Because there was always something there I didn't know about. *Always.*

One thing was certain: Miles was *never* found in the generic "D" section of the store's browser bins. He always had his own title card, and it always took up at least one full row. There was always plenty to choose from.

Since *The Columbia Years* provided the gateway, I started building my collection with the albums Miles released on that label. It turns out he had a solid back catalog from between 1951 and '55 on the Prestige label. But something in my brain led me to believe that those albums, with titles like *Walkin',* *Steamin', Cookin',* and *Relaxin'* would not be up to the Columbia label standards. Oh, Staggering Ignorance … does your idiocy know no limits? (6)

After *Kind of Blue,* I dug into records like *Round About Midnight, Milestones, Someday My Prince Will Come,* and *Miles Ahead.* The latter features a big band arrangement by the legendary Gil Evans, who first worked with Miles on *The Birth of the Cool* in '49. Gil had an ear Miles held in the highest regard. His ability to place instruments in the proper musical spectrum is unparalleled. The Davis/Evans collaborations, which include *Porgy and Bess* and *Sketches of Spain,* remain essential listening. (7) Evans's arrangements on these records serve as a master class on the art form. Miles, meanwhile, played with more emotion than I thought was possible.

Not only was Miles writing and playing incredible music, he was surrounding himself with top-notch sidemen. Miles shared the studio and bandstand with pianists Red Garland and Bill Evans, bassist Paul Chamberlin, alto saxophonist Julian "Cannonball" Adderly, and drummers "Philly" Joe Jones and

Jimmy Cobb. Each of these men would go on to front their own bands or continue to provide solid backing for other well-known jazz musicians. If I could go back in time, it just might be to the period between 1955 and '68, where I would hope to spend a little time talking to or performing with some of these remarkable men.

Perhaps the most famous Miles Davis sideman from this era is tenor and soprano saxophonist John Coltrane. He brought to the band a sense of fire, dexterity and speed that served as the perfect foil to Miles's understated lyrical grace. Most fans will point to the period Miles and 'Trane worked together as some of the very best jazz there is. It's no accident that Columbia released a CD box set featuring the collaborative efforts of these two legends.

The two of them (along with Adderly, Evans, Chambers, and Cobb) achieve their creative zenith on *Kind of Blue*. More than a few books have been written about this album, and with good reason. It strikes me as positively hilarious how bands these days routinely take months if not years to record an album. The Miles Davis Sextet recorded the first half of *Kind of Blue* on March 2, 1959. They recorded the second half on April 22. That's right: *Kind of Blue* was recorded *in its entirety* in two days!

What's more, the vast majority of the music is *improvised*. Miles came to the studio with rudimentary sketches of the tunes, which served as a guide for the other musicians. Once the composition's theme was established, the band shot from the hip. The solos were made up as they went along. Most of the final product is the first complete take of each song from the band, which was recorded live in the same room!

Are you *kidding* me?

If ever there was a distinction between a "rock star" and a "musician," the definition is found right there.

***

After *Someday My Prince Will Come*, Miles's music was in a state of flux. Coltrane left the band to pursue a solo career (which produced legendary albums like *Live at Birdland, My Favorite Things* and *A Love Supreme*), and Miles began working with a revolving door of musicians. Still, Miles released some solid studio work, like *Seven Steps to Heaven* (released in '63). He also issued some killer live material like *Live in Berlin, Live in Tokyo, Four + More,* and *My Funny Valentine.*

The key to the success of these albums lay in the discovery of a batch of young, gifted and eager musicians who saw working with Miles not only as a choice gig, but as the calling of a lifetime. Coming into the fold were a young pianist named Herbie Hancock, bassist Ron Carter, and 17-year-old drummer Tony Williams. George Coleman provided a competent and serviceable tenor saxophone, but it was the discovery and recruitment of Wayne Shorter that brought it all together. To Miles, Shorter bore the closest musical resemblance to Coltrane. Once again, the trumpet master had his foil. Without question, this quintet is my favorite jazz combo of all time. (8)

The band released a string of albums I wouldn't trade for the world. Between '65 and '68, the band issued *E.S.P., Miles Smiles, Nefertiti, Sorcerer,* and *Filles de Kilimanjaro.* Each record saw the band stretching itself to the point where it is almost hard to believe the same group who produced the last record made the first one.

"Far out" would a popular term during this time, but that phrase didn't suit the band. They were far *in.* That is to say, these five individuals were locked in to one another, reacting to and augmenting what they heard coming from each instrument. This was the band that taught me the importance of *listening,* and how that characteristic was often far more essential than the ability to play.

Of all the quintet's records, *Miles Smiles* (released in '67) is my favorite. It is the perfect bridge between the modal style Miles favored in the *Kind of Blue* days, and the newer, freer style of playing being embraced by the younger band members. The songs are faster, groovier, and more adventurous. Shorter, Hancock, Carter, and Williams pushed Miles and forced him to rethink his approach. This couldn't have made the bandleader happier, as his playing shows.

The quintet took the music to an even higher level on the bandstand, which doesn't seem possible until the music is heard. In 2011, Columbia began to release a series of Miles Davis recordings it calls *The Bootleg Series.* Volume 1 is called *Live in Europe 1967.* It contains three CDs and a DVD of the band's performances in Belgium, Denmark, Germany, and France. The quintet positively *scorches* tunes like "Agitation," "Gingerbread Boy," and "Riot." They are nearly unrecognizable compared to the studio recordings. It's a wonder the stage never caught fire during these performances.

To miss this music is to miss jazz history.

***

I've never been one to focus on visual image as means of appreciating music or musicians. With that being said, I must say this: Miles Davis had *style*! I've always admired the cut of a quality suit and hope to own more than a couple before I leave this world. And if I were to emulate anyone from the music world, it would be Miles Davis from the '60s. The man was sharp as a tack wherever he went.

Even in black and white photos and video, there could be no doubt Miles was making the scene in beautiful custom-made suits of Italian design. The *Live in Europe* DVD shows the band looking fantastic in well-cut tuxedos. And then Miles takes the bandstand in a grey, double-breasted pinstripe suit that completely blows them away!

I shudder to think what a suit of that quality would cost, but I have no doubt it's worth it.

According to legend, around 1961, Miles took the stage in a midnight blue pinstripe suit from Brooks Brothers. At the time, pinstripes were largely out, having been associated with gangsters from 20 or 30 years before. When an audience member saw what Miles was wearing, he said, "Pinstripes are back. I've got to get me one."

Miles spent his entire career striving to look hip. His outfits in the '70s were a bit extreme for me, viewing them three decades down the road. But I have no doubt he set a few trends during that time, and young men ran to the stores to try and emulate what they saw Miles wearing.

Miles Davis was an icon on many levels.

***

I joined the Air Force in April of 1988. By May, I was stationed at Shaw Air Force Base, South Carolina. My Miles Davis obsession came with me.

Alas, there weren't a lot of choice record shops in Sumter, the closest town to the base. There was a shopping mall with one of the old Sam Goody record chains, but quality discoveries were few and far between. More often than not, trips to that store yielded a CD not far removed from corporate rock. It was not a good time for musical discovery.

There was one salvation. Columbia, location of the University of South Carolina, was only 45 miles away. Since I didn't own a car, I rarely got to venture far from my base. Most of my friends wanted to go to Myrtle Beach, which was a little more than 100 miles east. I was far more interested in Columbia.

Specifically, I wanted to visit the Five Points section of town. I had heard stories of a little independent record store called Papa Jazz, and I wanted to see what it was about.

I made three or four trips to Papa Jazz during my two years in South Carolina. It was a pretty cool place. It didn't seem much bigger than a broom closet, but it was well organized, and the people working there struck me as knowledgeable. I had more than a couple of good conversations. They were even able to custom order a couple of obscure titles for me and ship them to the base. The Miles Davis section was fairly well stocked, containing most of the staples I already had, and even a rarity or two. Alas, they too were unable to get ahold of a copy of *Star People*. My quest would have to continue elsewhere. (9)

***

By 1969, the great quintet had disbanded, and Miles had begun to explore the use of electric instruments in his band. To jazz purists, this was heresy. To me, this was another avenue to explore. While visiting Papa Jazz, I purchased copies of two classic albums, *In a Silent Way* and *Bitches Brew.*

I can still see the somewhat pained look on the store clerk's face when he saw that I was buying *Bitches Brew.* "Are you sure about this, man?" he asked.

"What do you mean?"

"Well, I don't know how much you know about Miles Davis, but this is probably his most controversial record. It's nothing like *Kind of Blue,* my man."

I laughed. "Yeah, I know," I said. "I've heard 'Miles Runs the Voodoo Down.' It's pretty wild stuff, but I'll adjust." The clerk, knowing he wasn't going to talk me down from this particular musical ledge, let it go. My new records and I made our way back to Shaw, my dorm room, and my record player.

Since they were released in sequence, I played *In a Silent Way* (released in '69) first. What I heard cemented the album in my top ten favorite Miles Davis albums. But not before I found myself floored by the fact the great quintet broke up just a year before this album was released. Because this music sounded *nothing* like what that band had been playing.

There are just two tracks on *In a Silent Way*. The album totals a scant 37 minutes. But it is an incredible use of time. "Shhh/Peaceful," which makes up side one, contains some of the best use of space on record. Where Frank Zappa's records were chock full of musical information, Miles went in the opposite direction. I was not fully versed in ambient or minimalist works, but Miles was giving me a proper introduction.

The tune opens with a relatively simple drone from the organ of Joe Zawinul. This is quickly augmented by a two-note bass figure from Dave Holland, a continuous sixteenth note hi-hat run by Tony Williams, and the angular guitar of John McLaughlin. Zawinul also stabs a series of chords here and there. The simple contribution from Holland and Williams is what first grabbed my attention. They play the same simple riff throughout the tune's 18 minutes. Yet it's perfect. Their contributions leave more than enough space for the electric pianos of Herbie Hancock and Chick Corea, Wayne Shorter's tenor sax, and Miles. "Listen to that," I excitedly told a friend one day. "There's so much *air* in there. The guys in the band can do whatever they want! There's more than enough room. Best of all, sometimes they don't do anything at all. They just let things flow." It was my first real experience with the concept of "nothing" being the best "something."

Things intensify on side two. "In a Silent Way," a Zawinul composition, begins with a beautiful organ drone, augmented with McLaughlin's slightly distorted chords. Soon after, Miles and Shorter join in, establishing a beautifully understated theme. The horn section's notes seem to float on a cloud for just a moment … and then the piece takes off. Williams propels the piece forward from his drum kit, while the keyboard players provide additional stabs and riffs. Then Miles takes over, riding atop the musical wave. His trumpet (no mute this on this album) rings out with clarity and intensity.

Meanwhile, Dave Holland's bass grabs the anchor and holds down "It's About That Time." Miles and company weave in and around Holland's rock-solid line. This is where jazz almost collides with heavy metal. Many credit this album with the birth of fusion. (10) Just when things seem on the verge of going over the top, the band dials it back, and we find ourselves back in the serene womb of the song's opening drone. The album fades out, and the listener is left longing for more.

In a Silent Way laid the foundation for Miles's music in the years to come. Still, there was no preparing musically for the other record I bought at Papa Jazz.

***

I had seen *Bitches Brew* before. It was in my dad's collection. As a teenager, I was captivated by both the title and the cover art. The upper left-hand corner featured an extremely dark-skinned black man looking out over the horizon to the ocean, where a storm is raging. I can only assume he is looking off the coast of Africa, for also illustrated on the cover are the profile and back side of a man and woman embracing. They are dressed (barely) in what appears to be traditional African garb. The woman's hair is shooting straight up, with some of the strands reaching the sky to form the funnel cloud of a tornado. In the lower left-hand corner is a beautiful pink flower, which happens to be on fire. As it turns out, the music was every bit as intense as the cover art. But I would not learn that as a teenager.

Dad steered me clear of *Bitches Brew*, telling me I would not like it. It was his least favorite Miles album, and he didn't think it would help my exploration of his music. At the time, I simply took him at his word. Since I was still on the fence about "Miles Runs the Voodoo Down," I wasn't 100 percent sure I was ready for what I was about to hear in my Shaw AFB dorm room. I only knew I wanted to try.

Dad fell into the same trap as many other Miles Davis fans at the end of the '60s. When *In a Silent Way* was released, many people revolted, saying that Miles had abandoned jazz. He had sold out, they said, in an attempt to make more money. Miles wanted a younger, hipper audience. He loved Sly Stone, James Brown, and Jimi Hendrix. He wanted to snag part of that audience with his music. The new direction was a reflection of that desire.

Interesting word, "direction." Had Miles's fans been paying attention, they might have understood what he was up to. The evidence hides in plain sight on the album's front cover, just above the main title. It's only six words, but it speaks volumes. The words are "Directions in music by Miles Davis."

It says "Directions in *music*." Know what it *doesn't* say? "Directions in *jazz*". And therein lies the distinction.

If you take the word "jazz" out of the equation, and listen to *Bitches Brew* for what it is, without label or personal expectation, there is a good chance you will have a transformative musical experience. Alas, like Dad and so many others, I didn't immediately pick up on the clue Miles gave me.

I didn't hate *Bitches Brew* the way Dad did. I didn't love it either. I just didn't get it. The music seemed to come from everywhere at once. I had trouble finding that one element, like a bass line or a drum lick, to hold on to. The album had the Zappa-like quality of having a metric ton of musical information. But it didn't seem to have Zappa's sense of organization. There were three drummers, a percussionist, a bass clarinet, electric pianos, a guitar, a soprano saxophone, and Miles on trumpet. *Bitches Brew* fell on me like a ton of bricks. And I wasn't ready.

***

One great thing about being a Miles Davis fan is there is always more music to explore. I was having trouble grasping *Bitches Brew*. No worries: there's always another train coming. So, when *A Tribute to Jack Johnson* arrived, I climbed aboard. It was a ride I enjoyed immensely.

The music served as the score to a film about the world's first African-American heavyweight boxing champion. (11) He and Miles were two peas in a pod, even if they were separated by a generation. Miles had a passion for boxing, and it was how he got his exercise. Like Johnson, Miles had a taste for the finer things in life like nice clothes, fast cars, and beautiful women. Like Johnson, Miles felt his success was stunted by his blackness, and his unwillingness to subjugate himself. The music of *Jack Johnson* overflows with attitude, which works with brilliant effect.

Once again, there are but two tracks on the album. Side one is called "Right Off," perhaps the most appropriately named song in the Miles Davis catalog. I say this because the song wastes no time establishing itself and moving things right along. Drummer Billy Cobham, saxophonist Steve Grossman and keyboardist Herbie Hancock are on board, and they do a fantastic job. But the key to this tune's success lies in the hands of bassist Michael Henderson. His lines are funky, and full of soul. Henderson didn't come from a jazz background. Instead, he cut his teeth with Motown. Miles seizes the opportunity to sound hip, and his trumpet soars over the toe-tapping grooves laid down by his rhythm section.

McLaughlin's guitar bounces between mild and moderate distortion, with chords and lead lines interjecting themselves throughout the piece. Grossman's soprano sax wails, and Hancock sounds like his is practically standing on the keys of his electric organ. "Right Off" is 26 minutes of unbridled fun. It's a tune I wish I could have seen being recorded. Of course, I probably would have been kicked out of the studio's control room, because it's impossible for me to sit still when I hear it.

Side two is called "Yesternow." Once again, Henderson sets the tempo with a relatively simple staccato bass line. McLaughlin joins in, firing off chords with the aid of a wah-wah pedal. The tune takes on an atmospheric quality slightly reminiscent of the sound of *In a Silent Way*. But where "Right Off" has the feel of a fast-paced run, "Yesternow" barely moves beyond a trot. It doesn't need to. Miles uses his trumpet to accent the groove at hand, rather than lead it. He may be the session leader, but he seems to let the other musicians run the show.

    A Tribute to Jack Johnson is a fusion masterpiece. It is an indispensable album.

***

    In September of 1990, I landed in Tokyo, Japan, set to begin a two-year stint at Yokota Air Base, located some 30 miles west. Going from the sleepy town of Sumter, South Carolina, to a city of 12 million people sent a serious shockwave through my system. It took more than a little while to adjust to the vastly accelerated pace. But at least I had my music collection to help settle things down.

    My military specialty was Public Affairs Specialist. Simply put, I was a journalist. As my primary duty, I wrote and edited articles for our base newspaper, the *Fuji Flyer*. Save for the occasional major feature, the writing was pretty dry, and didn't require a lot of conscious thought. As long as I made the subject of the story look good, all was right with the world. (12)

    While we wrote and formatted our newspaper on base, the actual production and final layout were executed at the offices of the military newspaper *Stars and Stripes*, located in downtown Tokyo. Every Tuesday, my editor and I would carry floppy discs of that week's edition of the *Fuji Flyer* to the *Stripes* office, where would spend between four and six hours finalizing the layout and correcting any last-second inaccuracies we discovered.

    While the task of putting the paper to bed was relatively dry, there was a side benefit to making the Tuesday trip. I was, after all, in a foreign country. The commuter trains were packed between 3 and 6 p.m. every day (a lesson I learned the hard way). So, I took this time to do a little sightseeing. I was rarely looking for anything in particular. I just wandered from place to place, in and out of one interesting shop or another. Eventually, I would find a place to eat, and then make my way back home.

    Over time, I got friendly with the *Stripes* staff members living downtown. We talked about our interests and what we did in our spare time. Inevitably, music came up. Once again, I found myself talking to the right person, and he was able to guide me in the right direction. I told him about my odd musical tastes, including Frank Zappa, King Crimson, and Miles Davis.

He nodded along with recognition. "You need to go to Wave," he told me with a smile.

"What's Wave?"

"It's in the Roppongi district. About three subway stops from here. It's on your way back to the base. It's a music store. Huge place! I think you'll enjoy it. But be sure to bring enough money." (13) I actually had dinner plans with a friend the day I was told about Wave. But I now knew what I was doing after work the following Tuesday, no doubt about it.

As luck would have it, my editor, Adam Johnston, and I finished our work early the following week. Usually, Adam went straight home, so he could spend time with his infant son. But on this particular Tuesday, his wife had taken the baby to visit her mother. So, he had a little bachelor time on his hands. "Where you headed?" he asked, since he knew I loved to explore before heading home.

"Roppongi," I told him. "I heard about a music shop. I'm gonna try and hunt it down." Adam was also a former guitar player, having played in a few punk oriented bands before joining the Air Force. He asked if he could come along. I was happy to have the company.

We took the subway and found the Roppongi district with ease. Now it was just a matter of following the map I had been given by one of the civilians working in my office and hoping I would find what I was looking for. I've got to hand it to the Japanese: they draw one hell of a map. I couldn't read 95 percent of the signs in Tokyo, but every landmark was precisely where my Japanese friend said it would be. Finding the store was a snap. It was only a 10-minute walk from the subway station.

Talk about your first impressions: my friend at *Stripes* low-balled the size of Wave. It wasn't huge. It was *gargantuan!* It was easily twice the size of any record store I had ever been in. (14) Then I found out I was only on the *first floor*. There were three more floors to explore. Each was packed from one end to the other with CDs, LPs, laser discs, and videocassettes (this was the early '90s, after all).

I was used to record stores where jazz might take up one section of browser bins. It certainly wouldn't take up more than 10 percent of the store. The jazz section at Wave took up almost the entire second floor! My head was spinning with excitement as I moved from bin to bin, taking in the massive amount of music available for sale. Adam couldn't help but smile at my glee. Naturally, I gravitated toward the Miles Davis section. At least, that was my plan. Only I couldn't find it.

I looked high and low, all throughout the "D" section. No Miles. What the hell? I wondered. How can you have an entire floor of jazz and have no Miles? That doesn't make sense. Then I saw the problem: the Japanese filed their musicians by *first* name, not last. With that, I made my way to the "M" section. It took about ten seconds to find Miles.

Next, I learned many artists, Miles included, released records exclusive to Japan. Columbia Records had a good-sized catalog of Japanese only releases. They weren't cheap, either. The average CD was priced in the $27 to $30 range. I'm sure this was no big deal if you were paid in Yen. For me, it was a bit of a problem. Still, I continued to flip through the CDs with glee.

There must have been 80 or so titles to choose from. I can usually get through a particular artist's available stock in no more than five minutes. I was in the Miles Davis section for half an hour.

I was nearing the end of my browse, having chosen a couple of reasonably priced CDs to buy. I remember looking up for a second to get a gauge on where Adam was. I found him on the other side of the same floor, and then looked back down at the browser rack. And that's when I saw it.

There, about five CDs from the end of the section, sat a brand-new CD copy of *Star People*.

Remember the screams teenage girls made when they saw the Beatles in person? Well, that was me right there and then, albeit in a slightly lower octave. I'm sure more than one person in the store thought I was being murdered. Adam literally dropped the CDs he was looking at and ran back in my direction. He certainly had no clue what I was talking about when he heard me shriek, "I found it! I found it!" over and over again.

Adam put his hands on my shoulders, either to calm me down or to keep me from launching myself straight through the ceiling. I was finally able to control myself long enough to hand him the CD, tears of joy running down my cheeks. My hand shook as I handed it to him.

Why I expected him to comprehend right away is beyond me. Adam just stared at me. He had no idea what I was going on about. It took a couple of minutes, but I was finally able to tell him the story of the *Columbia Years* box set, and my endless quest for this album. Slowly but surely, Adam began to understand. His inner musician surfaced, and he started to smile broadly. He got it. "Well, this is a helluva find!" he said, starting to sound as excited as I was. "You're sure this is the right album?"

My heart almost fell out of my chest. What if there was an error in the translation? What if this was some other Japanese only record with the same title? Oh, God ... I hadn't even considered that! Adam saw me starting to freak out, and quickly turned the CD over so I could see the song titles. The last song on the record, track number 6, was "Star on Cicely." (15)

I was home.

Adam and I made a beeline for the cash register. I guarded my new CD like a Secret Service agent watching over the president. There was no way in hell anybody was going to pry this CD from my hands. The CD cost 2,300 Yen, which was just over $20. The average CD usually cost me about $10 on base. But this was *Star People*, so I didn't give a damn. I would have paid $50 or even $100 for that record. I *had* to have it!

It was worth it.

***

Star People was the second album Miles released after coming back from his hiatus. He dropped out of the music scene after a '75 tour, primarily for health reasons. Injuries suffered in a serious car accident, badly arthritic hips, and years of drug abuse took their toll on Miles's frail-looking body. He was also creatively burned out. Most friends and band mates figured Miles would take six months or so away from the scene, and then he would come back with his batteries recharged. He was gone for five years.

His first comeback record was called *The Man With the Horn* (released in '81). The album sounds like a man trying to find himself again. The trumpet sounds hesitant and unsure, when Miles took the time to play it at all. There are a couple of interesting moments. Miles's confidence seems to return – however briefly – near the end of the opening track, called "Fat Time." Miles starts the tune playing through his trademark Harmon mute, while bassist Marcus Miller and drummer Al Foster lay down an intensely funky groove. At the tune's end, Miles removes the mute and gives full-throttled support to his fellow players as they tie a bow on the piece. But it's not Miles that makes "Fat Time" worth hearing. That distinction belongs to guitarist Mike Stern.

"Fat Time" is actually named after Stern. Or rather, the not-so-kind nickname Miles gave Stern upon seeing him for the first time. Attempts to capture a proper guitar solo for the tune were not going well. Stern's name was brought up, and the call was made. After Stern showed up, the tune was re-recorded. Miles and soprano sax player Bill Evans (no relation to the *Kind of Blue* pianist) soloed, then Stern stepped up to the plate, and knocked it out of the park.

Playing a moderately overdriven Fender Stratocaster, Stern blazed away over the band's changes like he wrote the piece himself. By the time the song was over, Stern laid waste to my speakers, leaving me gasping for air. Apparently, the vibe was similar in the studio. While "Fat Time" is the only song featuring Stern on *The Man with the Horn*, the guitarist was invited to join the band, and went on the road with Miles and company. Stern's contributions are best enjoyed on the live release *We Want Miles*, which was released in '82. He also made quality contributions on *Star People*, along with co-guitarist John Scofield. Both now rank among my favorite guitarists.

***

I had no idea what was going to happen when I put *Star People* in my CD player and pressed the "play" button. I knew it was possible Miles would still be trying to find his groove. I knew I could've just spent $20 on a dud.

I needn't have worried.

Whatever Miles was looking for when he came back he'd found by the time he stepped into the studio to record *Star People*. It is 60 minutes of modern music bliss. I'm hesitant to use the word "jazz" in this case, because the term doesn't really apply. It was certainly a form of fusion. But this was unlike anything I heard called fusion before.

The first two tracks are appropriately named, starting with "Come Get It." The tune opens with a gargantuan two-chord power stance (16), before settling in to a dense, hyperkinetic exercise in power funk. To my mind, the title implies Miles is really ready to go for it this time, unlike *The Man With the Horn*. Miles is strong and bringing the power, and he wants his listeners to come get some.

The direction changes abruptly with "It Gets Better," when Miles and the band slow things down a bit and open up a little space. It's not quite a shuffle, but the band is definitely marching toward an aim. The tone is playful, but seriously so. Miles definitely found his groove.

Things pick up again with "Speak," an intense, dense exercise in funk rivaling anything Sly and the Family Stone or the Isley Brothers did. The bass contributions from Miller and Tom Barney establish the groove. Miles kicks the tune in the ass by playing trumpet and keyboards at the same time. The trumpet establishes the lead line, while the keyboard provides wicked, dissonant supporting chords. Meanwhile, Scofield, Stern, and Evans hold their own, bringing great enthusiasm to their solos. Side one of *Star People* is among the more powerful LP sides in the Miles Davis catalog.

Side two begins with the album's title track. A swirling synthesizer gives way to 17 minutes of pure 12-bar blues, and the band eats it up. Miles rediscovered the power of his muted trumpet and spends the next several minutes reminding everybody just who the hell he is, and why he is The Man. Evans and Scofield do their part to keep things grooving, and then Stern very nearly steals the show again, his guitar wailing and crying out as he does. Miles comes back at the end to put a bow on things. He must have known they captured something, because Miles can be heard calling out to his producer, Teo Macero, as the tune ends. No doubt he wanted to hear the playback to confirm the band had captured excellence.

"U 'n' I" is a playful little tune that adds little to the overall scope of the album. It's not a bad song. It just … is. If anything, it offers a nice moment of transition between the epic scope of "Star People" and the record's finale, "Star on Cicely," which was still everything I remembered it to be.

I'm not sure if *Star People* is my favorite electric Miles record. That varies from day to day. But it is always part of the conversation. Which is the main reason why I cherish that day at Wave in Tokyo as one of the absolute highlights of my musical life. (17)

***

The music Miles released in the '70s is without question the most divisive of his career. It would seem that people either loved it or hated it. More often than not, where my friends were concerned, the latter seemed to apply. But if ever there was a time I sympathized with my friends and their inability to grasp a certain style of music, this was it.

The primary reason for this difficulty lies with the artist himself, and his fans' expectations. Miles is credited for changing the course of music no less than five times. But the first three major changes – Cool, Post-Bop, and Modal – all remain within the confines of straight-ahead, non-electric jazz.

The addition of electric instruments was too much for the jazz purists to bear.

That being said, *In a Silent Way* is a relatively easy introduction to electric Miles. *A Tribute to Jack Johnson* is also a cool pathway of entry. After that, things get tricky.

In 1970, on the eve of *Bitches Brew's* release, Miles told *Rolling Stone* magazine he could create the best rock and roll band in the world. Whether or not this was the goal is a question only Miles could answer. But the music produced between '69 and '75 definitely had a rock attitude. (18) Even now, the music produced by Miles during this period cannot be defined by the simple confines put forth by those seeking to label it. One thing is certain: it is not jazz.

After going electric, Miles played gigs in non-jazz venues like the Fillmore, both East (in New York) and West (in San Francisco). He even played the Isle of Wight Festival, sharing the bill with rock icons like the Who. Miles was reaching new, younger audiences previously untapped by jazz artists. He was becoming the counter-culture embodiment of hip. But the music he was producing didn't always hit the mark.

I've been searching for the appropriate word to describe the records Miles released in the '70s. I keep coming back to the same one: *uneven*. Miles could both beguile and baffle. In many cases, his music seemed to be trying to accomplish too many things at the same time.

Perhaps it was due to the seemingly endless revolving door of musicians Miles employed. Music of this nature requires chemistry, in the studio and on the bandstand. Chemistry requires time. So a rapid-fire change on the keyboard stand, for example, from Herbie Hancock to Joe Zawinul to Chick Corea to Keith Jarrett – which took place over just a couple of years – can cause a sense of musical awkwardness not easily glossed over, regardless of the editing Teo Macero did with the recordings.

As innovative as it may have been, Miles may have had too many musicians to deal with at times. One or two keyboardists, up to three guitarists, saxophone, bass clarinet, sitar, percussion … the musical soup was becoming a thick gumbo, which could have been made tastier by thinning out the mix a bit and allowing a smaller number of ingredients to bubble to the surface. Sometimes, less really is more.

The lack of written material may have also been a factor. Miles had a couple of pre-written pieces, like "Directions" or

"Right Off," but for the most part he seemed to prefer an improvised affair, including making things up as they went along on stage, in front of the audience. Jazz is highly improvisational music by its very nature, but even the best musicians like to have some kind of guide, starting with the established name and theme statement of a song. From there, they can get a better feel for what they are doing, and where they want the music to go. Some of the efforts of Miles's bands, while certainly well intended, come off as so much desperate noodling.

There can be no ignoring the possibility drug abuse was a factor as well. Saxophonist Dave Liebman has pointed to cocaine as a factor in music Miles produced in the '70s. It was present, and the leader and his band consumed their fair share.

But this is *Miles Davis* I'm talking about. So, he was able to create more than a few moments of magic during this period. The '72 release *On the Corner* comes immediately to mind. Although it was reviled by critics, it contains some of the grooviest, funkiest, rocking music Miles created in the '70s. The album's song titles, like "Rated X," "Honky Tonk," "Black Satin," and "Thinking One Thing and Doing Another," meant relatively little from my perspective. But the groove is undeniable. Any listener with an open mind should be able to find it with relative ease.

Aside from *On the Corner*, three live releases from this era stand out, and receive repeated listens. *Dark Magus* was recorded March 30, 1974, at Carnegie Hall in New York City. *Agharta* and *Pangea* were recorded on the afternoon and evening, respectively, of February 1, 1975, in Tokyo. These are dark, dense, eerily groove-laden recordings, labeled by one critic as "fully functional improvisational acid funk." The label fits. Miles and his bands were not only reaching toward the music of James Brown and Sly Stone, with a touch of Jimi Hendrix, but to the polyrhythmic grooves of Africa as well. Of all the music put forth by Miles in the '70s, this is the most consistent and satisfying. But that's not to say it's easy.

While fans of Miles continued to try and tune in to what he was doing, Miles dropped out. The music of '69 to '75 is still deemed ahead of its time. Something tells me it will remain that way.

***

If it were up to me, Miles would have continued through the '80s in the musical direction that produced *Star People*. But in true Miles Davis fashion, he shifted gears, and veered toward what has been considered his "electric pop" period. People who disliked his '70s material were nearly apoplectic by what they heard from Miles after he came back. Even I go back and forth on some of the material, which sometimes comes dangerously close to the definition of smooth jazz.

Miles decided it was time to create some new Standards. Jazz musicians had played tunes like "Autumn Leaves," "Love for Sale," and "My Funny Valentine" to death. In the '50s, they were considered pop songs, and jazz musicians used them as vehicles for their own expression. Miles attempted to update the catalog, turning tunes like Cyndi Lauper's "Time After Time" and Michael Jackson's "Human Nature" into new vehicles of musical expression. The studio versions, found on the album *You're Under Arrest*, come off as a bit clinical. On stage, however, Miles breathed new life into the tunes, and made them sound like his compositions. (19)

When Miles departed Columbia Records for Warner Brothers in '85, his sound got even more pop-oriented. Marcus Miller and Tommy LiPuma, who produced the albums *Tutu* and *Amandla*, respectively, gave the albums a pop sheen, making them a sure-fire hit on the contemporary jazz charts, but left me wanting. Even if it wasn't jazz in the strictest sense, the thought of Miles standing alone in a room, headphones on, reacting to and playing along with pre-recorded tracks strikes me as sad. It is the very antithesis of *Kind of Blue* and other landmark Miles recordings. I understand the ideal stating the artist should be allowed to evolve and follow the path he feels best suits him. But I find it hard to believe this was the best path imaginable.

Miles's final record was, in some ways, a sad testament to what he had become. *Doo-Bop* was an attempt to embrace hip-hop and incorporate Miles's sound into it. The results are mixed, at best. The record would have done well with additional recording and polish (and perhaps a better production team), but Miles passed away in September of '91, before this could be done. I suppose the best way to sum up *Doo-Bop* is to say this: my sister – who *never* wanted anything to do with the likes of Miles Davis – enjoys that album, and demanded I make her a copy.

Given our frequent musical opposition, that speaks volumes.

***

Since Miles's passing, Columbia has issued a slew of archive recordings, bootlegs and re-masters. They cover the entire breadth of his creative output. Naturally, I have purchased nearly all of them.

In some cases, Columbia has assembled and released the whole of Miles's output from certain periods and albums, such as his work with John Coltrane, *The Complete Jack Johnson* recordings, and *The Cellar Door Sessions,* featuring a series of 1970 gigs in the club of the same name. I even bought the box set that culminated in the album that baffled me the most, *The Complete Bitches Brew Sessions*. But not before I had a revelation.

The re-masters Columbia released are positively stunning in their sound quality. Material recorded in the '50s and '60s sounds as though it was recorded and released just a couple of weeks ago. I bought everything the label issued, replacing everything that was already in my collection. The day finally came when *Bitches Brew* was re-issued. Twenty-six dollars later, the CD was in my home.

I was never worried about how the CD would sound. I had no doubt things would be taken to the next level. And I was right. But how would I handle the *music*, which baffled me for so long? The answer came quicker than I thought it would.

It's hard to say what, if anything, changed in my mind as I listened to this music. The sound was definitely clearer. I was able to pick up instrumentation I hadn't heard before. There was a groove in place which had eluded me. "Pharaoh's Dance," which made up side one, and the title track, which comprised all of side two, provided some fascinating musical moments. Miles was playing with power and passion.

And then it happened.

Somewhere early on side three (CD 2), during a tune called "Spanish Key," it all clicked into place. Whatever it was I didn't understand before suddenly made perfect sense. I was *there*. I understood.

I remember a huge smile coming over my face. I was alone, but that didn't stop me from yelling out, "I get it! I get it!" to anybody passing by. The feeling of triumph was on par with dissecting and comprehending a complex math or science equation. My persistence had finally paid off.

I've found *Bitches Brew* is best enjoyed on LP. The act of getting up to turn the record over before the next tune starts gives the mind a chance to breathe and absorb what has just taken place. By the time the needle drops again, I am ready for the next section.

Bitches Brew makes sense. And because of that moment, it now ranks among my ten favorite Miles Davis records.

***

The impact Miles Davis had on me cannot be overstated. One look at my music collection makes it obvious. I'm not just referring to his records, but the recordings of artists who played with him, and the bands they went on to form. Like King Crimson and Frank Zappa, the musical family tree of Miles Davis has many branches.

Miles introduced me to saxophone players like John Coltrane, who became a legend in his own right. 'Trane recorded landmark albums like *Giant Steps, My Favorite Things, Africa/Brass,* and *A Love Supreme.* Miles also employed Wayne Shorter, Julian "Cannonball" Adderly, Dave Liebman, George Coleman, and Kenny Garrett. All have recorded remarkable albums as bandleaders. All are represented in my collection.

Keyboard players Red Garland, Bill Evans, Wynton Kelly, Herbie Hancock, Joe Zawinul, Chick Corea, and Keith Jarrett all had tenures with Miles. Evans deft touch and haunting melodies make up part of one of my favorite piano trio albums, *Portrait in Jazz.* Zawinul joined forces with Shorter to form one of the most popular bands in fusion, Weather Report. Corea and drummer Lenny White (another Miles alum) formed Return to Forever, my favorite fusion band. Chick also made some fantastic acoustic albums. Herbie Hancock has become a jazz legend, recording landmark albums on the Blue Note label in the '60s like *Maiden Voyage* and *Takin' Off.* He also formed the Headhunters, a revolutionary fusion band, in the early '70s. Hancock's composition "Rockit" was the first instrumental to take MTV by storm in the '80s.

From the bass stand, Miles employed great musicians like Paul Chambers, Ron Carter, Dave Holland, Michael Henderson, and Joseph "Foley" McCreary. Carter is one of the most revered bassists in jazz, leading and supporting hundreds of sessions. Holland, too, has become a legend, influencing artists the world over, including another one of my favorites, drummer Bill Bruford. Foley revolutionized his instrument by taking on the role of "lead bass" within Miles's band. His instrument was tuned an octave higher, giving it the qualities of a guitar. It was a distinctive sound, and Miles made the most of it.

Legendary drummers "Philly" Joe Jones, Jimmy Cobb, Max Roach, Jack DeJohnette, Lenny White, Al Foster, Billy

Cobham, and Tony Williams all spent time with Miles. Their impact on music in general, and jazz in particular, cannot be overestimated. Miles's second famous quintet (featuring Shorter, Hancock, and Carter) would not have been the same without the young Williams propelling them forward from the drum riser. Cobham joined the Mahavishnu Orchestra and make some great albums of his own. His composition "Spectrum" has become a jazz standard.

The most famous guitarist to play with Miles was John McLaughlin, who went on to form another of my favorite bands, the Mahavishnu Orchestra. His blistering speed and technique leaves jaws dropping wherever he plays. Miles also employed Pete Cosey, Mike Stern, John Scofield, and Robben Ford. Each went on to make a name for himself as a bandleader.

The influence of Miles Davis is boundless.

***

Icons like Miles Davis are few and far between. I am fortunate to have him come across my musical radar. I don't agree with everything he ever did or said. His drug abuse is problematic. The way Miles allegedly treated women could be outright appalling. Of the musicians I admire, Miles is probably the one I wanted to meet the least. Sooner or later, we would wind up arguing about something. (20)

But there can be no arguing his contribution to music. Take it or leave it, like it or loathe it, music is better because Miles Davis was on the scene. He is a third of my Musical Holy Trinity for a reason.

One thing is certain: Dad knew what he was talking about.

(1)   Many artists became part of the "smooth jazz" format, which I despise. This genre gave us Kenny G, and the artists like him. My tastes for jazz were more "traditional," when not rooted in fusion. I saw what Kenny and those like him did as instrumental R&B.

(2)   Like so many others, I read the newspaper on my iPad these days. So I often forget about *Parade,* and the other things that come with the Sunday paper. The magazine is available on line, but I've never taken the time to go to their site.

(3)   I recall the "regular club price" being rather expensive, even for the mid '80s. Albums from Columbia House ran three or four dollars more on average than the record

stores. AND I had to pay for the shipping. Still, Columbia House (and BMG) helped form a good chunk of my record and CD collection until about 1990.

(4)   One of my fondest memories is going with my dad to see Delfeayo Marsalis at what is now called Jazz at the Bistro in St. Louis. This was in about '93, not long after I got out of the military. I will forever cherish the memory of the Hendrix Gentlemen in their best suits, sitting 12 feet off the bandstand, having the time of their lives. And it was more than acceptable for me to take advantage of the two-drink minimum. That's the first time I ever bought my dad a drink.

(5)   How many versions of this record have I bought over the years? It's only mildly embarrassing. First on LP. Then on CD. Then a re-mastered CD. Then the mp3 download. Then a 180-gram vinyl LP. Finally, there is the 50th anniversary box set, featuring yet another re-mastered CD, a 180-gram BLUE vinyl LP (which I played exactly once), a bonus concert CD, and a DVD. When I tell friends about this, they just shake their heads. All I can say to them is, "Worth it!"

(6)   Eventually, I purchased a CD boxed set of the earlier Miles works, called *Chronicle: The Complete Prestige Recordings*. Naturally, they were incredible. *Walkin'* ranks among my favorite Miles Davis records. So far, I have only bought two LPs and two CDs each of this recording. I must be slacking.

(7)   Davis and Evans also released a Bosa Nova album called *Quiet Nights*. The album was mostly marginalized by critics. I have yet to get around to hearing it. Although ultimately, I will.

(8)   A close second is the John Coltrane quartet of the early '60s. 'Trane on tenor and soprano sax, McCoy Tyner on piano, Jimmy Garrison on bass, and Elvin Jones on drums. This group achieves legendary status on *Live at Birdland*. The opening track, "Afro Blue," never fails to get me moving. It's not uncommon to hear me yelling, "Go 'head, fellas!" to my speakers as this tune plays. Never mind the fact the gig was recorded five years before I was born. It's a safe bet they can't hear me encouraging them.

(9)   During my time in South Carolina, I got to travel more than a little, due either to special assignment or because

I was visiting old friends. This meant I got to explore record shops in Virginia, North Carolina, Maryland, Florida, and Puerto Rico. I always found some Miles, but never the record I was looking for.

(10)   This assumption is not entirely accurate. Tony Williams, along with McLaughlin and organist Larry Young released *Emergency* by the Tony Williams Lifetime shortly before Miles released *In a Silent Way*. There could be no doubting the rock elements in Lifetime, and Williams and McLaughlin took those influences to Miles's sessions. Therefore, I credit Williams, et al, with the birth of fusion.

(11)   One of these days, I must get around to finding and watching that film.

(12)   There was no "hard journalism" to speak of. I wasn't going to win any Pulitzer Prizes. My job was to inform military members about what was going on around the base and make them happy to be there. Bad news was seldom reported, and almost never by me.

(13)   The U.S. dollar was not at its strongest during my time in Japan. My uncle told me stories of the early '70s, when a dollar fetched some 360 Yen. During my time there, the average rate was closer to 115. It never got higher than 136, and once bottomed out at around 96. Simply put, Japan was an expensive place to be a tourist, especially as a young enlisted man making maybe $1,200 a month.

(14)   The Virgin Records store in the Shinjiku district was also pretty large. Not quite as large as Wave, but very impressive nonetheless. Still, I liked Wave better, because it managed to maintain an Indie vibe, despite its size.

(15)   The song titles were also written in Japanese. I actually noticed that first. After a quick second, I realized the English titles were right there as well, underneath.

(16)   In fact, they are the same two power chords that open "Back Seat Betty," the second track on *The Man With the Horn*. Only this time, the chords take the band in a completely different direction.

(17)   Ironically, *Star People* is a much easier record to find now, 30-plus years after its release, than it was less than a decade removed. I'm sure Miles's death played into that, as well as the extensive re-mastering of his catalog.

I would say I am now able to find a copy of *Star People* – on CD or LP – one out of three times I go looking for it, just for fun.

(18)   Potentially the greatest Jazz/Rock collaboration is history never came to pass, but it was discussed. Miles met and befriended Jimi Hendrix, and the two reportedly discussed making an album together. Alas, Jimi died in September of '70, taking the dream recording with him.

(19)   Since Miles never played a show anywhere near me during the '80s, I never got to hear what he did with those pop songs on stage. I owned one concert video, *Miles in Paris*, which showcased the material. During the Internet era, more and more concert clips began to surface, and I was able to gain a new appreciation for the songs in question.

(20)   I must confess: I would have been honored to hear Miles call me a "motherfucker." Nobody – and I mean NOBODY – has used that word with more skill and eloquence. Except maybe Samuel L. Jackson.

*Rob Fetters is one of the most talented singer/
songwriters in pop music. Yet not nearly enough
people know who he is. But when I talk about pop music,
this is whom I'm thinking of.*
(Photo courtesy of Rob Fetters)

Track 12
Nobody's Talking 'Bout My Pop Music

In 1979, Top 40 group M scored a hit with a single called "Pop Muzik." The group was under the impression everyone was engaged in conversation about the sound they held most dear, be they in New York, London, Paris, or Munich.

I was engaged in whatever it was seventh graders in St. Louis were into at the time. And while my musical tastes continued to evolve, there was still a little room for popular music.

For the most part, the radio and television were still guiding my musical choices. I'd been listening to my parent's 45s since I was six. I had been exposed to various radio formats playing rock and roll, rhythm and blues, and easy listening. My musical week was incomplete if I missed *American Top 40* with Casey Kasem. Television exposed me to music by way of *Soul Train, American Bandstand, The Midnight Special*, and *Don Kirshner's Rock Concert*. Within a couple of years, I would be swept up in the phenomenon known as MTV. If it was popular, I'd probably heard it, and probably liked it. Like many people before or since, I maintained a simplistic mindset where popular music was concerned: "The radio plays that song all the time. So it *must* be good!"

I had a lot to learn.

As I matured, so did my musical tastes. The pop music I liked grew more sophisticated. Unfortunately, the songs being made popular on the radio didn't seem to keep pace. The music I enjoyed was well-played, sharply written, and expertly sung. The stuff on the radio ... well, not so much.

The King Crimson Revelation of '85 had a profound effect. I began to see through the load of crap commercial radio was feeding its listeners. There are infinite possibilities in the world of music. Top 40 wanted to narrow those avenues down, and few of them were any good.

The themes became shockingly obvious. There were sugary sweet love songs warbled by twenty-somethings, with all the sincerity of a campaign promise; songs of heartbreak and remorse, warbled over the same pedestrian 4/4 tempo; revenge songs so on-the-nose, they might as well come with a restraining order. Party songs that made sense on no level other than "shake your ass, and don't worry about what's being said." Tons of music pumped through the speakers, and most of it sucked. Yet its popularity could never be denied.

My biggest problem with Top 40 was its inherently disposable nature. People flock to record stores in droves to buy the latest single from Johnny Teenbop, making him the most important thing going in the music industry. Months later, Johnny's records are in the record store's "one dollar or less" bin, and those who bought the record find themselves asking, "What was I thinking?"

As the singles fly off the shelves, I find myself shaking my head in disbelief. My friends were confused by my derision. "You know, it really is a bad song," I say to them. "Have you really listened to it?" The dirty look sent my way tells me I will be unable to save my friend from his fate. Months later, when I mention the song or album in passing to the same friend, I hear something like, "I don't really play it that much. Are you happy?" The truth be told, I'm not.

Well, maybe a little.

***

The best music, pop or otherwise, has a timeless quality. It doesn't get dated easily. Even if the music does sound of its era, it incorporates the best elements of that era, which makes it palatable. The Beach Boys released *Pet Sounds* on May 16, 1966, six months before I was born. Yet the record sounds incredibly fresh. Conversely, there are hit songs from the '80s that make me cringe within seconds. The music smacks of the clichéd sounds of the era, used in the worst possible ways: Simmons electronic drums, key-tars, over the top synthesizers, and so on. It can be positively horrifying. I've seen fans of those plastic-sounding '80s tunes bury their faces in their hands when those songs come on the radio. Nobody does that when they hear "God Only Knows." That song has such depth, it still brings a tear to my eye.

The modern pop industry seems to go out of its way to reward sub-standard artists for singing sub-standard songs. People are quick to fawn all over the latest "American Idol," or the winner of "The Voice." These shows are little more than glorified karaoke contests. And once these contest winners release their own albums, we learn how limited their songwriting talent is. There are a couple of exceptions, of course. But they are rare.

Meanwhile, true singer-songwriters, who labor long and hard over their own music, go largely ignored. For the longest time, this irritated me to the point of being stressful. It took the wisdom of one of my favorite singer-songwriters, Adrian Belew, to bring me out of it. And he did it in just two sentences. "You know," he told me via Internet chat one day in '98, "Most good songs are not hits. And most hits are not good songs."

And just like that, the modern music industry made perfect sense.

***

Like so many others, I learned to appreciate pop music by way of the Beatles. The three- minute gems recorded and released by the Fab Four between '63 and '65 were the stuff bubble gum was made for. Songs like "I Wanna Hold Your Hand," "She Loves You," and "Love Me Do" had the girls screaming their brains out. Their boyfriends, meanwhile, just wanted to mirror the image created by John, Paul, George, and Ringo, especially after they appeared on *The Ed Sullivan Show* in February of '64. The Beatles spawned countless imitators and pretenders to the throne. Their influence on the artists following them should never, ever go without saying. (1)

While my loyalty to the Beatles is beyond reproach, I appreciate the music they made after '65 most, starting with *Help*. The primary reason for this becomes obvious quickly: the band came off the road. Once they were no longer limited to sounds that had to be replicated on stage by two guitars, bass, and drums, the Beatles' music took on an entirely new level of sophistication. Their songs made use of exotic and unusual instrumentation; they made the most of layering their recordings via multi-tracking; and they employed sounds and tricks that simply could not be duplicated on stage. In other words, they turned the studio itself into an instrument. The albums produced during this period – *Rubber Soul, Revolver, Sgt. Pepper's Lonely Heart's Club Band, Yellow Submarine, Magical Mystery Tour, The Beatles* (aka *The White Album*), *Abbey Road*, and *Let it Be* – showed fans a band maturing before its eyes and ears, with stunning results. Singles not included on those LPs were culled into separate collections called *Past Masters. Volume 1* focused on the early, bubble gum records. *Volume 2* (my favorite, needless to say) shows the band at its most sophisticated, having come into its own and at the peak of its compositional and performing abilities.

If there was any benefit to being introduced to band in the '70s, it's that I was able to absorb the band's entire catalog at once. It's funny when I think of the Beatles as having gone through periods, because it makes it seem as though the band was around for decades. The group released its entire recorded output (save for post-breakup collections) in *seven years*! Most modern bands consider it perfectly normal to put three to five years in between releases. The Beatles were pumping out new material every *six months*. And the music got better with each subsequent release.

Unreal.

***

The distinction between lighter and more sophisticated pop from the Beatles affected my choices when it came to other bands. I'd be lying if I proclaimed I sought out and discovered the bands who have shaped my Intelli-pop life. More often than not, I stumbled across these bands via the recommendation of friends, or purely by accident.

Once King Crimson came into my life, it seemed hard to believe I would find any use for modern pop music. But then Dave introduced me to XTC, and I knew I'd found an exception to my rule.

Adrian Belew (it always seems to come back to him, doesn't it?) has a fine ear for pop music, and is equally skilled at writing and performing it. And why not? Adrian is a dyed-in-the-wool Beatlemaniac. He has often spoken about having to "de-bug" his songs, when he realizes where a clever lick or chord change he wrote actually came from. Within the confines of King Crimson, Adrian hangs it out over the edge musically with the best of them. His pop sheen reveals itself here and there in songs like "Heartbeat," "Matte Kudasai," and "Man with an Open Heart." He calls one of my favorite Crimson songs, "Dinosaur," an epic pop song. And he's right.

Adrian's pop side fully reveals itself on his solo albums and with the Bears, the group he formed with co singer-songwriter and guitarist Rob Fetters, bassist Bob Nyswonger, and drummer Chris Arduser. I've been asked more than once to describe the Bears music. When "intelli-pop" doesn't do the trick, I say, "It's the Beatles on steroids." That usually drives the point home.

Fetters has produced some positively astounding solo albums in his own right since the late '90s. His albums *Lefty Loose/Righty Tight*, *Musician*, and *St. Ain't* rank among the finest in my collection. Given the opportunity for exposure in a fair and just world, I have no doubt Fetters would go home with more than a couple of those Grammy awards given to lesser artists over the years. But this is not a fair and just world, and most good songs are not hits. I have to keep reminding myself of that.

In '77, I stumbled across a band called the Electric Light Orchestra. I learned the driving force behind the band was Jeff Lynne, who wrote the vast majority of the songs, and frequently played most of the instruments in the studio. Eleven-year-old me didn't make the connection between Lynne and one of his biggest influences. By the late '80s, when Lynne was a member of the Traveling Wilburys (along with George Harrison, Roy Orbison, Bob Dylan, and Tom Petty), 20-something me took just a few moments to proclaim, "Holy crap! That sounds just like the Beatles!" Indeed, Lynne is a major fan. I can only imagine how he handled having Harrison in the Wilburys with him. (3) Lynne's first solo release, *Armchair Theater* (1990), drove the point home. The album is filled to the brim with clever lyrics, dynamic arrangements, and marvelous studio effects. It's no coincidence that *Armchair Theater* ranks among my favorite albums of all time.

While he is commonly recognized for his virtuoso abilities on guitar and keyboards, Mike Kenneally's sense of pop is as fine-tuned as any in music. Whether as a solo artist or with one of his bands, Keneally is just as musically comfortable singing and playing delightfully quirky pop tunes as he is weaving his way in and out of complex compositions by Frank Zappa, Steve Vai, and Joe Satriani. Recently, Keneally teamed up with Andy Partridge (of XTC) to produce an amazing album called *Wing Beat Fantastic*. Both the title track and my favorite tune on the album, called "I'm Raining Here, Inside" sound as though they came directly from an XTC album. That makes perfect sense, because Partridge wrote the song's lyrics. But it's Keneally's voice bringing the songs to life.

I was particularly impressed with the way "Raining" came together. "Andy had those lyrics sitting around for ages," Keneally told me. "He couldn't find a suitable melody for them. I read the words, and instantly heard the song in my head. I had the melody written out in about 20 minutes."

Timeless, high-quality pop music is possible in the modern music era. I wish more artists would strive to create it.

***

What separates intelli-pop from its Top 40-oriented brethren? I suppose it's mostly in the eye of the beholder. For me, it frequently comes down to a simple factor: most Top 40 hits are inherently danceable. Most intelli-pop isn't. Artists like Lynne, Fetters, and Belew are more focused on creating lasting lyrical phrases than making people move their hips. I can think of more than a few occasions when a turn of phrase would almost slip past me, causing me to stop the song mid-flow to ask, "Wait … *what* did he just say?"

I understand there are tons of people who simply do not give a damn about the clever nature of an artist's lyrics. If it gets them moving in the club, or serves as the perfect icebreaker, make out, or make up song, that's all they need. Taylor Swift seems to have made a career out of dating and breaking up with the men in her life, then writing about it. It has made her a millionaire. Good for her. I need a little more.

Instrumentation plays a key role in the nature of intelli-pop. Top 40 is more beat-oriented, and that rhythm is frequently driven by a computer or drum machine of some sort. That's all the better to get the rumps shaking, I suppose. My kind of pop music is driven most often by the guitar or piano, usually of the acoustic variety. The best songs seem to have some variation on a band consisting of an acoustic guitar, an electric guitar, bass, keyboards, and drums. It's a much more organic sound that leaves plenty of open space for meaningful lyrics that are meant to be heard throughout the song. If there's one thing I've noticed about Top 40, it's that fans rarely know all the words to their favorite songs. They know the hook, or a portion of the chorus, but little else. And that's all they need to know. Even I can sing the hook to a Black Eyed Peas song or two. I prefer not to, but I can.

But lyrics from a song like "Long Way Down (Look What the Cat Dragged In)," written and performed by Michael Penn, permeate the listener's soul. One has no choice but to absorb the singer's anguish. I understand some people don't want to listen to music to feel sad. But I would hope most people use music to get in touch with a side of themselves they may not otherwise pay attention to. It's difficult to make art without a little pain.

Nobody digs into that dark psyche quite like Aimee Mann. She entered my musical life in a big way in the year 2000. I'd heard of her before, when she fronted the band 'Til Tuesday. They scored a moderate hit in '85 with a song called "Voices Carry." For a time, it was in rotation on MTV. That song was all right, but it didn't hold my attention. I was deep in to prog and jazz by then, and the blonde woman with the big, spiky hair may have had a song with a nice hook, but she wasn't what I was looking for.

Mann released a couple of solo albums (called *Whatever* and *I'm With Stupid*) in the '90s. They achieved critical acclaim, but she remained an underground sensation. Things changed in '99, however, with the release of the soundtrack from the movie *Magnolia*. Mann wrote the vast majority of the music for the album, and it turned heads. I was trying to deal with the quirky nature of the film, when it dawned on me just how good the music was. It started with a fantastic cover of Harry Nilsson's "One." The woman singing the song sounded familiar, but I couldn't quite put my finger on it. Later in the movie, two additional songs, called "Save Me" and "Wise Up," tore my musical world asunder. They had the emotional depth I loved in a quality pop song. Every word of the lyrics had meaning. They conveyed the emotion of the film to a "T." I had to find out who this woman was! I've never stared at movie credits so carefully. In the end, I found I was listening to Aimee Mann. Within 24 hours, the *Magnolia* soundtrack was in my CD collection.

If there was any doubt I was about to become an Aimee Mann fan, that doubt was removed when I heard *Bachelor No. 2.*, which was released in 2000. The only thing more shocking than the quality of the songs on that CD was the fact Geffen, her label, didn't want to release it. (4). Songs like "Deathly" contain some of the most heartfelt lyrics I've ever heard. In the song, a woman meets and goes on a date with a man for the very first time. She likes him so much, she feels compelled to reject him, for fear he will see how deeply flawed she is. "Now that I've met you/Would you object to/Never seeing each other again?/'Cause I can't afford to/Climb aboard you/No one's got that much ego to spend." (5)

Holy crap!

Bachelor No. 2 showed songs like "Deathly" were no aberration. This was what Aimee Mann wrote about, and she did it remarkably well. I made it my mission in life to follow this woman musically, and I continue to do so.

Coincidentally, Aimee Mann is married to Michael Penn! What an odd feeling it must be to write a great song in the breakfast nook one day, only to learn you're not even the best song writer *in the house* for a given period. I wonder if Aimee and Michael ever compete over who writes the best song? Maybe one of these days, I can ask them. (6)

In 2013, Mann teamed up with singer/songwriter Ted Leo to form a band called the Both. They released a self-titled CD the following year, which rapidly became a favorite. Songs like "The Gambler," "Milwaukee," "You Can't Help Me Now," and "Honesty is No Excuse" showed off not only Mann's overall songwriting ability, but her collaborative skills as well. They are a band I'm dying to see live, as I have enjoyed seeing Mann in person twice already.

Bands like XTC have shown me what is possible in pop music, if the consultants and programmers would allow music of that caliber to leak through and reach the ears of the masses. I can only wonder, just what are these programmers afraid of? Do they worry that their audience might suddenly realize the music thrust upon them actually sucks? If so, why is that a bad thing? Why not elevate the thinking of the average consumer, rather than pander?

But there can be no stopping that which is "catchy." And I've found more than a few musicians I admire don't have a major problem with it. To those inside the industry, "bad" pop music is just one of those things that comes with the gig. Deborah Holland confessed to me a love for the Black Eyed Peas song, "I Gotta Feeling." She couldn't remember the name of the song, but she sang me the chorus. Part of me wanted to freak out. But my more rational side understands once a song resonates, it stays there until it runs its course.

I spent a good year coming to terms with my enjoyment of some of the material by the Black Keys. Their hooks had a way of doing just that: hooking the listener, and drawing him in. I admit, I resented them a little bit for it. But I was able to find a way to live with them, thanks to what I call the "Hipster Clause." This allowed me to explore the Black Keys earliest works, *like The Big Come Up, Rubber Factory, Brothers*, and *El Camino*. These albums had a raw, lo-fi sound I came to call "gutbucket." It was the sound of two guys making killer sounds in their basement, or whatever primitive room they were using, with cheap gear and minimal studio tricks. Once the band came above ground and they were able to afford top-flight studio time and producers, I lost interest. But at least I can feel like I was there from the beginning.

Jack White and I are also coming to terms with one another. (Well, since Jack has no idea who I am, I guess the resolution is only going one way.) I was never a huge fan of the White Stripes. When your drumming idols are Bill Bruford, Neil Peart, and Tony Williams, it's very hard to take Meg White seriously. I'm not saying I could do a whole lot better, but I don't have a professional recording contract, either. Still, the group's last record, *Icky Thump*, resonated with me. Now and then, I like to break away from the elite, precise sound that comes from jazz and prog so that I can embrace something a little more elemental and grounded. Jack White's guitar has that sound. His boutique guitars and custom effects produce a "high-end, lo-fi" growl I would love to replicate now and then. It just sounds … fun. And so, I swallowed my pride (snobbery?) and bought the album. As it happens, I like it just fine.

In fact, the further away Jack White is from the White Stripes, the more I enjoy his work. His solo albums, *Blunderbuss* and *Lazeretto*, are lo-fi gems. His solo work is steeped in the blues, with a dash of soul thrown into the mix. It's a fascinating sound. So, too, is his band the Dead Weather. They personify the lo-fi, grimy, indie groove I need now and then. Bands like them are the ultimate palate cleansers when I need to get away from layered instrumentation and alternate time signatures.

And every now and then, I hear them on the radio.

***

Once in a while, a band with chops and sharp songwriting ability sneaks through the cracks, if only to become a cult favorite over the years. English pop band Squeeze comes to mind. They were able combine playing ability, soulful vocals, and solid lyrical material to create a small stream of hits, including "Tempted," "Pulling Mussels (from a Shell)," and

"Black Coffee in Bed." The band did its best work in the '80s and '90s.

It should go without saying any band Adrian Belew is compelled to produce becomes worthy of my time. This is how the Irresponsibles came across my radar. Based in Boston, the band entered a songwriting contest, and Belew was one of the judges. By the end of the competition, Belew had reached out to primary songwriter Peter Montgomery, saying the veteran artist wanted to work with them. The end result was a '99 CD called *When Pigs Fly*, which has the pop sensibility and snark of XTC, the production value of the Beatles, and the occasional instrumental quirk of Belew himself. I got to see the band open for their producer. It was as close as I will come to seeing XTC on stage. I wish they could have broken out nationally.

***

There is good pop music being made. You just can't rely on radio to find it. Thanks to modern phone applications like Bandcamp and SoundCloud, the task is not as difficult as it was. The chances of modern radio coming to its senses and offering up songs of depth and substance are minimal, at best. With just a little more effort, music consumers can find the albums they can be proudly display on their media shelves and avoid asking "What was I thinking?" ever again.

(1)   Anyone claiming not to appreciate the Beatles should take their music collection outside and set it on fire. There is scarcely a single aspect of music – be it playing, arranging, or recording – that doesn't contain at least a shred of something the Beatles did first, or perfected after it was introduced by someone else. This is especially true when you factor the band's producer, Sir George Martin, into the mix. Diddy, Rick Rubin, and Kanye West should hit their knees at least once a week and thank the music gods for the Beatles.

(2)   Full disclosure: organized religion and I don't completely see eye to eye. All I will say is this: I was raised Baptist and baptized Catholic. I love reading Buddhist books. I consider myself spiritual, rather than religious. As far as I'm concerned, if your faith (or lack thereof) prevents you from shooting up a schoolyard full of kids or flying a jet plane into an office building, whatever works for you is fine by me.

(3)   In fact, Lynne handled it pretty damned well. He wound
        up producing the new tracks on the Beatles *Anthology*
        releases, "Free as a Bird" and "Real Love." Both are
        rock solid songs.
(4)   A saga covered elsewhere within these pages.
(5)   "Deathly," by Aimee Mann. Published by Aimee Mann
        (ASCAP) Copyright 1999
(6)   This is far from surprising, but both Michael and Aimee
        are Beatles fanatics. On the soundtrack for the movie *I
        am Sam*, the two perform a wonderful duet of "Two of
        Us," a Beatles classic.

College rock came above ground in a big way in the '90s. This was probably the last commercial trend I truly embraced

Track 13
The Alternative Approach

In everyone's life, there are a few "JFK" moments. These are events so profound, you remember exactly where you were when they happened.

I was still three years from being born when John F. Kennedy was assassinated, so my first JFK moment took place in January of '86, when the space shuttle Challenger exploded, killing the seven astronauts on board. I distinctly recall being in my college newspaper office when I heard the news. And, of course, I will never forget September 11, 2001, when the world turned upside down.

It will surprise no one to learn more than a couple of my JFK moments were musical. The "discoveries" of artists like King Crimson, Miles Davis, and Frank Zappa were profound moments with lasting after-effects. It can be argued the music I was listening to at the time was preparing me for each subsequent moment. There was no possible preparation for the lightning bolt that struck in October of '91.

There weren't many entertainment options at Yokota Air Base, Japan, where television was concerned. In fact, our "cable" television system consisted of about eight channels, with only two of them broadcasting in English. The Armed Forces Radio and Television Service (known as AFRTS) controlled both those channels. On the plus side, there were no commercials. (1) Programming deemed suitable entertainment for military personnel consisted mostly of stale sitcoms and corny movies. The exceptions were the occasional sporting event, *Star Trek* reruns, and episodes of *Saturday Night Live*. Since I spent most of my non-working time playing tennis, I recorded these programs on my VCR for later viewing. For us, *Saturday Night Live* aired on Sunday afternoon.

One fall Sunday, I was in my dorm room having a pleasant chat with my roommate, Steve. *SNL* had just ended, and we were talking about whatever it is two airmen talk about the day before they have to go back to work.

Since there were no commercials, programs usually ran short of their normal allotted time. So AFRTS would insert some sort of filler, like a music video or two, to eat up the remaining time before the next show aired. Had my TV not been running through my VCR, and had the VCR not been connected to my home entertainment system, enabling us to hear the audio in stereo, the moment might have passed us unchecked. Instead, Steve and I heard a few jangly guitar chords that might have fit nicely into an old song from the band Boston. What followed was a sonic avalanche I was stunned to learn was produced by a power trio.

Steve and I stopped our conversation mid-sentence and turned our attention to the television. What we saw looked like what I can only describe as pep rally in purgatory. Cheerleaders wore black uniforms with the encircled "A" of the anarchists. The teenagers sitting in bleachers were about as far away from peppy as can be imagined. An elderly janitor swayed rhythmically while grasping a mop handle, the business end still in its bucket.

At the center of attention was the power trio, fronted by a man in his twenties with stringy, dirty blonde hair falling into his face. His vocals were, for the most part, unintelligible. The bass player stood to his right, jumping up and down, barely containing himself. The drummer sported a mop of long black hair and played with the energy level and intensity of Animal from the Muppets.

Steve and I sat in place, open-mouthed, for nearly five minutes. The song crashed over us in wave after wave. By the time it was over, I think I was sweating. When the last note faded away, I looked at Steve. "What … the hell … was *THAT*?" I asked.

Steve looked at me blankly, slowly shaking his head. "I have no idea," he replied. Then he grinned. "But I want to hear it again." We looked at my VCR, hoping that it was still running from the *SNL* broadcast. To our delight, the red light was still glowing, with the letters "REC" showing clearly in the display window. I practically dove for the remote control and pressed the "rewind" button.

After watching the song again, we actually bothered to read the end credit, where we learned the band was called Nirvana. The song was called "Smells like Teen Spirit." What that title had to do with the song, I have no idea. More importantly, I didn't care. What I heard shook me to my musical core. This was something new. It was a much welcome departure from the "hair metal" that had taken over the airwaves in the mid- to late-'80s. That, combined with the introduction to King Crimson, Frank Zappa, and college radio, drove me away from commercial music. Nirvana had given me a reason to start paying attention again. But I didn't tune in to the radio again immediately. I went to the Base Exchange, and found Nirvana's CD, *Nevermind*. That was enough for now. The genuine return to radio wouldn't come for another year-and-a-half.

***

I was discharged from the Air Force in October '92. After spending a couple of weeks hanging out in Sacramento, California, I went home to St. Louis. Naturally, I made my way to the old record haunts. It was nice to see some of the old, familiar faces. Some of my friends had moved on, but many were still there. And they were talking about Nirvana and the new musical era they ushered in, called "Grunge."

The music being produced by the Grunge movement was fine and dandy. But the look of the musicians ran completely against everything I had been taught in the previous five years. Baggy, untucked plaid shirts with dirty t-shirts underneath, long hair, goatees and beards, torn jeans, and scuffed shoes were the norm for the musicians. Their look nearly caused my military-conditioned head to explode. (2) The epicenter of this movement appeared to be Seattle, Washington. Like Detroit, Washington, D.C., London, and Athens, Georgia before it, anything and everything coming out of Seattle was deemed worthy of nearly instant worship.

Nevertheless, I continued to ignore commercial radio. I stuck with my jazz station. The college radio station had changed, but I did my best to hang with it all the same. Once in a great while, I would tune into the classic rock station, KSHE, a St. Louis institution since 1967. But the corporate rock of the '70s and '80s was still a little stale to my snobbish musical mind. I was all but prepared to return to commercial radio seclusion.

In late '92, I got word a new radio station was to debut in February of '93. KPNT, situated at 105.7 on the FM dial, was being dubbed, "St. Louis's new alternative." They called themselves "the Point." They would specialize in Grunge and similar sounds. Music from the mid '80s back would be left for the classic rock stations to tread over redundantly. This station would be something new, boldly going where other radio stations feared to tread. I was wary, but I certainly believed this new station was worthy of at least a little of my attention.

For quite a while, I wasn't disappointed. The Point was everything I hoped it could be. The radio station immersed me in all things Grunge, and then some. The Alternative movement was much bigger than I thought, and was coming from all directions. Seattle was the epicenter, yes. But there were bands chiming in from as far away as Australia.

The point rooted itself in Grunge. The most popular bands being aired were Nirvana, Pearl Jam, Soundgarden, Alice in Chains, and Stone Temple Pilots, all Seattle bands. Still, it would be improper (and incorrect) to simply lump all these bands together because of their hometown. Each act had a distinctly different sound, even if it was rooted in heavy guitars.

To my ears, Nirvana had the attitude and approach of a punk band, while Pearl Jam seemed to come from the classic rock styles of bands like the Who or Led Zeppelin. Stone Temple pilots had a swagger I always admired, and reminded me of an updated version of the Rolling Stones. Alice in Chains seemed to base itself in heavy metal, coming across as Seattle's answer to Black Sabbath. I liked them all, and I liked them all for different reasons. 1993 was shaping up to be a heady period for Alternative radio.

Meanwhile, there were other artists trying to make a mark on the scene. Bands like Soul Asylum, Silverchair, and Collective Soul came close to the Grunge sound, but added their own flavor. In the early days, the Point was unafraid to explore the sounds of artists who rose in the late '80s, like Midnight Oil, U2, and R.E.M. Bands I had fallen in love with on the left side of the radio dial were now starting to make their mark on the right. The late '80s club bands were now playing arenas. What fun it was to hear the likes of Suzanne Vega, 10,000 Maniacs, and Tori Amos with the full power of a major FM radio station behind them. Of course, things changed over time, thanks to consultants. But it was fun while it lasted.

***

There was so much music playing at KPNT between '93 and '99, it made my head spin. Dare I say it? The Point was making commercial music fun again.

I was being introduced to an eclectic array of sounds. Bands like Toad the Wet Sprocket couldn't be farther away from the Grunge sound of Nirvana. But their conscious-driven, intelligent pop music was not to be ignored. More punk-driven bands like Ned's Atomic Dustbin also held my attention, for they sounded unlike anything I heard before. The driving, heavy metal sound of Helmet may have been a little redundant, but there could be no denying the power of their hit single, "Unsung." That tune still gets me through the occasional workout.

There were horn-driven bands like Reel Big Fish, Squirrel Nut Zippers, and Cherry Poppin' Daddies. They weren't necessarily something I wanted to hear every day, but they were a nice change of pace. There were heavier bands like Anthrax, Dinosaur Jr., and Ministry, the latter of whom helped bring in the relatively short-lived Industrial age in alternative music. I was introduced to some of my favorite female-driven bands and artists, like Liz Phar, the Cranberries, Paula Cole, Portishead, Mazzy Star, No Doubt, and Ani DiFranco. Those lovely feminine voices were cutting through sounds as diverse as metal, ska, punk, pop, folk, and electronica. I found a new bass hero in Les Claypool when his band, Primus, broke on to the scene. A music critic once described the band as "King Crimson meets the banjo player from (the movie) *Deliverance*." That's completely accurate, and totally awesome. I've been hooked ever since.

The early days of KPNT were amazing, because I didn't know where the DJ was going next. There was so much variety – so many interesting and unique sounds – it was nearly impossible to get bored. The songs in "heavy rotation" weren't repeated that often, so it was no big deal to spend most of my day playing the Point.

***

Of the popular Seattle bands, Pearl Jam was my favorite. From the get-go, they sounded like a band in it for the long haul. Their creative output over the past quarter century has been a slow burn, unlike the comparative flash and fade of other acts from that region.

In the '70s, record deals were structured so an artist or band had time to develop his craft, and build an audience. Bruce Springsteen, for example, didn't really break until he released his third album, *Born to Run*. Rush didn't take off in a major way until its *fourth* release, *2112*. Had either of those acts tried to establish itself at that pace in the '90s or beyond, they never would have made it. The record label would have dropped them like a bad habit.

The modern music industry demands hits *now*, rather than down the road. If the artist can't score a hit right out of the chute, the record label is pretty much done. Even if the artist does score a hit right away, chances are, the label will look for that artist to merely duplicate that formula and bleed it dry. An artist trying to grow or expand his musical vocabulary finds itself marginalized, pushed aside for the "next big thing." The fans don't help. A band scores a major hit, and that's what the audience wants to hear in concert, new material be damned. Does anyone remember the last time Rush toured without playing "Tom Sawyer," which was released in '81? I don't. A band trying to move beyond its hit frequently finds itself wearing out its welcome with the very people who ardently supported them shortly before.

I'm reminded of a line spoken by the "Harvey Dent" character in Christopher Nolan's *The Dark Knight*. Dent was discussing his belief that Batman did not want to be Gotham City's hero forever. Sooner or later, Dent determined, people would stop appreciating his efforts. "You either die a hero, or you live long enough to see yourself become the villain," Dent opined. Popular music acts suffer a similar phenomenon.

Stone Temple Pilots broke up, mostly due to the actions of lead singer Scott Weiland (who ultimately died from an overdose). Nirvana's leader, Kurt Cobain, committed suicide just three years after *Nevermind* was released, and his band died with him. Soundgarden broke up not long after scoring huge with its album *Superunknown*. Alice in Chains flamed out, for the most part, after the death of its lead singer, Layne Staley. The commercial run of each of those bands was relatively short. Still, each band remains highly regarded by fans and commercial radio.

Pearl Jam keeps plugging along. But while radio stations are still eager to play material from the band's first three records (*Ten*, *Vs.*, and *Vitalogy*), the music released since then isn't held at the same level of esteem. Is the newer music inferior? Not to me. There are plenty of exciting moments to be found in newer Pearl Jam albums. But the audience has moved on, and the radio is doing nothing to help. People I once knew to be fans now look at me with mild disdain when I ask whether or not they have checked out Pearl Jam's latest musical efforts. This is something I do not understand. People are more willing to let trends dictate what they listen to, rather than the music itself.

To the modern music industry, Pearl Jam has outlived its usefulness. And that is a crying shame.

***

While Pearl Jam is my favorite band to come out of Seattle, my favorite album actually came from Soundgarden in '94. *Superunknown* is 70 minutes of the finest rock and roll produced in the '90s. There are 15 songs, and there's not a dull moment to be found. The album comes out swinging and doesn't let up.

Soundgarden laid the groundwork for this album on their previous release, *Badmotorfinger*. The record featured blistering songs like "Rusty Cage," "Outshined" and "Jesus Christ Pose," which feel like they just might melt the eardrums. Unlike other Grunge bands, Soundgarden chose to make the use of alternate guitar tunings, which gave the instruments a heavier "crunch" when played. They also deviated from standard 4/4 time, giving the band a prog-like sense of musicianship. This foundation served them well on *Superunknown*.

It's difficult to fathom a band playing metal in alternate tuning and odd times having a hit single, but that's exactly what Soundgarden managed to do. Songs like "Fell On Black Days," "The Day I Tried to Live," "Black Hole Sun," and "Spoonman" were in constant rotation on the Point. I love that the drum break on "Spoonman," played by Matt Chamberlin, was in 6/4.

Legendary guitarist Steve Vai said that everything he was doing came to a stop whenever he heard "Black Hole Sun" on the radio. I can't say I blame him. The song's hypnotic guitar opening, played by Kim Thayhil, draws the listener in and holds him mesmerized throughout the song. But it's the voice of lead singer Chris Cornell that brings the song together. Whether crooning softly or belting out a guttural roar, Cornell's voice is the perfect icing for a very heavy cake.

There was a time when I would buy a CD based on hearing a single song. As I got older (or as money got tighter), I would hold off until I had heard at least two or three songs I liked. The decision to purchase *Superunknown* was a no-brainer. I knew from the get-go that I liked at least four songs on the CD. Still, I was stunned at the level of musicianship on the rest of the album. And the louder I played it, the better it got. My only regret is that I have not yet gotten around to buying the 20th anniversary re-master, which features rarities and B-sides from the *Superunknown* sessions. I am slacking!

***

If the Point did anything for me, the radio station introduced me to four bands who remain among my all-time favorites. Seldom does a week go by without at least one of them finding their way into my CD player or being cued up on my iPod.

Rage Against the Machine is a rap/metal band based in Los Angeles. I've often thought hip-hop acts like Public Enemy or N.W.A. would be more exciting if they had the full weight of a live band playing behind them. Rage made my case for me. Guitarist Tom Morello, bassist Tim Cummerford, and drummer Brad Wilk played some of the heaviest, funkiest, hard rocking licks going. The grooves seemed relatively simple on the surface, but they hit with all the subtlety of a sledgehammer. The groove was topped by the vocals of Zach DeLa Rocha, who waxed poetic about the social and political issues of the day with a level of intensity that led me to wonder if the man ever laughed about anything. Come to think of it, I'm still wondering.

Of course, there won't be many smiles associated with songs like "Guerilla Radio," "Freedom," "Bulls on Parade," and "Calm like a Bomb." There could be no doubting that these four young men took the stage with something to say. The fans took to it with relish. I have a great love for concert videos, and one of my favorite sights is a Mexico City crowd jumping up and down in unison while Rage tears through "Bulls on Parade." It's all I can do not to join them.

The political view of Rage is pretty far to the left. So far left, I didn't always agree with what they were saying. (3) But there was never any doubting the band's sincerity. Regardless of one's individual point of view, Rage made the listener think rather than just blindly following the popular crowd. Their first two albums, *Rage Against the Machine* and *Evil Empire*, do the best job at provoking thought.

Around the same time I first heard Rage, I was introduced to Nine Inch Nails. Largely the work of Trent Reznor (who played most of the instruments and sang in the studio), NIN was about tapping into the deep, dark areas of the psyche often best left untouched. Most people spend a minimal amount of time getting to know the darker side of their personae. Reznor not only visited that dark area, he pitched a tent and made himself at home there. Soon, millions of fans followed him into the dark, myself included.

Nine Inch Nails' first hit, "Head like a Hole," got past me. I'm sure the Point played it now and then (Lord knows they wore it out later on). I just wasn't paying close attention. The song was the feature cut of the debut album, *Pretty Hate Machine*. To be honest, it's my least favorite NIN record. It sounds dated, with drum machines and synth effects that sound like they came straight from a '80s hip-hop session. Still, there are some interesting moments, and the album gets occasional time on my CD player.

Trent Reznor really got my attention when he released *The Downward Spiral* in '94. The first single, "Closer," defies description. I've heard it played in Goth-type clubs and yuppie discos. Somewhere, there is a couple who refers to "Closer" as "their song." Given Reznor's declaration in the song's chorus, "I wanna fuck you like an animal," I can only wonder what a romantic evening at home is like for these couples. On the other hand, I don't want to know.

The Downward Spiral was my introduction to a musical style dubbed "Industrial." The music had a metal foundation but was somehow darker. Elements of noise, generated by keyboards and samples, provided a key element. A deeply disturbing or otherwise dystopian-type music video also proved essential.

There could be no dismissing the power of the music. Reznor used all the anger, pain and misery in his psyche to bring forth an album appealing to the manic-depressive in all of us. Imagine my surprise when I learned one of his guest musicians was none other than Adrian Belew! With that in mind, the music of Nine Inch Nails gained that much more credibility.

Nine Inch Nails's pathos reached critical mass with the *The Fragile*, released in '97. Reznor was still miserable, and he wanted everyone to know it. But the songs, blunt and brutal as they could be, were also more melodic. Songs like "We're in This Together" showed near optimism, while "The Big Comedown" reminded everyone there were still demons to conquer. There were also some remarkable instrumental passages, like on "Just Like You Imagined." Some believe a two-CD set was overkill. I am not one of those people. *The Fragile* ranks among my top 10 favorite albums the '90s.

Reznor's newfound sobriety helped lift a layer of darkness from his subsequent albums. That's not to say he's completely lightened up. His album *With Teeth* is appropriately named, because it has more than a little bite to go with the new grooves he was creating. With each subsequent release, Reznor appears to be pushing himself to expand his sonic palate, which I find more than a little admirable. Of course, radio (and more than a few fans) couldn't care less and have since moved on. I'm guaranteed to hear "Closer" on the Point at least once a week, even 20-plus years on. But I don't get to hear much else from Nine Inch Nails. What a shame.

Normally, I've never been one to go gaga over remixes. They strike me as a bit gimmicky. If you didn't want a particular guitar part on the original tune, or wanted to add a syncopated bass line or some sample, why not do that in the first place? But then I stumbled over Trent Reznor's Nine Inch Nails remixes, starting with *Further Down the Spiral*. They are fascinating to the fan who enjoys deconstructing music, and then putting it back together. Now any time Nine Inch Nails releases something new, I'm also on the lookout for the remix.

It would seem Trent Reznor always has something to say. I, for one, am always eager to hear it.

***

I enjoy heavy metal, even if demographics say I shouldn't. I've loved bands like Led Zeppelin from the first time I heard them. I also enjoy bands like Black Sabbath and Metallica. Hair metal bands like Poison, Ratt, Warrant, and Motley Crue were lost on me, mainly because I was deep into prog and college radio. Plus, from a musicianship standpoint, the hair metal artists were a lot of sizzle and not much steak, from where I was sitting. Still, I have no problem enjoying a band cranking the Marshall amps up to 11, and letting loose with a sonic tsunami. Whether or not this prepared me for Tool remains debatable.

While I can't declare the discovery of one of the heaviest bands I've ever heard as a JFK moment, Tool established themselves as favorites all the same. They registered as a blip on my musical radar with their '94 release, *Undertow*. It featured two unusual tunes garnering more than a little airtime on the Point, "Sober" and "Prison Sex." The songs were plenty cool, but I didn't rush out to buy them. Tool was one of those bands that made me turn up the volume when I heard them on the radio, but little else. That changed two years later.

In '96, Tool released *AEnima*, which is the epicenter of the sonic earthquake that is the "nu-metal" movement of the '90s. The thunderous riffs of guitarist Adam Jones, bassist Justin

Chancellor, and drummer Danny Carey hit like a freight train, left a mark, and lingered for a while. The vocals of Maynard James Keenan brought an air of gravitas to the heavy proceedings.

I am wary of any band making the first song on the record the first single. Tool did just that with "Stinkfist." They also put my personal fears to bed quickly. The lead single was worth the price of admission on its own. Before long, I learned "Stinkfist" was just the tip of the sonic iceberg. "Forty Six & 2," "Eulogy," and the title track provided more than enough excitement in a record clocking in at more than an hour long. Best of all, these cats could flat-out play! It would come as no surprise to learn the musicians in Tool cited King Crimson among their biggest influences. (4)

I've often said Tool is the band I turn to when I'm in a bad mood, or I'm trying to "get through some stuff." Their music has a sense of controlled aggression that enabled me to face up to life's difficulties, and plow right through them. More than one person has told me they've seen my expression darken a bit when I play a Tool CD. Given the sonic weight of the music, I believe that's appropriate.

Undertow showed that Tool made heavy music. *AEnima* showed they had chops. Those elements came together on *Lateralus,* which Tool released in '01. While I will never be mistaken for a "headbanger," this album gave me no alternative but to do just that. Rare is the band with the ability to combine deft touch and blunt-force trauma, but Tool does it, often, during the same song.

Starting with "The Grudge," the band comes out firing. The listener is greeted by the sound of a mysterious machine firing up, followed by the blistering riffs of Jones, Chancellor, and Carey. The riff drops out without warning, leaving space for Keenan's vocals (much less processed on this album) to enter the fray. That gives way to a gut-punching "drop-D" tuned lick alerting all involved this band is at the peak of its prowess. "The Grudge" is a sonic roller coaster, topped off by Keenan turning a primal scream into a lengthy, high-quality musical note. I remember thinking to myself, there's no way he can pull that off on stage. I learned just how wrong I was a few months later, when I saw the band in concert. Damn!

Another highlight of *Lateralus* is a song called "Ticks and Leeches." Danny Carey's polyrhythmic drumming opens the proceedings, followed shortly after by Chancellor's driving bass.

Adam Jones kicks in the side door by dragging his guitar pick along the strings before unleashing a Les Paul-driven wail. And then in comes Keenan, delivering a banshee howl bringing everything together. It is a blast to listen to.

Naturally, my favorite moment on the record never made it to the radio. It is a seven-minute instrumental called "Triad," which closes out the album. The piece sounds like something that came together during a jam session, particularly since the song begins by fading in on the band running at full-throttle. Carey, Chancellor, and Jones have established a heavy-footed groove, which Jones breaks from some 90 seconds in. His Marshall and Diezel amplifiers (known for their ability to channel massive amounts of distortion) are turned up to a Nigel Tufnel-like "11" as he pushes his Les Paul and wah-wah pedal to the breaking point. Afterward, the band falls back into the original groove, augmented by drop-D power chords which cause any listener's head to spontaneously "bang" away. Halfway through the piece, blunt force gives way to deft touch again, as the guitar and bass take a step back, leaving Carey room to show off his understated drum genius. Drum rolls are nothing new. But hearing them fired from Danny Carey's feet and the "kick" drums, rather than his hands and the snare, takes things to a different plane. Just when you thought it was safe, back comes the drop-D groove again, which the band runs to its conclusion. Just describing that tune causes my forehead to bead with sweat. It's 100 times more fun to listen to. (5)

While Tool have said King Crimson is a major influence on their writing, it can be argued that the statement goes in both directions. Look no further than Crimson's instrumental "Dangerous Curves," from their album *The Power to Believe*. Its groove can easily be seen as an extension of "Triad." What fun it would have been to hear the bands play these tunes back-to-back on stage. I wonder if anyone contemplated that idea when they toured together?

It was six years before Tool presented us with *10,000 Days*, the follow-up to *Lateralus*. The first half of that record is absolutely worth the wait. The band picks up where "Triad" left off, delivering one gut-busting riff after another on songs like "Vicarious" and "Jambi." But by the end of the title track (about halfway through the album), the band appears to be running out of creative steam. The rest of the record isn't bad. It just doesn't have the impact of the first half. Within the confines of a single record, Tool became a victim of its own success.

As I write these words, eight years have passed since Tool has released an album. The band has been mired in legal issues with its former record label, which ground all musical output to a halt. But the band is supposed to be close to finishing its next album. Considering the Beatles released their entire recorded output over the span of eight years, I'd say the fans have waited long enough. (6)

Yes, the Point plays Tool's music. But, as would seem to be the norm, they seem to be stuck on the earlier works. They spend most of their time – when they even bother – playing tracks from *AEnima*. By comparison, tracks from *10,000 Days* were on the air for about 15 minutes. Commercial radio moves forward. Whether or not it brings along the bands that helped them attain popularity is debatable.

***

I have obsessed over no '90s music quite the way I have obsessed over Radiohead. I am almost stalker-like. I have no desire to hang out with the band, but I want to hear every note they play together. Which is funny, because I was aware of their presence for a good four years before I truly felt their impact.

The Point brought Radiohead into my life by way of a single called "Creep," from their debut album *Pablo Honey*. The song is all well and good, and proved to be quite popular in modern rock circles. This is probably why it didn't take hold in my mind. "Creep" was a song I didn't mind hearing on the radio, but I didn't feel the need to rush out and buy the album.

Radiohead's second album, *The Bends*, established them as a force to be reckoned with. It was chock full of songs built for the left side of the radio dial, like "High and Dry," "Fake Plastic Trees," and Street Spirit (Fade Out)." Critics were beginning to take notice. The Top 40 crowd, personified by Alicia Silverstone's character in the movie *Clueless*, dubbed their sound "Complaint Rock," which I thought was hilarious. Their hatred of Radiohead's sound helped endear them to me. Alas, *The Bends* was released around the same time King Crimson came back. The discovery would have to wait.

The Bends got Radiohead off the launching pad. But their third release, *OK Computer*, released in '97, sent the band into the stratosphere. Suddenly, Radiohead was everywhere! A British reviewer noted, "The world had attached its collective tongue to the band's zipper." Awards flowed like water. The band moved out of theaters (which is where *The Bends* landed them) and into arenas. Critics lost their ever-loving minds.

Record store employees couldn't stop raving about them, which is how I found out about the album. When I asked what was new and exciting in music of late, my friend Kim wouldn't let me leave Streetside Records without taking a copy of *OK Computer* home with me. I trusted her judgment and went with it.

I made the mistake of multi-tasking the first time I played the CD. What I heard was plenty decent. It was very interesting music. I particularly liked "Karma Police." But I was also cleaning my apartment at the time. That, combined with the fact *OK Computer* was CD number three out of the five I loaded in my player that day, meant that this revolutionary music had been relegated to background noise. It is for this reason that I would call for a ban on multi-disc CD players. It may be convenient to be able to load and play five or more hours of music, but something gets lost. Knowing I would have to turn my LP over in 20 minutes or less sharpened my listening focus. When I buy my ultimate stereo set, the CD player will have a single-disc deck. The bottom line is this: I may have listened to *OK Computer*, but I didn't *hear* it. That would come a few months later, on a plane trip to Baltimore.

As always, I struggled with my CD selection before that four-day trip. I grabbed *OK Computer* almost as an afterthought, figuring I might have time to check it out while I sat at my friend's house in the country. The plane ride was just short of two hours long. Naturally, I had my Discman at the ready. As it turned out, Radiohead's CD was at the top of the stack when I opened my music case. It must have been a sign. No time like the present, I figured, and loaded the disc. I was free of distractions and could now focus entirely on the music.

It didn't take long to understand what all the fuss was about. This was unlike anything produced thus far in the '90s. The opening strains of "Airbag," the albums first track, put the listener in a distinctly different headspace. Thom Yorke's singing voice is far from operatic. But is precisely what this music needs. The same can be said for each of the musicians in the group. Yorke, guitarist Jonny Greenwood, guitarist Ed O'Brien, bassist Colin Greenwood, and drummer Phillip Selway each bring a set of skills to Radiohead's table and makes them more powerful as a band than they are as individuals. There was a similar phenomenon within the dynamic of the Beatles. I liked their solo efforts, but they never really came close to what the four of them did as a group.

I was just catching my breath from the opening track, when "Paranoid Android" kicked in, and took things to the next level. I could make a Tool-like "deft touch, blunt-force trauma" statement for Radiohead. But theirs was a distinctly different type of force. Their sound didn't batter the listener over the head as much as it pulled him along urgently for the ride.

In the documentary *Meeting People is Easy*, Thom Yorke claims the members of Radiohead hate progressive rock. Something tells me that quote was pulled out of context, because there can be no mistaking the prog influence washing over this band, particularly during this album. One magazine even referred to them as "Punk Floyd," which was highly appropriate, since Radiohead was bringing the youthful sneer of punk to an ethereal soundscape. It was, to say the least, an interesting combination.

OK Computer is a deeply emotional album. But where the music of bands like Tool and Nine Inch Nails seemed to come from anger and aggression, Radiohead was operating from pain and despair. In the documentary, a British television host – who clearly didn't get what she was hearing – referred to Radiohead's sound as "music to cut your wrists to." Even I had to laugh at the line's snarky nature. There was no denying that Radiohead would never be confused with uptempo bubble gum Top 40.

The flight gave me enough time to listen to *OK Computer* twice. My musical foundation had been shifted once again. By the time I met my friend at the airport, the album was pretty much all I could talk about. She did what she does best when I go on about music: she nodded and smiled. I don't remember if I played the CD for her or not. I probably didn't. I know when I have an attentive audience, and when I don't. Nevertheless, Radiohead had a new, die-hard fan. But that fanaticism nearly ground to a screeching halt a couple of years later.

In the year 2000, Radiohead released its much-anticipated follow-up, *Kid A*. Like many others, I was expecting a sequel to *OK Computer*, a sonic foray into revolutionary, but familiar, territory. It was here I learned the true meaning of a lesson taught to me years before: expectation is the prison in which we dwell.

Kid A couldn't have sounded less like *OK Computer*. The sound I had fallen in love with was gone. I was so busy lamenting what was missing, I failed to hear what was there.

This is where a key element in my relationship with Radiohead was established: I will not always get what the band is doing right away.

With *Pablo Honey*, Radiohead established themselves as a straightforward guitar/bass/drums rock band. Their sound was indie, with a touch of punk. With *The Bends*, the format was essentially the same, but small electronic elements were finding their way into the mix, via synthesizers and effects pedals. *OK Computer* brought the electronic noises to the forefront, sharing space with the guitars. *Kid A* was, with the benefit of hindsight and objectivity, the next logical step. The guitars moved to the background, and electronics carried the musical load. As a guitar player, I was annoyed. So were many of my guitar-playing friends. What the hell was going on here?

Once again, I was listening without hearing.

Eventually, I did what I should have done in the first place. I sat down in my apartment, turned out most of the lights, and put on my headphones. Then I gave *Kid A* my undivided, objective attention. That's when it hit me. The album was a work of pure genius!

I can't think of a better album opening than the first five notes of "Everything in its Right Place," which ring out beautifully via electric piano. Four single notes and a chord transport me to the perfect mental place to receive the music.

At times, I wonder whether I am truly hearing something revolutionary, or am I simply being obtuse? I felt much better after speaking to Mike Keneally, a musician I hold in the highest regard. We were discussing albums we considered perfect, and Radiohead came up. I mentioned the opening of "Everything in its Right Place," and Keneally's face lit up. He knew *exactly* what I was talking about.

So it's not just me, after all.

"Everything …" and the title track set the album in motion. Things really take off with the third track, called "The National Anthem." Rest assured, it has absolutely *nothing* to do with Francis Scott Key and "The Star Spangled Banner." This particular anthem is driven by Colin Greenwood's bass and Phil Selway's drumming. The rest of the band circulates in and out of the groove with unconventional keyboard stabs and other sonic oddities while Yorke takes his relatively simple lyrics and turns them into high art. The song reaches its crescendo with the aid of a horn section starting out with a baritone saxophone playing a conventional riff. That line is augmented by additional saxophones, trumpets, and trombones. The horn section descends into what I can only describe as organized cacophony. The sound can be harsh on the ears when taken out of context. But within the confines of the song, the noise makes sense. Eventually, the sound trails away, giving way to one of my favorite tracks. The song, called "How to Disappear Completely," is the sonic opposite of "The National Anthem." A synthesizer sculpts a lush soundscape, followed shortly after by the lush acoustic guitar of Thom Yorke, who sings some of my favorite Radiohead lyrics. The song's chorus, "I'm not here/This isn't happening," speaks to me and other fans on a multitude of levels. I've never taken the time to learn what Yorke actually meant, because it would spoil the song for me.

"Idioteque" is my other favorite song from *Kid A*. The lyrics make little to no sense, but that is beside the point. It's the groove that makes the tune. Most of the vibe comes from the electronic drumming of Selway. Meanwhile, Jonny Greenwood is having a ball wiring and re-wiring patches on his analog synthesizer as the rest of the band does what it can to keep up. I figured it would be a struggle to play live. Naturally, Radiohead proved me wrong, as I watched them perform the tune on *Saturday Night Live*.

I was still trying to absorb *Kid A* when Radiohead dropped their next album, *Amnesiac*, in '01. Urban legend says the new record was a collection of B-sides from the previous album's sessions. The band denies this, but there can be no questioning the similarity of the two albums. No matter, the material is still remarkable.

Without question, *Amnesiac*'s personal highlight is "Pyramid Song," a piano-driven tear-jerker that never fails to captivate me. The funny thing is, I can't definitively establish the time signature! My love of progressive rock has put my brain in a place where "odd" time signatures like 6/8, 7/8, and 5/4 don't seem odd at all. But try as I may, I couldn't nail down the time of "Pyramid Song." I discussed my problem with Julie Slick, a remarkably talented bassist who handles odd times with Adrian Belew's band all the time. She, too, is a Radiohead fan. And she, too, struggles with the time signature in "Pyramid Song."

"I think it's an uncommon division of 8/8 – divided as 3, 3, 2 – in which the eighth notes are swung," she told me. "It can also be expressed in 16/8 as 3, 3, 4, 3, 3. OR you can follow the drum pattern – which is 5/4, 4/4, 4/4, 3/4 – that repeats throughout the song." Perhaps the mystery of the time signature is part of what makes "Pyramid Song" such a joy to listen to.

Electronics continue to dominate the band's sound on *Amnesiac*. There is also a return engagement with the horn section that graced "The National Anthem." Their playing is a little more straight-forward this time, but it still fits the arrangement nicely.

Apparently, Radiohead felt they had pushed the electronic boundary far enough by the end of *Amnesiac*. When the band returned two years later with *Hail to the Thief*, the guitars and drums had muscled their way back to the forefront. In fact, on songs like "There, There," the drum duties were handled by not just Selway, but by Jonny Greenwood and Ed O'Brien as well!

Hail to the Thief struck me as a near perfect balance of acoustic and electronic sounds. It was a creative and sonic step forward in the band's development. Just how creative this band was, I would learn a little further on down the road.

As it turns out, *Hail to the Thief* was the last album Radiohead made for Capitol Records, their original label. Eager to squeeze every penny it could from the band's catalog, Capitol re-released the first six Radiohead albums, including bonus discs featuring live tracks and B-sides. Naturally, I snatched these collections up as quickly as they were released. Because of this, I was given a whole new reason to love and appreciate Radiohead.

I've listened to enough B-sides and outtakes from my favorite artists to learn the vast majority of what hits the cutting room floor is best left there. Certain songs don't make the final version of the album for a reason. Of course, there are exceptions to this rule. And Radiohead seems to fit those exceptions. The material the band relegates to the cutting room floor can be positively stunning. The B-sides from *The Bends*, for example, leave me to wonder why the band didn't release a double album the first time around. I can certainly understand the need to trim the fat from what may sound like a bloated album. But the fat trimmed from *The Bends* is very lean and meaty. It must have been tortuous trying to decide what would make the album, and what would have to go. There are remarkable moments within the B-sides of *OK Computer* and *Hail to the Thief* as well. I must confess: I would like to have been able to listen in on the decision making process that went into sequencing these albums.

No adjustment period was necessary for *In Rainbows*, which Radiohead released in late '07. I was smitten with the album from the first downbeat of the opening track, called "15 Step." The identity of the tune is established by Phil Selway's drums, which skitter about in 5/4. The rest of the band seems to play just a hair behind Selway's beat, leaving room for the song to breathe and groove deeply with what sounds like minimal effort. This tune helped establish Selway as one of my favorite drummers, not because of what he plays, but because of what he *doesn't* play. Selway is the antithesis of the over-the-top-drummer, playing precisely what the song needs, and nothing more. More than a few drummers could learn something from listening to Phil Selway.

If the band was laying back for the album's opener, they roar back to the forefront once the second track, "Bodysnatchers," kicks in. Thom Yorke's Gibson SG establishes the song's mood, and the rest of the band falls right in behind him. Once again, I can't help but notice Selway, kicking the tune square in the ass by doing no more than firing off 16th notes with his right hand on the ride cymbal. This tune never fails to make me smile.

In Rainbows does a great job of running the emotional gamut, musically. In this way, the album reminds me of the emotional roller coaster that was *The Bends*. But as it turns out, *In Rainbows* is much closer related to *OK Computer*, released a decade before. It took an unexpected Internet posting to drive this point home.

The craze was loosely labeled "01100110," which is based in the binary code of computers. The *OK Computer* album represented 01, while *In Rainbows* was 10. Fans were encouraged to create a playlist alternating tracks from each album, starting with "Airbag," and then "15 Step," and so on. To my ears, the results were stunning. These two records, created a decade apart, flowed together like the perfect double album! How intentional this was is anybody's guess. If I'm ever fortunate enough to be in the same room with a member of Radiohead, I'll be sure to ask them about it.

***

Alas, the Point (or, more likely, their consultants) seemed apathetic about Radiohead's later musical output. "Creep" would find its way on the air most often, while material from *The Bends* was reserved for the radio station's "Way Back Weekend," when it featured music from the late '80s and '90s.

Once in a great while, I might hear something from *OK Computer*. When the later records were released, the Point might play a single or two for a brief period, but the songs never made it to heavy rotation. *In Rainbows* was pretty much ignored altogether. I remember the surprised reaction from one of their DJs when I called the station and requested "Bodysnatchers." In fact, I *dared* him to play it! He did, saying on the air he was surprised anyone actually knew about the record. At first, I didn't understand what he meant. In time, I figured it out: radio is a fickle place for bands these days. Today's sensation is tomorrow's overrated annoyance. The station had moved on, leaving one of my favorite acts in its wake.

This was particularly true by 2011, when Radiohead released *The King of Limbs*. If I heard the Point play more than one song from this album, and they played that song more than a half-dozen times, I would be positively amazed. Admittedly, this album had to grow on me. The band decided to bring the electronics back again, this time trying to balance them with the analog sounds. While it's not a bad album, I would still call it a small step back from *In Rainbows*. In fact, the best song from this period wasn't even included on the album. It's a B-side called "Staircase," which does a wonderful job of balancing the analog and digital musical domains. Why this song isn't on the album proper is a complete and utter mystery.

These days, I've heard more than a couple of Point DJs virtually sneer at the name Radiohead, as though the band is some aspect of the station's past it must endure in order to propel itself forward. I find this annoying. The music the station plays these days is barely half a step above complete and utter crap. It's formulaic, condescending, and – worst of all – flat out dull. One of the great things that distinguished the Point from other radio stations was its music was rarely heard on other local radio stations. It was truly "alternative." Lately, I hear older Point material played on the local Classic Rock station, and the newer material can also be found on some of the Top 40 stations. I can live with the former aspect. The latter makes me more than a little nauseous. And once again, I blame the consultants.

The Point, it would seem, is losing its edge. Not that my opinion matters to them, or radio stations like them. As long as the ratings are decent, and the advertising revenue continues to roll in, what happens on commercial radio is fine by those in charge.

Consultants come in to the commercial radio stations and learn what is most popular. Who is drawing the most phone-in requests? What concerts are selling out the fastest, and where are they playing? How can the commercial station make this work for them?

The sense of musical individuality appears to be going out of the Alternative format. The same thing is happening in other forms of music. The trend started early, and only got worse. Why have just one Pearl Jam, when the market could bear five more bands sounding just like them? This not only created weaker music from the knock-off bands, it lessened the impact of the original artists. But it didn't matter, because the ratings were decent.

This "cloning" formula had another unfortunate side effect. Since there were now five or six bands who sound like, say, Pearl Jam, an artist with a different sound could not get any airplay. So artists with unique sounds were pushed aside, relegated to overnight play or Sunday night specials where their music might be heard once. This is hardly the way to expose people to new music. But that's not what commercial radio is for, is it?

Bands like Radiohead, Pearl Jam, and Tool will continue to make music as long as they feel they have something to say. I suppose they know their fans will continue to support them, even if we won't be able to hear them on commercial radio as much as we'd like. Luckily, technology has brought us Internet and satellite radio. We'll be able to enjoy the music of Alternative's prime to our heart's content.

And I can always look forward to "Way Back Weekend" on the Point.

(1)   Instead of commercials, AFRTS ran a never-ending series of public service announcements and military-oriented educational commercials. Some of them featured "acting" by AFRTS personalities stationed with me. As a military journalist, I spent more than a little time working with these people, so I would never say so at the time. But now that a couple of decades have passed, I think I can say it: most of those spots were HORRIBLE. But I'm sure they meant well, and did the best they could.

(2)   Admittedly, the first act of post-military rebellion is usually to grow a beard, since such a thing is a no-no

while on active duty. I made more than one ill-fated attempt to grow a goatee. It looks much better these days, even if there is gray in it.

(3)   This is not a book about politics, and I intend to keep it that way. For the record, I am a bleeding-heart pluralist. Some issues I'm conservative about. With other things, I'm more liberal. My political life is all about finding the balance that works best for as many people as possible.

(4)   The two bands are connected in more than a couple of ways. David Bottrill produced and engineered Tool's *Aenema*. The year before that, he did the same on King Crimson on *Thrak*. In 2001, Crimson opened for Tool for a few shows when they toured together. Danny Carey made a guest appearance on two of Adrian Belew's solo albums, *Side One* and *Side Three*. It's a small world, sonically speaking.

(5)   At my guitar-playing zenith, I bought a Schecter guitar, which I had outfitted with high-output humbucking pickups. It wasn't a Gibson Les Paul, but it wasn't bad, either. I tuned my low-E string to D, and set about trying to play "Triad," which I wanted my band to play on stage. The song is a testament to Tool's ability to make the tricky sound simple. I never got 100 percent of Jones's nuances down. But I like to think I got close.

(6)   At the risk of sounding cynical, I'm honestly wondering which will be released first: Tool's next album, or this book? It's going to be close.

SIDE THREE

Contrary to popular belief, there are a few ladies in my musical life.

Track 14
Coffee House Sirens

By 1989, I had settled in to life at Shaw Air Force Base in South Carolina. One day, out of the blue, I got a call from an old high school friend. "Hey, man," he said, "I'm getting married in a few months."

"That's great!" I replied. "Congratulations! I'm really happy for you."

"I'd like you to be one of my ushers. Is that cool?"

"Well, sure. I'd be honored. Just give me a date, and I can arrange to take some leave."

My friend filled me in on the details. And then he added one more wrinkle. "Listen," he said, "You like music. How would you like to be our DJ at the reception?"

I was taken aback. "Me? Well … sure! Why not? I could put something together, I guess. You sure you don't want to go with a professional?"

"Nah. You'll be perfect. I'm sure you can handle it. I know you have great taste. And I know you have a lot of music." And just like that, my friend sold me. (1) For one night, I would be a DJ.

I knew I had a monumental task on my hands. I may have been a music nut, but my collection came almost completely from the left side of the radio dial. Commercial music and I had gone our separate ways. Mine was not the collection people referenced if they wanted to get things going on the dance floor.

I enlisted the help of my friend Reggie, who had the ability to straddle the line between popular and niche music. One

Saturday, we found ourselves pouring through my records and CDs, trying to assemble about four hours of danceable music. Reggie also brought along a few items from his own collection. As he looked over my music, I could see his brow furrowing.

"What's the problem?" I asked.

He let out a chuckle. "Man, you are a misogynistic bastard when it comes to music," he said.

I was a military journalist, but Reggie used a word I had never come across. "Say what?"

"You hate women. Or at least, your music collection does."

I was flabbergasted. "That's ridiculous," I exclaimed defensively. "Look in there! I've got ... well, I've bought ... that is to say ... I'm in to ..." My voice trailed off when I realized I couldn't name a single female artist who had recently caught my attention.

How had my music collection, which I prided myself on, become almost completely devoid of women? What happened? It took a bit, but I figured it out.

Prog happened.

The discovery of music for musicians led me down a path dominated by men. Genesis, Rush, King Crimson, Emerson, Lake & Palmer ... I was listening to a lot of well-played notes. However, women were playing none of them. It wasn't intentional. That's just the way it was. (2)

Luckily, Reggie saved the day. The two of us put together a nice collection of tunes filling three 90-minute cassettes. My friend was kind enough to provide me with enough female representation to keep the reception guests from asking too many questions. I was complimented on my good taste and sense of musical variety. I came home from the wedding with a newfound desire to add more feminine voices to my musical catalog.

I suppose it was natural to gravitate toward familiar R & B vocalists. But while I respected the work of Aretha Franklin, Chaka Khan, and Gladys Knight in the '70s, their '80s material didn't do much for me. (3) There wasn't much happening in the pop world, either. I respected what Annie Lennox was doing with Eurythmics, but her music was becoming more and more formulaic, and simply couldn't hold my attention. I got into jazz because there were no vocals to deal with. So while I had nothing but respect for Ella Fitzgerald, Shirley Horn, Billy

Holliday, and Diane Schuur, I didn't feel the need to collect their material.

The "college rock" movement of the mid-'80s offered a ray of hope. It was there I first heard the harmonic voices of Kate Pierson and Cindy Wilson of the B-52s, who's sound provided the perfect counterbalance to Fred Schneider's unique voice. Long before they struck commercial gold with a song called "Love Shack," I was digging on songs like "Rock Lobster" and "Private Idaho." The B-52s had a quirky, fun sound that never failed to get people moving.

The late '80s brought me into contact with bands like the Sugarcubes, and their mercurial lead vocalist, Bjork. Admittedly, I often didn't know what exactly they were singing about. But the band's approach was loud, fast, catchy, and hard to ignore. Conversely, Cowboy Junkies vocalist Margot Timmons caused me to freeze in place, hypnotized. Her voice was haunting, lilting, and mysterious. I couldn't help but listen, because I had to know where she was going with each song.

Natalie Merchant helped cement my social consciousness via her songs with 10,000 Maniacs. She touched on issues from a feminine standpoint, which caused me to rethink more than a couple of opinions I thought would never change. This opened the door to other vocalists from a similar vein, like Tracy Chapman and Suzanne Vega.

Deborah Holland is one of the most talented singer/songwriters around. Listening to her music is a privilege.
(Photo courtesy of Deborah Holland)

While I appreciated these women, I was still looking for a female voice that worked with the "music for musicians" style I loved. My musical prayers were answered in late '89, when I learned about a group called Animal Logic.

Two of my all-time favorite musicians, bassist Stanley Clarke (from Return to Forever) and drummer Stewart Copeland (from the Police) got together and formed a band. After listening to more than a few audition tapes, they happened across a talented young woman named Deborah Holland and her two-song demo. Clarke and Copeland were blown away by the singer-songwriter, and hired her almost instantly. Within two weeks of Clarke and Copeland hearing the tape, Holland was on the road with Animal Logic.

The band combined the best of both worlds, from my musical standpoint. Holland possessed not only a dynamic singing voice, but also a knack for writing highly intelligent pop songs. Songs like "There's a Spy (In the House of Love)," from the band's self-titled debut album, wasted no time getting my undivided attention.

I got into Animal Logic thinking Holland's vocals would serve primarily as a companion to the chops of Clarke and Copeland. But the more I listened, the more taken I was with Holland, to the point where the other two band members were almost an afterthought. Clarke and Copeland must have had similar thoughts during recording, because their instrumental pyrotechnics are kept to a minimum, while Holland's voice soars over them. They knew where the musical emphasis needed to be, and it wasn't with the men in the group.

This made even more sense once I realized Holland wrote the band's songs. Clarke and Copeland handled the arrangements, but the substance of the songs came from this unheralded singer-songwriter. I was floored by the intensely personal nature of songs like "I'm Through with Love," "I Still Feel for You," and "Someone to Come Home To." As it happens, the songs seem personal for a reason. "(The lyrics) always come from a place of being autobiographical," Holland told me. "And then they get exaggerated."

Equally impressive is how Holland is practically savant-like when it comes to writing songs. They seem to pour out of her. "I write the music, lyrics, and everything, editing as I go," she said. "I try to finish a song in one sitting. The majority of it comes out in an hour or two. I may spend another week fine-tuning it after that."

While the men – particularly Clarke – upped the musical ante on *Animal Logic II* by displaying heavier chops, Holland's songwriting seemed relatively unfazed. In fact, she digs in with them. "In the Garden," the second album's opener, and "Through a Window" show the listener Holland's voice and Clarke's thumping bass lines were made for one another. Copeland's airtight snare (one of my favorite musical sounds) and seamless kick drum propel them forward. Even the relatively silly lyrics behind "Stone in My Shoe" can be forgiven, because Clarke unleashes a bass solo straight out of his Return to Forever days. It's the last thing one would expect to hear in a pop song, but there it is. And it kicks ass! By the time the album ends, fans are left wanting more. Clearly, this was a band building up to something!

Sadly, it wasn't meant to be. Not long after the release of *Animal Logic II,* the band broke up. I asked Holland why, expecting a lengthy answer involving the intricacies and complications of the music industry. The answer I got was much more basic. "It was a lack of success," she said. "The records just didn't do as well as we hoped they would." There was a thoughtful pause before she continued. "Plus, Stanley's career as a film composer was taking off. Did he want to stay (at home) and make $100,000? Or did he want to go out on the road and make nothing?" Holland could barely contain her laughter at the thought of making such a choice.

"Stewart would have hung in there," she continued. "He knew from (his time with) the Police the way you break a band is you get in a van, go out on the road, and play 200 dates. If we had a single that took off, (the band) would have stayed together."

One of the great tragedies of the music industry is it's positively littered with bands who could have been, who never were, or who never will be. The tragedy seems to befall the supremely talented more than anyone else. It infuriates me, but professional musicians take it in stride. It's all just part of the game.

Still, I couldn't help but express to Holland my disappointment in Animal Logic not becoming bigger. I told her I still break those two records out every few months when I need to hear some high-caliber pop music. She let out a laugh, a combination of pride, modesty, and defiance toward the industry. "They're pretty damn good records, aren't they?" she asked rhetorically. "When I go back and listen to them now, I think, 'Wow! That's really good!'"

If only more people knew about them.

***

I lost track of Deborah Holland in the '90s, before the Internet made it possible to track the musical movements of my favorite artists. She continues to move forward, mostly without the support of a major record label. But where my musical misogyny was completely accidental, her career was being undermined intentionally by the industry.

It's not that I never enjoyed music with women in the band. Quite the contrary. In addition to the women of soul and R&B, I've enjoyed a feminine presence in rock. One of my favorite classic rock songs is "White Rabbit," sung by Grace Slick with Jefferson Airplane. I respect the vocal abilities of Janis Joplin, even if I didn't own any of her records. Ann and Nancy Wilson made the music of Heart fun to listen to (and Nancy is an absolute *badass* on guitar), and I enjoy the voice of Debbie Harry with Blondie. Fleetwood Mac's *Rumors* was one of the best albums made in the '70s. That wouldn't be the case without the talents of Stevie Nicks and Christine McVie. One of the first 45s I ever bought was "Heartbreaker," by Pat Benatar. That song just flat-out rocked! There were quite a few musical women in my life.

And then there weren't any.

I'm sure there were plenty of women fronting rock bands in the '70s and '80s. But radio wasn't exposing me to them. According to Holland, record labels virtually refused to sign women. And that was by design. "It was sexist, just as it is now," Holland said about the music industry. "I don't think it's any different.

"At the time (in the '70s), if you shopped your demo to, say, Chrysalis Records, you were told, 'Well, we already have Pat Benatar. We don't want people to have to choose between Pat Benatar and you, so we can't take you.' That kind of stuff still goes on!" Holland's frustration was palpable, and more than justified. "I play in a band called the Refugees with two other women. When I took our demo to a label – which I won't name – I was told that they already had a band that was a trio of women." Needless to say, this label did not want to take on another similar act. Holland and her cohorts were out of luck.

Holland sighed. "I'll always be known as a Female Singer-Songwriter, as opposed to just a singer-songwriter."

The next group of women to capture my ear did so by accident. I wasn't looking for them. Rather, I just kept stumbling over them. Lucky for me.

In '92, Peter Gabriel released an album called *Us*. Shortly after, he took a band on the road, created and released a concert video called *Secret World Live*. In the studio and for the first leg of the tour, Gabriel hired Sinead O'Connor (who had a moderately successful solo career) as his backing vocalist, where she shined on songs like "Blood of Eden." When O'Connor left the band, Gabriel hired a relative unknown named Paula Cole, who handled not only O'Connor's parts, but those of Kate Bush as well. It was Bush who sang the stirring bridge in "Don't Give Up" from Gabriel's *So* album in '86. Those would not be small shoes to fill.

I watched, mesmerized, as Cole positively *nailed* the parts of her predecessors, making them her own. I made a note to myself then and there to keep my eyes and ears open for the musical efforts of the dark-haired woman in the black summer dress and Dr. Martens boots.

Cole would go on to become a solo artist, scoring her biggest hit with an album called *This Fire*. It contained her biggest single, called "Where Have All the Cowboys Gone," which was all over Adult Contemporary radio in '97. It peaked at number four on the adult top 40. It was one of those very rare times when the pop chart and I crossed paths. Naturally, the hit song was not my favorite. Instead, it was a tune called "Throwing Stones," four minutes of blistering piano-based power pop containing the most beautifully sung use of the word "motherfucker" I have ever heard. It was incredible on CD, and ten times better live when I caught her performance at Mississippi Nights.

Meanwhile, the Alternative movement unleashed a few new female voices. O'Connor, Bush, Natalie Merchant, and Bjork were carried over from the college rock scene of the late '80s. There was a brief surge of angry young women who emerged, post-Nirvana. Singer-songwriters like Alanis Morissette, Courtney Love (with her band, Hole), and Liz Phair – my personal favorite – injected their own form of raw aggression into the music scene, producing some interesting music in the process. (4) But there was another form of music rising in the distance. I never would have found it if I didn't enjoy a good book.

The mid-'90s saw the rise of the coffee shop in America, and St. Louis was not immune. I didn't feel the need to hang out in a coffee shop, but I do love to read. Somewhere, somebody decided it would be a good idea to put a coffee shop inside a bookstore. What better way to enjoy a gourmet cup of Joe than while enjoying a good book?

The Geniuses in Charge decided to add a new layer: music! A young artist or two would set up their microphones and acoustic guitars and serenade the coffee drinkers and book shoppers. I read with music on in the background all the time. The only difference now was the band was playing 25 or 30 feet away from me.

The bands were mostly folk-oriented. This wasn't necessarily my favorite style of music, but it fit the surroundings nicely. The singers were mostly women, and their songs were both passionate and unobtrusive. It was just as easy to tune them out as it was to absorb their sounds. I absorbed more than I tuned out.

This was around the same time I became a permanent resident at Streetside Records. The assistant manager, Kim Peterson, and I had become quite friendly. She was always telling me what was going on in the music world. Once she learned my tastes, she always had a knack for leading me right where I was dying to go, even if I didn't know it yet.

Kim sported a couple of tattoos here and there. It was one of those things that I never brought up in conversation, but my subconscious logged that information away. When I came into the store one day, I heard music playing over the store's speakers that would have fit in nicely at my favorite bookstore. There was an acoustic guitar, acoustic bass, and drums, topped by a spirited vocalist who definitely meant what she was talking about. Naturally, I asked Kim whom I was listening to. "Her name is Ani DiFranco," Kim said. "She's amazing! And she runs the record label she records under, on top of writing all her own songs! I'm a huge fan!" The CD's jewel case was sitting on the counter where Kim was working, so I picked it up. It only took a second or two to realize how deep Kim's fandom ran. My friend was sporting one of DiFranco's tattoos!

While I didn't forget about Ani DiFranco, I wasn't instantly drawn in, either. That happened a few weeks later, when I was watching television. I don't remember what channel was on, though it was most likely VH1, since they still had the audacity to show music videos, which MTV had long-since given up on. A video came on between whatever shows were being broadcast, and it captivated me almost immediately. The song opened with an acoustic guitar soon augmented with a Hammond organ. The stand-up bass and drums fell in line quickly afterward. The whole band was playing a funky, staccato-laden groove I couldn't help but bounce to. And there, at the front of the band, stood Ani DiFranco, preparing to launch into a song called "Jukebox." The next four-and-a-half minutes are a blur. I only know I couldn't get to Streetside Records fast enough.

It was as though Kim knew I was coming. I told her about the song, and she just nodded and smiled as she walked to the appropriate browser bin. "Yep. I knew that was your kinda song," she said, simultaneously tossing me a CD called *Up Up Up Up Up Up*. "You're gonna like that whole record, I'm sure." She wasn't wrong.

DiFranco is a singer-songwriter of remarkable depth. "Jukebox" was the fourth song on the CD (a good sign), so I had to absorb a couple of tunes before I got to my favorite. It was worth the wait. The album opens with an anthem called "'tis of thee," which seems like it would be ultra-patriotic. Instead, DiFranco rips into the underbelly of American society, pointing out the problems of racism and classism. That song wasn't an aberration. DiFranco is a passionate activist. And while I may not agree with everything she says, I have never doubted her conviction.

I also didn't realize DiFranco was a major champion of LGBT causes. I figured it out when I went to see her in concert. Not only was I one of very few men there, I was one of even fewer *straight* men there. No matter. As far as I'm concerned, your sexuality is your own business, and the concert was absolutely amazing. I've seen her twice more since then, and added more than a few of her CDs to my collection.

***

My musical desires continue to fluctuate from one place to another, but there will always be room for women. More often than not, they provide the soft-touch counterbalance to the heavy-handed sounds that come from the men I listen to. It can be the power pop sounds of Deborah Holland, Paula Cole, or Aimee Mann. It could be the raw aggression of Liz Phair or Bjork. It might be the soulful voice of Me'Shell Ndgeocello, Jill Scott, or Eryka Badu. Or it could come from the staggering talents of two more recent discoveries in Rhiannon Giddens and Courtney Swain.

Giddens came out of nowhere. I recorded a Showtime documentary about a one-off project called *The New Basement Tapes* in 2014. Legendary producer T-Bone Burnett unearthed lyrics to several songs written by Bob Dylan. The words had no melodies, so Burnett recruited a crack group of singer-songwriters to bring the songs to life. Included in the sessions were Elvis Costello; Marcus Mumford from Mumford & Sons; Jim James from My Morning Jacket; and Giddens, who played in an African-American bluegrass band called the Carolina Chocolate Drops. I was already a huge Costello fan, and that was what held my initial interest. But it wasn't long before my focus shifted. I didn't know Giddens from a hole in the wall. When she first came on screen, I barely noticed. And then she started to warm up her voice.

I nearly fainted.

The sounds emerging from her throat defy description. I could probably start at Heaven-sent, and then build from there. But any description I put forth would be underselling it. I hadn't heard anything that soulful, that *powerful*, since Aretha Franklin. Where had this woman been all my life?

As good as Giddens was with the New Basement Tapes, her debut solo record, called *Tomorrow is My Turn* (released in '15), took things to the next level, which I didn't think was possible. Giddens made it abundantly clear she was not to be pigeonholed into any one style of music. Her album deftly covers bluegrass, jazz, soul, gospel, and pop with a seamless ability reserved for the supremely talented. The record must be heard in order to be believed. Her blistering take on a song called "Waterboy" is worth the price of admission on its own. She performed the tune live on David Letterman's show, and blew the minds of everyone in attendance, particularly the host. It wasn't just that he couldn't stop saying, "Wow." It was the way he kept saying it. Letterman knew he was in the presence of greatness. I eagerly look forward to any bit of music this young woman brings forth. Had I heard her in the coffee shop, I don't think I ever would have gotten any reading done.

Courtney Swain, meanwhile, fronts one of my favorite modern bands, a Boston group called Bent Knee. They came to my attention courtesy of music journalist Anil Prasad, who simply would not – or *could* not – stop talking about them. It didn't take long to understand why.

The band's music defies description. It has pop sensibilities, but doesn't spend a lot of time in that realm. Avant-garde, prog, metal, and God-knows what else makes its presence felt within the context of the band's music. While the band members proclaim themselves a musical democracy, Swain's voice is the glue holding it all together, augmented by keyboards, guitar, violin, bass, and drums. The Berklee College of Music graduates are a force to be reckoned with. I only hope Swain doesn't find herself getting bigger than the band, which has been known to happen.

Bent Knee would probably be too much for the coffee house, but I suppose that doesn't really matter. The bookstore/coffee house phenomenon faded out almost as quickly as it arrived. That's too bad, but I suppose all things end. It was fun while it lasted.

I wish I could tell Reggie about all the amazing women in my musical life. I wonder what he would think?

(1)   He sold me, and also saved a great deal of money. I never asked to be paid for my services. My friend, God love him, was always a bit of a cheapskate. I didn't make the connection until later.

(2)   For that matter, I wasn't listening to a lot of African-American artists in this genre, either. But that was the furthest thing from my mind. I loved the notes being played, and that's all that mattered.

(3)   The entire R&B movement of the '80s did very little for me. It sounded far too "plastic" for my personal tastes. Organic horn sections had been replaced by keyboards synthesizing the sounds, though not with the same impact. Drums had been largely replaced by beat boxes, which seemed hard-pressed to push beyond 90 beats per minute and seemed to have the same rhythm. I called it "The Pedestrian R&B Beat," and it bored the hell out of me. The entire genre had been "produced" to death, and it was a long time before I came back around to R&B.

(4)   Many have argued Courtney Love only became famous because she was married to Nirvana leader Kurt Cobain. To be honest, I have trouble arguing with that. Hole was never a favorite band for me, and I wonder if I ever would have heard them if not for Cobain and his tragic end.

T.J. DuPree was a dear friend, and one of my favorite people in the world. Alas, this is the only photo I have to the two of us together. It was taken the day we graduated from the police academy, May 3, 1995.

Track 15
T.J. DuPree and the Return of the Crimson King

By December of '94, I was a month from starting my career with the St. Louis Metropolitan Police Department. I was also temporarily unemployed, since I exhausted the hours available in my last part-time job. I was a man with more than a little time on his hands. My new job required I move out of the suburbs and into the City of St. Louis. I didn't have much money, but that didn't stop me from exploring the new record stores I found via the Yellow Pages.

One of my "discoveries" was Euclid Records, located in the City's Central West End. It was a decent enough shop, even if it did put off an aristocratic air. (1) The store had a nice assortment of vinyl, which was starting to become scarce in the CD era. There was also a decent assortment of non-commercial music, appealing to my left-side-of-the-dial mindset. The prices were 10 to 20 percent higher than the stores I was used to, but no matter. I could make this place work.

It didn't take long before I did what I always did when I entered a record store for the first time: I made my way to the CDs featuring bands that started with "K." There was no guarantee that the store would have a King Crimson section, as I found out more than once before. But if I didn't look, I would forever wonder. The King Crimson title card took less than a minute to find. Next would follow the usual exercise in futility, where I would leaf through the three to five CDs and learn I had everything the store had in my collection already. Then I could move on. I'd probably find more exciting stuff in the jazz section, anyway.

To its credit, Euclid Records had as many as ten King Crimson CDs. But I wasn't finding anything new. Got this. Got that. Seen that before, but wasn't really interested. Yeah, this is going pretty much how I –

Wait a minute. *Holy shit!*

My fingers ran across a CD sporting an unfamiliar red cover, with gold lettering. I figured it must be some low-quality bootleg of a concert from years past. But that wasn't the case at all. I lifted the CD out of the bin for a closer examination. The title of the CD was *Vrooom*, and I knew I had never seen it before. Was this new? The sticker on top of the CDs cellophane wrapper provided the answer to that question.

The sticker told me who was in the band. There were the four names that brought joy to my heart: Adrian Belew, Robert Fripp, Tony Levin, and Bill Bruford. This was my band! Hallelujah! There were also two new names: Trey Gunn and Pat Mastelotto. Who were *these* guys? And why did my favorite quartet need them? I still hadn't grasped the most important edict of being a King Crimson enthusiast: trust Robert Fripp and his vision.

The CD contained a mere six tracks, clocking in at a scant 31 minutes. It was hardly a full-length album. *Vrooom* was an EP, designed to generate revenue for a forthcoming full-length CD. That was fine and dandy. But Euclid Records wanted 20 dollars for the CD I had in my hands. Seriously? Twenty bucks? I wasn't sure where my post-Christmas, pre-police academy meals were coming from. This was not the best time to invest 20 bucks on a thirty-minute CD.

I asked one of the store's employees (who barely acknowledged my presence when I came in) whether or not there were more copies of *Vrooom*. That employee pointed me in the direction of another worker, who was no doubt their version of Prog Guy. After recovering from the mild shock he experienced from seeing a twenty-something black man asking about King Crimson, Prog Guy informed me I was holding the only copy of the CD in the store, and it would sell quickly. *Vroom* was a

Japanese import, a royal pain to order, and not getting any cheaper.

My decision was made for me. I'd figure out how to eat later. There was new King Crimson at hand!

***

I raced home to my tiny apartment, located just a stone's throw from the world famous Anheuser-Busch brewery. (2) My hands almost shook with excitement as I plugged *Vrooom* into the CD player. Not wanting to disturb my landlord, who lived upstairs, or the kindly old lady next door, I decided it would be best if I used my headphones for this musical adventure. I turned off the external speakers and pressed "play," on the CD deck, eagerly awaiting the return of the band who shaped the '80s for me.

They never showed.

The band vibrating the daylights out of my eardrums was an entirely new animal. If '80s King Crimson reached me by way of flanking maneuvers, this band delivered a full-on frontal assault. The music was heavy, almost to the point of brutal. God help anyone who stood in the path of this sonic freight train. He was going to be blown apart on impact.

"Vrooom," the EP's opening track, not only blasted the senses out of me, it showed me the importance of trusting the musical vision of Robert Fripp. (3) With this "Double Trio," as Fripp coined it, King Crimson was able to find a path back to '74's *Red* sound, while still remaining firmly rooted in the mid-'90s. The sound was heavy, but required a degree of touch to execute. The thunder of two guitars, two basses (or Chapman Sticks), and two drummers almost overwhelmed my headphones. One could also sense King Crimson had not yet perfected this material. They were playing quality notes, to be certain. But the compositions were not complete, overall. The band was still searching for musical answers.

The "new guys" in the band were Trey Gunn (Chapman Stick) and Pat Mastelotto (drums). I would be lying if I said I could distinguish their parts right away. But I would get to know these musicians over the next few years, and I would come to respect and love their work. The new rhythm section members infused a bit of youth into the stalwart Old Guard that is King Crimson. Levin and Gunn made for a fascinating low-end combo. Theirs was not to duplicate bass lines, but rather to offer a sense of counter-point for the other to react to. The situation was similar for the drummers. In fact Bruford and Mastelotto would later refer to themselves as Elvin Ringo. One drummer would be Ringo Starr, the timekeeper. The other would be Elvin Jones, the jazz drummer firing off unpredictable fills and inverting the beat. Bruford and Mastelotto would switch these roles from song to song. The result was a great deal of excitement from the drum risers.

Vrooom served as a link to the band's past and its future. The title track invoked the mindset of *Red*, while songs like "Cage" and "One Time" kept the listener connected to the King Crimson of the '80s. There was even an improvisational piece, jokingly called "When I Say Stop, Continue." This band was off and running. I couldn't wait to hear what happened next.

The EP was released a good three years before I bonded with the World Wide Web. So finding information on anything Crimson-oriented was a difficult task on the best of days. I had all but given up on *Rolling Stone* magazine around the same time I gave up commercial radio. Yet I found myself leafing through an issue sometime before Christmas. Lo and behold, there sat a six-paragraph article on my favorite band, situated in the "Briefs" section. It was there I learned Crimson's full-length album was scheduled for release in April of '95. I circled the date on my mental calendar and waited with great anticipation. In the meantime, I continued to play the hell out of *Vrooom* and the rest of the Crimson back catalogue.

***

One of my best friends was a man named Terrence Joseph DuPree. I met T.J. in the police academy. I had a feeling I needed to get to know this man within a day or two of walking into class. I could feel his level of intellect. He was someone I knew I could learn from. In fact, that's the first thing I ever said to him. He was flattered and humbled. We wound up having lunch together. Inevitably, the talk turned to music.

As I've said, I have a knack for surrounding myself with the right kind of musical people, even if I don't know it at first. So when I told T.J. that I had odd musical tastes, he challenged me to name an artist. I went with Frank Zappa. Without missing a beat, T.J. broke into the opening verse of "Penguin in Bondage," from Zappa's *Roxy and Elsewhere*. That was one my favorite albums.

I knew then and there I had a friend for life.

A couple of days later, we were walking out of our classroom, headed to the gym. For no apparent reason, I asked him who his favorite drummer was. T.J. and I had yet to speak about King Crimson, so when he said, "Bill Bruford" without hesitation, I nearly went into shock. He was equally shocked when, in front of God and classmates, I embraced him warmly. I had found a kindred spirit. T.J. picked up on that immediately. The shock faded, and he laughed and hugged me back. He understood.

The two of us formed a study group. There were five or six of us, but T.J. was the only family man. He lived about 10 minutes from me, in a pleasant south St. Louis home with his wife and two children. I developed a couple of "knacks" during this time. One, I always got to the study session a little early, so T.J. and I could talk about music before the rest of our classmates arrived. Over time, I learned my friend not only had a very impressive collection of vinyl, but he also played guitar and piano. For quite some time, he played in a band called the Bucketmen. Like I said, I'm just drawn to these people.

I always swore the other "knack" was not intentional, but the subconscious is a powerful beast. Even after we graduated, I developed a thing for showing up at T.J.'s house just before dinnertime. His wife, Brenda, always seemed to be setting the table just as I rang the bell. And even if I was only coming by to drop off a CD, she insisted that I come in and eat with the family. What sane single man passes up a home cooked meal?

Our academy days could be grueling, with the seemingly endless study of bone-dry material and rather intense physical exercises and drills. But T.J. had not only the intellect and drive but the sense of humor that made it easier to get through those 16 weeks.

My friend was also the very definition of a "family man." The pay isn't very good in the academy. It's not much better after graduation. Every penny T.J. made went toward providing for the people under his roof. There was no such thing as "disposable income" for him. So, when I told him the new King Crimson CD would be released a couple of weeks before we graduated, I didn't get the reaction I anticipated. "I won't be able to get it," he said with a pained expression.

"What do you mean?" I asked, not quite comprehending. "I won't cost more than 15 bucks."

"I've got a wife, two kids, and a mortgage. It might as well cost a million."

I hurt for my friend. I decided then and there he would not be deprived of such a special musical moment. I lived alone in a tiny one-bedroom apartment. (4) I wasn't rich, but I certainly had a little more budgetary room for error. So, when King Crimson released *Thrak* in April of '95, I walked out of the record store with two copies.

I wasted no time playing my CD. In fact, by the time I got to the academy the following morning, I played it three times. I couldn't wait to tell T.J. about it. I found him in the break room about 10 minutes before class started. I can still see and hear our conversation like it was yesterday. "So, I got the new Crimson," I said within seconds of saying hello.

T.J. tried to look disinterested. "Oh, yeah? Well, how is it?"

I took a little pause for dramatic effect. "Well ... you know how you really look forward to something, and when it finally happens, it doesn't quite live up to your expectations?"

My friend looked a little puzzled. "Yeah ...?"

I waited another beat, and then smiled broadly. "Well, this is *not* one of those times! It's an awesome record. Positively *awesome!*"

T.J. couldn't help but laugh. "Well, I'm glad," he said. "Next time you come by for dinner, you should bring it with you."

"Why not tonight?"

"Can't do it tonight. Got something going with the kids. I won't be back until late."

"So check it out after you get home," I said insistently.

"How am I gonna do that? Brenda won't want anybody knocking on the door when we're putting the kids to bed."

My smile broadened. "That won't be a problem," I said.

"What are you talking about, dude?"

With that, I reached into the blue binder I was carrying. Out came a copy of *Thrak*, still tightly wrapped in cellophane. I handed the CD to my friend. I can still see the stunned look on his face.

"Ced, I *told* you. I can't afford this! There's no way I can pay you back!"

I just held up my hand, as if to cut him off. "I think you can afford free, man." T.J. still looked befuddled, so I added, "How many times have you fed me in that past four months? Think of it as an early graduation present."

This time, my friend hugged me.

***

It wasn't long before T.J. and I were trading notes on the latest effort from King Crimson. The band we knew and loved was back! And they were copping a serious attitude! Neither one of us could get enough of what we were hearing. Once again, Crimson gets the ball rolling with "Vrooom." The poking, plodding, heavy version originally played on the EP had been replaced by a smoother, sleeker model. Whatever the band had been looking for, they seemed to have found it. Perhaps the most impressive aspect of *Thrak* is knowing there are six musicians performing on the album, yet the mix allows the listener to hear each of them! (5) On this particular track, the Double Trio is split within the stereo spectrum. Robert, Pat, and Trey can be heard in one ear, while Adrian, Tony, and Bill clatter away in the other.

"Vrooom" is an aggressive, menacing piece of music, broken up by a pair of light arpeggio sections picked by Fripp, which are augmented by the guitar stings and swells of Belew, the tender fretless bass of Tony Levin, and the thoughtful single-note stabs of Trey Gunn's Chapman Stick. The end of the piece was also slightly re-worked and dubbed "CODA: Marine 475." It lurches along a la the EP, while maintaining a slightly lighter air about it. This new record was off to an amazing start.

What follows qualifies as my all-time favorite individual King Crimson moment. It takes place over seven-and-a-half minutes in the form of an "epic pop song" (Adrian's term) called "Dinosaur." When Belew and Fripp first assembled the tune, Adrian recalled being inspired by the Beatles "I Am the Walrus." (6) I'm willing to go out on a limb to say "Dinosaur" outdoes that classic Beatles tune.

The song opens with a string section generated by Adrian's guitar synthesizer. But any thoughts of a tranquil, pastoral piece of music are shattered quickly by the downbeat of Bill Bruford's drums and the thunder of Tony Levin's five-string bass. They drive the band forward (surprisingly, in 4/4 time) until Adrian presents his vocals, loaded as always with clever wordplay.

The song follows the standard verse/chorus/verse/chorus/bridge format, then takes a quick turn toward left field where Adrian and Tony engage in an interlude, giving the song a moment to breathe. Adrian re-engages his guitar synthesizer to replicate the sound of an oboe, and Tony briefly grabs hold of his NS electric upright bass. (7) The two engage in a lovely duet that gives an otherwise heavy song an air of regality.

I thought the song ended there. I was wrong. The rest of the band comes storming back, led by Robert Fripp's searing guitar solo. Finally, Adrian puts a nice cap on things with one more take on the chorus, and a series of "dinosaur roars" deftly executed with his hands, effects rack, and Fender Stratocaster. "Dinosaur" elevates pop music to the highest level.

The band must have known its audience needed a moment after a song that heavy. So they followed "Dinosaur" with a tender ballad, called "Walking on Air." It was T.J.'s favorite song on the album. The song's title is appropriate, since Adrian's lead guitar and vocals (where he seems to channel his inner John Lennon) seem to float above the rest of the band, who laid a tranquil, almost jazzy foundation for him.

I remember going to T.J.'s house one day, where I found him in the back yard, grilling. His back was to me, and he didn't hear me coming. But I heard *him*, as he sang "Walking on Air" to himself while flipping chicken and applying barbecue sauce. I stood behind him and said nothing for a good 30 seconds, soaking up the sound of his rock-solid singing voice. The memory never fails to bring a tear to my eye.

King Crimson may give the audience time to breathe, but not *that* much time. *Thrak* picks up the pace again with "B'Boom," which features a guitar synthesizer intro from Fripp giving way to a wicked drum duet from Bruford and Pat Mastelotto. Elvin Ringo is in full effect as the drummers weave their lines around each other, making their eight active limbs sound more like 20. The drums give way to the album's title track, a remorseless stomp over all that is peace and tranquility in music. The middle section is improvised, or at least has that feel (8) as the band offers a series of points and counterpoints, each musician offering up a musical thought as they move forward. "Thrak" is not for the musically faint of heart.

The rest of the album contains more than a few enjoyable moments. "People" is a nice bit of funky pop, "One Time" is a solid ballad, featuring a beautiful interlude that could help prove the existence of a higher power. "Sex, Sleep, Eat, Drink, Dream" is just quirky Crimson fun. In case anyone forgot what skilled musicians played in this band, "Vrooom Vrooom" serves as a nice reminder. I particularly enjoy hearing this number performed live, so I can watch the faces of the band members. It's not hard to pick up on how much fun they're having.

Thrak is a more than competent return of the band I fell in love with a decade before. It was also the center of conversation for my friend T.J. and me for quite some time.

***

While I will never stop extolling the merits of *Thrak*, I will also admit the record does not feature the band playing its music to the fullest potential. Robert Fripp has often said that a King Crimson record is a "love letter." A Crimson gig, on the other hand, is more of a "hot date."

There is something to be said for this comparison. I remember thinking about how much I loved King Crimson's '80s output. The albums were rock solid, and well worth the endless hours I spent playing them. But when I heard *Absent Lovers*, a live performance of the same material, I knew that the music I knew and loved had been taken to a new level. The band *played* the material in the studio, and capably so. But they *owned* the material on stage. King Crimson's music became a living, breathing organism, laying waste to all in its path.

The Double Trio took the material from *Thrak* and made it sound considerably less sterile on stage. It's one thing to perform while isolated from fellow musicians, wearing headphones, and not being able to interact with one another in a studio environment. Imperfections and errors can be corrected and overdubbed, sometimes taking a bit of the "soul" out of a band's performance. On stage, once the song starts, there is no going back. King Crimson digs in and goes for broke. Some musicians might see playing complicated songs without a safety net as cause for trepidation. Not this band. A Crimson musician tends to thrive in this setting, sounding more like he can't wait to show not only the audience, but his band mates, just how up to the task he is.

Fortunately, the King Crimson Collectors Club (accessible via the band's official website at www.dgmlive.com) makes experiencing the live Double Trio possible. A concert video, called *Deja Vrooom*, is available on DVD, and is well worth the viewing time. I can't count the number of times I have played this video (recorded in Tokyo), and continue to be amazed by it. I have also collected performances from New York City, Mexico City, and London. Not only are there occasional shifts in the band's set list, the listener can pick up on the increased intensity coming from the band as they get more and more comfortable with one another. While the New York performance is probably my favorite, each gig has merit and never fails to entertain.

King Crimson is a group of world class musicians. Each member of the band has been eagerly sought by other artists to contribute his talents to non-Crimson bands. (10) It seems hard to believe any Crimson member would be overly impressed, or even surprised, by something his band mate does. Yet within the Double Trio, there was always room for a little shock and awe.

A prime example occurs during the performance of "Elephant Talk" on the *Deja Vroom* DVD. Adrian plays a sizzling solo toward the end of the piece, playing notes that seem to come from everywhere while employing numerous hand and picking techniques. At the end of the solo, the camera quickly pans to Adrian's left, where Tony Levin appears awed by what just happened. He looks behind him, toward Bill Bruford's drum riser. Levin's facial expression clearly says, "Did you *see* that?" If Tony Levin can be amazed – even after playing hundreds of gigs and sessions with Adrian Belew – then so can I.

***

T.J. and I graduated from the police academy in May of '95. Our district assignments took us to opposite ends of the City. We did our best to call one another, and scheduled the occasional outing or barbecue. Alas, our schedules became more and more convoluted. Getting together got harder and harder to do. I desperately wanted him to come with me to the HORDE Festival in August of '96, where King Crimson was opening the show. But we just couldn't make it work. Instead, I had to tell him about my near miss with Adrian and chat with Pat over the telephone. (9)

Around this time, I started playing guitar. It wasn't long before I was talking to T.J. about it, telling him we would soon form a band, and that band would cover more than one King Crimson tune. My friend was always agreeable, but rarely available. It was the story of our lives.

In similar fashion, King Crimson struggled to find its musical groove as they attempted to follow up on *Thrak*. Fripp was finding the Double Trio to be a logistical nightmare, as getting six busy musicians to assemble in the same place at the same time to work on new material was becoming counterproductive, and incredibly expensive. When they did come together, the results were mixed, at best. A couple of "official bootlegs" of these rehearsals were released via the King

Crimson Collectors Club. Naturally, I ordered them both. Neither, however, proved to be musically revolutionary.

Perhaps the "fault" can be laid at the feet of Fripp, the band's leader. It is both a blessing and a curse Robert did not want to repeat Crimson's musical efforts. This would prompt him to try and re-invent the wheel, as he put it. This is easier said than done. Ideas seen as extensions on what had been done an album or two before were rejected out of hand, perhaps out of fear of repetition. I have never had the pleasure of sitting in on a King Crimson writing session, so my knowledge is limited.

Putting six musicians in a room was not working. Normally, this would lead to a band's demise. Fripp, however, had another idea. Rather than assemble the whole of the group, he created a series of sub-groups he called "FraKctals." These bands would come to be known as The ProjeKcts. They served as research and development toward the creation of new material.

While Fripp, the band's primary composer, may have had some ideas to present to the group, very little material was pre-written. ProjeKct One consisted of Fripp, Gunn, Levin, and Bruford. They set up their equipment on stage at the Jazz Café in London on the last day of November '97. There was no rehearsal. Each musician tested his gear to make sure it was working properly, and then left the venue. ProjeKct One took the stage eight times over four nights between December 1 and 4, performing full sets of improvised music.

Like any other musicians in an improvisational context, ProjeKct One struggled from time to time. But when they hit on something, the results could be positively stunning. Highlights from these gigs were released on a single CD called *Live at the Jazz Café*. I continue to play this recording with a sense of awe and wonder.

Of the original sub-groups, ProjeKct Four is my favorite. The band featured Fripp, Gunn, Levin, and Mastelotto. They played a series of gigs along the west coast of the United States, shaking its stunned audience to the core. Most of the excitement comes from Pat, who brought (at Fripp's behest) tons of electronic percussion, beat boxes, and samplers which he used to push the band in a "Drum 'n' bass" direction fancied by younger artists. Tony took advantage of the grooves by laying down a monstrous low end, while Trey's Warr Guitar (an instrument very similar to the stick, but with a body designed for strumming and picking, in addition to tapping) provided chords and double-stops on top of the rhythm. Meanwhile, Robert dug in and let his guitar wail over the din created by his band mates. Not every moment is perfect, but there is more than enough featured on the CD *West Coast Live* to keep the listener coming back for more.

***

Naturally, I did all I could to keep T.J. in the loop where the ProjeKcts were concerned. Nothing was more fun than watching his flabbergasted face as our favorite musicians tore off toward musical lands unknown. "How do they do it?" he asked me one day while ProjeKct Four ripped holes in his speakers. "My God! These guys have no limits!"

All I could do was laugh. "It certainly seems that way," I said.

Before Robert Fripp FraKctal-ized King Crimson, T.J. and I appeared to be on the verge of a professional comeback. In the summer of '96, T.J.'s partner left our department to pursue an opportunity with another law enforcement agency. My friend's work was highly regarded by his commanders, and they told him he could pick his next partner. He was free to choose any officer in the city. T.J. chose me. After a few months of command-level hemming and hawing, I was transferred from District 8 to District 3 in March of '97. I don't think I've ever been happier professionally than the day I walked into roll call, and saw my friend standing there, waiting for me. We were all set to live the dream. Unfortunately, that dream lasted just six weeks, as T.J. was forcibly transferred. Things weren't the same for either of us after that.

***

The transfer sent T.J. went into a funk all the quality music in the world couldn't fix. I did the best I could to be a friend when he needed me, but those moments were few and far between for a while. Sometimes, a man just has to work things out for himself.

Meanwhile, my guitar skills were slowly improving. My repeated viewings of the *Deja Vroom* (which I played along with for the first 30 minutes) gave me the impetus to form a band. My group would be heavily influenced by the music of King Crimson. There was no getting around that. In fact, it became crucial to name my band after a Crimson song. Eventually, I settled on The Sheltering Sky.

I remember telling T.J. of my grand plan. He was amused, but too busy to be part of it. The Family Man was still doing what he had to do to provide for his household. This meant working not only a ton of overtime with his new unit, but taking on secondary security jobs as well. This didn't leave a lot of time for band rehearsals with his obsessed, unmarried friend.

Still, we hatched a scaled down plan, a la a Crimson ProjeKct. We thought it might be fun to perform as an acoustic duo playing the occasional open-mic night, or opening for some other band in a club. We even sought to learn a couple of King Crimson tunes, like "Frame By Frame." Once again, I pushed to name us after a song from our favorite band. The choices were narrowed down to Three of a Perfect Pair or Neil and Jack and Me. Both were perfectly ironic for a duo.

The plan got as far the two of us sitting in his living room (after dinner, of course), picking and strumming our way through a few songs. Needless to say, the material was quite challenging. I remember T.J. stopping halfway through one of the songs and looking at me with the most sober expression.

"What?" I asked, a bit confused.

"You realize," he said at last, "there can be no drinking while we perform."

I produced a snort that turned into a chuckle. "Well … yeah! Of course not!" And we went back to playing.

Our duo never came to pass. I did manage to form the Sheltering Sky, but not without great difficulty. The story of that band is a saga in and of itself.

At least King Crimson found a way to move forward.

***

While the ProjeKcts helped Robert Fripp find a way to make new music under the Crimson banner, there was also an unexpected side effect. Bill Bruford, who played drums in Crimson since '72, decided he'd had enough, and left the band. Bruford was one of my favorite musicians of all time. The thought of King Crimson without him left me cold and wary. I liked Pat Mastelotto, and respected his abilities as a drummer. I just didn't know whether he could handle the gig by himself. (12) To make matters worse, Tony Levin would also be unavailable, as gigs with Peter Gabriel, among others, beckoned. He was a bassist in demand, and there were jobs being thrown his way. The next version of King Crimson would be a quartet, or as Fripp cheekily called them, a Double Duo. Robert and Adrian would now move forward with an entirely new rhythm section for the first time in almost 20 years. Things were about to get interesting.

Robert Fripp often says King Crimson is not a band, but a way of doing things. One of those things involves the way new material is presented. While most bands record a new album and take the material on the road, Fripp preferred to come at it from the opposite direction. He and his band mates "play in" the new material in front of an audience, tweaking and perfecting it from gig to gig. By the time the music reaches its boiling point, the band is ready to record it. For King Crimson's next record, called *The ConstruKction of Light*, Fripp decided to take the "traditional" approach. It can be argued the music suffers a bit for it.

The music created by the ProjeKcts gave Fripp more than a couple of avenues to explore toward the new album. So by the time he, Belew, Gunn, and Mastelotto gathered at Adrian's house outside Nashville, Tennessee (where the basement makes up StudioBelew), the ideas were flying. Still, the band members would find themselves recording to "click" tracks, or smaller portions of what would make up the final arrangement. It's a completely different vibe, compared to playing live. The music the Double Duo made, while certainly competent, comes off as a little stiff.

More than a couple of my friends told me they don't enjoy King Crimson's music because it lacks "soul." While none of those friends were ever able to give a precise definition of the word in a musical context, I've taken it to mean a sense of feel largely derived from making the "wrong" note sound "right," usually during a period of improvisation. There is plenty of room for "soul" in blues, jazz, or rock contexts, where solos are often improvised, and not played the same way twice. Progressive rock rarely does this. Like classical music, the song is designed to be played just so. The quest for perfection can at times deprive the music of a bit of personality.

It's hard enough to make notes played at 140 beats per minute in 11/8 time sound right when a musician is interacting with his band mates. Sitting alone in a recording booth, wearing headphones, and playing along to a "click" makes it even harder. The sound of "stiffness" in all likelihood comes from the drive for perfection. It is a musical walk along a razor blade, and it is easy to get cut.

Pat Mastelotto's exclusive use of electronic percussion (at Fripp's behest) does not help. Pat has a rock-solid sense of groove, but the absence of warm, well-tuned, acoustic drums prevents the music from obtaining a much-needed "organic" feel. The quality drummer with a solid sense of feel is reduced, in a way, to a rhythmic computer.

The ConstruKction of Light is not a bad record. It simply doesn't live up to the potential of its four top-flight musicians. Trey Gunn described the album as "The map, but not the treasure." I will never come up with a better description.

Still, the album is not without its moments. During the title track, Fripp and Belew revert to '80s era form, and resurrect their interlocking guitars. It never fails to send me into a burst of unrestrained "air" guitar. (13) Fripp ratchets things up a notch or two with a blistering guitar run on "FraKctured," an update of fan favorite "Fracture," from '74's *Starless and Bible Black*. About two thirds of the way into the piece, Fripp unleashes a guitar solo that will serve as the centerpiece of any clinic given on the man. Even at the height of my guitar playing mania, I knew I would *never* be able to play this solo, no matter how much I practiced.

Adrian gets another chance to show off his remarkable ability with words, combined with his quirky sense of humor, this time in a tune called "The World's My Oyster Soup Kitchen Floor Wax Museum." In the midst of his verbal joy, Belew also unleashes an atonal guitar solo that seems to have no real place in the context of the song. Therefore, it fits perfectly. Fripp also adds a distinct solo, using his guitar synthesizer to create the piano solo from hell, while Gunn and Mastelotto stomp rhythmically all over the place, with and against the lead lines provided by the guitarists.

For me, *TCOL*'s high point is "Larks Tongues in Aspic, part IV," a continuation of a song idea found on the '73 album *Larks Tongues in Aspic* (which housed parts I and II) and '83's *Three of a Perfect Pair* (where part III can be found). The tune features everything the King Crimson enthusiast loves about the band: a grueling minor key riff establishing the theme, tricky time shifts, and another breakneck guitar run from Fripp, the interlude giving the audience time to breathe, and what I believe to be one of the best guitar solos of Adrian Belew's Crimson career.

It's no secret that the band's front man had been under more than a little stress during the recording of this album, mostly as a result of reading *Elephant Talk*, a now-defunct Internet forum extolling all things King Crimson. For reasons which continue to elude me, there are more than a few people in cyberspace who believe Adrian had no place in Crimson, and they spent a great deal of time ripping a very nice man to shreds. (14) Adrian committed the cardinal sin of trying to engage these basement dwellers, as Fripp called them. Not only did he not help his cause, Adrian probably made things ten times worse for himself. In cyber space, anonymity breeds ignorance.

The "Larks IV" solo had a much heavier attitude to it, from my standpoint. It growled, roared, and seared the landscape while the rest of the band laid down a solid foundation for Adrian to play over. He'd probably never admit it (being the nice person he is), but I think Adrian was telling more than a couple of people what they could go and do with themselves, where his position in the band was concerned.

I'm torn between favorite solos, where this song is concerned. The studio track is incredible, but the King Crimson Collectors Club offers a gig from Nashville in '01, where the band takes the tune up yet another notch. Belew is very much in the moment, and shreds his solo once again, this time without a safety net. I have rewound and replayed that solo more than a few times. The hair on my neck never fails to stand up.

***

The ConstruKction of Light could have ended with "Larks IV" and its coda, called "I Have a Dream." But King Crimson took an unusual step from its usual *modus operandi* by adding a bonus track. This tune, and the album it was a part of, put an electric charge of excitement into Y2Crim the *TCOL* album could not quite attain.

The tune, called "Heaven and Earth," was attributed to ProjeKct X, which was mostly the brainchild of Trey Gunn, Pat Mastelotto, and Bill Munyon, Mastelotto's drum tech. "Heaven and Earth" is seven minutes, 46 seconds of what I call 22nd century King Crimson. Yes, it seems that far ahead of its time.

While Crimson hashed out ideas for the *TCOL* album, the rhythm section was collecting unused song snippets, jam sessions, false starts, and samples, which they augmented with fresh rhythm tracks and ideas that didn't quite fit in with what the band was playing toward *TCOL*. Pat was playing anything he could hit with a drumstick – including Adrian's garage door – to get the grooves he was looking for. The new pieces were assembled and mixed in the small apartment Gunn and Mastelotto were renting.

The album, also dubbed *Heaven and Earth*, is positively stunning. Gunn, Mastelotto, and Munyon push Crimson in directions Fripp and Belew probably never fathomed, let alone attempted. (15) It is the sound of a band looking for the music's outer edge, locating it, and tap dancing along said edge without teetering over. I have to play that album at least once a month, just to remind myself of what is possible in music, given the creative outlet and the opportunity.

***

My friend T.J. DuPree found the music intriguing, too. We saw less and less of each other after his transfer. It was as though someone was conspiring to keep us from enjoying each other's company.

When we found a window of opportunity, I jumped through it. Once again, I found myself at his house around dinnertime. After another quality meal, we adjourned to his living room, where I put *TCOL* on the CD player. Like me, T.J. found the record interesting, though not revolutionary. "They're searching for something," he said to me without prompting. "I don't know if they've found it yet. But they're definitely headed in the right direction." All I could do was nod and smile at my friend's remarkable insight.

T.J. whistled a different tune when I played ProjeKct X. Once again, I saw my initial reaction in him. I can still see him smiling and shaking his head in absolute amazement. "My God!" he exclaimed, almost cackling with glee. "This is it! *This* is where they should have gone! That's the sound of musicians flat-out *going for it!*" *Heaven and Earth* contained 15 tracks, totaling just over 72 minutes. I have no doubt I played each piece at least twice, and a couple of them three or four times. There was just no getting over what we were hearing. It was affirming to me, since I knew I wasn't the only one hearing what I believed to be the next evolution of King Crimson.

***

The stiffness I heard on *The ConstruKction of Light* loosened up when the band took the material on the road. Despite all the technical and precise aspects of its music, King Crimson is a band built to show its ability live, on stage. Even Mastelotto's electronic percussion seemed to have more room to breathe.

The band released *Heavy ConstruKction*, a three-CD set featuring live performances from their European tour. Not only did Crimson have its new material securely under its collective fingertips, but aspects of ProjeKct X appeared to be rubbing off on them as well, as the band took two or more opportunities to improvise music during its sets. A couple of these improvs are featured on the first two CDs of the live set, and then the third CD features improvs from all over Europe, showing the band in blistering form.

The collector's club also offered multiple recordings from that tour. My favorite shows took place in Prague, London, and Nashville. As T.J. observed one day while listening to *Heavy ConstruKction,* the band seemed to be getting closer and closer to what they were looking for. After taking a much-needed break, King Crimson re-convened, and began making strides toward its next album.

This time, Fripp and company reverted to form, playing in the new material on stage, tweaking it as they went along. Unlike before, however, the band offered up CDs that seemed to serve as a testament to their progress toward the next album. *Level Five* came first in '01, offering up rough versions of tunes called "Dangerous Curves" and "Virtuous Circle."

Wisely, Pat Mastelotto re-inserted acoustic drums into his kit. The electronics were still very much a factor, but now they were augmenting his sound, rather than driving it. The difference was night and day. Songs sounding stiff and clinical now sounded loose and organic.

King Crimson took its next step in '02 with the release of a new EP called *Happy With What You Have to Be Happy With.* The title track found Adrian having fun with the songwriting process once again, using the clever song title as the chorus to a song about writing a song. Belew was also writing song lyrics in haiku form, while Fripp continued to add to his sound arsenal, using a rack unit he dubbed the Lunar Module. Trey Gunn was also expanding his sound palate, making the most of his Warr Guitar and associated effects rack.

King Crimson's sound was getting more aggressive, heading toward metal. Touring as the opening act for nu-metal stalwarts Tool no doubt had an effect on the band as well, as the two groups shared a mutual admiration for one another. The average age of the members of King Crimson was in the mid-50s. The music they were playing sounded 15 to 20 years younger. The band was also gaining a new, younger audience, thanks to exposure to Tool fans.

Adrian told me about walking amongst the audience after a Tool gig. He was able to move about anonymously, since most of the audience had no idea who he or King Crimson was. Two people were walking in front of him, talking excitedly about the show they had just seen. While one went on about

Tool, his friend chimed in, "How about those other guys? They played some tricky shit, too!" Adrian laughed at the comment. "So you see, King Crimson is now known for playing tricky shit!"

***

Something big was coming from this band. I could feel it. I remember telling T. J. as much during one of our all too infrequent phone conversations. He seemed to sense it, too. Our beliefs proved accurate in '03, when King Crimson released *The Power to Believe.*

I've listened to a lot of King Crimson over the years. I've always listened with great anticipation. Still, I keep in mind what Fripp said about expectation being a prison. I make a conscious effort to clear my mind before playing new music.

It's not unusual to be surprised by what King Crimson springs forth. This was different. My thoughts go back to the parade ground at Fort Lee, Virginia, and pressing the "play" button on that Walkman as – for the second time – what poured out of my speakers stopped me dead in my tracks.

The album starts innocently enough, with Adrian singing a verse from "The Power to Believe" *a cappella.* That pleasantness ends quickly, and King Crimson unleashes hell. The next tune is an updated and perfected version of "Level Five." It never fails to leave my jaw dragging on the floor. One thing is certain: this wasn't the '69 King Crimson. Not by a long shot!

I went to the show Crimson played in support of this album in November of '03. (16) I remember standing in line before the doors of the Pageant opened. Standing in front of me was a man in his 50s, sporting a gray ponytail and a tie-dye t-shirt. He was talking to his companion and wondered aloud if the band would play tunes like "In the Court of the Crimson King" or other material from the early '70s. I couldn't help but snort, and concealing my laugh was impossible. It got his attention. "What's so funny?" the man asked me.

I kept smiling in spite of myself. "My man," I said to him, "If that's what you're looking for or expecting, you might want to leave *right now.*" I made a conscious effort to keep an eye out for that guy during the gig. When the band launched into "Level Five," I looked his way. He must have felt my stare, because he turned his head my way. He looked at me with a stunned expression. I just mouthed the words "I told you."

"Level Five" is a vicious piece of music. Everyone in the band is taking his ability to the next plane. Pat's drum kit strikes the perfect balance between the acoustic and the electronic. Robert's guitar moves deftly and precisely from one stage to the next. Trey's bass propels the tune forward. Adrian is apparently still carrying a chip on his shoulder from *TCOL*, because his guitar wails like a banshee. (17) It didn't take long to realize King Crimson found the treasure it was seeking.

Other album highlights include "Elektrik," where Fripp and Belew interlock their guitars once again, but not before using their guitar synths to replicate a woodwind section. The tune balances tenderness and aggression in a way not easily attained by other bands. "The Power to Believe II" is the official re-working of "Virtuous Circle," with the band locating and maintaining the groove it sought on the *Level Five* EP. My second favorite moment after "Level Five" comes on a tune called "Dangerous Curves." It's a 6/4 stomper that is equally calm, funky, and foreboding. From a technical standpoint, it's a relatively simple song to play. What makes the song is its intensity, starting out quiet as a church mouse, and gradually building to a deafening roar. The song builds and builds until its crescendo, a dissonant chord from Belew, leading into an edited version of "Happy with What You Have to Be Happy With."

"The Power to Believe" parts III and IV close out the record, the latter being Adrian ending things as he started them, singing an *a cappella* verse. The overall experience is the most satisfying I've had since *Discipline*.

***

The new album had me so excited, I couldn't even describe it to T.J. I just begged him to find the time for me to come over, so I could play it for him. It took more time than I imagined, but he finally found some time for me to come by. Once there, I didn't waste time talking the album up. I just plugged it into the CD player.

I realize my objectivity is questionable where my favorite band is concerned. This is particularly true when I get a new record. It takes time before I start hearing the possible "flaws." T.J. had a way of cutting things to the bone, even if he liked what he was hearing. How I felt about a record was validated by his feelings. Which is why I enjoyed what happened next so very much.

T.J. was standing when "Level Five" kicked in. Within 30 seconds, he was sitting. I watched as the music flowed over him, seemingly making it impossible for him to stand again. Instead, he just stared at me. Clearly, my friend was hearing what I heard. He verified this by looking at me and mouthing the words, "Oh, my God." All I could do was smile and nod my head quickly in understanding.

This went on over the next 50 minutes, and then we played the CD again. T.J. and I found ourselves asking the same question: "How do these guys *do* it?" I suppose the question was rhetorical, because we never came up with a sufficient answer.

I still don't have – or need – one.

***

There are many bands and musicians who love to interact with fans. Whether it's through pre-scheduled "meet-and-greets," post-show autograph sessions, or chance encounters on the street, there are plenty of musicians happy to make time for an autograph, a photo, or just a little idle chit-chat.

Robert Fripp is *not* one of those musicians.

This is not a secret to most King Crimson fans (or "enthusiasts," as Robert prefers to see us). As far as Robert is concerned, the money plunked down for a CD entitles the buyer to precisely that. A concert ticket gives the consumer the opportunity to experience Robert Fripp and the band he formed in a live performance. That's it. The other members of the band may be willing to interact with fans, but the band's *de facto* leader wants no part of it.

I would not presume to speak for Robert and attempt to explain why he feels this way. Based on his online interactions with fans in King Crimson forums and on his own DGM Live web site, I would surmise he has little to no tolerance for the banality coming from meeting someone who offers him nothing on a personal or intellectual level.

More than a few people are put off by this point of view. I have no problem with it. I have a couple of autographs from the musicians I admire, but they are not essential to my appreciation of their music. One of two autographs I did want is from Adrian Belew, and I have that more times than I care to say. (18) Fripp made his personal code clear, and I find it easy to adhere to. I have never sought him out after a King Crimson or solo show. I assumed he would be there to perform, and he always showed up.

Perhaps that's why I cherish my eight-second encounter with Robert Fripp so much.

On November 7, 2003, King Crimson was in town to support *The Power to Believe*. They were playing the Pageant, a pleasant room holding about 1,500 people. The sightlines are good from just about anywhere, and the sound is better than average, depending on the sound engineer. Naturally, I had to be there

I invited T.J., of course, but the Family Man didn't have the cost of a ticket in his budget. I can't be mad at him. The man had his priorities straight. Instead, my friends Ian Good and Trey Adams came with me.

I'd gone to more than a couple of concerts at the Pageant, and I ultimately learned the best place to view the show was not from the front, next to the stage. Rather, it was toward the back of the room, behind the mixing console. Sure, it was back a ways (at least 20 yards or so), but you were perfectly centered on the stage, and in between the PA speakers hanging some 10 feet up on either side. Best of all, the mixing console was sunk into the floor, which made it easy to see over the soundman, even if you were seated. From there, I could see and hear *everything*. Why would I want to elbow for room up front with everyone else?

A series of stately pillars adorned the rear of the room, in line with where my friends and I were standing. I imagine the view is picturesque from the stage, which elevated some four feet off the floor. I hadn't given the pillars a lot of thought until that evening, but they did give more than adequate space for a concertgoer to lean back and enjoy the show.

The opening act was Living Colour. It was my first time seeing them live, and they did not disappoint. The way Vernon Reid and company tore into their set, I almost forgot I still had King Crimson to look forward to! The audience was equally impressed, shouting support during and between songs throughout the set. It was as good an opening act as I can ever recall seeing.

About 40 minutes in, I felt Trey nudging me with his elbow. I turned to my right and looked at him, my face saying "What?" without actually speaking. He leaned in to insure I could hear him.

"That dude over there," Trey said. "He looks just like Robert Fripp!" Without pointing, Trey gestured to my left. I craned my neck to nine o'clock. There, a mere ten feet away, leaning on one of those stately pillars, was a familiar figure. He was wearing a blue dress shirt and black slacks, and I can vividly remember seeing the yellow plugs he had in his ears. The trademark glasses, coupled with the English accent he produced while urging Living Colour on (quite loudly) were the final giveaway. I grinned in spite of myself.

"That's because it *is* Robert Fripp," I told Trey after turning back to him. Trey's eyes lit up, and he smiled broadly. I also saw his body start to shift in a way that said, "I'm gonna go over there and talk to him." Before he could build up any momentum, I reached out and gently – but firmly – grabbed hold of my friend's arm. He looked at me again, and I slowly shook my head.

Trey was not as familiar with the Fripp rules as I was. He seemed a little confused at first, but he saw in my eyes how serious I was. Slightly crestfallen, Trey nodded understanding, and turned back to watch the rest of Living Colour's performance.

I don't know if Robert saw this or not. I have a hunch he did. A minute later, I looked to my left. At almost the same time, Robert turned to his right, and we made eye contact. I wanted to show my respect, admiration, and appreciation without leaving my space in order to violate his. On a whim, I balled my right hand into a fist, and placed it over my heart. I accentuated the move by bowing slightly in his direction. Amused, Fripp grinned warmly, and returned the gesture. And with that, we returned to watching Living Colour.

It was one of the coolest moments of my life. Crimson's show was pretty awesome, too.

***

Of course, I told T.J. about this moment, which tickled him to no end. "That was a classy move," he told me over the phone. "You said it all without saying a word."

I remember thinking King Crimson could stop making records after *The Power to Believe*. I didn't believe they were going to get any better. It would seem the Double Duo would have no choice but to quit, anyway. Not long after the '03 tour, Trey Gunn quit the band. Coupled with Robert's legal struggles with the record label over royalties and Adrian's return to the Bears and his solo career, I assumed that was that. So be it. It was one hell of a musical legacy.

But the Crimson King never truly dies. Robert resurrected the band briefly in '08, with Tony Levin returning to the bass chair. He also added a drummer in Gavin Harrison, an Englishman who made his mark in the progressive rock band

Porcupine Tree (19). Along with Adrian and Pat Mastelotto, the band embarked on a brief tour, performing material mostly from the '80s forward. A Collector's Club download from a show in Chicago was made available. I rarely play it. It doesn't do a lot for me. When I listen to the performance, the word "under-rehearsed" runs through my mind. There are "clams" (musician-speak for "mistakes") in many places, and the timing seems a bit off now and then. That's not to say I could play the music any better. I just demand a little more out of my King Crimson, and this wasn't reaching the established standard. That bothered me, but Life was about to show me there were bigger things to worry about than the sound of a band, and whether or not it lived up to expectations.

***

I fucking *HATE* cancer.

Not that I believe anyone loves the disease. But it really sticks in my craw. Cancer killed my paternal grandmother, and her mother before her. Cancer grabbed hold of a young lady I dated. It took its toll on one of my uncles. Cancer has affected the lives of people I worked with. It has entered the lives of friend's siblings and parents.

Cancer came for T.J.

I don't remember the exact circumstances of learning of my friend's condition. I do remember it hitting me like a ton of bricks. T.J. didn't always have the best luck in the world. There were times when I swore the man couldn't catch a break. It's like the old blues song, "Born Under a Bad Sign:" If it wasn't for bad luck, T.J. wouldn't have no luck at all.

It's not my business to discuss the intricacies of my friend's medical condition. I will simply say cancer came for T.J. more than once, and he never failed to stand up to it with courage, dignity, determination, and good humor. My friend fought tooth and nail for his life. For a time, it appeared he was going to win. Unfortunately, cancer had the last say.

Never mind our desires to play in a band together, or just go to more gigs. What mattered more than anything to T.J. was seeing us retire from the police department together, preferably as watch commanders. It wasn't meant to be.

Music was the best way I could think of to keep T.J.'s spirits up. I would bring CDs to his house, we would share downloads, and talk endlessly about what we loved to hear. We never stopped introducing one another to the bands crossing our musical radars. And of course, we never stopped talking about

King Crimson. I don't know how much good I did, but our evenings always ended with a smile and a hug. Hopefully, that was worth something.

In 2007, Adrian Belew and Rob Fetters brought the Bears to town. They played the Duck Room, my favorite place to catch a gig. Naturally, I invited T.J. to come with me. He was too ill to attend. It bummed me out, because I knew we were running out of chances. Still, I made the most of the evening, enjoying an intimate but rocking set along with 200 others, which was about all the Duck Room would hold.

After the show, I bought a second copy of *Eureka*, the album the Bears were promoting (I ordered one months before, when it was released). The band came out to meet with the fans and sign autographs. Adrian Belew, Rob Fetters, Bob Nyswonger, and Chris Arduser each heard about my friend T.J. DuPree and why he couldn't make this show, even though he desperately wanted to be there. Each band member was kind enough to sign the CD for him. I recall Rob being especially kind, telling me, "You be sure to give T.J. my best, and bless you for being such a good friend." It wasn't about me, of course. But it was nice to hear.

T.J. was grateful when I presented him with the CD, even though he didn't say a lot. He didn't have to. The look on his face spoke volumes. It was the look of a man who appreciated a small gesture, because he had been going through so much, and it was wearing on him. T.J. was putting up a good fight, but even he knew he was fighting a losing battle. I remained in denial for a while longer.

The day I presented T.J. with that CD was one of the last good days we got to spend together. There were other days, of course, but the disease was taking its toll. Eventually, things got to the point where T.J. had to retire from the force. He simply wasn't able to do his job. I went to a gathering at our police union hall for him. Plenty of people stood up to talk about what a good police officer T.J. was. I was the first to stand up and talk about what a good friend, and more importantly what a good *man* he was. That means so much more.

I suppose it's natural to wish I had spent more time with my friend toward the end of his life. But there was always something in the way. He was busy with his family, and now I had one, too. My work as a detective kept me incredibly busy. But when Brenda called to tell me the end was near, I dropped what I was doing and made my way to the DuPree house.

T.J. was unconscious when I got there. It wasn't certain he would wake up again. His family surrounded his bed. They were kind enough to give me a few minutes alone with him. I can still hear his labored breathing, which cut through the high-pitched whistle of the air conditioner in the nearby windowsill. I took a moment to gather myself, and then leaned forward so that I could whisper in his ear. I said what I needed to say to my friend, trying not to focus on the "coulda/shoulda/woulda" weighing heavily on my mind. When I finished, I stood up and left the room, making a beeline for the front door. I took time to hug Brenda and exchange a quick word or two with T.J.'s parents. Then I was out the door and back at home, trying desperately to get on with my life without lingering over what I knew was coming. I didn't have to linger for long. Four hours after I got home, Brenda called me again.

T.J. was gone.

Our conversation was brief. Brenda informed me of the funeral arrangements, which I acknowledged. I remember her thanking me for coming by. I hung up the phone and stared off into space for a very long time.

***

I have many regrets, but one of my biggest will be not attending T.J.'s wake. I just couldn't bring myself to go. I knew what I was missing, and I know I should have been there. I should've spent some time with my cop family, swapping stories, laughing like hyenas, crying like babies, and getting drunk as a skunk. But I didn't. Something in me would not let me move. Instead, I spent the afternoon playing King Crimson CDs.

I focused on the '80s and '90s material, which created a bond with my new friend in the police academy all those years before. Adrian Belew was singing, but I could imagine T.J.'s voice taking his place. I thought about the songs we were going to cover as an acoustic duo, like "Three of a Perfect Pair," "Frame By Frame," and "Walking on Air." I imagined T.J. and me standing on stage with the rest of King Crimson, amazing them with our knowledge of the band's material. I smiled at the thought of thrilling a small club crowd at the Venice Café, or one of our other favorite band-watching sites. More than anything, I missed my friend.

I did make it to the funeral. In fact, I wound up sitting next to our mutual friend, Tory Z Starbuck. It was Tory who recorded us when I covered Adrian's "The Rail Song" on my first CD. I played guitar, and T.J. sang. It remains one of my favorite music-playing memories.

***

King Crimson returned to service in 2014, this time as a seven-piece band featuring *three* drummers and no Adrian Belew. I wanted to talk to T.J. about it. He would understand how baffled I was by Robert Fripp's latest vision for his band. I can see him smiling at me, saying, "Trust Robert, Ced. He knows what he's doing." Now that I've heard what the band can do, I believe – for the most part -- T.J. is partially right. Robert Fripp *mostly* knows what he's doing. (20)

The band is more than competent, even though they lack a true frontman, like Adrian. I suppose this was done by design. Damned if I know why. The group seems less like King Crimson and more like Robert Fripp and the Six Studio Aces, since no one other than Fripp really had anything to do with writing the material they play. I don't mind the return of Mel Collins on saxophone and flute, but there were times when I questioned his necessity. This is particularly true of the flute parts. On heavy songs like "Red," the flute completely sucks the weight out of the low-end growl in the bridge. I also didn't believe it was necessary at the end of "The ConstruKction of Light," which was ethereal enough. Now it sounds dangerously close to Muzak. The re-arrangement of "Level Five" could stand a little scrutiny, as well. The middle of the song – as played on *The Power to Believe* – is *incredibly* heavy. The new band – particularly the drummers – seems to have overthought it. There is sound where there should be silence, and silence where there should be sound.

More than a few people have told me what a "transformative" experience the new Crimson has been. I think they're just happy to hear the early material again, because they've been clamoring for it since the '80s. Likewise, I think Fripp finally found a way to bring the '69-'74 sounds to life in such a way that he doesn't mind playing them again. But that material still sounds dated to me. It doesn't *pop* the way the '80s, Double Trio, and Double Duo material does. The music, as played by the current band, lacks personality. And that personality is Adrian Belew.

More than anything, I wish this new Crimson would focus on doing something *new,* instead of just regurgitating older songs. There were a couple of new pieces featured on the last tour, but nothing particularly jaw-dropping. This may be where

Adrian's absence is felt the most. He was, after all, a key co-composer. More than anything, the new Crimson sounds like an easy-listening version of its former self. Perhaps this is deemed age-appropriate, since most of the band members (and many of their fans) are in their 60s. Perhaps there is a reason I have not obsessed with this version of the band the way I have all others since '81. I hate to use the term "cash grab" where my favorite band is concerned. But if I'm really honest with myself, I must consider that a possibility. Maybe T.J. would have seen it differently, since he had a more sentimental attachment to the early material than I do. Somehow, I think he would see things the same way.

I am not a religious man. My idea of heaven is a great seat in an acoustically perfect room. The room will have the ultimate stereo system, and I will have access to every note played by every artist I have ever admired. The King Crimson collection will be *massive*.

My friend T.J. DuPree is setting things up for me. When I get there, we're gonna have a blast!

(1)   Since the Central West End contains houses that sell for a million dollars or more, the somewhat snooty attitude made sense.

(2)   Not the best smell in the world when I was downwind from there, by the way.

(3)   The lesson didn't stick. I would question him again in the years to come. He always won.

(4)   Good God, what I wouldn't give to pay $275 a month for a place to live again. Did I mention heat was included?

(5)   Admittedly, the sound of Trey Gunn's stick can get lost every now and then. The trick, I learned is to identify Tony Levin's bass. Push his sound aside, mentally, and what remains is Trey.

(6)   Adrian Belew is a die-hard Beatlemaniac. He has said in interviews he has to "de-bug" his songs at times, because the Beatles influence is far too obvious. Robin Thicke and Sam Smith could learn something from that.

(7)   If I ever win the lottery, it will be hard for people to tell until they enter my 48-track music studio. Among my first instrumental purchases will be a NS electric upright bass, and a Roland Guitar synthesizer. I swear it.

(8)   "Thrak" really shines when King Crimson plays it live, as the improv sections continued to morph and evolve with each gig. A compilation of some of these improvs, called *ThrakAttak*, was released in '96. It was savaged by critics. They had no sense of the song's context, and therefore did not completely understand what was happening. It was like walking into the middle of a movie and bitching about not understanding the plot. Even I struggled with the album at first. But it has grown on me, and I appreciate its scope and beauty.

(9)   Details of this adventure can be found in the Adrian Belew chapter.

(10)   For example, a Peter Gabriel album or tour is essentially a non-starter unless Tony Levin is available to play bass. Levin has been in control of the Gabriel low end for more than 30 years. That won't be changing any time soon.

(11)   I should have been there, too. As it happens, I attended a training seminar that day instead of reporting to my usual assignment. I can only wonder if things would have gone differently had I been there.

(12)   I was more familiar with the drumming ability of Pat Mastelotto than I realized. He played in the '80s band Mr. Mister, and did session work with the Rembrandts and XTC, among many others. I had always loved the driving drum track on XTC's "The Mayor of Simpleton." Only years after the fact did I learn it was Pat.

(13)   I got caught "playing" this part by none other than Pat Mastelotto during a 2001 Crimson gig in St. Louis. I was in the very front row at The Pageant, leaning on the stage. I was standing directly in front of Pat's drum kit. When "TCoL" started, I "played" along, with my right hand on the stage. Pat saw me, and even motioned to Trey, on his right, to check me out. They both had a good laugh over it. I saw it, but was oblivious to the fact they were talking about *me*. After the show, when the two came out to sign autographs, Pat complimented me on keeping good time. "I got lost for a second," he told me. "So I just looked at you." I figured he was just putting me on, but then I met Trey five minutes later. As I handed him a CD to sign, he looked at me and exclaimed, "The Timekeeper! You did a great job,

man!" I was immensely proud and horribly embarrassed at the same time. I'm just glad my buddy Ian Good was there to see it. Otherwise, you might not believe me.

(14) I spent more than a little time defending Adrian on *Elephant Talk*. Not that he needed my help. Some of the people could be unbelievably dopey. Over time, I realized it was useless to engage in a battle of wits with an unarmed man (or woman) and his anonymous keyboard. *Elephant Talk* – and later my police department's *CopTalk* – tuned me off anonymous message boards forever. Life is too short to deal with stupid people.

(15) A year or so after ProjeKct X, Mastelotto and Munyon, using the moniker BPM&M, created a similar album called *XtraKcts and ArtifaKcts*. It is every bit as intriguing as PX, incorporating more "Drum & Bass" aspects to Crimson-oriented sound snippets. I like it a lot, and it is worth seeking out.

(16) As a matter of fact, it was November 7, the day before my birthday. My friend Ian Good's birthday was that day, and he went to the show with me. Living Colour was the opening act. It was one hell of a double bill.

(17) Anyone questioning Adrian's place in King Crimson should watch the live DVD from this tour, called *Eyes Wide Open*. Watch Robert's expression when Adrian launches into his "Level Five" solo. The sly grin on the Englishman's face speaks volumes. Adrian is his guy, no doubt about it.

(18) The other autograph I covet is from St. Louis Cardinals pitching legend Bob Gibson. I actually had it as a child, after my dad gave me a baseball with his moniker on it. Guess which 10-year-old idiot decided to use it for a game of catch with his friends? Moron. Well, maybe one of these days …

(19) I "discovered" Porcupine Tree after I learning Adrian had a couple of guitar cameos on their album, *Deadwing*. Robert did a cameo or two on a subsequent album. Eventually, I realized just how amazing Porcupine Tree was, with or without the King Crimson members.

(20) That doesn't make me miss Adrian any less. He's still my King Crimson front man, come hell or high water.

From the outside, J. Gravity Strings may not look like much. But what waits within has fueled a two-decade obsession with the guitar.

Track 16
The Unsung Heroes of J. Gravity Strings

Now that the guitar was a part of my life, it stood to reason that sooner or later, I would find myself in a guitar shop. It's a safe bet I visited nearly every store in the St. Louis metropolitan area at least once. Each trip was an adventure, and some held more meaning than others. In the beginning, there was simply no telling which store would get the most of my time and money.

The aspiring guitarist could find just about anything he wanted in one of the larger, corporate stores. But from a "service" standpoint, I never felt like more than a number. There was no connection. Other stores were smaller and more intimate, but the employees dismissed you as a "poser" or a "wannabe," once your lack of knowledge or experience was revealed. I would leave these stores not only without buying anything, but also with the stigma that I was unworthy of being there to begin with.

My guitar explorations weren't more than a few months old the first time I set foot in J. Gravity Strings, located at 1546 South Broadway, just south of downtown St. Louis. At first, I could only come up with one practical reason for visiting the place: it was 10 minutes from my apartment. That seemed like as good a reason as any to do a little exploring.

The store was opened in 1978. To my eyes, it seemed like it had been there a lot longer. The building itself is nondescript: just another old brick building, probably built in the '20s, if not before. The green façade was well weathered and in need of a touchup. The building didn't seem to be more than 12 to 15 feet wide. Two storefront windows housing vintage guitars and amplifiers that looked like they came out of a '50s era Sears and Roebuck catalog flanked a standard wood door with a large glass windowpane. (1) I found it hard to believe I was about to encounter anything, or anyone, special on the other side of that door.

Once again, I am reminded of the hazards of judging a book by its cover.

The store's interior resembled a single, long corridor, known as a "shotgun" layout in St. Louis real estate parlance (damned if I know why). A single doorway, located about 30 feet from the main entrance, divides the long corridor. That doorway leads to the store's repair shop. It would be some time before I was able to make my way to the other side of that door.

A real estate agent might describe the store's main showroom as "cozy." Others might call it "claustrophobic." The walls on either side were laden with guitars and basses hanging from specialized hooks. The floor was not exactly built for high-volume pedestrian traffic. A three-foot wide area rug showed the customer where his feet belonged. The rest of the space was for gear. More instruments sat on stands along the length of the floor to the left. Where there were no instruments, there were amplifiers, large and small, stacked one on top of the other. There was no danger of any of this equipment tipping over, but that didn't make me any less paranoid about running into it. On the right were two glass cases, which housed the effects pedals and other gear. There were still more guitars and basses hanging behind the first 10-foot case. Where the case ended, the next stack of amps began.

Between the amps and a second glass case was a 30- or so-inch opening, which allowed the employee to get behind the register (which sat atop the second glass case) and gave access to a door that led upstairs, where lessons were given. I would become more than a little familiar with this door. Just past the second glass case was a seven-foot long wooden counter, which served as a "triage center" for sick instruments. It was here where the crestfallen musician would place the case or gig bag holding his baby, and he could tell the employee what the trouble was. That counter and I would also get to know each other very well, but not for musical reasons.

My first visit to Gravity Strings (nobody uses the "J" after the first couple of visits) was relatively uneventful, and pretty brief. I walked in to the store carrying a cheap pawnshop guitar fashioned to look like a Gibson Les Paul. I had it in my head the instrument needed new pickups, even though I wasn't completely sure how pickups worked, or why I needed them. The first employee I met, named Tam, knew what he was dealing with from the moment I started talking. He was kind and patient, tolerating my lack of knowledge with a cool aloofness I've come to expect from the musicians I encounter. By the time our talk was over, Tam had convinced me to try new strings, which would be a much cheaper sound-changing option than new pickups. It turns out he was right. This was the first of many times something like this would happen. Tam doesn't work at Gravity any more. (2) Of all the people I met in that store, I would get to know him the least. The rest of the guys became like a surrogate family.

***

It didn't take long to realize I wouldn't be able to teach myself the guitar the way I did tennis. It was time to take a lesson. I made a few phone calls, looking for a teacher that worked for a reasonable rate, and also understood my exotic musical interests, even if he didn't share them. I found what I was looking for at Gravity Strings.

Like the record stores I loved, each person at Gravity performed a specific function. Like the record store, I gave each person a nickname. Unlike the record store, however, I got to know each of these men personally.

THE BLUES MAN

When I came into the store to inquire about lessons, I was sent to Billy Barnett. I found him where I would come to find him nearly every time I walked into Gravity Strings: seated on a bar stool, merrily riffing away on his or one of the store's guitars. His fingers moved with blazing speed and dexterity, yet his actions seemed effortless.

Billy can strike an intimidating pose. He stands some six feet four inches tall, with a stocky build and gait that implies he has been around the block of Life more than a couple of times. To be certain, I want him on my side in a bar fight. But given his jovial nature, it's highly doubtful that bar fight will ever take place. I have never met anyone who gets more pure, unabashed joy out of making music than Billy Barnett. It's impossible to *not* have fun making music with him.

Billy comes from musical parents. His mother was an organ player, and his father was a vocalist. He's been playing guitar since age nine. His first record was Aretha Franklin's cover of Simon & Garfunkel's "Bridge over Troubled Water." Talk about great first impressions! From there, he was introduced to Black Sabbath and Jimi Hendrix. He played his first gigs in VFW halls at age 13, and continues to play professionally into his late 50s.

His experiences put him on the road with various blues/jazz-oriented bands. He has recorded at least 10 CDs with his own band, and worked as a sideman for many others, including a stint with violinist Shoji Tabuchi in Branson, Missouri. I wondered if the life of a professional musician ever wore thin on him. "There are times I think, 'Oh man, I *have* to do this,' as opposed to *getting* to do this," he said. "But then I remember how lucky I am to have been able to do this for so long. I still love it, and I still have a passion for it."

I think Billy and I bonded balmost immediately. I'm not sure what exactly he was expecting from me, but when I mentioned my love of King Crimson, Miles Davis, and Frank Zappa, his eyes lit up. He saw someone looking beyond the simplistic. During one of our early lessons, when he was teaching me how to play an Adrian Belew song, he stopped and laughed. When I looked at him, he said, "One thing is certain: you don't wanna learn any 'see Spot run' music, do ya?"

Billy is a true musician. He can play just about anything you put in front of him. And I mean *anything*! I've never found a quality so deeply admirable and maddeningly infuriating at the same time. This may have something to do with him being in a serious car accident back in '77. Confined to bed, he found himself playing his guitar for eight hours a day, every day. The work paid off.

I remember wanting to learn to play an incredibly complex guitar part by John Petrucci on a song called "Paradigm Shift." The song's opening, performed by the supergroup Liquid Tension Experiment (3), defies explanation. There are notes flying all over the place at break-neck speed. I played the track for Billy, certain I was going to trip him up. He listened to the opening riff carefully. "Play it again," he said when it ended. I complied. By the time the song's opening had ended, Billy had his guitar in hand. "Oh, I've got it," he said nonchalantly. "What he's doing is this ..." And just like that, Billy fired off Petrucci's riff, note for note, without breaking a sweat.

Damn!

I studied under Billy as much as I could over the next couple of years. He provided the grounded, theory-oriented Yin to the otherworldly, rules-be-damned approach of Tory Z Starbuck's Yang. I was one lucky student.

Billy seems most at home when he was playing jazz or the blues. He had the technical proficiency to move through any scale or mode with absolute precision. "I'm comfortable playing the blues, but I can get tired of playing in (the key of) E and A," he said. "I have a keyboard background, so I'd like to play in B-flat every now and then." He also loves taking apart complex songs and learning to play them. "It's like working a crossword puzzle," he says.

Billy plays with more heart than anyone I know. The listener can feel each and every note he plays. None of them are wasted. Billy strikes me as the kind of player Stevie Ray Vaughan was, meaning he never plays things the same way twice while he *channels* the music more than he plays it.

My teacher also unwittingly taught me one of the cruelest lessons in the music business: *talent means nothing.*

When I first heard Billy play, I thought about the people I saw on MTV and heard on the radio. Their playing skills didn't amount to a bucket of spit next to Billy's. How is it, I wondered, that those people were rich and famous, and my friend and teacher wasn't? It didn't make any sense.

The truth is there is a lot more to fame and fortune in the music industry than the ability to play. I knew this already. After all, I *am* a King Crimson fan. But it's something else entirely when you know the person being screwed over. So many other factors come in to play: the right look, the right connections, timing ... everything matters. And it all has to happen under the perfect set of circumstances. When people ask me who the best musicians are, I tell them those guys are toiling away in guitar shops, teaching lessons and making repairs. And they've rarely had so much as a sniff at a record deal. These days, that's less of a factor. "The internet has made it possible for people to get their music out there without management and record labels," Billy observed. "Look at someone like Ani DiFranco. She's doing all that stuff on her own."

Oh, they might have gotten "fame adjacent." Artists like Billy pick up a loyal regional following. Or they spend time in a band with someone who has managed to become famous. My teacher auditioned for blues singer Keb' Mo' and the Blue Man Group. I can only wonder how good the other guitarists were, since Billy didn't get the gigs. And sometimes the high-profile gigs aren't all they're cracked up to be. Billy described his time in Branson with Shoji Taguchi's band as, "The most money I ever made being miserable." He was working seven days a week, the band's singer was a diva, and he wasn't allowed to play music with other musicians in what little spare time he had. It's not the kind of band I would clamor to play in, but this also taught me the second cruel lesson of the music industry: *A gig is a gig*. And when it's offered to you, take it.

Speaking of fame, Billy makes sure to show me his prized woodgrain Fender Telecaster. The guitar is not one of his regular gigging instruments, but it does contain the signatures of at least 75 of his favorite musicians. I've lingered over this guitar more than once. I've identified autographs from Carlos Santana, Jeff Beck, B.B. King, Pat Metheny, and countless others. At this point, it's more about who's *not* on the guitar. "Eddie Van Halen, Eric Clapton, and Chuck Berry have been unapproachable," Billy says.

Of all my friends at Gravity, I've seen Billy perform live the most. He had a regular Tuesday gig in a bar and grille located near my apartment for 15 years. For the longest time, I was there nearly every week. I think I was trying to muster up the courage to sit in with his band, which he always invited me to do. I never quite got there. When the bar became part of my beat, I would pop through in uniform. Billy would be there, singing and playing away. And without fail, he would gesture as though he was being handcuffed whenever he saw me walk in. I knew it was coming, and I still smiled every time.

Ironically, Billy came to refer to his regular Tuesday gig as his "golden handcuffs." Yes, it was a steady paying job. But he saw his fan base start to dwindle, because he was always there. "It got to the point where people weren't showing up, probably figuring, 'I'll just see him next week.' It's good to be able to play at different places and keep things exciting."

As time has passed, Billy's playing style continues to evolve, which is yet another mark of a true musician. "I'm editing myself a lot more these days," he says. "I try not to play as much as I used to. If the song calls for something tricky, I know I've got the gas to get it done."

I don't spend nearly as much time in Gravity Strings as I used to. But when I do go in, Billy is almost always there to greet me with a warm smile and a huge, nearly blackout-inducing embrace. Our conversations pick up like they never ended, even if I haven't seen him in months. He's still going at it, day in and day out. He sells gear, he records, he gigs. That is the life of Billy Barnett. He doesn't lament his lack of fame. "I may not get paid back for my efforts in this life," he says. "But maybe I will in the next one. I'm still playing, so there's still a chance something will happen." And so, on he goes.

I don't see it changing any time soon.

Jimmy Griffin

THE ROCK STAR

Thanks to Jimmy Griffin, I can say I know someone featured in a video on MTV. Granted, I didn't know him at the time, and the video had long since gone by the wayside by the time we met. But still …

Like Billy, Jimmy is a musical "lifer." He will make this vocation work for him, come hell or high water. I've seen and heard him play in various guises and styles, but in the end, the sound is always Jimmy.

I think we get along so well because he embraces my desire to absorb all kinds of music. "That's one of the things that draws me to music (fans)," he said. "The people who really love music are a little bit … different. That's a beautiful thing, and the beauty of music. It accepts you. It draws you in. It binds to you."

Jimmy is only a couple of years younger than me, so in many ways, I feel like I grew up with him. Jimmy's six-foot, two-inch lanky frame could easily have been covered with a plaid flannel shirt, opened to reveal the latest concert t-shirt from Rush, AC/DC, or Black Sabbath. It's not even a remote stretch to imagine my friend in bell-bottom jeans and big, chunky Colorado hiking boots. His mop of neck-length black hair always looked as though he'd just rolled out of bed. By the time we met, it was easy to imagine him playing in a band like Nine Inch Nails, grinding away on an Industrial guitar part in between stage dives.

But as a musician, Jimmy is much more. I love watching his eyes light up when we talk about artists like Johnny Cash or Tom Petty. He plays in El Monstero, one of the best-known Pink Floyd tribute bands in the Midwest, and Celebration Day, a remarkable Led Zeppelin tribute band. And even with all that heaviness under his belt, Jimmy had a great sense of intelligent pop, as he and I are the two biggest Michael Penn fans I know, outside of Aimee Mann. (4)

That sense of intelligent pop reveals itself best within the confines of Jimmy's band, the Incurables. Albums like *Songs for a Blackout* and *The Fine Art of Distilling* allow Jimmy to channel his inner Penn in a husky tenor, singing songs of love, life, and loss. It's music that should be played on radios nationwide. Once again, justice has failed to assert itself.

Of all the musicians I know and call friends, Jimmy was the closest to the myth non-musicians refer to as "making it." In the early 90s, his band – called King of the Hill – was signed to SBK records, enjoying all the spoils that came with it. This included shooting a music video called "I Do You," which has the feel of late '80s hair metal colliding with horn-induced funk.

Had I still been in America at the time, I probably would have seen the video on MTV. Jimmy was 19 when he joined King of the Hill. By age 22, he'd made his MTV appearance. "I had gone from what I thought was the pinnacle of fame to being done by age 23," he told me. "As a kid, that's what I wanted. I wanted to be on MTV. I wanted to be a rock star."

I had known Jimmy for years before I even found out about King of the Hill. It was a while longer before I saw the video. I couldn't believe I actually knew someone that had been on the channel that occupied a great deal of my early- to mid-'80s time. But there was Jimmy Griffin in all his glory, singing backup vocals and blazing away on his guitar. His jet-black hair was considerably longer, but I had no problem recognizing him as he wailed and ground away on his guitar, sometimes against a large stack of Marshall amplifiers and speaker cabinets. They were the moves of a rock star. I couldn't help but smile.

Jimmy's appearance on MTV taught me the third cruel lesson of the music industry: *Fame, such as it is, is fleeting.*

It's a common misconception that a band appearing on MTV or another international medium has "made it," and nothing but fame and good fortune awaits. King of the Hill was touring Europe, eating catered food, and enjoying the spoils of that level of near-stardom. So, what happened?

"Grunge," Jimmy said flatly. "Grunge happened."

While the '90s musical style that produced Pearl Jam and Nirvana was fine by my friend, it proved to be his band's undoing. "Things literally changed overnight," he told me. "Our band was cool when we left for Europe. The whole band was in a hotel room in England together when Nirvana's 'Smells like Teen Spirit' video came on. I remember saying, 'Man, they listen to some pretty cool shit over here.' Somebody said to me, 'Dude, that's like the number three record in America right now.' By the time we got back, everyone was wearing Doc Martens, they cut their hair, and had tribal tattoos. King of the Hill had already established its sound. (our) look and sound were now completely uncool."

So, Jimmy came back home, and ground it out around St. Louis (after spending a year in Miami), like so many other musicians. He worked a series of day jobs in guitar shops, like so many other musicians. He played in a ton of bands, like so many other musicians. And he's in it for the long haul, like so many other musicians. Now that his moment of international fame had come and gone, his focus shifted, and he developed new ambitions. It became less about the popularity of the music, and more about its variety and quality. "I've played in punk bands, hip-hop bands, and Americana bands," he said. "I've liked all the things I was doing. I've made good music with good people."

The King of the Hill experience taught Jimmy about the different levels of the rock and roll lifestyle. As a burgeoning rock star in his early 20s, Jimmy experienced the royal treatment that came from touring on a bus. "When we got on the bus (after a show), 80 percent of the time we were headed to the next gig," he said. "That meant you got to stay up, play video games, smoke a little weed, then go to bed. When you woke up, you were in the town you were playing in next. You checked into a nice hotel, showered, ate free food, hung out all day, and got to the venue in time for sound check. We were opening for Extreme, so that meant we played for about 45 minutes, and then repeated the cycle."

The scaled-down life of traveling in a van was much different. Jimmy did this while working as a guitar tech for Jay Farrar, who played in a band called Uncle Tupelo. The group made its mark throughout the Midwest. "Riding in a van in your 30s is a *lot* harder," Jimmy said, laughing. "You're up at eight and driving until three. Then you load in the gear and set it up, do a sound check, eat something, the doors open at seven, you're on around 10 (since Farrar's band was headlining), you're off at midnight, and packing up the gear until about one. Then you go to a cheap hotel and start over the next day." Griffin also learned the importance of saving money by using a van, as opposed to a tour bus. "King of the Hill spent about $15,000 a week on the road," he said. "We were only making about $4,000. But we didn't care, because we were kids!"

Griffin remembers traveling in the Farrar van, and thinking back to how King of the Hill made fun of bands traveling that way. "We said we weren't gonna ride around in a van like a bunch of fuckin' losers!" Jimmy said, laughing at himself. King of the Hill wound up almost $2 million in debt. Whereas the Farrar tour actually *made* money.

When I met Jimmy, he was playing in a band called Neptune Crush. That band's sound reminds me of a hybrid between Nine Inch Nails and Nirvana, with a touch of glam thrown in for good measure. I still break that self-titled CD out now and then. It never fails to entertain. Not long after, he was part of an Americana band called Nadine. And then there were the tribute bands, which continue to keep him busy.

Jimmy and I don't always see eye to eye, musically. Our debates are spirited, passionate, and fun. Eventually, I learned the secret to introducing Jimmy to a band I liked: they had to have a singer. Instrumentals were simply *not* his thing. Without fail, I would start chattering away about a new band I was digging, and I would be eager to share a sample of that group's music via YouTube. "Does it have a vocal?" Jimmy would ask me with a grin. I would feign a huge groan and grin back. "YES, Jimmy! It has a damned vocal!" And then we could sample and talk about the band.

My friend was kind enough to break his "no instrumentals" rule when he recorded a guitar solo for a song I wrote called "Trouble Looms on the Horizon." The song appears on my band's CD. What I remember most about that appearance is the fact that Jimmy used my primary guitar – a '96 Fender Stratocaster – to record the solo. It sounded like a completely different instrument in his hands! That speaks volumes to the power of his abilities.

Like many others, Jimmy expresses annoyance at the modern aspects of music consumption. Specifically, the lack of money exchanging hands for musical efforts. I thought it might be something the music business could be held responsible for. "I don't think it's the industry," he replied. "I blame the people. They say, 'I want my music for free.' I buy software to record my music, and these young people look at me and go, 'Dude why did you pay for that? You could've gotten a cracked version for free.' It's happening throughout the entertainment industry in general. People are so de-sensitized by it all at this point. It used to be going to see a band was something special. Now there's somebody making music every ten feet, usually with a computer!" Still, he finds a way to remain optimistic throughout the modern changes. And he continues to make himself a part of the scene.

Like the others in the shop, Jimmy has had his share of brushes with famous people in the music industry. And like the rest of them, he doesn't like to talk about it very much. He mentions briefly holding Brian May's guitar at the Hammersmith Odeon in London. The Queen guitarist was jamming with Extreme, and Jimmy had become friendly with May's tech. "I strummed an A chord, and put (the guitar) right back in the case!" Jimmy said. "I just kept picturing myself falling down and breaking it." Ultimately, he sums up his encounters with famous musicians simply. "They're just people," he says.

Two decades have passed since Jimmy and I met. The aspiring rock star has become a husband and – very recently – a father. It's not really about fame any more. "The main thing is to be able to continue doing this, and have fun doing it," he said with a wistful smile. "That, to me, is success at this point And I'd like to see other people do my songs."

I've seen Jimmy perform almost as much as Billy, but in more contexts. But each performance – be it solo, with Neptune Crush, with Petty/Cash junction, or with the Incurables –has one thing in common: anyone coming to watch my friend does so with a sense of awe and reverence reserved for rock stars.

As well they should.

David Smith

THE PROFESSOR

Of all the guys in Gravity Strings, David Smith and I came closest to sharing musical DNA. If I liked a band or song, there was a very good chance Dave liked it, too. There were times we would find ourselves trying to introduce one another to an obscure track, only to find that we both already knew and liked the song.

Our primary shared interest was progressive rock. This seemed perfectly appropriate, as Dave's mop of hair and eyeglasses made him resemble King Crimson founder Robert Fripp. Dave and I could talk endlessly about odd time signatures, lengthy instrumental passages, and unorthodox guitar solos. He was the music teacher I wish I'd had in school.

Dave found his way to J Gravity Strings by way of another guitar shop in town. At that store, he was well paid for his efforts. But dealing with the personalities of his bosses became too much. He came to Jimmy Gravity, hoping to find a job. "My interview consisted of Jimmy asking me, 'Are you tired of (the other place)?' and me saying yes. Then Gravity says, 'Well, let's go across the street.' There was a McDonalds there back then. And we had lunch." Dave started on a probationary basis, working at Gravity Strings three days a week. But it didn't take long before he was managing the store.

I was aware of the quality vibe coming from the store. Dave knew exactly what I was talking about, and where it came from. "We're all good friends," he said of the people in the store. "It's almost a family situation. I'd seen all those people over the years in different places. I remember seeing Mike in his band, Fairchild, and Billy and I both went to (Southern Illinois University) in 1980. I remember him coming to my place, where

I put on a record by Pat Matheny called *American Garage*. I asked Billy if he knew about it. He picked up my guitar and started *playing* it! So I guess he knew it pretty well."

I never doubted Dave's abilities as a guitarist, even though of all the people working at Gravity, he was the one I heard play the least. His primary gig at the time was with a wedding band called Spectrum. Like most groups, they played just about anything under the sun. For a time, Dave also took on the role of the Edge in a U2 tribute band. We spent more than a few hours discussing just what went in to making the Edge sound like the Edge. I was never bored.

I did a lot of my actual gear shopping when Dave was working, because his honesty was precisely what I needed. He knew what I was into, and had no issue with steering me away from a piece of gear I thought I wanted or needed. That's saying something for a man who received a commission on what he sold! Anyone more interested in making me musically happy than turning a buck was all right with me. It got to the point where I would pick up an effects pedal or guitar, walk it over to Dave, and say, "Talk me out of buying this." And he would, without hesitating.

My trust in him was unwavering. This stemmed from his understanding how to approach people. "We have what we call the First Rug Rule in the store," he told me. "Jimmy would buy these area rugs from flea markets and what not and put them on the (showroom) floor. When people came in, we gave them the first rug to "take everything in." Once they moved past that rug, I would gently approach them." The method seems to work. "I've never seen anyone get mad, or storm out of the store," Dave said. "Well, maybe three or four times in 20 years. But that's a helluva success rate!"

The success comes from the quality of work done by Gravity and Mike Newman. "Jimmy is the best repair guy in four states, easy," Dave said with a sense of awe. He also seems convinced the boss will never actually retire. "Jimmy is gonna die behind that bench," Dave said, referring to his boss's sense of focus and dedication. I mention it would probably happen right after Gravity completed the very last detail on the very last repair job. Dave laughed at the notion. "That would be perfect!"

Dave was the primary sales face at Gravity Strings when I hung out there. Because of this, he had to deal with all kinds of people walking in to the store. These people came in with all kinds of questions. "I'd get asked, 'What's the best guitar you have in the store?'" Dave said. "I'd say, 'I'm sorry, but I can't show it to you. It costs $35,000.' Or they say something like they want to play the same guitar as Eric Clapton. I have to ask; do you mean when he played with Cream? Or his Strat from the '70s? Or his (Gibson) 335? It's not that they're ignorant. They're just uninformed."

The same problem crops up when people come in for repairs. "You have to gently school them," Dave said. "You don't treat them like they're ignorant. By the same token, there are guys who come in here knowing as much as I do about repairs, if not more." But conflicts are few and far between. "Because of the nature of the business, and the ambience of the place, people are usually very comfortable," he said. "And we always remind ourselves that the customer may not always be right, but he *is* always the customer."

Dave's musical knowledge was something I fed off for a very long time, be it in sales or musical knowledge. Rare was the day we would talk about a complex piece of music when I wouldn't learn something. We were both huge fans of vintage Genesis, in general, and the opus "Supper's Ready," in particular. I complained to him more than once that I had trouble counting the "Apocalypse in 9/8" section of that song, which made me crazy because it was my favorite part. Patiently (and more than once), Dave would walk me through it. "The trick is in the off-beats," he told me. "You have to count them out loud until you have it. It's one-two-three-AND one-two-AND one-AND, over and over." Eventually, the concept sank in, and I was able to take my enjoyment of the section to a whole new level, because now I truly understood the rhythmic complexity.

Dave's approach to music may seem academic on the surface, but underneath lies a great deal of soul. I'm sure of this despite the lack of hearing him play. He admits to being blown away with Billy's skills to the point where he doesn't see the point in playing, too. "He'll try out these new strings, and just blaze away," Dave says. "Then he'll try to hand the guitar to me and say, 'Here. Try these.' I'm like, no, that's okay. I'll take your word for it."

Even during the time he demonstrated gear for customers, he kept things brief. "I would never play for more than 30 seconds," Dave says. "And I would never try to show up anyone looking to buy something." His technique seems to work. I've seen people buy things within seconds of Dave's demonstration. And the customer walks out with a big smile on his face.

Dave struck me as a guy more interested in chasing his musical muse than any form of fortune and glory. Given our mutual love for prog, that makes perfect sense. The value of the musical note, to us, goes far beyond anything monetary. Dave was truly in it for the art. His is a rare type, indeed.

Mike Newman

THE JUKEBOX

It was pretty much a given that each staff member at Gravity Strings was a talented musician. It's one thing for a customer to admire the abilities of one of the guys working there. It's something else entirely for one staff member to inspire awe from another, especially when they're around each other most every day. It's not something you see all the time. In fact, I only saw it once.

I was in the front of the store, having one of my chats with Jimmy Griffin. Meanwhile, Mike Newman – one of the two occupants of that mythical, mysterious back room – was doing one of his many daily guitar set-ups and repairs. Before long, Mike started strumming a few chords, to the point where we could tell he was working on a 12-string electric guitar. Jimmy and I continued to talk. Suddenly, Mike started playing a note-for-note perfect solo I recognized as George Harrison's seminal moment in the Beatles' "A Hard Day's Night." From there, Mike continued to riff on something of his own, firing his way up and down the guitar's fretboard.

Jimmy and I stopped talking and were now both staring at the doorway leading to where Mike riffed away. I'm pretty sure both of our mouths were open. Eventually, we turned to face each other again, and I saw Jimmy mouth the most supreme compliment one musician gives another.

"Mother*fucker!*" Jimmy mimed, shaking his head and smiling broadly. I couldn't help but laugh, because I knew exactly what he meant.

Not long after, I invited Mike to play at my neighborhood's block party. I didn't put forth any rules, other than show up and have a good time. Mike showed up with just an acoustic guitar, leading me to wonder if that would be enough to entertain the people milling about. I needn't have worried. Using just his voice and hands, Mike Newman put forth a cavalcade of hits, spanning from the '60s though the 21st century. I heard songs from the Beatles, Stevie Wonder, and countless others, sung with gusto and perfection. It was a sight and sound to behold. *My God*, I thought. *This guy is a one-man jukebox.*

You wouldn't know that by looking at the man. In the dictionary under the word "unassuming" sits a picture of Mike Newman. He has face and stature of an "everyman," putting one at ease almost immediately. He's the kind of guy you start a casual conversation with in a bar and realize an hour or two later you've been talking to one another the entire time.

I mentioned to Mike how impressed I was with his musical vocabulary. He just gave me a sheepish grin. "I suppose that's what happens when you've been playing the guitar for 50 years," he said. I just knew his math was wrong. But Mike is a little older than me, and I was pushing 50 at the time of our conversation. Damn! I guess he's right!

Mike started playing guitar at 13, mostly out of desire to join in with his peers. He was the kid who listened to the radio all night and took his guitar to bed with him. And like so many others, he was deeply influenced by the British Invasion of the mid-'60s. By '65, he was playing in his first band.

Nothing other than playing guitar mattered to Mike. "I stopped going to the roller rink, and spent all my time practicing," he said. "No sports. I had tunnel vision. This is what I wanted to do. It brought joy to my heart. It felt right." He honed is chops further by playing fraternity parties, church dances, and Teen Town gigs. "I learned a lot playing those shows," he said. "They were good for me." But like so many other musicians, Mike found it difficult to make a living doing what he loved. Ultimately, he found himself selling heating and air conditioning units on the road.

There was a dramatic shift in '78, when Mike got a call from a friend named Dan, who asked if Mike was available to play in his band. They had a month's worth of club gigs lined up, but that was just the beginning. "Dan told me I was going to need to rehearse, because in a month, we would be opening for Robert Palmer at the Keil (Opera House)," Mike said. So the band – called Fairchild – became Mike's top priority, air conditioners be damned. He played gigs with the band for free, just so he could learn. By the time the Robert Palmer show came, he was ready.

Mike laughs at the memory of seeing Robert Palmer that fateful evening. "He got out of his limo wearing this immaculate blue suit," he said. "And then came on stage wearing a pair of jeans and a t-shirt." As for his work with Fairchild, things went very well. So well, in fact, Mike stayed with the band for the next 30 years. When the band broke up, Mike found he couldn't bring himself to stop playing. So he continued as a solo artist, playing mostly solo acoustic gigs. The work continues to satisfy him. Plus, he was able to pick up another skill.

A little after he joined Fairchild, Mike met Jimmy Gravity at R & D Music, where Jimmy replaced the pickups in Mike's guitar, and shaved down its neck. This opened up an entirely new avenue of self-exploration and education for Mike. When Jimmy opened up his own shop a short time later, Mike followed him. "I had to make myself a part of (what Jimmy was involved in)," Mike said. The two started a friendship that continues to grow. "He's as close to me as anyone else in the world," Mike said.

Mike eventually found himself employed at J Gravity Strings. First, he was a sales associate. Then in '97, Mike took his place by Jimmy's side (well, across from him anyway) in the repair shop. They have been two peas in a pod ever since. They are a universal constant. Water is wet. The sky is blue. And Mike and Jimmy will fix your broken guitars, making them sound better than ever.

Mike takes his job seriously, to the point of personally. He understands the intimate relationship between a musician and his instrument. "When I set up a guitar, I set it up so I *know* I can pick it up and play it," he said. This statement seems obvious, but that intimate relationship makes the task far more difficult than it seems. "We know we're not just working on someone's guitar. We're working on their psyche. If the instrument isn't right, then the musician isn't right. So we want them to leave with *exactly* what they want."

There is another added benefit to the time Mike spends behind the desk. He beams when he tells me about it. "I get to practice every day," he says. This makes sense, because he has to make sure the guitars are playing properly before he returns them to their owners. Needless to say, the guitars and basses undergo extensive testing. "*And* I get to listen to other people play all day. I actually get paid to do that."

Mike's laughter is infectious.

THE BOSS

At first glance, Jimmy Gravity doesn't strike me as the kind of guy who owns and operates a guitar shop. If I saw him on the street, I would be pretty confident he worked with his hands. But I would also be certain he was building houses, pouring concrete, or welding large beams of steel together. Well, Jimmy Gravity does work with his hands. But he's rebuilding guitars, pouring his heart and soul into delicate necks, and soldering electronic wiring. His are the hands of a surgeon.

I wasn't sure who Jimmy was the first time I saw him. His face can wear the kind of gruff expression that dares some unfortunate soul to test him. And while not particularly tall, his muscular frame is as hard as a coffin nail. I don't know what gym Jimmy Gravity goes to, but I'm pretty sure he lifts at least half of it.

That gruff expression prevented me from going to the back room for a long time, even when I was invited. But my trepidation was unfounded. You would be lucky to meet a kinder soul than Jimmy Gravity. He'd give you the shirt off his back. He's the only person on this planet who can call me "Cedsie," and have me not only smile in reply, but welcome the name when I hear it. What would annoy me coming from anyone else is a badge of honor coming from Jimmy.

It's fascinating to watch this man work. Jimmy Gravity is a study in focus. I've watched the man sand away deficiencies in guitar bodies, set and repair broken necks, add just the right amount of glue to a 50-year-old instrument in dire need of repair, and file a fret to within a millimeter of its life. I've lost track of how many instruments I've watched him work on over the years. I'm quite certain he lost count long, long ago. Mike Newman estimates he and Gravity have worked on an average of 2,000 instruments a year. Multiply that by three or four decades, and it adds up to a *lot*.

It's one thing to be a music fan. It's something else entirely to stretch that passion into playing an instrument. Jimmy has the drive and energy to repair instrument after instrument once it comes into his shop. It's a different level of commitment altogether. Jimmy has had that level of commitment for more than 40 years.

Jimmy Gravity (not his real name, but it is as far as everyone else is concerned) found that focus not long after coming out of the military in 1970. He had already been playing guitar since age 11, influenced largely (surprise, surprise) by the Beatles. After the service, Gravity took his musical ambitions as far as Niagara Falls, where he went to play in a band with friends. During that time, he discovered he had a knack for repairing instruments. Save for some time spent at the St. Louis Institute of Music, he is largely self-taught, as there were not a lot of manuals (except for one Japanese book he read repeatedly) to rely on. Instead, Gravity relied on the scientific methods known as "Trial and Error" and "Learning by Rote."

Gravity is the epitome of the self-made man. His career path is that of one driven to make it on his own. Perhaps that's where his gruff exterior and intense focus come from. He's had many business partners over the years, and speaks of each of them glowingly. But in the end, Gravity is his own man. Make no mistake about it. His work with partners lasted between '71 and '78. I think of that time as his apprenticeship. Now, he is the master.

I came into the store one day to find Jimmy working diligently on a mandolin. He wasn't being particularly chatty (which happens from time time), so rather than engage in small talk, I made my way back to the main showroom. Dave wasted no time walking over to me. "Did you see what he was working on?" he asked me.

"Yeah," I replied, thinking nothing of it. "It was a mandolin."

"But do you know who it belongs to?"

I shrugged a no, and Dave showed me the box Jimmy would use to ship the instrument once it was done. It was headed to Athens, Georgia, I saw. Then I noticed the three letters near the top of the address. They read "R.E.M." Dave smiled at me.

"It's Peter Buck's mandolin," Dave said proudly. "Pretty cool, huh?" I nodded in enthusiastic agreement.

Another time, I was doing the old "cock and bull" with Dave, Billy, and Jimmy Griffin when a gentleman walked in carrying a bass guitar case. He looked older, perhaps in his mid-to late 50's, with a well-worn face, a mop of unkempt black hair similar to Jimmy's and a goatee. There was no doubt this guy had been around. Jimmy saw him first, and his eyes lit up. Before anyone could say anything, Jimmy was waiting on the gentleman. When the man spoke, I detected an English accent. He was showing Jimmy a well-worn Fender Precision bass guitar. Shortly after, Griffin raced past us to the back. Within seconds, Jimmy Griffin was making his way to the showroom, where he greeted his customer warmly, and listened to Englishman's needs. Griffin, meanwhile, had slowly made his way back to our group.

It was clear Griffin was excited about something, but damned if Dave, Billy, or I knew what. Finally, Griffin said, "Do you guys know who that is?" We stared back at him blankly. "It's Geezer!" he said excitedly. Poor Jimmy continued to receive blank stares. "*Geezer Butler!*" Nothing. I thought Griffin might have a stroke. "From BLACK SABBATH!" And then we caught on. To a man, we all mouthed, "Ohhhhh," and stared over to where the bassist and the Boss were talking. Geezer must have felt us looking, because he turned toward us and waved. We all grinned and waved back. It was one of those moments I thought only took place in a sitcom.

It really doesn't matter whose instrument Gravity is working on. He treats it like one of his own. "I've worked on the guitars of some super players," he told me. "When I would go to work on their instruments, they were unplayable (by normal standards)!" Or so it seemed. Even without extended "formal" training, Gravity's approach to guitar repair is very academic. "I have a logical brain. I like to look at an instrument and figure out what I need to do to it," he said.

Apparently, Gravity is doing the job correctly. His list of satisfied customers is endless. The only person not happy with the work is Gravity himself. He has a mile-wide perfectionist streak. "People will come up to me and say, 'Man, you really made my guitar sound good.' That's nice, but I'll be thinking of all the things I didn't do when I had the chance."

He'll have plenty of opportunities to practice. The store is positively littered with guitars, basses, mandolins, and other stringed instruments in various states of disrepair. Gravity told me if he stopped taking new repair jobs today, he'd still need two to three years to complete all the repairs he has planned and sell everything off.

And then there's String Man.

I've been in and out of the Gravity Strings repair shop so often, I've stopped seeing the boxes and boxes of used guitar strings lying about. But they're everywhere, and Gravity has a plan for them. "I'm gonna make a String Man (sculpture) out of all of them," he says of the miles of used wire. "There's a ton of voodoo in that pile."

Gravity is enamored with the music business. Doing repairs is his way of being a part of it. "Being in a band was not my calling. But I'm still welcome backstage," he said. "I want to make sure the musician is confident in his gear. It's nice to see people waiting to talk to a musician as he comes offstage, but the musician goes past them, because he is eager to talk to me."

To be certain, Gravity is the Boss. But to his employees, he's more like a father. He sees his guitar shop as a family-run business. "Profits take second place to family," he said. As he spoke, I was able to briefly see through the gruff exterior, and directly into the heart of one of the kindest people I've ever met. "My goal is for the people who work for me to make it to Social Security. Then I can think about closing or selling off the shop (and retiring)."

The man's heart knows no bounds.

***

As it turns out, visits from well-known musicians are rather commonplace at Gravity Strings. The guys are by no means jaded by these encounters. Nevertheless, it makes for an interesting job perk. Dave told me a story about being eager to close the store one day, when the phone rang just before closing time. The caller wanted to know what time the store closed. When Dave informed the caller he locked up at six, a disappointed voice on the other end of the line asked, "Well, can't you stay open for a while longer? It's Jackson." A tired Dave didn't make any kind of connection, and curtly asked Jackson who? "It's Jackson Browne." David decided he could make time for a little after-hours shopping by a legendary singer/songwriter.

What amuses me is not the number of musical legends who have come through Gravity Strings, but the casual nature by which Jimmy Gravity rattles them off. "I've worked on a couple of basses for Van Halen," Gravity said casually. "Al Caldwell brought his bass here while he was working for Vanessa Williams. I've done some work for Bachman Turner Overdrive, Lenny Kravitz, Tom Petty, and AC/DC. I sold Danny Gatton a guitar, which he played in a video."

There were many others, but Gravity wasn't really interested in naming them. Sometimes, they don't even see the musicians. They see the musician's guitar techs. "We may not see the musician," Gravity says casually. "But we see his stuff." He talks about celebrity appearances in his store the way I talk about violent crime scenes. To outsiders, either of those things would be fascinating, and an endless source of conversation. To us, it's a Tuesday.

***

I haven't done the math, but I'm reasonably certain J. Gravity Strings' prices are five to ten percent higher than most other guitar shops. And you know what? That's just fine by me. It's worth it. I walk into a franchise guitar shop, and the employees barely seem to care. I walk into Gravity, and I feel like Norm walking into Cheers:

"Afternoon, everybody!"

"CED!!!"

It's nice to not have to explain my influences over and over again. It's nice to have a sales staff who not only knows me, but knows what makes me tick. There were days I would casually stroll into the store out of a lack of anything else to do. Billy, Dave, or Jimmy would have a new CD for me to listen to, a new article on one of my favorite musicians to read, or a new piece of gear. These things were never forced on me. They were merely shown. I don't know how many unintentional casual sales those guys made, but something tells me it was more than a few.

For a couple of years, Gravity Strings was actually on my patrol beat. (5) My guitar shop became an unofficial police sub-station, where I hand-wrote my accident reports and summonses until I was transferred a few years later. Jimmy Griffin used to tell customers who saw me sitting on one of the shop's bar stools scribbling away on one form or another, the store was my donut shop. "Only the glaze here is a helluva lot more expensive," he'd joke. Contrary to popular belief, I almost never picked up a guitar while I was in uniform. It's not because I didn't want to play. It's because I was deathly afraid of scratching up an instrument with my brass belt buckle.

My playing ground to a halt in 2007. Only recently have I decided to pick it up again. Alas, I've only wandered into J. Gravity Strings a scant few times in the past decade. Jimmy Griffin and Dave have moved on (6), but Billy is still there. That vice-like handshake and midsection-crushing bear hug is always waiting for me when I walk in. Jimmy Gravity and Mike are still in the back room, doing what they do best. Jimmy's baritone voice still bellows out, "How ya doin' there, Cedsie?" every time I come in. It never fails to make me smile. I find comfort in that level of consistency.

Gravity hinted he may be thinking about retiring soon. While I understand the desire to move on after 40-plus years, I hope he doesn't rush. Jimmy Gravity is an unsung hero. I'm willing to bet he and his staff have never been mentioned by name on stage by a prominent musician. But there can be no denying the influence these men have had on the thousands of people who have wandered into 1546 South Broadway. Whether they left with a brand-new instrument, a newly repaired instrument, an effects pedal, or just a good bit of advice, the customers of J. Gravity Strings saw their playing experience enhanced. Hopefully, more than one of those people took just a moment, looked up from his instrument, and said, "Thanks, guys."

I do it all the time.

(1)   More than a few people have tried to buy the guitars and amps in those windows. All have been quickly rebuffed. That gear is not for sale, now or ever. Period.

(2)   There is an interesting tale behind Tam's departure. But it's not my tale to tell. I can't tell you much more, because he was gone almost as quickly as I met him.

(3)   It doesn't get much more virtuoso than Petrucci, Jordan Rudess on keyboards, Tony Levin on bass and stick, and Mike Portnoy on drums. Their albums, *Liquid Tension Experiment* and *Liquid Tension Experiment 2*, are not to be missed.

(4)   Since Aimee is married to Michael, I'm not even sure that counts.

(5)   I called my on-duty visits to Gravity "therapy breaks." I would deal with a violent offense, a robbery, or some asinine call. Once that was done, I would head to the guitar shop, where I almost instantly relaxed and felt better about the world.

(6)   Jimmy Griffin now works at a shop called Killer
        Vintage, located in south St. Louis. Believe it or not, I
        patrol *that* area now. I've been known to take the
        occasional "therapy break" there. Jimmy and I chat like
        we never missed a beat.

*Thanks to gigs at more intimate venues, I've been
able to interact with the musicians I admire,
like legendary bassist Victor Wooten.*

Track 17
Up Close and Personal

Live music is the best.

Don't get me wrong: I have the utmost reverence and
admiration for studio records. The recording studio is a place of
awe and wonder, and musical miracles emerge from there all the
time. My media shelves are lined with these little miracles. I
cherish them, one and all.

There are certain musical feats that have no business on
a concert stage. I have trouble imagining the Beatles reproducing
Sgt. Pepper there. Todd Rundgren can't do everything himself in
a live setting. A lot of the best hip hop is captured in the studio,
and rarely translates perfectly to a live setting.

But the stage … man. There's just something about the
bandstand and how it pushes all the right buttons in my musical
soul.

From the time I walk into a concert venue, my heart
begins to race. Never mind the fact the band won't be occupying
the stage for at least an hour or two. The equipment is here! I'm
a big enough fan of certain bands to know what kind of musical
instruments and effects they prefer. So I can tell who's going to
be where on stage just by looking at the setup. The only thing
cooler than knowing Tony Levin will be standing *right there*, or

Vernon Reid will be picking up *that* guitar, or Mike Portnoy will soon be sitting behind *that* drum throne is when the musicians actually walk on stage. There's nothing else like it.

Playing live is the ultimate test of musical skill. There are no take-backs. There's no starting over. If the musician makes a mistake, he has to deal with it in real time. The musicians I admire take it a step further and eschew what they did in the studio in favor of spontaneous compositions (particularly during solos) right there on the stage. "Is this gonna work?" the musician wonders. "Can I pull this off? I guess there's only one way to find out!"

***

King Crimson founder Robert Fripp understands the elemental differences between studio and live recordings. He likes to view the studio recording as a "love letter," while a live recording is more like a "hot date." Both have benefits. But it's ultimately a question of what kind of thrill is the fan in the mood for.

In the recording studio, nearly every element of the session is controlled. There are few surprises. Musicians spend hours setting up their equipment and microphones so things sound just right. I've heard of recording sessions where the first day (usually 10 or 12 hours) is nothing more than the drummer setting up his gear and microphones, positioning everything to get just the right level of natural reverb. Baffles and sound absorbing panels are placed throughout the room to make the drums sound as "organic" as possible. Once this is done, the drummer himself comes in, and pounds on each and every drum until everything sounds perfect. Meanwhile, the producer and engineer sit in the studio's control room, twisting and turning the dials on the multi-track recorder until they hear the perfect "thwack" and "thump" from each of the drums. Once this is done, the other musicians come in, and the process repeats.

On stage, the soundman's job is more challenging. He must adjust to the ambient conditions of each new room. He has to hope the bodies there to see the show absorb sound just the way he planned. He has to accept the background noise of chattering fans, where once there was silence. He has to make the band loud enough to be heard, but not so loud it deafens the audience. It's a delicate balance, and it frequently needs to be adjusted on the fly.

For the musician, the challenge can be even more daunting. The studio provides a perfectly controlled environment. Nothing is left to chance. The musician can bring as many guitars, basses, keyboards, drums, and amplifiers as he deems necessary to capture the right sound. If something goes wrong, all he needs to do is grab another instrument and keep moving forward. After getting a do-over, of course. Speaking of do-overs, the musician is free to use as many takes as needed to capture just the right sound. When all else fails, a good engineer will be able to edit together the best sounds of multiple takes and make everything sound just right.

On stage, it's a different ball game. Musicians tend to bring only their two or three favorite guitars or basses. He must try to coax a relatively foreign sound out of a guitar that may not have been built for that purpose. Sometimes, a string breaks or a drumhead pops. This is rarely cause for a do-over. The musician must keep propelling the tune forward, as though he knew it was going to happen the whole time. These moments are met with either triumph or disaster, as Rudyard Kipling might say. Either way, it's going to happen in real time.

When Herbie Hancock played piano for Miles Davis, he recalled hearing Miles tell the members of the band, "I pay you to practice on the stage." On the surface, that sounds insane. You want to be perfect in front of the people, right? That's what they came to see! But Miles didn't see it that way. "Miles wanted the music to be as fresh as he thought it could be," Hancock said. Keyboardist Chick Corea said something similar about playing with Miles. "Our first gig was in Boston," Corea said. "I called Miles and asked him if there was going to be a rehearsal. He said, 'Nah. Just play what you hear.'" My stomach sank at the notion on Chick's behalf.

One chance to get it right: It doesn't get much more fun. I suppose that's easy for me to say, since I have always been on the viewing end rather than the performing one. But I can't recall seeing any of my favorite performers was having a rough time on stage. Things go wrong, to be certain. But I haven't seen anything catastrophic. Once, when I saw Adrian Belew perform live, something went wrong with his effects rig. He never verbalized it, but I've seen him perform enough to know he was irritated about something. But he got through it, and the show went on. I'm much more likely to see the smiles exchanged between band members when they know the music is cooking and everyone is firing on all cylinders. I've only had that thrill during rehearsals, but I know it's a rush. It goes straight to my head and manifests itself as the most ridiculous grin. It's a great place to be.

***

Concerts come in all shapes and sizes. My personal level of enjoyment is almost directly proportionate to the size of the venue. Even the band's performance can be tied into this factor. Here are the levels of concerts I've personally experienced, and the levels of enjoyment connected to them:

BAR/SMALL CLUB GIGS: Usually attended by 50 to 200 people. The band is usually unknown, but on the rise. Tickets for the show are relatively cheap, if there is any cost at all. The band is normally hungry, both figuratively and literally, and living hand-to-mouth, one gig at a time. They play with a level of ferocity and purpose almost guaranteed to garner attention. Few people know the band's original songs, so the set is peppered with covers within the same musical genre wherever possible. Interactions with fans are frequent and meaningful, as the group is trying to build a following. Chances are, the band has an EP available for sale, with hopes of recording a full-length album with any money made from this tour. **Personal Excitement Level:** Maximum

CLUB GIGS: Attended by 200-1,000 people, depending on the size of the room. The bands playing here usually have a devoted cult following and at least one full-length album under their belts. Tickets aren't terribly expensive, and the band can usually afford a decent hotel (provided they share rooms) and at least one non-fast food meal a day. The band plays with the joy and energy saying they know who they are and what they're aiming for. They may even have a little label support behind them. They will play most of their new record, a smattering of that first EP, and maybe a cover or two. Club bands interact with the fans eagerly, as they understand the fickle nature of the music industry and want to maintain that positive rapport. In addition to CDs, you'll probably be able to purchase a t-shirt or baseball cap from this band. **Excitement Level:** High

THEATER GIGS: Attended by 1,000-3,500 people. This band is either getting its first taste of the big time, or is scaling back from its previous major success. Ticket prices are not unreasonable, but may require advance planning on the fan's behalf. The band has released at least three albums, and there is one hit song they play at every gig none of them really wants to perform any more. But they play it, because they want to maintain their momentum. Chances are, they have a tour bus and spend at least a few hours a day in a decent hotel. They know where the decent restaurants are and try to catch a meal there either before or right after the gig, before they pile back on the bus and head to the next town. The music is still played with passion, with the emphasis on the catalog that helped make them what they are. The band will sneak in new music here and there, just to remind fans there is more to them than "The Hit." Fan interaction will consist of at least half the band, but usually not all of them. The encounters will be brief, regardless. CDs, hats, t-shirts, and other swag (like coffee mugs and key chains) will be available from a well-stocked merchandise table. **Excitement Level:** Moderate to Good

ARENA/AMPHITHEATER GIGS: Attended by 3,500-20,000 people, depending on the venue. This band has arrived! They have a decent-sized following and a solid catalog of at least four albums, and possibly a "Greatest Hits" set. They've been on the radio more than once, and fans are getting tired of that one song. Tickets are a little pricey, meaning only true fans will seek them out. The band is trying to convey a sense of fun, but it's getting harder, since barricades and security personnel are keeping them separate from the audience. The band got here via a really nice tour bus, with the road crew riding in separately. Sometimes, the lead singer flies in separately from the rest of the band. Meals are no problem, since the band probably has a chef on the payroll. The bands set will focus on hits, with a new song sprinkled in here and there. Fan interaction will only be possible via special VIP passes, which will add another $50 to the price of a ticket. Even then, the encounter will be little more than a quick handshake and/or a picture. A staff member staring intently at his watch will monitor the encounter. Nobody gets much time with the musician. The meeting has all the charm and ambience of an assembly line. **Excitement Level:** Low, at best

STADIUM GIGS: Attended by 20,000 or more. This is the band at its most self-indulgent. Ticket prices in the hundreds of dollars are necessary to finance the massive stage, adjoining set, video monitors, custom light show, and pyrotechnics. After paying all that money, it will be a miracle to see the band on stage without binoculars. The band might have a new album, but it will largely be ignored, since this throng of people came to hear their favorite songs from the band's massive back catalog. The biggest surprise will be the group digging out a rarely played chestnut from the very first record. Chances are, the band flew into town on a chartered or private plane, while the crew came in with a convoy of 18-wheelers. The hotels are top-shelf, with suites being the order of the day for the band members, even if they don't spend more than four or five hours there. The band employs a chef, a masseuse, a personal trainer, a publicist, and a life coach to help them get through those times when they can no longer stand one another. Encounters with the fans are extremely rare, and usually involve some kind of unattainable VIP pass or the smoking hotness of the fan in question. Anything holding band's name or signature logo is available for sale at one of the many merchandise tables located around the venue. Major credit cards will be accepted. **Excitement Level:** Zip. Nada. None.

***

Here is a universal constant of concert attendance: the bigger the venue, the less the band has to do with the event. Therefore, the less I will enjoy it. I'm sure there are exceptions to this rule. I'm just hard pressed to think of any.

Like pretty much everyone else, my first concert experiences were in large venues, like hockey arenas. I just assumed it was the way concerts were supposed to be seen and heard. Anyone playing a smaller room wasn't worth troubling myself with, right?

Well, wrong.

Concerts in larger venues are more social events than anything. The band is almost incidental. I've heard more than a few conversations from people who went to a stadium gig. The conversations go something like this:

"Dude, remember when we saw the Stones at the Big Stadium?"

"Aw, man! That was so awesome! I got totally wasted! And my girlfriend took her top off!"

"Yeah, and that couple in front of us? Were they out of control or what?"

"No kidding, dude! That was a killer show!"

The conversation goes on for another minute or two, but one thing is certain: barely a word is spoken about the band or its performance.

Conversely, a club gig has the fan babbling almost ceaselessly about the performance he just witnessed:

"Man, Living Colour tore the roof off the place last night! What a show!"

"Yeah, Vernon was on fire! And Corey really sang his ass off! The whole band was air tight from the get-go! They haven't lost a step after all these years! My ears are still ringing from being that close to the amps. But it was worth it!"

I suppose it's a question of priorities. For some people, a concert is about the people going and the party that ensues from it. Whether the band is good or bad – or even present for that matter – is just an added layer to a social event. The music has always been what mattered most to me. It is my primary focus. How well I was able to maintain that focus ultimately came down to the size of the room.

***

As it happens, the best and worst concert experiences I ever had (in terms of sound) both took place in Tokyo, Japan. I saw jazz guitarist Stanley Jordan perform at the Blue Note on my birthday in 1990. As gigs go, it was a good time. Jordan played incredibly well. Unbeknownst to me, the show was being recorded. It was released less than a year later as a live album called *Stolen Moments*, which made its way into my collection. (1) I saw Sting perform at Budokan, the venue made famous by Cheap Trick, who recorded their legendary '78 live album there. Sting's band (featuring guitarist Dominic Miller and drummer Vinnie Colaiuta) was remarkable, and our seats were decent, even though they were behind the stage. I almost felt like I was sitting on Vinnie's drum throne, and Sting made his way back to us on several occasions, making us feel like part of the show. It was a lot of fun.

The worst concert I ever attended was Billy Joel at the Tokyo Dome. This was my second time catching him (the first being at a hockey arena in St. Louis), and for the record, Joel bears NO fault in my poor experience. It was all about the room.

Tokyo Dome was home to the Yomiuri Giants, the legendary baseball team. They are the New York Yankees of Japan. The stadium is made of concrete, which does absolutely nothing to capture sound. In fact, it makes things ten times worse! Our seats were high up and way to the right of the stage. This meant the sound was projected *past* me, rather than toward me. Once said sound raced past, it ran into the big concrete wall at the back of the stadium, causing a horrible echo. (2)

From where I sat, I couldn't see drummer Liberty DeVito. But I could hear him. *Twice.* In rapid succession. During the *same* song! So instead of hearing his bass drum go, "Boom! Boom! Boom!" I was hearing "Boom! (boom!) Boom! (boom!) Boom! (boom!) It was *horrible*! My friends didn't seem to notice. Or they didn't care. It's been said more than once: few people listen to music the way I do. I was annoyed from the first note to the last, and it was a two-hour show. That was my last stadium gig.

The best sounding show I ever attended took place in a college auditorium I have long since forgotten the name of. I think it might be the Nippon Plaza Hall, where the 2003 version of King Crimson recorded a concert video called *Eyes Wide Open*. The show I saw was jazz based, featuring Herbie Hancock on piano, Wayne Shorter on sax, Stanley Clarke on bass, and Omar Hakim on drums. It was a powerhouse of musical talent. (3) And the sound of the room made it that much better.

The venue held about 1,500 people. The seats were angled stadium-style, so nobody had to suffer the indignity of looking at the back of someone's head during the show. Our seats were about halfway back, a good 25 yards off the stage. But we were in the middle, which was a good break. As I took my seat and examined the room, I noticed the way the ceiling was angled, which struck me as odd. I also noticed unusual-looking panels, about eight feet high and half as wide, lining the walls on either side. Once the show started, I forgot all about these things. In retrospect, they make complete sense.

My Japanese friend would tell me later the hall had been acoustically engineered. It was designed to house symphony orchestras and chamber musicians. The ceiling was angled to reflect the sound toward the sidewalls. The panels I saw were sound baffles, designed to absorb excess noise. The same things can be found in the finest recording studios. Within the confines of this venue, the same principles had merely been extended into a larger space.

The sound of the band was absolutely *perfect*. I could hear every note from each musician with crystal clarity. It sounded like I turned the volume of my stereo up just a little higher than usual. But the extra volume was distributed throughout the hall in such a way that it was impossible to complain. Was the gig 90 minutes long? Two hours? I honestly don't remember. I just know I didn't want it to end. I've never heard a concert like that before or since.

***

I have reached the stage where I despise seeing concerts in large venues. Anything larger than a small theater, and you can probably count me out. It wasn't always this way. There was a time when I did my best to make a big room work for me.

At the Hollywood Casino Amphitheater (4), the trick was, quite simply, to buy tickets early, or on the day of show. This got me my 11th row tickets for Dave Matthews, a few weeks after I was in the third row for the H.O.R.D.E. festival, where I saw King Crimson. Of course, this plan has also backfired on me. But I'll get back to that.

At Scottrade Center (the home of the St. Louis Blues hockey team), I defeated the rush of people standing on the floor by staying away from them, and standing in front of the mixing board, which was back at about center ice. I could see the band just fine without dealing with the crush of humanity, and I was centered between the PA speakers, so I could hear everything perfectly as well. Of course, the mix was almost always a bit too loud. But what the hell … it *is* a hockey arena.

At the Fox Theater (now the outside limit of my tolerance), being on the floor level is fine. But if that fails, a seat along the railing on the balcony level works just as well. It was from there I enjoyed Australian Pink Floyd. Admittedly, I've passed up on a couple of choice gigs, like Jeff Beck and Return to Forever, when they played this venue. I just like being closer to the artist. If I have to sit way back, I may as well buy a DVD. It's cheaper than a ticket, I can see the show as many times as I want, the views are better, and there's no line for the bathroom.

As it stands, The Pageant works just fine for me. It's bigger than a small room, but not too big. The sound can be controlled, although a few have failed in their attempt. There are no really bad views of the stage, and I'm pretty sure I've covered just about every angle. It's not necessary to get right on top of the stage for a good experience. And getting in and out of the venue is relatively easy. I've seen acts as diverse as Medeski, Martin, and Wood, Aimee Mann, and Jeff Beck in that building. It's a cool place to catch a gig. But it's no Mississippi Nights.

***

Without a doubt, Mississippi nights was THE concert venue in St. Louis, particularly during the '80s and '90s. It can safely be said anybody who became somebody in music played that room. The club was situated just west of the Mississippi River, on Laclede's Landing. It's walls were quite literally littered with the faces who played there: Stevie Ray Vaughan, Wynton Marsalis, Midnight Oil, the Black Keys, Joan Jett, My Morning Jacket … and so on and so on. My God, how I loved the place.

Yet if you pinned me down and forced me to answer the question, "What was so special about Mississippi Nights?" I don't think I could come up with any one specific answer.

On the surface, there was nothing special about the club. It held about 1,000 people, give or take. There was seating available on either side of the large, open floor plan, or from the middle of the room back. For the best view, you had to stand. There was a bar on one side of the club, and another toward the back. The lighting in the place was subpar, at best. But what did you really need to see other than the band on stage?

There was nothing distinctive about anything in the club. But it had a *vibe*. It could be felt from the instant I walked through the dual sets of double doors. Something special was about to happen in that room. I just *knew* it! For that matter, so did everyone else. Any band playing there seemed to raise its game a notch or two while on the Mississippi Nights stage. It was the perfect combination of location, ambience, audience, and music. Everything met in harmonic convergence at 914 North First Street.

Vernon Reid. Paula Cole. Me'shell N'degeocello. Morphine. Ozric Tentacles. Chris Duarte. John Scofield. Gov't Mule. Buckethead. I saw a lot of quality acts at Mississippi Nights. I'd still be seeing them had The Pageant not taken its place in '07. I'm still feeling that loss.

***

In the late '90s, Laclede's Landing was a great place to check out bands on a nightly basis. As it happens, my job actually accommodated my club hopping. My shift hours rotated between 10 a.m. to 6 p.m. and 6 p.m. to 2 a.m. every three weeks. During my time on "days," I was free to catch a shower, have dinner, and make my way to the club of my choosing. The shows usually started at around 8, and could run as late as 1 a.m. Even if I stayed until closing time, I could be home in bed by 2, which allowed me to sleep until 8:30 and wake up fresh as a daisy for my next shift. Being single helped as well.

Mississippi Nights was the club of choice on the Landing, but that was where the "name" acts played. There were other clubs in the immediate area featuring local acts. I can't count the number of times I wandered into Kennedy's or the Trainwreck Saloon, paid my cover charge, ordered a Diet Coke (5), and found a nice spot in the corner to enjoy the band of the day. Sometimes, I was watching a cover band recreate the

Grunge hits of the day. Other times, I was fortunate enough to catch an exciting young band on the rise.

The clubs on Laclede's Landing afforded me the opportunity to see bands like New World Spirits, the Love Hogs, Great Big Everything, Sinister Dane, Tuff Nutz, Sky Bop Fly, and the Urge. Some of these bands were able to score major record deals. Others eventually collapsed. At least one of them – the Urge – is still out there, on a part-time basis, plugging away for their legions of fans. (6) Nearly all the musicians in those bands are still out there, playing gigs, in other groups. The desire to make music never dies, even if the band they're playing in does.

If there was nothing happening on Laclede's Landing, I could make my way west into Downtown, where I could hang out at the Galaxy or the Creepy Crawl. More than a few up-and-coming acts (like Radiohead) played the Galaxy. It had the feel of a grungy dive bar, but there was no denying the musical vibe and energy coming from that room. The Creepy Crawl was even grimier, to the point where I questioned whether or not I should actually sit in one of its chairs. But I caught some decent gigs there. That was where I saw my friend Tory Z Startbuck perform for the first time. That gig sticks out in my mind not because of Tory, but because of his warmup act. I don't remember the guy's name, but he was a performance artist, whatever the hell that means. He read from a book of poetry. At the end of his set, he stripped completely naked before walking off. I'm not sure what purpose the act served, but I'm guessing it must have been cold on the stage.

The Galaxy was the embodiment of why I prefer club gigs to anything else. In 2001, I finally got a chance to see Prince in concert. For $60, I got to sit way up and way left in our hockey arena. When Prince came to the front of the stage to sing, I got a perfect view ... of his PA speakers. The gig lasted a scant 90 minutes, and that was pretty much that. A few days later, I saw Mike Keneally at the Galaxy. For 10 bucks, I stood less than three feet from the man, occasionally leaning on his monitor wedge. I spoke to Mike for a good 20 minutes after the show, where he signed a CD I bought at the merchandise table for $15. I also had three Diet Cokes, costing a total of six dollars. Mike came on stage at around 9 p.m., played for 90 minutes, and then came back onstage to play Frank Zappa tunes with Ike Willis and Project/Object. They were still going strong when I left at

1:30. I spent half as much money at the Galaxy and got three times the entertainment I got at Scottrade Center.

If Downtown wasn't happening, I might make my way to the Soulard neighborhood, where I could spend time at clubs like Mike & Mins, Hammerstone's, or the Great Grizzly Bear. My favorite place was 1860s Hardshell Café, which I visited nearly every Tuesday because my friend and teacher, Billy Barnett, had a regular gig there. There was no cover charge, and Bill played for the better part of four hours, starting around 9 p.m. The place had good Cajun food, and the drinks were relatively cheap. It was a great way to spend an evening. (7)

There was also the Way-Out Club on Cherokee Street, another semi-dive bar with a killer vibe. I caught more than a few shows there. I loved spending time at the Venice Café in Benton Park. It was practically around the corner from my apartment. I had no idea it was there until my friend T. J. DuPree told me about it. We got the chance to hang out there more than once. The Venice often featured one of my favorite local bands, called Funkabilly. Their music is described by the name of the band. They were highly versatile, and a lot of fun to listen to. I still treasure the autographed CD I have from them, recorded at that very club. The Hi-Pointe was another cool room, and a great place to catch a band. That's where I saw Jimmy Griffin live for the first time, with Neptune Crush. The University City Loop offered up not only the Duck Room, but the Red Sea and Cicero's. Most of the acts were local, but the energy was always high.

There were so many clubs. There was almost always something going on. I'm sure there are a couple of places I have since forgotten about. For a while, there was a running joke between me and my fellow officers, one of whom would inevitably ask me, "Where the show tonight?" Without hesitating, I would come back with the name of the club and the band I was seeing. My friends would just shake their heads.

The Creepy Crawl moved to a new location a few years ago. It's much better lit, and nicer to visit. Naturally, that sucked the vibe right out of it. It's been quite a while since I've been there. Kennedy's and the Trainwreck are gone, too. When Mississippi Nights closed, the impact was felt all over the Landing. The area has become a bit more run-down. There was talk of putting a football stadium in that area just before the Rams decided to move back to Los Angeles. For now, the area just sits there, devoid of action.

What a waste.

***

I understand the need for bands to reach as many people as possible on a tour stop. This is what makes arena and stadium gigs necessary. But I no longer get any enjoyment from these shows. None. My rationale comes down to one word: Radiohead.

I am a huge Radiohead fan. I love just about everything about the band. *OK Computer* and *The Bends* rank among my favorite albums. I didn't really know a lot about them when they toured behind *The Bends* in '94, when they played the Galaxy. By the time of *OK Computer,* they moved up to hockey arenas. I learned about the band after they had already come through St. Louis. My loss. The band released *Kid A* and *Amnesiac* without me catching them live as well. Tickets for the band went fast, and I made the mistake of slowing around. Our paths were finally able to cross when Radiohead released *Hail to the Thief* in 2003. This time, when the concert was announced, I was on top of it, and would not be denied my chance to see them.

The gig was at Riverport, which did *not* make me happy. But Radiohead was a big-time band, and it stood to reason they would play the appropriate-sized room. I would have to grin and bear it. This, I decided, would be worth it. Tickets went on sale on a Saturday morning. As it happened, I had the day off. I made my way to a local grocery store who sold concert tickets on behalf of Ticketmaster, Metrotix, or whoever was brokering the gig.

The ticket window opened at 10:00 a.m. Needless to say, there were more than a few people cued up to purchase seats. I was there at 9:00 a.m. and was surprised to see how many people beat me to the punch. But the vendor (like for so many other big concerts) was using a "line ticket" system. Potential concert goers would gather and be issued a line ticket number. Once each person had a number, the vendor would draw a number from a bucket or some other container. Whoever had the lucky number would be the first to purchase tickets, with everyone else lining up sequentially afterward. I don't remember what my number was, but I wound up being about the fifth person in line. Not too bad, all things considered.

This is where things go off the rails.

I understand Riverport is a large venue. It holds around 20,000 people. I understand my purchase point wasn't the only one in town. I understand tickets could also be purchased online.

I understand ALL of this. That being said, I had two tickets in my hand (at $45 each) six *minutes* after they went on sale. And where were my seats? In row XX. The seated rows went out to row ZZ. That put me 49 rows off the stage! Five deliberate steps backward, and I would be on the lawn! Unbelievable!

Things didn't get any better the day of the show. I thought I might try the old "Purchase Better Seats" gag, a la H.O.R.D.E., a few hours before we were due there, but there weren't any available. I would learn later Clear Channel, the radio conglomerate (and bane of my musical existence) purchased box seats and nearly everything in the first few rows, making it impossible for anyone to get an up-close view of Radiohead without going through them. These seats were given to VIPs, corporate lackeys, friends of the band, and "Lucky Caller number 15" in those radio station giveaways. My step-son and I were stuck with the seats we had.

I did my best to keep a positive attitude. I was going to make the most of these seats. After all, how many chances was I going to get to see Radiohead? Still, it didn't take long to sour my mood. After paying $20 to park my car and walking for what seemed like ages to get into the venue, we made our way to our seats. It was every bit as bad as I imagined.

The reserved seats are covered by an overhead pavilion, which comes in handy should it rain. But the pavilion only stretches out to around row UU. That put us a few rows *behind* the damned pavilion! If it rained, we were going to get wet! When you buy lawn seats, it's understood that can happen. The purpose of buying reserved seats was to stay out of the weather. So much for that.

And still, it got worse.

For a show like Radiohead, it is widely assumed to fans will be standing for the majority of the show, whether they have seats or not. I can live with that. Still, I have to hope I'm not stuck standing behind someone considerably taller than me. Well, guess what happened?

On a good day, I consider myself to be 5'10" tall. Normally, a standing gig isn't much of a problem. Usually, I'm at least as tall as the person in front of me. When Rob and I arrived at our seats, the ones in front of us weren't taken. They stayed empty until shortly before the opening act took the stage. For a while, I thought we might have an unobstructed view of the stage. But then the owners of the seats in row WW arrived.

And the guy in front of me was 6'4", easy. I'd have better luck trying to watch Radiohead through a brick wall.

There were large video monitors set up on either side of the stage. By the time Radiohead came out, I realized I paid $45 to watch one of my favorite bands on television, even though we currently occupied the same space. A great sounding show was ruined, because I was unable to see it.

I had a chance to see Radiohead again in '07 when they were touring behind *In Rainbows*, my second favorite of their albums behind *OK Computer*. Once again, the show was at Riverport. Once again, the experience was a Greek tragedy, even though my ticket was free. There's a long story behind this, but I don't think it's entirely mine to tell. The friends I went with suffered a personal tragedy the morning of the show. We never should have gone to the gig, but they insisted on the diversion. In the end, we were very late, I missed the live performance of the one song I wanted to hear above all others ("15 Step"), and our seats were so far off to stage right, I couldn't see half the band. I love the way Phil Selway plays drums. I was really looking forward to seeing him in action. After two attempts, I'm still waiting.

I swore then and there I would never attend another show at Riverport. A decade on, I have remained true to my word.

***

Tony Levin is a master of the bass (both upright and electric) and the Chapman Stick. But until I saw him up close in 2011, I'd never seen him BOW the Stick before. Seeing him play in the Old Rockhouse (a nice, intimate venue) gave me the perfect vantage point to see a maestro at work.

I feel bad for musicians playing large rooms. It can't be easy to connect with fans when playing in front of more than, say, 500 of them. I understand the money is better when the artist plays a larger room. But as a part-time musician, I would be equally, if not more, interested in making the connection with my audience. In live performance, the connection is crucial.

One of the best parts of being within ten feet of my favorite musicians is the eye contact. There were times when Adrian Belew was looking right at me as he played my favorite songs. That's the stuff dreams are made of! It's as though he was playing "Dinosaur" or "Big Electric Cat" just for me. That feeling is indescribable. Of course, the artist is usually performing with a spotlight in his face, which makes looking out into the audience challenging. At times, I wondered if Adrian knew I was out there at all.

"Oh, yeah! I could see you just fine," Adrian told me with a grin. "It looked like you were having a pretty good time!" Those are the meaningful moments. Mike Keneally caught me playing "air" guitar to one of his tunes at the Galaxy. He smiled at me and said, "Oh, you know that one!" once the song was complete. I could only grin sheepishly and nod. I don't get moments like that watching a show at Busch Stadium.

When I watch concert videos from artists like the Police or Eric Clapton, they are playing in front of audiences of 20,000 or more. Even fans in the very first row are still 15 or 20 feet off the stage, with a metal barrier and a row of security staff in front of them. It's safe to assume the band will be at least another 10 to 15 away from the front of the stage. Nothing strikes me as colder and more impersonal. Can the musician possibly be enjoying himself? I wonder.

I recently watched a video of Miles Davis playing the Isle of Wight festival in England in 1970. It's estimated there were 600,000 people in the audience. There were 400,000 people at Woodstock. Can anyone say with a straight face those gigs were all about the music? How could anyone possibly connect with what was happening on stage? It eludes me. As I've said, at some point the gig becomes less a concert and more a social event. I guess it's just a question of priorities.

Given the choice, musicians seem to prefer the intimacy of clubs over arenas. When I asked Deborah Holland what size room she preferred, the question had barely left my lips before she answered. "A small club, absolutely! The best aspects of playing live are hearing an audience laugh at my jokes and visibly seeing them appreciate the music by seeing their faces and hearing their applause. I also love interacting with them."

"I was the first-born child. So I got used to hearing applause for just about anything I did," Jimmy Griffin told me. "I still enjoy that. I love connecting with someone in the audience and getting them off through my music. I love being able to reach people emotionally, particularly kids, when I play for them at hospitals. They still look at musicians with a sense of awe."

Live performance doesn't just allow the musician to connect with the audience. Musicians are also able to connect to one another in ways not possible in the studio. One of the worst aspects of recording my band's CD was the lack of musical intimacy. There were at least four musicians on each song. Yet the four of us were never in the same room at the same time at any point during the recording. *Never*. Not once. I recorded my guitar parts to a "click" track. Trey recorded his guitars to the click and what I had done. Terrell used the click and our guitar parts. Larry used the click and about a third of what had already been recorded. That it worked is a musical miracle. But it's far from what I wanted.

Even professionals have to deal with similar conditions, particularly in rock-based situations. Normally, a rock song's parameters are laid out by the time recording starts. The musician knows what he wants to play, so he goes about making it happen. Since there is no real spontaneity, there is no need for more than a couple of band members to play together. In jazz, the situation is more fluid, which is why the musicians traditionally record their basic tracks together. They already know the central theme of the song in question, but they leave room for improvisation when it's time to solo. If another take is necessary, then everyone in the band plays. I would prefer to see more of that in rock-based recordings as well. It's just more exciting!

"It's a special dimension," Billy Barnett, who specializes in jazz and blues, told me. "One golden gig makes you forget about the 10,000 shitty ones. When everything clicks, spontaneously, it's as close to heaven as we mortals can attain."

"There are many things I love about performing," said Adrian Belew. "Things like trying to do something to perfection, and knowing each performance is one of a kind, a moment shared with your audience. Or the 'oneness' you feel with your band mates, like you can finish each other's thoughts."

Upon hearing those words, two examples of that "oneness" sprang immediately to mind. Not surprisingly, one of them involves Belew.

The '80s King Crimson will always be my favorite, because they were my entry into a new musical world. The albums the band released during the '80s rank among the most important in my collection. But since the band broke up a year before I even knew they existed, I never got to experience them live. That changed by way of DVD and archive CD.

Robert Fripp's DGM Live label released a couple of concert videos from that era in a compilation called *Neal and Jack and Me*. One gig was from '82, recorded in France when Crimson was opening for Roxy music. It's a marvelous gig. The band is tight and plays one of the best versions of "The Sheltering Sky" I've ever heard. (8) But at under an hour, I didn't think the total might of the '80s Crimson was properly captured. The other video was recorded in Japan two years later. There was no doubting the band's chemistry, as they were deep into finishing each other's thoughts. But there were a couple of equipment glitches and a missed cue or two, throwing things off a bit.

The '84 tour was the last for this version of the band. They recorded the final gig, which was played in Montreal. The show was broadcast on radio long before I ever knew about King Crimson. It was released as an "official bootleg" by DGM, called *Absent Lovers*. (9) According to Sid Smith's Crimson biography, *In the Court of King Crimson*, the band didn't know they were breaking up until Fripp informed them the morning after this show. But if the way they played was any indication, the band may have felt something was up. As such, they left it all on the stage.

Songs like "Larks Tongues in Aspic, part 3," "Thela Hun Ginjeet," and "Waiting Man," which were difficult to execute in an ideal studio setting, were absolutely laid to waste by the band on this marvelous evening. Guitarists Belew and Fripp, bassist Tony Levin, and drummer Bill Bruford took no prisoners, playing as though their very lives depended on it. I heard the material 14 years after it was recorded. It took at least that many months to remove my jaw from the floor.

The other moment took place 10 years before I was born. In fact, it was recorded on my mother's 12th birthday: July 7, 1956. The artist was the legendary Duke Ellington and his orchestra. The gig took place at the Newport Jazz Festival in

Rhode Island. It was recorded and ultimately released as *Ellington at Newport*.

The highlight of the evening was a number called "Diminuendo and Crescendo in Blue." Admittedly, I have never heard a studio version of this piece. Not that it matters. The live recording will always blow it out of the water. The piece becomes special not because of Ellington, but because of his tenor sax soloist, Paul Gonsalves.

Ellington gave his musicians a chance to shine via their own solos, but Gonsalves took things beyond that mythical next level. In jazz, a soloist is usually given three or four "choruses" (12 4/4 bars) to show off his abilities and wow the crowd. For most musicians, it's a chorus to warm up, a chorus or two to blow up, and a chorus to come back down. A really hot musician may get an extra chorus or two, but is usually reeled back in before things can get out of hand. For Gonsalves at Newport, the exact opposite happened. He came out smoldering, caught fire, and never stopped burning! Rather than reel him in, Ellington and the band can be heard shouting encouragement to Gonsalves, who caused a near riot amongst the relative staid jazz crowd. About a quarter of the way in to the 27(!) chorus solo, a young blonde woman in a black cocktail dress leapt up and started to dance. Seeing this, the band fed off her, sending the crowd into an even bigger frenzy. For a total of 324 bars, Gonsalves raised the art of improvisation to an all-time high. By the time he finally came back to earth, the crowd (and a young man shouting at the stereo speakers in his living room some 32 years after the show was recorded) was completely out of hand. Ellington's band had to play an unplanned ballad after the tune was over, just to bring the crowd back under control. I cannot imagine something like this happening in the sterile setting of a recording studio.

That is the power of live music.

I don't think Adrian knows a great deal about Duke Ellington. I'm almost certain he's never heard the Gonsalves "Diminuendo in Blue" solo. Nevertheless, he manages to capture precisely what that solo is about when he told me his two favorite things about playing live. "Sometimes while you're playing, you can get lost in what you're doing, like time stands still," he said. "And in those moments you may actually play something you didn't know you were capable of. I guess it comes from all those years of practice.

"The amazing surge of pure energy you feel onstage when the audience is excited ... there's simply nothing else like it," he continued. "I'm sure that's why so many 'elder' rock people are still out there when they no longer have to be.

"There are times when I'm about to take the stage, and I feel completely worn out from the long travel day and maybe even concerned that I have enough in my tank to make it a great concert. But once I feel the energy from the audience, I feel like a little kid bouncing around happily, and then time seems to fly by. And it's over before I want it to be."

I'll say it again: live music is the best.

(1)   Like an idiot, I "purged" that CD along with many others in 2006. When I tried to re-acquire it, I got nowhere. It turns out the CD was only released in Japan, where I bought it in the first place. There are times when I could wring my own neck.

(2)   Billy Joel's band is easily among the *loudest* bands I've ever heard, much to my amazement. And this is coming from a guy who's stood ten feet from Vernon Reid's guitar rig, and has seen A Perfect Circle, Tool, and Rush!

(3)   I'm guessing this band was an offshoot of the Manhattan Project, a 1990 Clarke/Shorter band featuring Michel Petrucciani on piano and drummer Lenny White. I found their CD in Japan. It never fails to knock my socks off.

(4)   The venue was originally named the Riverport Amphitheater. That's what I always call it. The name has changed several times, depending on what company owned the naming rights. My alternate name for the place is the Corporate Whore-Atorium.

(5)   While I enjoy a beer or a quality scotch now and then, I'm not a big drinker. It takes away from my enjoyment of the show. I didn't show up at these gigs to "party." I was there for the music, period. Plus, there's that whole "potential for a DWI" thing, which is frowned upon by the Chief of Police, whom I work for.

(6)   Sinister Dane, New World Spirits, and the Urge all scored major label deals. Unfortunately, with record deals come musical compromises, and these groups collapsed under the weight of those compromises. Sometimes, it seems the worst thing that can happen to a band is they get noticed by a label.

(7)   Billy always said he was going to have me sit in with him at 1860's. I wish it could have come to pass. It's my own fault. I never felt my chops were up to snuff. He would probably say otherwise. Self-doubt is a powerful beast.

(8)   In fact, it was this version of the song which motivated me to name my band after it. In my mind, I wanted to capture the precision and cool of King Crimson as they played it. Alas, we never quite got there.

(9)   I love this CD. And yet, I purged it. My idiocy knows no bounds. By the time you read these words, I'll have it back in the fold.

The legacy of the Sheltering Sky comes down to a beat-up box full of unsold CDs and liner note pages. The music still makes me smile. And cringe.

Track 18
D.I.Y via the Sheltering Sky

My quest to make music began because my ability to play tennis ended. While music has always been a constant, the desire to create my own tunes took time to take hold. In the summer of '96, I was still all about playing tennis, a sport I took up in earnest in the mid '80s. I had actually gotten pretty good at the game. I believed I could get good enough to walk on to a college tennis team somewhere after I got out of the Air Force in October of '92. My last coach (who held the number one singles spot on the U.S. Air Force tennis team) believed I was a solid backhand return of serve away from achieving that goal.

The dedication I gave tennis might have given an Olympic athlete a run for his money. I woke up early every day and rode my bicycle around the perimeter of Yokota Air Base, which was about eight miles. After a quick shower, I was in the 475th Air Base Wing's Public Affairs office by 7:30. Breakfast was something light and quick, and almost always enjoyed at my desk. Three hours later, I would have a light lunch, also at my desk. I did this so that I could spend my "lunch hour" at the fitness center, where I would spend that time lifting weights. After another quick shower, I came back to the office, where I finished my work for the day. At 4:30, I left the office and headed straight to my dorm room, where my roommate might or might not see me during the 15 minutes I spent there. After a quick change of clothes, I was back out the door, and headed for the tennis courts, which were a five minute walk away. That's where I would spend the next three hours. My tennis practice routine was the stuff of legend, but I'll spare you the details. Let's just say it was grueling. After that, it was home for yet another shower, dinner, and maybe a little television or music before I dozed off for the night.

This was my routine for about 10 months out of the year. Weekends were reserved for tennis tournaments or casual matches. I probably spent ten hours every weekend on the tennis court. Sometimes, I went to the movies or hung out with friends, assuming I wasn't at home pouring over videotapes of tennis matches I used to gather tips and strategies.

Near the end of my Japanese tour, I picked up yet another interest: baseball. I spent my last four months on base dividing my time between tennis and the Yokota baseball team, where I played outfield. It was a blast, and I still miss it. I also stumbled into having a girlfriend, who took up more than a little of the time I was supposed to be using to sleep. Oh, the things one can do with youth.

Alas, October of '92 arrived, and I decided that I had given the military all I had to offer. It was time to go back to the real world.

My original plan was to stay in St. Louis long enough to say hello to my family, then make my way back to South Carolina, where I would try to attend the University of South Carolina, and perhaps walk on to the tennis team. But that girlfriend of mine caused me to alter my plans. I was now all about starting a professional life (not in tennis), so I could get married. Life can really be funny sometimes.

By the winter of '94, my hopes of a professional life similar to that of the military had bitten the dust. My engagement fell apart, and my tennis skills began to erode, culminating with my failure to make a casual team I should have strolled onto with ease. I frequently found myself in the depths of despair. I managed to pull myself together long enough to pass the necessary tests to qualify me for entry into the St. Louis Police Academy. I began my training in January of '95 and graduated in May. The tennis-playing journalist was now a cop.

***

To me, there is nothing sadder than an athlete who has held on too long. I am forever wary of any jock that goes on television and declares that he has "one more good season" left in him. In '96, I became that athlete. I knew my best tennis was behind me, but I was sure I could conjure up the magic for one more season. I wish I could have heard myself objectively. But that's not where life's lessons come from.

In June of '96, I was preparing to do something I had always wanted to do as a tennis player: play on grass. I had spent about 99.5 percent of my playing time on asphalt courts, which was a major contributing factor to the degeneration of my knees. Once, while on a temporary assignment in Virginia, I got a chance to play on a clay court. It was a remarkable experience. It required a different level of grit and determination, since my serve (once clocked at 120 miles per hour) would be neutralized, and I would have to have the patience to play longer points. Grass, on the other hand, would make my serve even more of a weapon, since the ball would skid and stay low, enabling me to attack the net with my volleys. The tournament in Tower Grove Park, located in south St. Louis, would be the closest I could get to playing at Wimbledon, where I dreamed of playing against my hero, Stefan Edberg.

But like so many other dreams, this one simply wasn't meant to be.

A couple of weeks before the tournament, I was playing a set against an older gentleman on the hard courts of Tower Grove Park. I could see the grass courts from where I was. But things were not going well. I was losing, and it was pissing me off.

There is an old saying amongst tennis players: "Beware of the old man with the frayed shirt and knee brace." This veteran tennis player is to be feared, because he has the benefit of experience on his side. He may not look like much of a player, but he will run you to death without breaking a sweat, because he knows how to dictate the pace of a match. He knows how to put the ball precisely where he wants it, causing his opponent to run all over creation. I was learning this lesson the hard way.

I played tennis long enough to know I should *never* try to serve with maximum power before the third or fourth service game. My serve was my primary weapon, and I knew good and well how long it took to get it to maximum power and effectiveness. The first couple of service games were for putting more spin on the ball and dialing in my placement. Power would come later. By the time my serve was good and loose, I was confident that I would not be "broken" (lose my service game), and obtaining a single service break against my opponent would be more than enough to enable me to win the set. Yes, I was rather arrogant on the tennis court.

But my strategy wasn't working, and I had actually been broken twice already. I was down 0-4, and the old guy still looked as though he just strolled onto the court. How could this guy be kicking my ass? My emotions (which I had been taught to control at all times) were starting to get the better of me. It was time to teach this old man a lesson, I thought. It was time to flatten out my serve and put this guy back on his heels.

And so, a full-service game or two too early, I started trying to serve as hard as I could. The strategy lasted all of three points. At 15-all, I decided to blister my best, flattest serve right up the middle. I wouldn't even need to come in behind it, because there was no way he was going to get to it. I went through my routine, tossed the ball over my head, bent my knees deeply, and launched myself into the ball. I felt my racquet scrape the middle of my back as I cocked my arm behind me, and then brought the racquet up and through, full throttle. My wrist twisted just the way it was supposed to, and I felt the ball meet the sweet spot in the middle of my Wilson Pro Staff.

I also heard (and felt) a loud "pop" come from the back of my right shoulder.

The serve was perfect. It blazed right up the middle, kissing the center service line that separated the "ad" from the "deuce" court before smashing into the fence behind the baseline. The old guy never even moved. He had no chance at getting to it. I'm sure that serve broke my 120-mph record. I think the old guy even applauded the shot. I say "I think" because I don't remember seeing it. I was now focused on the intense pain coming from my shoulder. It was as if someone lit a blowtorch and was holding the flame right on top of the injured area. It hurt so badly, I couldn't think straight.

My best tennis days were over. Unfortunately, it took me a little while longer to realize and accept it.

A sane person would have stopped playing then and there. He would have walked to the center of the court, shaken hands with the old guy, told him what had just happened, and gone straight to the doctor. Alas, I was *not* that sane person. I had finally aced this son of a bitch. There was *no way* I was backing off now! I was determined to finish the match. I am male, after all. My shoulder, however, had other plans.

It didn't take long before I knew I could no longer serve flat and up the middle. Instead, I would focus on spinning serves in. I managed to win that service game, and one more. But three games into the second set, down 2-6, 0-3, I finally knew it was over. I could barely raise my right arm now. I finally took the walk to the center of the court and shook the old guy's hand. I packed up my gear and – head down – made my way to my car, and back home.

Did I go to the doctor? Nope. I spent the rest of the day applying ice packs and popping Tylenol like it was candy. After all, I had to work the next day! Over the next week, I went from pulling out of the grass court tournament to giving up competitive tennis to quitting the game altogether. I ignored a torn rotator cuff for the next seven years. The injury would patch itself together via scar tissue, only to come back apart again while doing the most innocuous of tasks, such as lifting a small, empty box over my head. I've always had a relatively high pain threshold (thanks to the constant aching in my knees), so I just did my best to ignore the agony in my shoulder. (1) In fact, I had both of my knees operated on before finally succumbing to the pain and allowing my orthopedist to repair my rotator cuff in 2003.

I'm a smart man. But sometimes, I do stupid things.

***

Tennis was over. It was time to find a new hobby. I spent my spare time watching movies and listening to music. One late fall day, a "911" call brought my partner and me to a pawn shop. The call itself was easy enough to deal with, but since it was cold outside, my partner and I lingered in the shop, chatting up the owner and his assistant.

As we talked, my eyes began to gaze along the walls, where I saw musical instruments hanging from hooks. It had been a long time since junior high school band. I couldn't read music any more. Still, I began to think that it might be fun to start playing again. Normally, an ambitious thought like that would stick with me for a few hours, and then I would move on to something else. But this thought took hold, and showed no sign of letting go. I was on to something.

But what instrument would I play? Jazz was still the dominant musical form in my life, even though King Crimson's comeback and the "Alternative" music format were having a major impact. At first, I thought the saxophone would be the way to go. I would play tenor and soprano, like John Coltrane,

Wayne Shorter, and Branford Marsalis. That would be cool! But wait … what about the guitar? After all, I loved a pretty wide variety of music. It seemed to me that it would be easier to bring a guitar to jazz than it would be to bring a soprano sax to prog or Alternative. I mulled the thought over for another week or so. Finally, I decided: I would get myself a guitar. Surely, my new friends in the pawn shop would have a bargain for me.

Just before Christmas of '96, I bought my first guitar. It was a hand-made instrument, shaped to look like a Fender Telecaster. I believe I paid $90 for it. I took it home, put it in the corner of my living room, and stared at it from time to time through the Holiday season.

In early '97, I decided to start making the most of my new purchase. I found a sheet music store about 15 minutes from my apartment, where I bought a couple of books. Like tennis before, I figured I could teach myself to play the guitar. I didn't take long to realize I'd figured wrong.

I really enjoyed playing guitar, even though I wasn't sure what I wanted to do with it. That changed during one of my visits to Streetside Records. I bought a VHS copy of *King Crimson Live in Tokyo*. It was concert footage of the newly formed Double Trio during their '96 tour. I was gobsmacked from the opening note. Then I knew what I wanted to do with my guitar playing. I wanted to be in a band. I wanted to make music that fired me up the way Crimson did.

Eager to become a musical sponge, I began taking lessons from both Billy Barnett at J. Gravity Strings, and Tory Z Starbuck, who worked at the Streetside Records. Billy was a student of theory and technique, showing me the scales, modes and rhythm techniques I needed to achieve the sound I was looking for. Tory, on the other hand, lived in the musical moment, chasing the Muse wherever it led him, and creating whatever music seemed to present itself in that moment.

Better still, each teacher told me to listen to and learn from the other. They figured they were molding the ultimate musician: a technically proficient thinker who wasn't afraid to let all that go in order to live in the musical moment. How close they came is not really for me to say. One thing is certain: I am slow to reject any form of music or style of play, thanks to Billy and Tory. Even if a particular style isn't my cup of tea, I will do my best to make it work before letting go.

Thanks to Billy and Tory, I was growing more confident in my abilities. Tory took things a step further, and decided it was time for me to start composing my own songs. The idea initially scared the daylights out of me. What could I possibly have to say that would be of any interest musically? I started thinking on chord progressions and scale ideas that might lead to something. Naturally, Tory rejected that mode of thinking.

"Here's what I want you to do," he told me at the end of one of our sessions. "Find a beat you like in your drum machine and build a rhythm part around it. Bring it back to me next week." I rifled through a couple dozen patches in my Boss DR-303 drum machine. Before long, I found a patter that held my interest. As I listened, I reached for my guitar. Before long, I was playing an unplugged rhythm along with the drum part.

I recorded my ideas onto tape using an old Tascam four-track recorder. I laid down the drum part, a rhythm guitar, and a rather crude lead guitar. Within two days, I had recorded my first song, which I called "No Relation." The title was a joke, acknowledging I am in no way related to Jimi Hendrix. (2)

My lessons with Tory took place in his spacious apartment in University City, a St. Louis suburb. A rear bedroom had been converted into his home studio. I presented Tory with my cassette, which he loaded into an identical Tascam recorder. While he listened, I fiddled with one of his synthesizers. Before long, I found a bass sound I liked. I played a pattern quietly, while anxiously awaiting my teacher's critique.

His remarks were positive, and he suggested minor adjustments. The advice made sense. As I absorbed what he was saying, Tory heard the "SynthBass" line I was playing. He stopped talking mid-sentence. "That's an interesting line," he said, and grinned a bit. "You need to put a song around that. In fact, that's your next assignment." I was shocked by how quickly the new idea manifested itself. Within a day, I had the foundation for a song I called "Creepin'."

Tory had me repeat this exercise six more times. I built a song around a favorite bass guitar line (which I had to play myself); I created a composition around a sound I heard every day (namely, my police radio); I wrote a song designed for acoustic guitar; I wrote a song based in pure ambient noise. By the time I finished, I had written 11 songs. It was enough material to complete my first album. This had been Tory's objective the entire time. He was smart enough not to tell me what he was doing.

I called the album *No Relation*. I hated the idea of leaving the songs as compositions where I was the only musician. That struck me struck me as horrifying. Wisely, I invited some friends to make "guest appearances." Billy played bass on "No Relation," and a blistering slide guitar solo on a tune I called "The Middle of Nowhere." A bass playing friend named Lynmann Stamps contributed a Larry Graham thumb-plucking bass line to a song called "A Joyful Noize." Naturally, Tory made a couple of appearances with his violin and other instruments. Best of all, my friend T. J. Dupree contributed his singing voice to my cover of Adrian Belew's "The Rail Song." That may have been my favorite moment of the entire recording experience.

Tory's wife, Venus, helped me design *No Relation*'s CD booklet and took photos. It was a surreal experience. I mean, what the hell was I doing with an album? Who was I going to sell it to? Who on earth would actually buy one? In the end, I realized the *No Relation* experience wasn't about making money. It was about building up the skill and confidence that would allow me to consider myself a musician.

The jury is still out on that one.

***

There are few experiences quite as horrifying as exposing your music to an audience, even if you know them. There are few secrets in a police department, or amongst musicians. And here I was, part of both circles. It didn't take long for people to learn I was playing guitar, and I was working on making an album. Naturally, curious ears were everywhere.

I played *No Relation* for a few friends and coworkers. I was rarely able to stay in the room with them while they listened. When Kim played it on the overhead speakers at Streetside Records one day (granted, it was before the store opened), I did all I could to be all the way on the other side of the store. On any other day, I would be sitting right next to her, chit-chatting or dancing along to whatever was playing. Now the 1,500 square feet separating us wasn't nearly enough.

About halfway through the disc, I mustered up the courage to walk within 20 feet of Kim. As I got closer, the store's phone rang. She turned the music down just enough to answer. It was one of the other store employees calling. What I heard was surprising, a bit embarrassing, and more than a little fulfilling. Naturally, I only heard half of what was being said. "Hey, what's up? Oh, nothing … Ced brought his CD in … Yeah, I'm playing it right now … Ya know, it's surprisingly

298

good ... Sure, it's got some weird stuff on it. You know him ... but I like the way he plays ... Yeah, he's on to something."

I was on a cloud.

Naturally, all of my "guest musicians" got a copy. Each seemed pleased with what he heard. The recordings were crude by modern industry standards. With only four tracks to work with, I was using exactly 1/12 the number of recording tracks traditionally used by professionals. My friends didn't always get was I was doing, but they seemed to appreciate the effort. One decided he was paying me the ultimate compliment by saying, "Dude it looks and sounds just like a real CD!" (3)

What the hell, I'll take it.

***

Eventually, the question was finally asked: "So when are you going to play this stuff on stage?" When the question came, I realized I hadn't given it a lot of thought. The time had come to give an answer.

I started thinking about putting together a band to help me support *No Relation*. But the last thing in the world I wanted was to be the center of a group. Even now, the thought of forming "The Cedric Hendrix Experience," or something like it, makes me cringe. I'm not worthy of that kind of attention. My mind was geared toward being a cog in the wheel of a larger band, preferably featuring four or five musicians.

The *No Relation* material was fine, but Tory instilled some newfound confidence into me, and I was itching to write a new song or two. While my initial pieces were geared around me as an individual, I now wanted to try to compose something for a full band. I borrowed a bass guitar from a friend and found myself fiddling about with it one day. The heavy gauge of the strings sent my mind in a different direction. Before long, I turned on my drum machine to accompany my thought process. What I was hearing in my head was ominous, dark, and foreboding. I was captivated. I slowly built a chord structure around the bass lines. Before I knew it, the lead line was staring me in the face. The bridge and solo sections practically wrote themselves. In what seemed like a flash, I had conceived, rehearsed and recorded a demo of my first song intended for a band. I called it "Trouble Looms on the Horizon."

Never one to take his impulses slowly, I was ready to charge ahead, obstacles be damned. I wanted to form a band. My initial thought was to form a quintet, featuring two guitars, two basses (or better yet, one bass and one Chapman Stick), and a drummer. We would have elements of progressive rock, electronica, and metal. King Crimson was my biggest influence, so I figured the band should be named after a Crimson song, preferably from the '80s band. I considered calling the group Three of a Perfect Pair. Then I changed to Neal and Jack and Me. Finally, the name right name descended. We would call ourselves The Sheltering Sky. Perfect! Now all I needed was like-minded musicians to join me on my great musical quest. How hard could that be?

Pretty damned hard, as it turns out.

I met more than a few musicians, some busier than others. I wrote out several possible band incarnations and started making calls. The story I got was pretty much the same every time: I had an interesting idea, but nobody had the time to help to get it off the ground. The band I had in mind would definitely be labor-intensive. Or, the musicians weren't as interested in the musical direction as I was. Some were really interested one day, but not so enthused the next time I spoke to them. Musicians, as I would come to learn, are a flaky lot at times.

In late '99, I met a guitarist named Trey Adams and a bassist named Eric Littles. They worked at Streetside Records, and we always found ourselves talking about making music together. We spoke the same musical language, which can be a very rare thing. I made sure to keep talking to those guys, about anything, just to stay on their radar.

Eventually, I invited the two of them to my apartment to discuss music, listen to CDs, and watch concert videos. In my own way, I was testing them to determine if I had truly found kindred spirits. Before long, the three of us were transfixed on the King Crimson video I bought a couple of years before. I took a moment to take in the scene before me, and it made me laugh. Naturally, my new friends wanted to know what was so funny. "Well," I said, "who would believe three black men would be sitting in the same room, captivated by a progressive rock band?"

It took several moments for the laughter to die down. Once it did, I was certain I'd found my band mates.

I gave Trey and Eric a copy of *No Relation*, and showed them which songs to focus on. We also came up with a couple of tunes we wanted to cover. Most importantly, I provided them with a copy of my "Trouble Looms on the Horizon" demo. That was the tune we would use to establish our identity as a band.

I abandoned the dual bassist idea. The Sheltering Sky would go forth as a quartet. The only problem was, we were currently a trio. We were missing a key element to our sound. The band needed a drummer. I spent weeks begging my friend – and fellow police officer – Larry Wilke, to join the group. He is, without question, one of the most talented drummers I've ever been around. I had no doubt he could handle any form of music we put before him. Alas, Larry is one of the busiest human beings I've ever been around. He simply didn't have the time needed to dedicate himself to playing in a band. I was forced to move on.

In the summer of 2000, I met another fellow police officer who happened to be a drummer. For the purpose of these pages, we'll call him Roy. The two of us spent a little law enforcement downtime talking about music and drumming. We didn't speak the exact same language, but it was pretty damned close. Roy told me he played all the time and was always looking for someone else to make music with. In fact, his drums were set up in a space that would more than accommodate himself, Trey, Eric, and me. "Why don't we give it a try one day," he said. "What do we have to lose?"

Sold!

And so, on a sweltering July day, the four of us found ourselves in the equally sweltering (and completely unventilated) storage area of a liquor store in South St. Louis. The first rehearsals of The Sheltering Sky had begun.

Things got off to a great start. Maybe it was even *too* great. Before we started playing, Roy – steadfastly adjusting his drum kit – dropped a cymbal on the floor. Without missing a beat, I shook an overdramatic fist at the sky, and yelled, "Damn, damn, DAMN!" I didn't have to tell anyone I was imitating Florida Evans from the classic TV sitcom *Good Times*. They knew, and the laughter seemed to go on forever. I had *definitely* found my kindred spirits.

Once the gear was set up, we started to jam. I don't remember who played the first note, but the rest of the group just dropped in with him. I can't describe the music we were making. We just *played*. And it worked! After about five minutes, I felt like it was time to move into the material we were planning to rehearse. So I raised an index finger into the air, a cue for the band to prepare to stop. I gave the stop cue, and the group halted on a dime. It was stunning. We spent a moment or two just looking at one another. And then we started laughing again. Yep ... this was the band. This was the Sheltering Sky.

I couldn't help the visions I saw in my head. I saw us jelling as a group, taking the *No Relation* material to the loftiest of heights. "Trouble Looms on the Horizon" was taking shape with minimal effort. I couldn't wait to bring in more material! We even managed to incorporate the theme from the movie *Shaft* into our repertoire. The first two or three rehearsals were a ball. I was sure we were on to something big. But now the hard part was about to begin.

Musicians make being in a band look like so much fun. Bandleaders, in particular, appeared to be having the best time. But there is one crucial lesson concert videos do not teach: leading a band is a royal pain in the ass.

***

While I don't mean this as an insult, it still needs to be said: the vast majority of my band-leading problems originated from the drum throne. When I think of the Sheltering Sky and its drummer problems, I can't help but equate us to Spinal Tap.

Things started to come unglued with Roy during our fourth rehearsal. About 45 minutes into practicing, he needed to take a break. No big deal, I figured. As it happened, Trey broke a guitar string, and now he would have the time to repair it. Roy left the room and made his way to the front of the liquor store.

We waited for Roy for several minutes, but he didn't come back. I was thinking about going to look for him, when Eric's friend, Yohannis Emica (who had come along to check out the band), asked if he could sit in on the drums. Why not? There was nobody else there, anyway.

Yohanis sat down and started playing. The next 20 minutes or so rank among the greatest I've ever experienced in music. Eric started playing a bass groove to his friend's beat. Since I was standing there, guitar draped over my shoulder, I decided to join in. Soon, the three of us were in musical lockstep. Trey had been slowly replacing his guitar string. Now he felt the need to pick up the pace. Before long, the four of us were playing together, in complete and total improvisational splendor.

Trey and I traded solos by merely looking at one another for cues. It was as though we had written the material beforehand. Eric and Yohannis saw fit to maintain their groove. We just kept playing. I always played with my back to the door. So I was slightly startled when I felt a human chin on my right shoulder while I played chords for Trey to solo with. I snapped my head to the right and found Roy grinning at me. "What song are you playing?" he yelled in my ear. I shrugged in reply. "I have no idea," I answered, and went back to finding my groove. But not before I turned completely around to see the owner of the liquor store, his co-worker, and at least half a dozen other people staring at us. They were captivated!

Eventually, things wound down. Roy took over for Yohannis, and the vibe changed. We finally stopped playing, and our makeshift audience applauded wildly. All we could do was grin and wave in acknowledgement.

This is where I learned the most valuable lesson in band management: *record everything!* There were no recorders running during that rehearsal. The improvisation vanished into the ether as quickly as it came. Attempts to describe what he had played were fruitless. The magic moment was gone forever.

Things didn't get any better when I remembered why the improv was necessary in the first place. I looked at Roy and asked, "Where the hell did you go?" All he could do was shrug and grin sheepishly. "I needed a break," was all he would say. What could I do? I let the matter pass, and we went back to working on our established tunes.

But Roy's longest break was yet to come.

***

I don't know how many drummers the Sheltering Sky saw during my decade of attempts to put the band into motion. But it was a LOT. My problems with them tended to spawn from one of three areas: 1. They were talented and equipped, but unavailable, 2. They were talented and available, but unequipped, or 3. They were available and equipped, but not talented enough.

This is where migraines come from.

My first headache came from Roy, and our next attempts at rehearsing. I'm a pretty laid-back guy, which tends to put people at ease around me. I like things that way. Still, there's being at ease, and there's flat-out taking advantage. When I set a rehearsal time, I assume that there will be the occasional delay. This is particularly true when dealing with policemen, since anything can happen at any time during a shift. Still, there were only two cops in the Sheltering Sky, and I was one of them. I managed to make it to rehearsals with minimal fuss. Roy, not so much.

I called our fifth rehearsal for 6 p.m. on a Saturday. Everyone agreed to be there. I got there 20 minutes early. Both Trey and Eric were 15 minutes late. I got over that pretty quickly. But 7:00 came and went with Roy nowhere to be found. Calls and pages went unanswered. The three of us noodled about as a power trio, figuring our drummer would wander in sooner or later. He never did.

I found Roy at the station a couple of days later. I asked him where he had been, and why he had missed rehearsal. He stumbled and stammered a bit before saying something like, "Oh, was that last Saturday? My bad, man. I thought you meant this Saturday." It was the lamest excuse I'd ever heard. But everybody gets to make a mistake in my book, so I let it go.

I called a rehearsal for the following Saturday. Once again, Roy failed to show. We scheduled our next practice for the following Thursday. Again, there was no Roy. I couldn't find him at work, either. I was growing well beyond pissed off.

One of my fellow officers heard me grumbling to myself, and asked what the problem was, since I was not known for grumbling. I gave him a brief rundown of the band's trials and tribulations. Here we had a perfectly good spot to rehearse in the back of a liquor store, and our drummer was flaking out on us. My fellow officer asked me who the drummer was. I told him it was Roy.

"And you're practicing in a liquor store?" he asked me.

"Yeah," I said, thinking nothing of it.

The officer chortled. "Well ... that makes sense." The look on my face told him I didn't follow. "You know Roy's a drunk, right?" The look on my face told him I had no idea. "Oh, man! He's notorious. He's showed up at roll call hammered. He drinks during the shift. He disappears and misses radio assignments. Word around the station is he's just this side of getting fired. You didn't know?" All I could do was shake my head. Suddenly, everything was starting to make sense.

When Roy put his chin on my shoulder the day of the Great Improv, I remembered smelling booze on his breath. But I didn't think anything of it. We all enjoyed a drink now and then. I just chose to enjoy mine after practice. And as long as you played your parts properly, I didn't care whether you drank during rehearsal or not. But now I was seeing the bigger picture. I was seeing Roy's bleary eyes on day tours at work. I was hearing his slurred speech when asking questions at rehearsal. And how had that cymbal fallen all those weeks ago? Did Roy genuinely drop it? Or did he simply lack the body control to hold on to it? I wasn't sure any more.

I was facing my first crisis as a bandleader. I was going to have to confront and most likely fire my drummer. His actions were holding us back, and Trey, Eric, and I were eager to move forward. I decided I would find him at work and let him down gently there. But I never got the chance.

As it happens, I left a piece of gear I needed at the rehearsal spot. I stopped by the liquor store to pick it up. The owner knew me by then and had no problem with me going to the back of the store. I walked down the hall to our rehearsal room, opened the door, and flipped the light switch. What I saw – or *didn't* see – stunned me.

Roy's drums were gone. Not so much as a drumstick remained.

I made my way to the front of the store and asked the owner if the drums had simply been moved. We had, after all, been talking about moving to a larger (and better ventilated) space upstairs. The owner looked perplexed. "Roy took his drums out of here a few days ago," he said. "Didn't he tell you?" I shook my head. "I don't know what the problem was," he continued. "He just said something about finding another space, and not wanting to be hot all the time. I don't know where he took them. He just got his stuff and left." Clearly, the owner could see how wounded I was. He tried to make me feel better. "Listen, I like you guys. You sounded real good. If you want, you can leave your stuff here, and play as much as you want." I thanked him for the offer and told him I would think about it. And then I drove home, calling Trey as I did. He was as floored as I was.

I was never able to see Roy at work, either. Apparently, he could read the writing on the wall, and resigned from the police department. Not long after, his phone was disconnected. I never heard from, saw, or spoke to Roy again.

After Larry Wilke, he became the second member of Category One.

I remembered the fun the three of us had with Yohanis as the drummer. I asked Eric to gauge his interest in joining the band. Eric was pumped about the idea and gave his friend a call. Sure, he was interested, came the reply. But there was a hitch: Yohanis didn't own any drums. And it would be a while before he could make that happen. Welcome to Category Two.

Once again, the Sheltering Sky was without a drummer.

***

I told Larry my tale of woe one day over lunch in late '01. Something needed to be done. I took a flyer and asked Larry again if he'd play with us. Nope, he said. Still too busy.

Still, I plowed forward. I was determined to make the record I had been slowly assembling, which came to be called *Valley of Shadows*. By '02, Eric had moved on. Terrell Carter, another friend and fellow police officer, replaced him. The three of us spent a great deal of time in the second bedroom of my house, where I had set up a home studio I called The Padded Cell.

There was a glimmer of hope that spring, when a friend of Trey's showed interest in jamming with us. He was incredibly talented, and more than eager. A jam session at his house with Trey and myself went remarkably well. He even learned "Trouble Looms on the Horizon" with very little effort, playing unexpected fills reminding me of Rush's drummer, Neil Peart. I was getting excited again.

But the music gods continued to mock us. Our new potential drummer kept running into barrier after barrier when it came to playing with us. Eventually, he pulled out of the prospect altogether, and the band was back at Square One, courtesy of another visit to Category One.

My lack of patience was beginning to get the better of me. By late summer, I had written eight solid tunes for *Valley of Shadows*. I was ready to get on with recording them. I bought a 16-track digital recorder, which replaced the Tascam 4-track model. While still only a third of what professionals used, I believed this would be more than enough space for the Sheltering Sky to get what it needed. Best of all, I could do the majority of the recording at home, which meant not having to pay for studio time.

At last, the time had come. On November 8 of '02 (my birthday), we began recording our album. By all conventional accounts, we went about recording *Valley of Shadows* backward. Traditionally, drums are recorded first, then the bass, and then the lead instruments. I went in from the opposite direction. I recorded my guitar parts with the aid of a "click track," Trey added his parts, and then Terrell added the low end. We still didn't have a drummer.

Eventually, we found an interested and equipped drummer. After moving his gear into The Padded Cell and playing our tracks for him, we started recording him. It didn't take long to discover he fell into Category Three.

The drummer who eventually recorded the tracks was Larry. Ironically, he agreed to participate in the recording because he heard the efforts of the previous drummer. He charitably offered up one day of his incredibly busy schedule (I'm not being facetious: the man was *incredibly* busy) and allowed me to take my recording gear to his house, where we could get what we could in five or six hours.

Anyone with recording experience will say that normally it takes five or six hours of studio time just to get proper drum sounds. And they'd be right. In fact, it often takes longer. Alas, I didn't have that luxury. So, after about an hour of setting up, we recorded drum tracks. (4) I got what I could and took it back to The Padded Cell. I must be honest here: I'm simply amazed it worked as well as it did. I knew Larry was a supremely talented drummer. But I also knew that we were recording this album backward. Timing could have been a serious issue, but I was able to sync all the recorded tracks with ease. In the end, Larry contributed drums to all but two of the 10 total tracks. The others were covered with my drum machines.

While I credited the entire band with writing the songs, I must admit I provided the foundation and impetus for about 75 percent of the material. More often than not, I recorded the basic tracks, and had the other musicians react to what I had already done. Jimmy Griffin, a friend and musician I hold in the highest esteem, came in and contributed a guitar solo to "Trouble Looms on the Horizon." He was stunned by the quality of the drums once I told him how I went about getting Larry's contribution. "That shouldn't happen," he told me. "The drums should be all over the place. But they're spot-on. You really lucked out." I can't argue with him. Or maybe I should have. Like I said, Larry is one hell of a drummer.

While hanging out in a music store, I met a Chapman Stick player named Tim Duggan. I wanted him to be part of my band, but he didn't have the time. One of the last tunes I wrote for Valley of Shadows was called "Fripp," a 6/8, high-speed homage to the founder of King Crimson. The guitar lines interlocked in the fashion of my favorite King Crimson music. The song begged for a Stick. Fortunately, Tim was willing to come by and spend the afternoon laying down the perfect part.

I can't help but wonder how great a band consisting of myself, Trey, Terrell, Tim, and Larry would have been. But that will just have to be one of those "road not taken" moments that may or may not wake me up in the middle of the night.

Despite the inherently backward nature of *Valley of Shadows*, I am proud to say that there is only *one* edit on the entire record. I've challenged more than one person to find it. Nobody has. I'm proud of *that*, too.

While I always revered their efforts, recording *Valley of Shadows* gave me even more respect for what musicians do in the studio. I can't even begin to calculate the number of hours I spent in that room, recording track after track, sometimes over and over again. I distinctly remember trying to nail the guitar solo on the title track before going downstairs for dinner. I finally got it right on attempt number 23. And my dinner was very cold. It was worth it.

By the spring of '03, the finishing touches had been recorded, the songs were mixed, and the CD was complete. While it didn't sound exactly what I heard in my head, it was pretty close. King Crimson member, Trey Gunn, once called one of the band's records "the map, but not the treasure." That was exactly how I felt about *Valley of Shadows*. I was proud of it, particularly when I realized the band's four primary musicians were never in the same room at the same time at any point of the recording process. In fact, Larry, Trey, Terrell, and I played together live only once, several months after the record was complete. But I knew the full potential of the music could be reached on stage, in front of an audience. Once the lights went up, we would be able to take this music to the next level.

But this, too, would never come to pass.

***

I talked *Valley of Shadows* up to friends in St. Louis with club connections. I planned to take the band on what I called "The Five-Hour Tour." If we could drive there in five hours or less, then we would play there. Kansas City, Chicago, Nashville, and points in between were all possible destinations. I even made a minor connection in the San Francisco Bay Area, giving me the wild idea of playing seven shows over ten days in California.

I use the term "show" loosely. I wanted nothing more than a 35-45 minute slot, opening for a more established act. I just wanted to get our sound out there. I knew we weren't going to make any money. But this was never about money. I longed for the adventure of going out on the road with a band. I was still young enough to be idealistic about the concept, even if I was old enough to know better.

And there was still that nagging constant that came with The Sheltering Sky: we lacked a drummer.

I thought we might have lucked out when Trey's friend resurfaced, and he seemed eager to have another go with the group. But that fell apart rather quickly. Eventually, we found another guy willing to sit in the drum throne. He was a nice guy, and eager to please. But despite his best efforts, we found ourselves saddled with another member of Category Three.

By this time, I was recording all band rehearsals, should another happy accident take place. Our new drummer lacked the raw aggression the material required. What does it say when I can stand right next to the drum kit, guitar in hand, and not be able to hear the drummer over two guitars and a bass? On one of the recordings, I can hear myself yelling, "*Hit* the fucking drum, man!" No, this wasn't going to work at all.

The funny thing is Larry played *the very same drum kit* when he came over to rehearse with us. After tinkering with the kit for several minutes, we launched into "Trouble Looms on the Horizon." From the moment Larry started playing, everything else fell right into place. I remember looking at Trey and Terrell as we played. We couldn't wipe the smiles from our faces. The Sheltering Sky had arrived, once again. Unfortunately, it only lasted a few hours.

Frustration set in, and the band soon found itself saddled with the priorities that come from being an adult, like day jobs, families, and bills. Making music slid down the priority scale, and our plans to "tour" fizzled out. The band, such as it was, fizzled as well.

Sales of *Valley of Shadows* would be geared around live gigs. I would create a web site, hype the band, and make a few audio samples available. More than anything, I would talk the band up to anyone and everyone willing to give us a stage for 30 to 45 minutes.

In the end, I wound up giving copies away to those who couldn't believe I was part of a recording project. Feedback has been generally good, and those who heard *Valley of Shadows* were eager to hear what we could do with it on stage. What a disappointment it was to tell people we probably wouldn't be taking the stage any time soon. And so, the web site was never built, and the remaining CDs were collecting dust in my attic. I stumbled across them while looking for something else. Reading those liner notes and thinking about the effort that went into that music pretty much defines the phrase "agony and ecstasy" for me.

The Sheltering Sky wasn't dead. But it was definitely on the "critical" list.

***

In early '07, I tried to resurrect the Sheltering Sky. I had some ideas for a new record, which I was calling *The Jungian Compass*. I recorded a few demos and invited Trey and Terrell to offer their input. Their enthusiasm for the new music gave me hope. But there was still one small problem. Yep, we had no drummer.

In the fall of that year, I completed a musical Hail Mary. I sent a copy of *Valley of Shadows* to King Crimson's drummer, Pat Mastelotto. I spoke to him a couple of times after Crimson's St. Louis shows, and found him to be a very nice and receptive man. I can still see his critique in my head. "I expected the music to be more derivative of Robert [or Crimson]," he wrote. "But you have your own thing going here. Sonically, I would make a few adjustments. But on the whole, it's very good." I was thrilled. And since it was my first time ever mixing a recording, I was more than happy to hear what he had to say about the overall sound. But the bottom line was this: a member of King Crimson dug my music! It couldn't possibly get any better. Or could it?

On a whim, I emailed Pat and asked if he might be interested in producing the Sheltering Sky. At first, he said it depended on his availability, potential resources, and his feelings toward the music. After hearing the first CD, he informed me that he would, indeed, be open to producing our next effort.

Quickly realizing I could kill two birds with one stone, I asked him if he would be interested in drumming for us. "Oh, that would be the fun part," his reply read. "Sure. No problem." My heart still skips a beat when I think about that reply. I wish I had printed out that email.

Pat and I roughed out an approximate fee, and I informed my band mates of my musical coup. Enthusiasm ran amok. The price was not cheap, and we would have to travel to Austin, Texas, to get the recording done. What's more, we would only have about a six-day window to record. But who cares? Pat Mastelotto wanted to work with The Sheltering Sky! Trey, Terrell, and I agreed to begin rehearsing in January of '08, with plans to travel to Austin and begin recording on October 24.

But even as I began to prepare for rehearsals, a sense of dread came over me. Somehow, I knew this grand plan would never come to fruition. In fact, I didn't practice nearly as much as I should, because I knew it wouldn't make any difference. The night before our first rehearsal, I was proven right.

I had stressed to my band mates the importance of rehearsals. But I never really questioned their total commitment, which was necessary. I just assumed they understood and would make any and all family members aware of this commitment. I was wrong.

Terrell called me and informed me our current plan would be problematic, where his family was concerned. I had always said that I would never tell a band member to put music before family, and I didn't tell him to do so now. I'm not psychic, but somehow I knew the problem Terrell was having was worse than he was letting on. Unfortunately, I was proven right. Within 24 hours of the first call, Terrell had left the band.

Trey secured both a rehearsal space and a practice drummer. Within a day of my telling Trey about Terrell, Trey told me both our rehearsal space and our practice drummer had been lost. He didn't say exactly why, and in all honesty, I didn't want to know.

The thought of breaking in yet another rhythm section to learn the Sheltering Sky's material nearly reduced me to tears. I'd had enough. In early January of '08, I permanently disbanded the Sheltering Sky. Before long, I stopped trying to make music altogether. It was just too depressing.

I should have known better than to put all of my musical eggs into one basket. But I've always been a dreamer, and I figured that somehow, some way, this dream of being in a moderately successful part-time recording and touring band was going to work out. But reality can be a cruel mistress, capable of crushing even the most realistic-seeming dreams. I should have been ready, willing, and prepared to go in a different musical direction. I wasn't.

There was one more cruel irony left to encounter. On the evening of October 24, 2008, I sat at a computer terminal in my office, working a robbery case. For reasons I can't recall, I needed to refer to my pocket calendar. Looking at the date, I saw I failed to erase the note I had made for that day: "Recording, Day One." I was supposed to be in Austin, making a record with Pat Mastelotto and the Sheltering Sky. The thought was still on my mind when my cell phone rang. It was my sister, informing me that our dad had passed away.

Even if I had gone to Austin, I wouldn't have been able to stay. Chances are, I might not have gotten the message that first night. Once I learned the news, I would have packed the gear back into our van and driven straight home to bury my father. This is where someone would tell me everything happens for a reason. It's hard to argue with that, even if it is difficult to hear.

The Jungian Compass remains a rather interesting – if slightly painful – thought in my mind. Perhaps one day, I might do something with it. Not too long ago, I sat in Trey's home studio, where we listened to demos I recorded what seems like a lifetime ago. I could still hear their potential. Trey asked me if I wanted to revisit the material and make something of it. I couldn't say no. Now all we need is the time to make it happen.

***

At one point, I had eight guitars, a couple of basses, two synthesizers, and about $10,000 worth of beat boxes and other recording gear under my roof. Over time, I sold off just about everything, including my beloved '96 Fender Stratocaster, signed by Adrian Belew. My daughter's private school tuition needed to be paid, and the gear was serving little to no purpose in my home. All logic aside, I came to regret that decision in much the same way I regret the Great CD Purge of '06.

Not long ago, the urge to make music hit me again in earnest. I was inspired by one of my new favorite bands, Umphrey's McGee. I was also digging sounds made by Tortoise and the Miles Davis bands of the '70s. It might be fun to make music like that, I thought. I even went as far as to send an email to Trey and Terrell, telling them about what I was thinking. They showed a little interest. But we never talked much about it after that. Before long, I was obsessed with golf. I didn't have to rely on anyone else to enjoy that activity.

There is still music in my head. *The Jungian Compass* could be a great record. I've plotted another solo CD, called *Exposing Person*, for years. It would be a shame if neither of these projects came to pass. But it wouldn't be the end of the world, either.

It would be easy to blame my band's failure on the people I surrounded myself with. But I place the lion's share of the blame on the guy I see in the mirror every day. I never doubted my commitment to the Sheltering Sky. But I should have questioned the commitment of my potential band mates much harder than I did. Future vetting processes, should they come to pass, will probably be somewhat brutal. But it will be for the greater good.

Most likely, there will be no band in my future. Instead, I prefer the idea of joining someone else's jam or recording session or inviting someone over to record with me for a day or two, tops. The thought of trying to find three or four other guys with the same level of musical commitment – especially given my age – is nightmarish, at best. Chances are, we would all be far too set in our ways to make it work. "People don't realize a band is like a marriage," Jimmy Griffin told me. "Being married to one person is hard enough. Now imagine being married to *three or four* other people, each with a strong personality, and being confined to cramped spaces like the inside of a van for extended periods of time. That's more than a lot of people can handle." I certainly saw his point. And my group never even got on the road.

Still, the dream has not completely abandoned me. Not long ago, I bought another Stratocaster. And I have since purchased to small amplifiers perfect for rocking out in my den, playing along with CDs, or recording on a smaller scale. I've even rebuilt my effects rig. I am ready to play whenever the Muse decides I am worthy of the effort. Something tells me that day is coming and coming soon.

(1)   A couple of days after the initial injury, my partner and I arrested a couple of guys who bailed from a stolen car. My shoulder was already killing me from the weight of the bullet-resistant vest I had to wear, but I did my best to hide it. Once we had the bad guys in custody, my sergeant arrived on the scene. He was so pleased with our effort, that he gave me a huge clap on the back, squarely at the center of my injury. To this day, I'm sure he thought he was seeing tears of joy coming from my eyes.

(2)   As a nod to Jimi, I begin the song with the opening riff from "Voodoo Chile (Slight Return)," but that's where any relation between me and Jimi Hendrix ends.

(3)   I don't have the original cassette master for *No Relation* any more. God only knows what happened to it. But I still have a few CDs left. Maybe one of these days, I'll

re-assemble the package and re-release the CD. Or I'll just give it away via download. We shall see.

(4) We almost weren't able to record, because Larry nearly deafened me by accident. I was setting up a microphone near his marvelous Drum Workshop bell brass snare drum. I was underneath the kit, and he forgot I was there. The snare drum is not only remarkably crisp, it's incredibly *loud*! My left ear caught the full brunt of several aggressive strokes. I screamed out, and punched Larry in the leg. He stopped playing, but it was at least an hour before I could hear anything properly out of that ear. It made earphone monitoring ... interesting, to say the least.

Adrian Belew, my musical hero **(Photo courtesy of Adrian Belew)**

Track 19
My Guru Belew

Someone once said a fan should never meet his hero, because the worshipper will only be disappointed. Clearly, that person wasn't talking about Adrian Belew. I have been fortunate enough to share the same space with my all-time favorite musician at least a half-dozen times, and I have never walked away disappointed. In fact, my faith in humanity is always elevated.

When people learn I'm into music, they ask who my favorite musician is. When I tell them Adrian Belew, I am almost always greeted with the same response: "Who?"

My reply to that question is always the same. "You may not have heard of him," I say, "but you *have* heard him."

Adrian's diverse musical talents, mostly by way of his guitar, have appeared on hundreds of records by dozens of artists. Turn on the radio for long enough, and there's a good chance that something Adrian played on, wrote, or produced is bound to start playing.

That horn section on Paul Simon's "You Can Call Me Al" is actually a guitar synthesizer, and Adrian is playing it. Who was imitating Bob Dylan and singing "Flakes" and "City of Tiny Lights" with Frank Zappa? That's Adrian. Who was making those wild guitar sounds heard on records from Nine Inch Nails? It was Adrian. Who made those otherworldly noises heard in the background (and sometimes the foreground) of Talking Heads records in the early '80s? Yep, it's Adrian.

Remember the Crash Test Dummies? They had a hit in the '90s with "Mmmm, Mmmm, Mmmm." Jars of Clay had a hit with an album called *Flood*. Take a wild guess who produced those records? Laurie Anderson, Herbie Hancock, Bela Fleck, David Byrne, and David Bowie have each benefitted from the talents of a smart, humble, unassuming man from Covington, Kentucky.

***

Years ago, there was a popular parlor game called "Six Degrees of Separation." This game morphed into "Six Degrees of Kevin Bacon," one of the more popular actors in Hollywood for some time. The idea was that any actor or director in movies could be linked to Kevin Bacon within six or fewer acquaintance steps. The results were both accurate and hilarious.

Upon looking at my CD collection, I realized that I could do the same thing with Adrian Belew. Little effort was needed. To prove my point, I pulled six CDs off my shelves at random, and made the associations. For example:

Miles Davis: Herbie Hancock played with Miles, and Adrian played with Herbie.

Led Zeppelin: John Paul Jones plays bass for Led Zeppelin. Robert Fripp was a guest musician on one of JPJ's solo albums. Adrian played with Robert Fripp in King Crimson.

Eric Clapton: Phil Collins produced records for EC in the '80s. Collins played in Genesis. Bill Bruford played drums with Collins in Genesis. Bruford played with Adrian in King Crimson.

And so on, and so on, and so on. By the time I pulled my seventh artist, and made the connection in less than four steps, I was laughing. Within the confines of music in general, and my CD collection in particular, Adrian Belew was *everywhere!*

***

Adrian's career is a testament to hard work, perseverance, and perfect timing. He started out as a drummer, which led him to play in his high school marching band in Ludlow, Kentucky. Not long after, he found himself playing drums and singing Beatles songs in a band called the Denems. The impact the Fab Four had on Adrian cannot be understated.

He was all set to become a music teacher before seeing the Beatles on the Ed Sullivan show in 1964. Then and there, everything changed. Adrian was now eager to become a professional musician.

In the mid '70s, Adrian was laboring away in a Nashville bar band called Sweetheart. The band played covers of the popular tunes of the day while wearing vintage "zoot" suits. Adrian considered himself to be a literal starving artist, and he was beginning to think about quitting his attempt to make a career in the music industry.

One day in '77, Belew found himself on stage at a biker bar called Fanny's, when Frank Zappa and his entourage walked in to the bar. Zappa was in town headlining a show and was looking for something to do afterward. His limo driver directed him to the bar where Sweetheart was playing. Zappa and his friends watched the band for a while, then the composer made his way toward the stage as Sweetheart played "Gimme Shelter," a Rolling Stones classic. Zappa was taken with Adrian's playing abilities and told the young guitarist that he would get Adrian's contact information from the limo driver, and then audition Belew for Zappa's next band.

Belew was forced to wait for nearly six months before the call from Zappa finally came. "I thought Frank Zappa was a big liar!" Adrian exclaimed with a laugh at an acoustic show he gave in Nashville in '97. But Adrian soon found himself flying to Los Angeles (his first time on an airplane, by the way), where he went through an arduous audition for the demanding taskmaster that was Frank Zappa. Despite being unable to read music (a requirement for Zappa band members before and since), Adrian won the job, most likely because of his unique approach to the guitar and his positive attitude. The fact that Adrian spent hour after hour of extra time learning the complex Zappa compositions (while staying at Frank's house) speaks volumes about his persistence.

After that, the instances of impeccable timing began.

Adrian toured the world with Zappa. Most of those musical efforts can be found on Zappa's album *Sheik Yerbouti* and the concert video *Baby Snakes*. The band eventually found itself playing in Germany. During one of the concerts, Adrian happened to notice David Bowie standing in the wings, watching the show. An avid Bowie fan, Adrian made his way over to the superstar during one of Zappa's signature guitar solos.

Adrian introduced himself, telling Bowie how much he admired his music. Without missing a beat, Bowie replied, "Well, how would you like to join my band?" As it happened, the Zappa tour was winding down and Adrian was looking at the very real possibility of a return to Sweetheart. Instead, he accepted Bowie's offer.

Another world tour followed, and Adrian found himself playing on Bowie's studio album, *Lodger,* as well as his live release, *Stage.* The producer of *Lodger* was Brian Eno. As fate would have it, Eno was also producing Talking Heads, a band looking for a guitar player. Timing struck again, as the Bowie tour was winding down and Adrian would need another job. Eno suggested Adrian to Talking Heads, and the return to Sweetheart was put off yet again. This time, it was for good.

Adrian's guitar sound, to my ears, was relegated more to the background with Zappa and Bowie. He could be heard, to be certain. But his signature abilities had not yet started to truly manifest themselves. That all changed within the confines of Talking Heads.

On the landmark album *Remain in Light*, Adrian's Fender Stratocaster cried, wailed, dive-bombed, and shrieked all over the Talking Heads soundscape. The album (one of my personal all-time favorites) was a series of single-chord jams finding the core Heads (David Byrne, Chris Franz, Jerry Harrison, and Tina Weymouth) breaking remarkable ground with Adrian and other musicians, giving themselves a funkier, edgier sound that produced hit songs like "Once in a Lifetime." But to truly appreciate Adrian's contributions to Talking Heads, the second disc of the live release *The Name of this Band is Talking Heads* must be heard. The listener cannot help but notice Adrian, who positively loses his mind musically during the set. His cries and wails can be heard all over the music as both point and counterpoint, sometimes seemingly at the same time.

There is video from this tour, showing a scrawny Adrian Belew standing stage left, his guitar appearing to weigh more than he does. But even from that peripheral position, one can sense the band feeding off of his energy. By the time they launch into "Crosseyed and Painless," things appear to have gotten out of hand in the best possible way. I have often dared friends to sit still while that song plays. It simply cannot be done.

Adrian's playing caught the attention of Robert Fripp, who had previously played with and produced Talking Heads. Not long after, Adrian was offered a spot in the soon-to-bereformed King Crimson. Once again, timing proved crucial, as Talking Heads appeared to be in turmoil. Adrian took Fripp up on his offer, and the nucleus of the band I "discovered" while walking across a parade ground in Richmond, Virginia had been formed.

* * *

Why is Adrian Belew my favorite musician? At least part of the answer lies within the question. Adrian is more than a mere guitar player. That point of view is far too simplistic. Adrian is a true musician, with genuine ability to play the guitar, bass, drums, piano, cello, and other instruments as well. Most of his solo records are one-man affairs. Adrian is a solo taskmaster who knows precisely what he wants his songs to sound like. And more often than not, in his mind, he is the only person that can produce that sound. (1) This is not to be viewed as a form of egotism, because when Adrian does choose to let others help him make his records, he gets the best of the best. Bassists like Les Claypool and Julie Slick, drummers like Danny Carey and Eric Slick, and vocalists like David Bowie are among those that have made appearances on Adrian's albums.

While Adrian is definitely among my favorite guitarists, to say that he "plays the guitar" is also low-balling it considerably. Yes, he plays chords and melodies on his instrument. But he also goes miles beyond that.

Most guitarists look at their instrument and go about the act of doing the most they can within the confines of the guitar's abilities. Adrian doesn't see the instrument that way. In fact, he seems to go out of his way to create sounds that clearly had nothing to do with the original intentions of the guitar's designer.

Adrian employs techniques with his hands that often defy description. The sounds produced by these techniques are equally unbelievable. Like many other frustrated guitarists, I have leaned toward the stage to get a closer look at Adrian's hands in an attempt to figure out how he does what he does. And like those other guitarists, I remain baffled.

In Adrian's hands, a guitar can suddenly sound like an elephant, a rhinoceros, or a seagull. Car horns and sirens come wailing forth from Adrian's amplifier, based on what he does with his hands and with the help of select effects pedals. And the sounds aren't simply superfluous noises added to an already complete song. Instead, they are often the center of the song, with the rest of the music supporting the unorthodox sound.

I have often found myself trying to describe Adrian's guitar playing to the uninitiated. I tell them that there are guitarists who root their sound in the basics, and others tend to stretch out, taking the guitar to unexplored places. Adrian has a knack for doing both at the same time. "Yes, yes. That's all well and good," one of my exasperated friends said. "But can he *play*?"

Adrian might not be the very first guitarist I call for a blues or jazz jam. But I assure anyone the addition of Adrian Belew to one's band invites colors and tones that make the music in question ten times more interesting. And regardless of the guitar, amplifier, or effects he is using, Adrian's sound always finds a way to shine through.

"The first time I heard Adrian play was in 1978, in a small rented apartment in Hollywood," said Rob Fetters, Adrian's co-guitarist in the Bears. "He was practicing with a Stratocaster plugged directly into a tiny Pignose amp, no special effects or gizmos. Now he uses what may be one of the world's largest and most advanced effects chains, but it really sounds only 10 percent different from that place on Franklin Avenue. Adrian's magic is in his mind and hands, not in his tools."

Adrian's methods are not only exciting to hear, but they are highly versatile as well. The list of artists he has collaborated with is testament to that. How many other musicians can fly to Los Angeles and spend several days making wild, dark, "outside of the box" sounds for Trent Reznor and Nine Inch Nails, and then pack up and head to New York to spend a few days in session with Paul Simon? Adrian has done just that.

Within the confines of his own music, Adrian defies easy categorization. His love of the Beatles has given him an uncanny knack for clever pop pieces. But he is also at home assembling a piece of "*musique concrete*," a la Frank Zappa. Sounds seem to come from everywhere, both musical and otherwise, blending into an audio soup that appears to have no discernible sequence. That is, until the listener takes the time to examine each ingredient in the soup, and he realizes that all the pieces fit together perfectly.

Adrian is also comfortable in metal-type settings, as his efforts with the 2000-era King Crimson and Porcupine Tree signifies. And while he claims to have little knowledge of the realm, Adrian can be found holding his own in jazz settings, too, as his work with Bela Fleck has shown.

The bottom line is this: to employ Adrian is to enhance whatever type of music is being played. Because Adrian isn't thinking about what kind of music he is contributing his talents to. His only concern is what he can do to make that particular piece of music better. And he does that as well as almost anyone else.

***

I was listening to and captivated by the music Adrian made throughout the '80s and '90s, but it had never occurred to me to try and meet the man. It wasn't a priority. I had the music, so what more did I need? Besides, in my mind, musicians were untouchable, like professional athletes. You might get to see them in passing, and perhaps get an autograph. But that would be the extent of it. And since I've never been an avid autograph seeker, there was no need for me to worry about it.

What's more, for at least the first year of my avid Adrian Belew fandom, I had no earthly idea what he looked like! The King Crimson records from the '80s – *Discipline, Beat,* and *Three of a Perfect Pair* – featured minimalist artwork. The album credits were printed on the LP's back cover. The song lyrics were printed on the inside sleeve that housed the record. But there were no photos of the band, or anything else. While King Crimson did appear on the ABC variety show *Fridays*, and they did have a video for the song "Sleepless" on MTV (most likely in the late-night rotation), I missed both of these. Talking Heads landmark movie *Stop Making Sense* was filmed after Adrian left the band. And I didn't see Zappa's *Baby Snakes* video until 2000 or so. YouTube did not yet exist.

I have joked that Adrian could have sat next to me in a bar and asked me to pass him the cocktail peanuts. In spite of my avid love of his music, I would have simply passed the peanuts to him and then gone back about my business. I would have been none the wiser.

Of course, this finally changed when I got my hands-on Adrian's first solo record, *Lone Rhino*. There he was, resplendent in a red suit, sporting the beat-up sunburst Stratocaster I later saw him playing with Talking Heads. Did seeing Adrian's face add anything to the music I was enjoying? No, not really. But it was good to see that the person making all of those wondrous sounds did in fact exist.

Still, I wasn't looking to have a chance to occupy the same physical space Adrian did. I didn't see the point. But that changed, beginning in the summer of '96.

***

Between 1982 and 2016, Adrian released 17 solo records. It will surprise nobody to know that I enjoy all of them. But the records Adrian released between '90 and '96 are the ones I hold closest to my heart. They contain some intensely personal music with lyrics that often reached me in such a way that at times, I thought Adrian was talking directly to me.

In September of '90, my Air Force duties saw me transferred to Yokota Air Base, Japan. This meant exploring the exchange (where military members and their families did their shopping), and discovering they had a record store. It was much better than I anticipated.

I did what I do every time I walk into a record store for the first time: I looked for my favorite artists. Miles Davis, Frank Zappa, and King Crimson were present, and in stock. How exciting! But what were the odds that they had anything from Adrian Belew? I headed to the appropriate section, to see what could be seen.

It was in the "Misc. B" section that I found not only a CD from Adrian Belew, but it was a new disc I was unaware of. Ten minutes later, I was walking back to my dormitory with a copy of *Young Lions*. I played the daylights out of it. The album contains some of my favorite songs, like the title track, "Pretty Pink Rose," "Gunman," "Men in Helicopters," and a wonderful cover of the Traveling Wilburys "Not Alone Any More." Roy Orbison sang the original vocal. That man will never be described as an easy act to follow. Still, Adrian's performance is a rock-solid recording that never fails to entertain me.

While I thoroughly enjoyed *Young Lions*, I was surprised to learn Adrian declares it to be one of his weaker efforts. His primary complaint was that he only had ten weeks to record the album. This sounds like a great deal of time until it is understood that with the exception of a couple of cameos by David Bowie and a gentleman who called himself The Prophet Omega, Adrian sang every track and played every instrument. That kind of effort takes a great deal of time. And time was the one thing that Adrian didn't have, since he was slated to tour the world as Bowie's primary guitarist and musical director for the *Sound and Vision* tour in '90 and '91. Still, I think Adrian undervalues the album. It is well worth the time for anyone willing to give it a listen.

When Adrian came off the road, he wasted no time putting together his next album. *Inner Revolution*, released in

'92, is firmly entrenched amongst my top three favorite Adrian Belew albums. It is pop music played at the highest level, with instrumentation and lyrics that can go toe-to-toe with any other album from the "Inteli-Pop" genre.

Adrian has confessed that he struggles most with lyric writing. The process can be excruciating for him. But hearing the completed songs makes that seem hard to believe. Adrian is comfortable with addressing his joys and demons directly through song. He can use metaphor, or take on an issue straight on, depending on what the song calls for.

Inner Revolution starts with the title track. In the song, Adrian makes it abundantly clear that the best way to make your world better is to take on challenges yourself. "You can't fix it with a drug, You can't kill it with a gun. Inner Revolution, that's the way it's done," he declares. (a) I can't say exactly how many times this mantra has snapped me out of a deep personal funk, but it's a lot.

Adrian confronts a fear of flying (which he has since conquered) in "I'd Rather Be Right Here" and the pain of his divorce from his first wife, Margaret, in "The War in the Gulf Between Us." I've gone through more than a couple of breakups since first hearing that song more than two decades ago. Every time it happened, I could hear Adrian singing to me:

"What was the sense in keeping alive
Something that never made us satisfied?
Sometimes it's better to get on with your life
I don't believe in hurting each other all the time" (b)

It didn't take long to realize how right he was. And with that, I could move forward.

I was still coming to grips with the brilliance of *Inner Revolution* when Adrian released his next album, *Here,* in '94. The new record was lighter, and with good reason. *Inner Revolution* was about dealing with loss and fear. The new record found my favorite musician in love with Martha, who would become his second wife. The opening track, "May 1, 1990," is all about the day Adrian met Martha in Orlando, Florida, while he toured with David Bowie. *Here* is a sweet record that depicts a man who has found a new lease on life. It is a pleasant listen.

In between the pop albums, Adrian took the time to make himself part of the "Unplugged" craze of the time by releasing *The Acoustic Adrian Belew* in '93. Stripped down to his voice and an acoustic guitar, the listener gets to the very heart of Adrian's previously released material, now re-recorded in the most intimate fashion.

When I started playing guitar, I was told by more than one musician that a sure-fire way to determine whether or not a song was any good was to strip away everything instrumentally and play it on an acoustic guitar. Adrian's album sounded almost like a personal litmus test, showing that his songs (and the two covers he added) were worthy of consideration from those who may have ignored his music before. Biased though I may be, I have no doubt that Adrian passed this test.

By '95, Adrian's experimental side had reared its head. Fresh from a foray with a re-united King Crimson, Adrian's new guitar effects rig helped him to create *The Guitar as Orchestra*. On this release, a guitar synthesizer, all the way from the opening applause through the final notes, generated every sound. While not everything on the album works for me, there can be no denying the ingenuity Adrian shows on this project. "Laurence Harvey's Despair" is an absolutely gorgeous piece of music. It is worth the price of admission on its own. *Guitar as Orchestra* is not how I would introduce someone to the music of Adrian Belew. But the importance of the album in terms of his musical "big picture" cannot be ignored.

Everything Adrian Belew is as a musician comes together in one package on *Op Zop Too Wah*, his '96 release. I remember getting a copy of this CD as a 30th birthday present to myself and being completely blown away. God forbid I'm ever forced to live with just one of Adrian's records. But if forced to choose, this would be the one.

Op Zop Too Wah offers listeners "The Full Adrian." Pop songs, aggressive guitar, quirky experiments, guitar synthesizer, *musique concrete*, and all points in between are compacted into some 60 minutes. If there were any justice in the world, this album would have won the Grammy for album of the year for '96. Alas, that honor went to Alanis Morrisette for *Jagged Little Pill*. Go figure.

***

Before I could meet my hero, I had to endure two near misses.

The first came in August of '96. King Crimson was on the road in support of their latest album, *Thrak*. I knew that the band was touring in Europe, Asia, and Central and South America. I had even heard rumors that there would be some concerts played in the United States. But St. Louis is not known for bringing the more musician-driven bands to town. I figured that if I wanted to see Crimson, I would have to make my way to Chicago when the time came. Since I was still single, this seemed well within the realm of possibility. I would just have to wait.

As it turned out, that would not be necessary. The H.O.R.D.E. Festival was coming to town, taking place at Riverport Amphitheater. (2) Blues Traveler was the headliner, with Lenny Kravitz scheduled to appear right before them. There were at least 20 other bands scheduled to perform, both on the main and assorted side stages.

Normally, I wouldn't have given such an event a second thought. There weren't enough bands there to hold my interest and justify paying $30 for a ticket. (3). And I certainly didn't want to schlep out to Riverport, where I would be gouged for the privilege of parking my car and would then have to wait at least two hours to get off the parking lot when the event was over. Nah ... I could go along just fine without going to this gig. That thought was still in my head when I looked toward the bottom of the list of bands and saw a very familiar name.

Holy shit! King Crimson is playing the H.O.R.D.E. fest!

Suddenly, there was nowhere else I would rather be.

I read the announcement on a Tuesday. Tickets went on sale that Saturday. I spent the next several days attempting to rally a few of my friends so we could make our way to this event.

I had yet to see King Crimson live. The term "Bucket List" had not been coined yet, but seeing this band perform on stage was definitely something I had to do before I met my proverbial maker. I had to be at this show. I *had* to be! Who knows when I would get another opportunity? If we got our tickets quickly, then we would have prime seats.

My friends showed mild to moderate interest, but they weren't quite as fired up as I was. Seeing King Crimson was a much higher priority for me than it was for them. Still, I decided to be patient and wait for them to join me, even as Saturday came and went. By the following Thursday, there was still no pro-active movement from my friends. I heard all about family obligations, bills, and the hatred of the venue (4), but nothing about being willing to power through all the excuses and make our way to the show. It was time to act on my own behalf. On Friday, I went to Streetside Records, and purchased my own ticket. I was going to the show!

My seat was in row KK, which is not exactly next to the stage. I was a little bummed out by this, if only because I knew I could have gotten a much better seat had I just gone ahead and bought one the previous Saturday. My friend Kim sold me the ticket, and she could see my disappointment. She then let me in on a music industry secret. "Come back on the day of the show," she said. "Sometimes, the corporate sponsors give tickets back, and maybe you can get a better seat. I can't refund the ticket you have, though. It's up to you to decide whether or not you want two seats." I had several months to think about it, so I said that I would let her know.

Time passed, and the day of the show arrived. I can't begin to describe the level of my excitement. I remember thinking to myself, "By the end of this day, I will have finally seen my favorite band of all time." Perhaps it was that thought that spurred me to head to Streetside Records to see if there were any better seats available. If I had to pay for another seat to wind up in a better spot, so be it.

Kim wasn't working that day, but my friend Tony was. I told him what Kim said, and he nodded in agreement. "Let's go back to the ticket station and see what's available," he said and motioned me to the back of the store.

I admit I was skeptical as Tony began his search. I had my chance to get good seats, and I let it pass because I chose to wait for my friends. I would never make that mistake again, I vowed. It is a policy I adhere to even now. If I invite someone to a concert, they must be ready to act when tickets go on sale. Otherwise, I will move right along without them. It's nothing personal. But if I say that I'm going to the show, it's an ironclad lock that I'll be there!

The look on Tony's face a few seconds later told me that I might be in for good news. He confirmed my guess by saying, "Do you think you can live with third row, center?" Once the feeling came back into my legs, I was able to jump up and down with excitement. Another 30 dollars had to be spent. But now I was going to be infinitely closer to my favorite band, and my favorite musician in particular. I couldn't get to Riverport fast enough.

***

Crimson was scheduled to open the show. (5) They would take the stage at about 5 p.m. I parked my car at Riverport Amphitheater just before three. For reasons that elude me, I brought both of my tickets with me. But I made damn sure that my third-row ticket was in exactly the same place on my person all evening. There was no way on Earth I was going to lose *that*.

Even after showing the usher my ticket and being taken to the third row of the venue – some 15 feet off the center of the stage – I couldn't believe where I was. In just a couple of hours, I thought to myself, Adrian Belew would be right *there*. Wouldn't it be great if I could actually talk to him? What would I say? Would he sign the program I purchased? Perhaps I would find out soon.

I watched the King Crimson crew set up the band's equipment, trying my hardest not to drool all over myself. I could tell who would be stationed whereas the men worked. The Double Trio was the Crimson band of the moment. The back row would consist of drummers Pat Mastelotto and Bill Bruford on the left and right, respectively. Robert Fripp would sit in between them. The bass players, Trey Gunn and Tony Levin, would occupy the front line. Adrian would be in between them. I could virtually reach out and touch his microphone. But knowing I was looking at Adrian's microphone was nowhere near as exciting as when his flaming orange Fender Stratocaster was placed on a guitar stand, just behind and to the right of the microphone. Now it was real. Adrian was really going to be here.

That thought was resonating in my head when I realized the band was walking out on stage, preparing for a sound check. I saw Bill Bruford first. He sat behind his drum kit, fiddled with some of the equipment, and then picked up his sticks and banged on a couple of drums. He didn't need to do much, because he was active for what only seemed like a minute or two. Then he was gone, just as quickly as he came.

Mastelotto and Gunn came out next. Like Bruford, they spent a scant few minutes playing around with the instruments. But the Crimson crew is efficient, and minimal work was needed from the musicians. By the time Mastelotto and Gunn were finished, I noticed that Robert Fripp had made his way to his position. Sitting at his customary stool, Fripp strapped on his guitar, and then ran through a few sounds, fiddling with his effects rack as he did so. I must admit I was captivated by Fripp's actions, because they nearly caused me to miss the entrance of Adrian Belew.

He strode out from the back of the stage, wearing a blue suit coat, white t-shirt, blue jeans, and loafers. His receding hairline was countered by long, straight brown hair, grown down to his shoulders. Adrian seemed to be every bit as laid back as his album covers portrayed him to be. He struck me as being completely approachable. This was confirmed when he acknowledged the smattering of applause from fans by smiling and waving to them. He almost seemed surprised by the outburst, but he was clearly amused by it.

I was applauding, too. But the action taken by my hands was now independent of my brain. I was too busy wondering if I could have any meaningful contact with the man I called my musical hero. The answer to that question came seconds later, when after picking up his guitar, Adrian turned back toward the seats, and made direct eye contact with me.

The moment was at hand! I was eye-to-eye with my hero.

I couldn't think of a single word to say.

All I could do is manage a meager wave and a smile. Adrian must have noticed that I was star-struck, because he just grinned at me and nodded. Then he went to work, running the opening chords of "Dinosaur," my favorite Crimson song of the time, through his guitar synthesizer. Satisfied with the sounds he was hearing, Adrian ran through a couple more sound patches, put the guitar back on its stand, and walked off stage.

I had choked. Hard.

Anyone who knows me is aware I have the proverbial gift of gab. Talking to someone has never been a problem for me. Until now, that is. How utterly, albeit personally, embarrassing. Hot anger flashed throughout my body. But it didn't last. I realized quickly that I might have another opportunity to talk to Adrian once the band's set was complete. I was determined to try again. Plus, I still had a King Crimson performance to look forward to.

***

Because they were the opening act, King Crimson was only allowed to perform for an hour. (6) To their credit, the band took the stage promptly at 5 p.m., and played right up until 60 minutes later. It was an hour filled with fabulous music, featuring new songs from *Thrak* and several of my '80s favorites, like "Frame By Frame" and "Elephant Talk." Adrian expressed his disappointment with the required length of the set to us, saying that Crimson wanted to play for much longer, but they were not allowed. With that, the band performed a rather rushed, but entertaining, version of "Indiscipline" before leaving the stage to a standing ovation.

I was still annoyed about choking on my chance to talk to Adrian. But while I was fuming at myself, I remembered there was an entrance to the backstage area. It was the gate from a wooden privacy fence, located at the rear of stage left. I knew I couldn't get backstage, but the gate opened to the amphitheater grounds. Any artist coming out of that gate could roam around the area, visit concession stands, purchase souvenirs, or even mingle with fans.

Suddenly, I had a new purpose.

The next band up was Rusted Root. They had a minor Alternative hit with a song called "Send Me on My Way." I saw no need to stay in place for their set. And since I came alone, I was free to wander around the grounds as I pleased, and take my time doing so. This was my chance to head for that gate and meet my hero.

I went to the gate and waited. And waited. And waited some more. Only a couple of people came out, and none of them were Adrian. Meanwhile, Rusted Root was didn't sound half bad. I felt myself being slowly drawn back toward the stage, wanting to see what I was hearing. I wandered back, ducking and dodging around fellow festival fans, many of which could have used a shower. The H.O.R.D.E. festival was a great draw for the mid-'90s equivalent of the Hippie. They appeared to be following the festival, bringing their hacky sacks, Birkenstocks, and B.O. with them.

The festival had drawn a pretty good crowd, many of who were still making their way to their seats. I was weaving in and out of these people, while trying to watch/listen to Rusted Root and look for Adrian at the same time. I was about to re-enter the main pavilion, when I decided to check the gate one more time. When I did, I thought I saw a familiar hairdo.

The people in front of me distorted my view. So, I couldn't be certain that I had just seen Adrian enter the grounds by way of that gate.

I made my way there as quickly as I could, but negotiating the human traffic was no easy task. Finally, I got close enough to get a good look at the gate.

There was nobody there.

I took a minute to scan the grounds, hoping that I could determine which way the ponytail I thought I saw had gone from where I now stood. No such luck. If Adrian had been there, I had missed him. I started back toward my seat, feeling completely dejected. As I made my way toward the pavilion, I realized that the path was almost devoid of people, now that they had made it to their seats. It was almost as though the fans had conspired to keep me from meeting my hero. That is ridiculous, to be certain. But that's how it felt.

I made it back to the pavilion, reaching for my ticket as I did so. Just before walking back in, I took one more look at the gate, just in case.

And like magic, the gate opened.

My heart nearly jumped into my throat. The gate remained open for an eternity, with no one coming out. Finally, a figure emerged. It was King Crimson drummer Pat Mastelotto.

I had not even remotely considered talking to anyone else in King Crimson. My mind was focused on Adrian. I was a good 50 feet from the gate. Pat was walking out by himself. Whatever had taken hold of me and rendered me unable to talk to Adrian had vanished. I heard myself call out, "Hey, Pat!" And just like that, he turned right toward me.

I offered up a little wave, expecting little in return. Instead, Pat not only returned my wave, but he smiled and started walking right toward me! Figuring that he must have recognized someone behind me, I turned around. There was no one there. When I turned back, I was greeted with a warm smile and an extended hand, ready for shaking. "Hey, it's nice to meet you!" Pat said. "How are you? What's your name? Did you enjoy the show?"

I introduced myself and declared that I had just enjoyed my best hour while still fully clothed. Pat found that hilarious. He signed my program, and we talked for the better part of 20 minutes. He even introduced me to one of his friends, who sauntered up halfway through our conversation.

So, I got to spend some time with someone from King Crimson after all. (7)

***

The Internet is a wondrous thing. I've been surfing the web since about '97. How I went through the previous 29 years without that much information at my fingertips is beyond me.

It's only natural upon gaining access to the World Wide Web, people want to know as much as possible about what they love. So it didn't take long before I was gathering all the information I could about Adrian Belew.

One day, I found a great website that featured all things Adrian. Before long, I was visiting the site every day. The information I was getting from that site was better than anything

I was reading in *Rolling Stone* or any of the guitar magazines I was just getting into. Webmaster Rob Murphree appeared to be the first person I had ever come across who was more obsessed with Adrian's musical efforts than I was!

I was so impressed with Rob's work, I decided to drop him an email to thank him for his efforts. I got a reply from him just a few hours later. And just like that, a cyber-friendship was formed. Rob and I would chat at least three times a week for quite some time.

In late '97, Robert Fripp was actively trying to find the next course of musical action for King Crimson. The band wasn't making much progress as a "double trio," so Fripp tried something rather radical: he broke the band into small sub-groups, which he dubbed "ProjeKcts." They would then explore music both written and improvised, almost always in a live setting, which would theoretically forge the next path for the larger band to explore. It was announced that ProjeKct II would consist of Fripp on guitar, Trey Gunn on bass, and Adrian Belew on drums.

ProjeKct II struck its first blow almost by accident. Fripp and Gunn were visiting Adrian's house outside of Nashville. As it happened, Roland had just delivered a set of V-Drums to Adrian, and he had them set up in his studio, located on the lower level of his home.

V-Drums were the next generation of electronic percussion, supplanting the Simmons electronic pads used by drummers like Bill Bruford. In addition to being fully programmable, V-Drums felt more like acoustic drums, and they responded to the dynamics of the player's drumsticks. They were even shaped like acoustic drums, as opposed to the octagon pads used by Simmons.

Without plugging them in, the sound of a drumstick striking a V-Drum was that of a stick striking a beanbag. Run through a PA system, V-Drums sprang to life, taking on the characteristics of nearly any commercial drum kit available at the time.

Adrian, Fripp, and Gunn had been working toward new King Crimson material, when they decided to take a coffee break. Spotting the V-Drum kit in the corner, Fripp asked Adrian to give him a demonstration of "the mighty wonder tubs." Adrian obliged and sat behind the kit. Shortly after he started playing, Gunn and Fripp joined in. The trio's sound engineer, Ken Latchney, was savvy enough to press the "Record" button in the studio's control room. Twenty minutes later – to their immense amusement – ProjeKct II had recorded its first song. They went on to record enough material for an album, which they called *Space Groove*.

It was quite an adjustment for me to listen to Adrian as the drummer of a band, as opposed to the guitarist. While he played drums on his solo records, that was not his sole duty. So I listened to Adrian's drumming as part of the song's whole. Now I was listening to Adrian propel the band from the back, rather than the front. While my hero's drumming didn't do anything to make me forget Bruford, Rush's Neil Peart, Phil Collins, or Billy Cobham, there could be no denying the solid foundation that Adrian was laying down for Fripp and Gunn to blaze away over. ProjeKct II was a fascinating band. I wanted to hear more from them.

As if he heard me make the request, Fripp announced that ProjeKct II was about to embark on a tour of the east coast of the United States. Unfortunately, none of those stops would include St. Louis. (8) The closest they would get to me would be on opening night, when they played at The Cannery, a club in Nashville.

During one of our email chats, I expressed my disappointment to Rob, who lives in Alabama. What he wrote in reply shocked me. "You should come to Nashville," he wrote. "I'm going up there the day before to do some work for Adrian's site. I'll be at the show and hanging out with him afterwards. You're a big fan and a great guy. I'm sure he'd love to meet you. You can hang out with us."

Had I been drinking something, I would have done a spit-take. Meet Adrian Belew? Hang out with my hero? And all I have to do is come to Nashville? Sure! No problem!

The gig was around Valentines Day of '98. While my girlfriend was not a huge Adrian/King Crimson fan *per se*, she was open to more music than most women I had ever known. I believed I could sell the trip as both a musical and romantic getaway, since we had never been out of town as a couple. To my delight, she was open to the idea. Within minutes of gaining her approval, I went online and ordered a pair of tickets. One of the more exciting days of my life was the day those two tickets arrived in the mail.

Rob and I continued to make arrangements for our meeting via email. We would have dinner and drinks before the show. I made sure my work schedule was clear. My girlfriend wrangled a couple of days off. My sister was going to look after my cats. We were all set.

But it never came to pass.

The day before we were to leave, I began to feel sick. A nasty flu bug had been going around the police station, and my partner had fallen victim to it. I did all I could to avoid getting sick myself, but it would appear my efforts had failed. I tried to medicate myself, but the virus seemed to just smile and keep coming.

My girlfriend, a nurse, could see that I was getting sick. She also knew that the medication had been started too late. Before going to sleep that night, she began to prepare me for the fact that we weren't going to make the trip to Nashville. I stubbornly refused to accept this. I was certain I could sleep it off. I thought about dropping Rob a line, telling him I was sick. But that sounded defeatist to me. I would sleep and wake up tomorrow feeling right as rain.

Wrong.

I felt three times worse the next day. Fever, chills, dizziness, and nausea landed on me like a ton of bricks. I couldn't get out of bed, let alone drive a car for five hours to go to a concert. I never saw my girlfriend look sorrier for me than I did that day. My attempt to argue my case for going was interrupted by me vomiting into a trashcan. She took the can, laid me back down, and covered me with the blanket. I was scheduled off work for the next three days. I spent two of them in bed feeling like death on a soda cracker.

When I finally made my way to the computer, the emails from Rob were waiting for me. "Where were you, man?" the notes demanded. "I was looking everywhere for you. You missed a great show. It was a really good time."

That was bad. But what followed was infinitely worse. "I told Adrian about you," Rob's email sad. "He was really excited to meet you. We were at the club for hours, having drinks while he told stories. Man, you don't know what you missed. And Adrian's car almost got towed! I hope you're ok, and nothing bad happened to you."

I thought I was feeling better. That email set me back a little.

I sent Rob a reply, informing him of my health issues. When his reply came, it practically dripped with sympathy. "I'm sure you'll have a chance to meet him," he told me. "It will happen before you know it."

As it turns out, Rob was right. I just had to wait another year.

***

King Crimson began work on its next record, *The ConstruKction of Light,"* in 2000. The band was trimmed to a quartet, or "double duo," as Robert Fripp put it. Pat Mastelotto and Trey Gunn would now be the rhythm section behind Fripp and Adrian. But before diving back into the band, Adrian gave a little attention to his solo career.

With his 20th anniversary of joining Crimson coming up, Adrian decided that he wanted to compile a box set of his works, covering music he made as a solo artist, with Frank Zappa and other bands, King Crimson, and the Bears. The compilation was being called *Dust.*

In support of that effort, Adrian embarked on a solo tour throughout a portion of '99. He didn't even take a band out with him. In true Belew fashion, Adrian recorded some backing tracks, and played along with them in concert. For this tour, Adrian proclaimed he would have his "hands in the past and the present." I was excited by the idea of hearing some of my '90s favorites live. I couldn't wait to hear it.

Best of all, I wouldn't need to go to Nashville for this gig. Adrian was coming to me. The show was going to take place in the Duck Room at Blueberry Hill, a club located in the University City loop, just down the street from Vintage Vinyl. Perfect. I couldn't buy my ticket fast enough.

Having learned my lesson the first time, I attended the show alone. I would have been happy to take someone with me, but it just didn't work out. That's just the way it goes. Plus, I could get to the venue early, with no complaints from anyone about just sitting around, waiting for the doors to open.

Blueberry Hill is a bar and grille that gained its initial notoriety by being partially owned by rock and roll legend Chuck Berry. It's a nice place to go for a burger and a beer. The restaurant is loaded with musical memorabilia, not unlike a Hard Rock Café. The walls are lined with photos of the musicians and bands that have come through. Nearly every inch of wall space is covered.

The Duck Room is downstairs. For me, it is the perfect place to see a concert. The room holds about 250 people. It's hard to get a bad seat. Assuming, of course, there is seating in the first place. For some shows, the few tables and chairs are cleared out, and it becomes a "standing room only" venue. The stage is elevated, so having to see over or around someone taller is rarely an issue. The stage always struck me as being a little small, but every band I've seen there always seems to find just enough room for the musicians and their gear.

I arrived at Blueberry Hill some 90 minutes before the doors were due to open. To my amazement, I was not the first person there. Rather, I was about fifth. After buying a beer, I queued up with everyone else. We exchanged small talk, discussed our favorite Adrian moments, and waiting patiently. While we talked, we could feel the floor vibrating as Adrian conducted his sound check below us, and we played our own little game of "Name that Tune," in an attempt to gain a sneak preview of the show's set list. Eventually, the vibration stopped. Apparently, Adrian had what he needed.

How to describe the average Adrian Belew fan? Is there even such a thing? We come from all walks of life, but are predominately male, over 30, and intellectual. Even I can't help but describe us as being a little nerdy. I've stood in many lines for shows featuring artists like Adrian. There is not a lot of talk about sports.

There is, however, a small sub-group of fans that tend to distinguish themselves by having intricate knowledge of artists like Adrian. This fan could break down every album track by track, telling you who was in the band, or the ultimate meaning of the song. This fan could distinguish himself even further by having attended multiple concerts. While I could certainly hold my own on artist and song knowledge, I've never had the time or money to see an artist two dozen times or more on the same tour.

I listened with a combination of awe and befuddlement as a couple of fans talked about how they followed Adrian or King Crimson on tour in years past. As impressive as the achievement sounded, I still found myself very tempted to ask one of these Super Fans, "Don't you work? How are you paying for all of this?" Fortunately, I was always able to resist the urge.

It is in the fan's best interest to know what he is talking about, where the artist is concerned, before speaking. A show of ignorance may not get you shunned from the conversation, but your contributions will definitely be marginalized. I myself have done this to one or two people. In my defense, these people sounded like they got hold of a couple of free tickets, and they decided to come to the show as a goof. They were aware that the artist or band existed and might even be able to name one song.

Chances are said song was the artist's only hit or had been recorded at least 10 years prior.

I would rather the less-knowledgeable concert goer admit his ignorance up front and ask questions about who and what he was about to see and hear. The fan who does this is actually embraced by the rest of us, and we often go out of our way to bring the novice up to speed. By the time the doors open, the novice almost feels like an expert!

***

Not long after the sound check ended, the door leading to the Duck Room opened, and out came a couple of people who worked at the club. They were chatting about whatever it is that people who work at Blueberry Hill chat about. And then from behind them strode Adrian himself. I was even closer to him this time than I was at Riverport! This time, at least, I wasn't the only person in awe of the man.

Adrian waved at us and smiled. We waved back as he made his way through the restaurant, and off to points unknown. Somebody asked him to sign something, and he replied, "I'll sign whatever you want after the show, ok?" That was more than enough for us. Adrian has a knack for keeping the kindest part of his personality up front all the time. Fans can be annoying and self-entitled. They want what they want, and they want it NOW. If the artist doesn't deliver, then the fan sees the artists as a jerk, or worse. This has to grate on a musician's nerves.

Some artists have chosen to isolate themselves from their fans because of this. After all, a rock star is one snippy remark from seeing his fan base greatly reduced. But Adrian has always presented himself as being affable and accessible. All he asks of his fans is a little patience. And we are happy to oblige.

Those who don't understand the rules have found themselves incurring the wrath of the obedient fans acting as a barrier between the rude subject and the musician. The rude fan can find himself on the embarrassing end of a stern scolding, or escorted off the premises, should his actions go over a certain line. Yes, I have seen this happen. Yes, I have become a temporary escort.

The Adrian Belew/Prog Rock fan is *not* to be trifled with.

***

After what seemed like an eternity, the Duck Room's doors were finally opened. Unlike many major rock concerts in much larger venues, there was civility as the fans made their way downstairs. Nobody ran over anyone to get into the room. We simply walked down the stairs, turned right, and made our way to whatever spot we liked. There were a few tables toward the front, and I made my way to one of them. I found myself situated slightly left of center stage, about eight feet from Adrian's microphone. I was a happy camper.

The show started on time. There was a warm-up act called the Irresponsibles, a pop-oriented group Adrian produced. Promptly at 9 p.m., Adrian Belew came through the dressing room door, located stage left, and sauntered onto the stage. He looked enthusiastic and itching to play before his rabid fan base.

There was a lot of energy in the crowd, and Adrian picked up on it. His smile was infections, and he dug into tunes like "Dinosaur" and "Inner Revolution" with what appeared to be extra relish. He seemed to go out of his way to make eye contact with as many people as he could, including me. I was in heaven. I had loved these songs and this artist for 15 years, and now Adrian Freaking Belew was standing *right there*, bringing them to life! And he looked at me! I must admit, even that eye contact scared the hell out of me. He didn't know my name, where I was from, or what I was about. But it didn't matter, because I was digging his music. That was all we needed.

***

About 40 minutes into the show, Adrian stopped playing and announced that he would like to do a little "Question and Answer" session with the audience. I had seen him do this before at a solo show recorded in Nashville that Rob Murphree had been kind enough to share with me.

People always seemed to ask the same things. What was it like to work with So-and-So? When is your next record coming out? What's going on with King Crimson? I was determined to ask something different.

My hand shot into the air with what seemed like just about everybody else's. So I was more than a little shocked when Adrian pointed directly at me and said, "Yes, sir?" What followed immediately after altered the way I looked at Adrian Belew forever.

Apparently, my "thought" and "voice" wires got crossed, because my next thought after Adrian pointed to me was, "Wow! That was really fast!" Trouble is, I hadn't thought it at all. I had said it out loud! And without missing a beat, Adrian responded, "Well, you were first!" In that moment, whatever wall of fear I had of my favorite musician imploded on the spot.

I was no longer talking to Adrian Belew, Guitar Legend and Musical Hero. I was talking to Ade, Cool Dude I Can Have a Chat With. The butterflies that had been kicking a hole in my stomach magically vanished, just like that.

Still, I needed a minute to recover from my thought/voice mix-up. But I had the floor, and I needed to do something with it. So, I vamped, deciding that this was the perfect time to make a statement on behalf of the audience. I summoned my courage, took a deep breath, and spoke. "Well first of all, I'd like to thank you for coming here tonight, Adrian," I said in my best U.S. Air Force Spokesman voice. "We don't get nearly enough quality musical acts in this town, and I think we all appreciate you taking the time to play for us." Adrian offered up an "aw, shucks" grin he must have learned in Kentucky, while the rest of the room broke into enthusiastic applause.

After a quick bow, Adrian stepped back up to the microphone and said, "It's because of people like you that I'm happy to play these shows, so thank you. Now, what's your question?"

My moment was at hand. But now, I was not the least bit worried about blowing it. I just let it flow. "I was wondering," I asked, "When did you know you'd made the right choice to become a professional musician?"

The look on his face – quizzical yet intrigued – told me I had asked something new. He actually had to take a moment or two to think on it. He stared off into space for a heartbeat or two, and then re-engaged his microphone. Looking directly at me, he finally answered, "You know, I'm *still* not completely sure." The room erupted in laughter.

He could have left it at that. I would've been perfectly content. Instead, Adrian spent the next three or so minutes expounding on what he had just said.

He talked about just wanting to be a high school music teacher, and then seeing the Beatles on *The Ed Sullivan Show*. He talked about his time in the Denems and Sweetheart, and how he very nearly quit the music business altogether. And he talked about finally getting his big break, and how fortunate he was to have done what he had in music up to this point. It was a great moment. I felt like I had done my bid to help educate the audience about a great musician.

When the show was over, Adrian sat at his merchandise table, and took the time to speak to anyone who wanted to chat, and autograph anything a fan wanted signed. I had brought along my copy of *The Guitar as Orchestra*. While it was not my favorite music from that era, that particular CD did contain an excellent photo of Adrian sitting on a bench in his home. There was enough open space for an autograph along the top of the photo. Adrian must have been thinking the same thing. When I presented him with the CD, he started signing in the exact space I had hoped for.

I thanked Adrian for the considerate answer to my question. He smiled and said, "It was my pleasure. That was a really good question." Now that my fear and nerves had been cast aside, this seemed like a good time to engage in slightly deeper conversation with my hero. I told him that I was supposed to meet him in Nashville the year before, but the flu kept me from attending.

To my surprise, his eyes showed instant recall of what I was talking about. There was nothing but sympathy on his face. "Oh, *no*! I remember that!" he said. "Rob was telling me all about you. I was really looking forward to meeting you. He kept looking all over for you, but you weren't there." Adrian must have seen the shame rising in my face. "But if you're sick, you're sick, man. There's nothing that you could have done about it. I'm just glad we finally got to meet." Relief flooded back over my face. Adrian extended his hand again. "Thanks for coming out," he said as I shook it. "I really appreciate it."

I wanted to part ways on a lighter note. "I play a little guitar, too," I told him. "Maybe you could produce me one of these days."

Adrian laughed and said, "Give me a call. I'm reasonable." With that, I made my way out of the line, out of the club, and back to my car.

I don't think my feet touched the ground.

I've met with and spoken to Adrian at least four times since then. And we've exchanged emails a couple of times. He has never been anything other than gracious and kind. (9) I wouldn't presume to rate one encounter over the next, but I remember being incredibly happy after leaving the Duck Room with my favorite '96 Fender Stratocaster, shortly after Adrian had signed it. He also took a picture with me, still holding my guitar. I was positively giddy. And anyone who knows me will tell you giddiness is *not* my strongest suit.

It's the stuff that heroes are made of.

***

*I've been lucky enough to get VERY close
to Adrian while he's performed. I was so close to
him here, I had to lean back to get all of him
in the frame.*

What has enabled Adrian to remain my musical hero for three decades? What does he have that other musicians don't? If I were to put it into a single word, that word would be versatility.

Adrian's voice and guitar sound have the ability to move from one genre of music to another with minimal effort. Adrian not only rolls with the punches, but he lands crucial shots while he makes the music in question sound better.

His ability to switch musical gears, seemingly on a dime, comes from a never-ending series of ideas. "I understand music on a level where I'm able to fit into anything. I have ideas for anything you present me," Adrian said. "You can be Paul Simon and present me a song, and say, 'What would you do here?' And I'll have some ideas. You could be Trent Reznor with this strange, dark music, and ask 'Do you have any ideas?' Yeah, I've got some ideas!"

Adrian's "ideas" have shown up in more places than the average musician can take credit for. Some of the bands are relatively obscure or cult bands like Man on Fire or Porcupine Tree. He has shared the stage with jam-band favorites Umphrey's McGee. Everyone that thought they were enjoying an "original" Mariah Carey song in "Fantasy" were actually hearing the main riff of a song called "Genius of Love" by the Tom Tom Club. That band featured Tina Weymouth and Chris

Franz of Talking Heads, and their guitarist, a guy by the name of Adrian Belew.

Adrian has also appeared on recordings by Peter Gabriel and Stewart Copeland, the drummer from the Police. He played a prominent guitar role one the album *Strange Little Girls* by Tori Amos. He can even claim a *Star Trek* connection after adding his guitar to the songs of Captain Kirk himself, on William Shatner's release, *Has-Been.*

Musicians everywhere seem to understand: if their music needs a capable, affable guitarist with a never-ending source of original ideas, it's best to call on Adrian Belew!

***

As they get older, most artists tend to slow down and become more selective about musical appearances and releases. Sometimes they seem to remain in place. Adrian appears to be going in the opposite direction. His output has not only increased, but it has made its way across new artistic mediums.

The first part of the 21st century found Adrian hard at work with King Crimson, releasing and touring first behind *The ConstruKction of Light,* and then *The Power to Believe.* When Crimson finally came off the road, Adrian wasted no time diving back into making solo records.

One day while driving his sixties-era pickup truck, Adrian struck a dog that wandered out into the road, killing it. An avid animal lover, Adrian was devastated by the incident. But the incident also triggered something in the musician. He suddenly felt the need to paint the image of the dead dog tormenting him.

A trip into Nashville found Adrian visiting an art supply store, where he asked tons of questions, and then he came home with the equipment necessary to begin painting. Before long, his first painting, called "Dead Dog on Asphalt," was complete. That painting graced the cover of *Side 2,* the second of four releases that came out rapid-fire between '05 and '07.

The *Sides* albums found Adrian releasing his music in a format oriented more for the modern listener. With the advent of iTunes and the iPod, Adrian realized that the attention span of the average music fan had grown considerably shorter. Releasing records that lasted from 45 to 60 minutes no longer seemed viable to him. *Side One, Side Two,* and *Side Three* each lasted around half an hour. To Adrian, it was like listening to a single side of an LP.

The albums were also Adrian's definitive effort to form a three-piece band, which he dubbed the Power Trio. His first attempt, which utilized musicians around Adrian's age, fell apart shortly after its first tour. Adrian decided that he would be better off using younger musicians, whom he could mold and shape himself. Tryouts were held at his home, but the plan never came to pass. The bassist and drummer he hired simply lacked the chops to bring Adrian's visionary (and often complex) music to pass. For a time, all seemed lost.

In 2006, Adrian visited Paul Green's School of Rock in Philadelphia as a guest musician. The visit was going well enough, but Green insisted Adrian jam with a sister and brother rhythm section. They had already graduated from the school, but Green felt these were the musicians that Adrian had been looking for. Shortly after, Adrian found himself playing remarkably complex Frank Zappa music with bassist Julie Slick, then 20, and her 18-year-old drummer brother Eric. Not only were the Slicks not intimidated by Adrian's presence, they positively *nailed* "City of Tiny Lights" and other songs. There was no ignoring the vibe that had been created. Adrian had found the two members of his trio.

Julie and Eric took to Adrian's musical catalog with relish. Adrian upped the ante by creating a guitar rig that allowed him to loop his own guitar sounds, then play along with them. In other words, Adrian was doing the work of *two* guitarists, while the rhythm section blazed away behind him. The results of these efforts are apparent on *Side Four*, a live release issued in '07.

It didn't take long for Adrian to figure out he had an immense amount of talent on his hands. Adrian and the Slicks were making remarkable music, offering up blistering performances of Adrian's solo material and King Crimson tunes. Since he had the musicians who allowed him to catch lightning in a bottle, Adrian embarked on his most ambitious (and my favorite) instrumental work, which he simply called *e*.

"I wanted to write a piece of music that I thought would showcase the abilities of my young new trio," Adrian told me. "I wanted to write something I knew would be super challenging for them and would show off the talents they had, and the talents of the Power Trio. As it developed, though, it turned into a much longer idea, a much deeper idea. It went from one piece of music to, 'How about I do this more thematically?' After three years of very hard work on those separate ideas, it became a 43-minute piece of music in five sections."

Based on the quality of the music, not a moment of those three years was wasted. Naturally, Adrian acted as his own co-guitarist. His King Crimson-esque melodies were interlocked with stabbing chords and sizzling lead lines. He wrote challenging parts for his rhythm section as well. The Slicks tore into those parts with relish far beyond their years. I'm still trying to decide what amazes me more: the music's complexity, or the fact that the band recorded it *live* in Adrian's studio.

The advent of modern recording systems, like Pro Tools, make it possible for lesser musicians to make records by splicing together (via computer rather than reel-to-reel tape) performances from multiple takes in order to create a perfect whole. That didn't happen here. The Power Trio approach is much more organic. Adrian Belew wrote *e*, the Slicks learned *e*, and then the Power Trio recorded *e*.

The pieces were named alphabetically. The song "B3" would probably be deemed the most difficult on the album. Julie Slick told me with a smile that the trio dispatched the piece in a single take. Her pride is justifiable. I was certainly familiar with the track and impressed by it. But after learning that the song was completed in one try, I can't help but laugh with excitement as I listen. Even Adrian knew that his band was on fire. The "B3" section gives way to "C," my favorite piece. As the song builds to its crescendo, Adrian can be heard exclaiming "Yeah!" amongst the brilliant clatter of the trio. It sounds as though joy exploded out of him, and he just couldn't help himself.

I don't blame him.

***

Even for the best musicians, there are professional setbacks and disappointments. Adrian Belew is not exempt from these occurrences. The year 2013 appeared to hold significant commercial potential for my hero, for he had been tapped by Trent Reznor to join the touring edition of Nine Inch Nails. The band was about to head out on the road for a 15-month world tour in support of the new album, *Hesitation Marks*.

When Adrian made the announcement via his web site, my feelings were mixed. On one hand, here was a great opportunity for Adrian to raise his profile on a huge stage. Nine Inch Nails sold out arenas pretty much everywhere they went. Now people would actually be able to see them man who made all of those wild guitar sounds on NIN albums. There was also the potential for a pretty decent payday for Adrian. Any "outside" musician will remind fans cringing at a commercial project those obscure records must be financed in some way. A gig with Nine Inch Nails would no doubt help pay for a lot of future Adrian Belew solo records.

On the other hand, I for one had trouble picturing Adrian on stage with Nine Inch Nails full-time. To me, he just didn't fit the image, based on NIN shows I had seen both on video and in person. The music didn't necessarily offer the same level of precision as a King Crimson or Power Trio performance. And I was quite certain Adrian wouldn't tolerate being splashed with bottled water by Reznor, or do any stage diving, as NIN guitarists were known to do. So how would he fit in?

It turned out to be a moot point. One minute, Adrian was updating his blog about the special sounds he would be making for Nine Inch Nails. Then, just as suddenly, he was out of the band.

When I talked to him about it, I told Adrian I had trouble picturing him playing Nine Inch Nails music in the same fashion night after night. It turns out I wasn't alone in that feeling. "In retrospect, I wish that we had foreseen that, too," he said. "I kind of did. I said going into it for months before, as I was learning the tunes, 'I don't see how this is going to work.' Trent told me he and I were going to re-invent the sound of Nine Inch Nails. I was thinking what he meant by that was I would just be Adrian Belew doing new things in his music, not that I would be, 'Okay, now you play exactly what's on the record, and you're going to play exactly what's on the record exactly that way every night for 15 months.'

"By the time I realized it, I had learned 21 songs, and wasn't playing anything that was my own. He and I both came to the same realization: *what the hell am I doing here?* (Reznor) already had another guitar player who could do all that stuff in Robin Fink, who had been doing it for years. I really was not needed."

And just like that, Adrian went back to Nashville. But he holds no ill will toward Reznor or Nine Inch Nails. "I think our relationship is still in place," he said. "I hope so. I do like Trent. I like what he does on a sonic level. He's a good (musical) painter."

For a time, things seemed to go from bad to worse. In the summer of '13, Robert Fripp announced that King Crimson was reuniting, and would be heading back out on the road in the fall of '14. The new lineup featured three drummers (Pat Mastelotto, Gavin Harrison, and now Bill Rieflin), the return of saxophonist Mel Collins (who was featured on '70s era Crimson records), and Tony Levin on bass. Fripp would, naturally, hold one of the guitar spots. The second spot would go to Jakko M. Jakszyk, who would also handle the vocal duties. After 33 years, Adrian Belew was out.

King Crimson Mark VIII, as it became known, would focus primarily on the band's early catalog, from '69 to '74. It would lightly touch on the '90s and Y2Crim periods. The '80s material (which Adrian dominates) was, for all intents of purposes, going to be mothballed.

The news hit me like a ton of bricks. Adrian was part of my King Crimson "discovery" way back in 1985. I had never known the band to exist without him. How could they move forward? It wasn't fair! My Belew bias was firm. I decided that I would take little to no interest in this new version of King Crimson.

As it turned out, the "scorned" musician had a much more philosophical view on his exclusion than his fan. After speaking to Robert, Adrian simply decided, "Ok, that's fine. I wasn't really wanting to (play the older material) right now anyway. If I'm not fitting into the picture, that's ok. I have my things that I want to be doing."

Where I saw bitter disappointment, Adrian saw opportunity. "I've realized that I only have myself," he told me. "I'm Adrian Belew, a recording artist. I can't think of myself as Adrian Belew in a band (like Nine Inch Nails) or I'm Adrian Belew tied to something else that I have no control of (like King Crimson). I have to use what's left in my life to create my own music.

"I have no bad thing to say about any of it. I just feel like it's not for me. I think Robert did me a favor, really. He was right. I shouldn't be a part of it. If something seems like a real disadvantage, you have to learn how to turn it around 180 degrees in your favor"

And that's precisely what my hero did. He re-assembled the Power Trio, and took them around the world, playing to the delight of audiences everywhere. He even resurrected the '80s and '90s King Crimsom material via the Crimson ProjeKct, a band consisting of his power trio and Stick Men, which featured Crimson members Levin and Mastelotto, along with touch guitarist Markus Reuter, who handled the Robert Fripp guitar parts. The band performed with the complete endorsement and enthusiastic support of Crimson founder Fripp.

One of my favorite concert experiences of 2011 was the Stick Men/Power Trio Tour. It was a three-hour extravaganza. Stick Men opened the show, followed by a set from the Belew Power Trio. That was followed by a brief set featuring Belew, Levin, and Mastelotto, with the sextet Crimson ProjeKct making up the finale. For a fan introduced to King Crimson via the '80s band, this was nothing short of musical Nirvana.

When that was done, Adrian went home to Nashville, and dove back into the passion project that may very well serve as the most innovative part of his musical legacy.

***

It is impossible to count the total number of musicians who have been described as being "ahead of their time." In many cases, such a description might even be somewhat true. For Adrian Belew, the description can be considered quite literal. For my musical idol conceived what might be his musical legacy in the late '70s. Technology didn't permit him to bring it to life until the end of 2014.

One thing is certain: Adrian hears music differently from just about everyone else. The website bearing his name contains a blog. On June 5, 2013, Adrian explained to his fans just what it was he was hearing in his head, and what he wanted to do with it. That blog entry, unique format intact, follows:

"may 28, 1978. marseille, france.
on tour as a member of david bowie's band.
the night before we had played a concert at palais des sport.
it's a day off. I have never been to marseille before
so in the afternoon I wander down to the famous port area.
I sat outside between two cafes.
beautiful day. the cafes both had their doors open
and both of them had different radio stations playing.
in fact, one of the radios seemed stuck between stations
and seemed to be jumping from one thing to another.
one second it would be an accordion song, then static,
then it would turn into a cello performance,
then it would return to the accordion song, and so on.
in front of me was the harbor, full of activity.
the sound of boats, motors, water, seagulls,
people walking by talking in french (of course),

cars driving past, children playing, a boat bell ringing, and all of this interrupting the different types of music playing on either side of me.
I remember closing my eyes and listening
to this beautiful cacophony; the sound of life.
and I thought "this is how I want my music to sound someday.
music being interrupted by life being interrupted by music."
from that moment on I began working out how
that could ever be possible.
over time I added in other ideas.
what if, just like life, the music never repeated itself?
what if it was always different, surprising?
how could you do that?
over the decades since may 28, 1978 I returned again and again to this idea until it became a mild obsession.
I knew sooner or later it would be something I had to do."

What Adrian had to do ultimately became known as *FLUX: Music That is Never the Same Twice.* Technology has finally evolved to the point where the unique idea of a young musician enjoying a day off in Europe has manifested itself into a computer application that is being enjoyed by fans the world over.

With help from an Amsterdam-based designed company called MobGen, Adrian brought forth a new app (currently based in the Apple iOS format) that allows fans to experience his music via stream, 30 minutes at a time, in a completely different way each time it's played. The songs are intercut with ambient noises, *musique concrete*, and other sounds dropping out as quickly as they dropped in, leading to the next song. Sometimes, the listener gets to hear a full song. Most times, he doesn't. Adrian offers up fragments of the tune, like the rhythm tracks, background vocals, and guitar parts. Even if the same song is featured twice in 30 minutes, it's not heard in the identical fashion. There is much insight to be gained from hearing music this way. It can also be delightfully maddening. Adrian's album *Op Zop To Wah* comes very close to simulating the FLUX experience.

I've come to think of FLUX as the equivalent of an old FM radio tuner, where the stations are accessed via a large knob on its face. Starting from the left side of the dial, the listener turns the knob to the right, enduring static, idle chatter, and other noises before the tuner hones in on a song, which is usually already at least partially complete. Once the song is complete, the tuner's dial is turned to the right again, with more noise and static cutting through the speakers before the next song emerges. FLUX is a continuous left-to-right journey across that FM dial.

FLUX has proven to be quite successful and popular amongst Adrian's fans, and is certainly among the best 10 dollars I've ever spent. I can only imagine the app becoming more popular once he finds a viable and affordable method to release it to Android users. Currently, the app is only available to Apple users. Fortunately, no one will be left behind, musically. The music and ambient noises from FLUX will also be released in conventional CD fashion.

Naturally, I'll buy that, too.

***

As I write these words, Adrian Belew is in his mid-60s. We like to believe our heroes are going to live forever. But as many a sports radio host has noted, Father Time is undefeated. I really don't spend time thinking about the demise of my hero. But everything ends. I just hope it takes a long, long time.

Adrian continues to worship at the church I like to call "Our Lady of Perpetual Motion." His Facebook page is bursting with news of fresh songs and plans for CD releases, tour schedules, and paintings. Good Lord, so many paintings! It seems as though he only stops long enough to take in a meal at his favorite Mexican restaurant, and then it's back on the creative treadmill. I can only dream of having that much creative energy.

Adrian has said in the past he would like to pursue music until he is in his mid-80s, and then he would concentrate on painting. I suppose he sees himself painting until his very last day. I have no trouble envisioning that very scenario. Still, to my mind, there are only two acceptable ways for Adrian Belew to shuffle from the Mortal Coil, and join that Great Jam in the Sky (10).

Since Adrian possesses a deep, undying love for the recording studio, it seems fitting he would drop as the last note from the last song from his last album resonated through the control room speakers. Left behind would be his greatest studio work of all. It would be released shortly after his passing to the joy of his fans, old and new.

The second way makes even more sense. Adrian would be on his deathbed, having done everything he wanted to do. Family and friends surround him. (11) Adrian would be motionless, his eyes closed, arms on top of the blankets, and drawing slow, deep breaths.

The clergyman has just left the room. It would seem to be only a matter of time. Tears are flowing all around. Suddenly, a smile comes across Adrian's peaceful face, and his eyes flutter open. His hand rises from the bed, and he gestures to a relative, who quickly comes to his side, and leans in to hear what he has to say. Adrian's voice is dry and husky.

"I have an idea," he says to the relative. "Hand me my guitar ..."

Just before this photo was taken, Adrian said to the photographer, "This guy here? This is a good man." Hence, my goofy expression."

(1)   Artists like Prince, Jeff Lynne, Todd Rundgren, and Lenny Kravitz have also been one-man bands in the studio. All are very good at what they do. But from time to time, I have complained that these artists could have benefited from having a band with them in the studio, recording live. Once in a while, I've had similar feelings about Adrian. The more aggressive the material, I thought, the better off Adrian would have been with a band in the session. Yet I'm well aware the first two albums he made were recorded with a band, and I don't enjoy them as much as I do his other records. Go figure.

(2)   I don't remember what the acronym stands for, and I don't really care. It's not relevant where the story is concerned, anyway.

(3)   As it turns out, I was introduced to, and became a huge fan of, Me'shell N'Degeocello, who was playing on one of the side stages at this event. I was coming down from my "just saw King Crimson" high, when I took notice of this diminutive, dark-skinned, bass-playing woman with a shaved head just *tearing shit up* with her band. I stood in front of her bass cabinets, and I could feel the low-end notes going right *through* me. I instantly became a fan for life.

(4)   I'm not a fan of that amphitheater, either. As a matter of fact, Riverport Amphitheater is one of the reasons that I no longer go to concerts at large venues.

(5)   The very idea that King Crimson, a band of great skill and deep musical history, had to open the show for Blues Traveler, a jam band with a couple of minor hits under its belt, struck me as remarkably insulting. I'm sure the mainstream music fans will be quick to point out that there were less than 2,000 people in attendance when Crimson took the stage, and close to 20,000 by the time Blues Traveler finished its set. This means nothing to me, because Blues Traveler has been relegated to the "What was I thinking?" section of the music industry for many, while Crimson continues to plug away with its rabid fan base intact after more than 45 years.

(6)   I bought two $30 tickets, two $30 t-shirts, and a $15 program. I also spent $10 to park my car. This means I spent approximately $1.92 per minute to see King Crimson live for the first time. I have no regrets. It was worth every penny.

(7)   I actually had a moment of interaction with another member of King Crimson during the show. Early on, I realized I couldn't hear Tony Levin's bass. I was close enough that we could see each other clearly. When he made eye contact, I pointed to my ear and shook my head. He seemed puzzled, so I repeated the gesture. Understanding, he checked his bass, and saw that it wasn't plugged in properly. He shoved the cable's connector pin into the bass's jack-plate, and his five-stringed instrument sprang to life. Tony looked at me, and I smiled and gave him the "thumbs up." He smiled back, and all was right with the world as he went back to thundering away.

(8)   In fact, none of the ProjeKcts appeared in St. Louis.
       While I understand that Chicago is a larger town, and
       more receptive to experimental bands like this one, I still
       find it remarkably frustrating. For every interesting
       independent instrumental band that came to my town,
       there were at least five who didn't. This is why I am
       frequently heard saying St. Louis is the city where good
       music goes to die.

(9)   Adrian did manage to anger me once. But even that was
       handled with hero-worthy grace and class. We discussed
       the issue via email, and my anger vanished as quickly as
       it had arisen. (In my defense, I had the flu – again – at
       the time, and I was more than a little hypersensitive. I
       admitted as much to him.) We broached the topic again
       at our next face-to-face encounter. Within 30 seconds,
       we were laughing about it. What he did initially really
       doesn't matter anymore.

(10)   In an online interview conducted on his website, Adrian
       was asked whom he would like to perform with. He
       replied, "John Lennon and Jimi Hendrix, but I'm not in a
       hurry!"

(11)   I would not presume to believe that I would be one of
       the people in that room. But I'd like to think that
       someone there would call me shortly after leaving.

(12)   (a), (b) "Inner Revolution" and "The War in the Gulf
       Between Us" written by Adrian Belew. Copyright 1991,
       Saiko Music Co. All rights reserved.

SIDE FOUR

The iPod was supposed to be a musical dream. But in its own way, it became a bit of a nightmare.

Track 20
(Near) Death by Download

I was in the mood for a '50s era Miles Davis album. I thought it would go nicely with the book I was reading. So, I headed to my CD shelf to find what I needed. Alas, the disc wasn't there.

I checked in a couple of other places, to be sure I hadn't misfiled it. (1) But the CD was nowhere to be found. I took a minute to think, and then I remembered: The CD I was looking for left my shelves long ago.

"Damn," I muttered. "Another victim of The Purge."

The year 2006 was significant for at least two reasons. First, it was the year I turned 40. This is a significant age, because I am not a "kid" any more. Any attempts to hang with twenty-something people seemed less "hip" and more "creepy." It was time to embrace the onset of middle age with grace and dignity. The only time I might "skew" younger was in my music choices.

Secondly, '06 was the year I decided to invest in my first iPod. What seemed like a perfectly reasonable and thoughtful decision very nearly destroyed my musical world.

On the surface, there is nothing wrong with digital music players. The concept is nothing short of wondrous. Digital music files take up a fraction of the space and were stored on the internal hard drive of a music player like the iPod, making it possible to reduce an entire music collection into something that could be carried in the palm of his hand. What's not to like?

I didn't have an exact count, but my CD collection lingered somewhere in the neighborhood of 1,800 to 2,000 CDs. (2) As I neared 40, I yearned for space. Over the years, I had collected more than a little "stuff." This stuff was now taking up valuable space. The thought of opening up areas reserved for shelving by putting all that music into a hand-held device (as well as an external computer hard drive) seemed too good to pass up.

I love to travel. And where I go, music follows. I have no problem with packing, layovers, hotels, rental cars, or anything else that goes with it. What always made me crazy was picking my road music. At first, it meant picking 15 or 20 cassettes for my Sony Walkman. Over time, it evolved into picking the same number of CDs for the DiscMan. But the problem was always the same: my ever-shifting musical tastes made it very difficult to choose those records. The day I pack, I'm in a progressive rock mood. But the day I land, my focus will have shifted to jazz. And now I'm nowhere near my collection to rectify the problem. The iPod would render that problem moot.

In the fall of '06, I bought my first iPod. It was a 30-gigabyte model, which was the largest Apple sold at the time. Not long before, I purchased and Apple MacBook Pro. The stage was set for me to bring my music collection into the 21st century. I wasted no time getting home and plugging CD after CD into my computer, creating my first iTunes library.

Almost immediately, I ran into my first challenges.

I had nearly 2,000 CDs to deal with it. There was only so much hard drive space on my laptop, and my entire collection would not fit there. So, I had to stop what I was doing long enough to buy an external hard drive. This was a wise move, anyway. Computers are known to crash. And should that happen, the data they store goes with them. I needed some backup.

Which lead me directly to my second problem: the iPod wasn't big enough to hold my entire collection.

What good was having a device that stored your entire music collection if the entire music collection couldn't be stored there? I was back to my traveling problem, albeit on a larger scale. I had to pick and choose what would travel with me, and I had to choose carefully. Once the files mate with the iPod, it's for life. There's no moving stuff in and out. (3)

The external hard drive gave me more than enough space to store my music. Now all I had to do was pick what would go into the iPod. In the end, I found most of my rock-oriented material was making the cut. That was, after all, what I spent most of my time listening to. Since I was also a bit of an eBay junkie at the time, I was able to track down an earlier generation iPod at a reasonable price. That is where I put most of my jazz, blues, and R&B.

And so, the Monumental Music Collection – which took up large amounts of wall space in assorted dorm rooms, apartments, and houses over the years – was now stored on the corner of my desk, next to my computer. I had all the music, so there was no need to keep the CDs, was there? Thus, began The Great Purge of 2006.

Between three or four record stores, I sold CDs by the boxful. The everyday title netted me an average of three or four dollars. Rare and limited-edition CDs would get me twice that. On the whole, I felt I did well, considering I was making money on music I still had.

I was also finding Internet services that made it possible for me to add to my music collection without leaving home. This was even better than Columbia House, because I could get the music I wanted instantly. Primarily, I was dividing my efforts between iTunes and a monthly subscription service called eMusic. For a nominal fee, I had access to thousands of albums, which I was essentially purchasing one song at a time. No need to disappoint myself at the record store any more, where the friendly clerk would tell me the album I wanted was sold out or, worse yet, out of print. No more waiting weeks for a special order to arrive. The music was available right then and there!

I don't know how much downloading I did from those two sources, but it was a *lot*. My external hard drive filled up quickly. I soon needed a backup for my backup.

I should have been happy. I had more music than I knew what to do with. I had space in my home for recording gear and instruments. Things should have been just fine. But something strange happened.

I started to lose interest in music.

There were serious side effects to downloading, which I had not considered. For starters, I began to forget just what music I was collecting. Also, I could no longer see my music collection, in the form of jewel boxes on shelves. Therefore, in my mind, the collection ceased to exist.

When I go to a record sore, I know precisely what I bought. My collection was such that when I bought something new, I would store it on the media shelf, but leave it protruding slightly from the rest of the CDs. This served as a reminder I hadn't played it yet. While I got my music via eMusic, there was no tangible evidence I had bought anything. The new records simply became part of my external hard drive's trove of data. Since the music came from relatively obscure bands, and since I almost always bought more than one record at a time, it was not uncommon for me to lose track of what I was downloading. This was especially true if I was busy, and I didn't have time to check out the new records right away. I can't count the number of times I scrolled through my iPod and said, "Damn, I forgot I bought that one!"

I also hadn't realized how important the tangible aspect of purchasing music was. When I downloaded, there was a level of excitement missing. I loved removing the cellophane shrink-wrap and the protective sticker holding the top of the jewel box closed (which, thanks to my record store friends, I knew how to remove both quickly). I loved gazing at the LP or CD for the first time. If you held the LP up to the light at a certain angle, a prism formed from the vinyl surface. This also worked with the "data" side of a CD. There was something spiritual about that.

I've been told my need to possess the physical music product is little more than a "jewel box fetish." The need to physically obtain a record is little more than a mental tic, easily dismissed with time and practice. I disagree. There is more to it than that. The opening and examination of the package is just the beginning. There is another aspect of music collecting frequently absent from the mere download. I'm speaking of liner notes.

I am the guy who reads all about the recording he just bought. I like to know where the album was recorded. It's fun to discover how many albums were recorded at the Record Plant, Electric Lady, or Real World studios. I am equally fascinated to learn an album has been recorded at the artist's home studio, which is usually located in a basement, bedroom, backyard shed, or garage. I want to know who handled the recording and engineering, and mastering duties. I'm often amazed by how many times I come across names like Rick Rubin, David Bottrill, Alan Parsons, and Bob Ludwig (4). There are times when I'll take a chance on an unknown artist once I find out one of these people is involved in the project. After all, I respect their work enough to know they wouldn't waste time on a sub-standard musical endeavor.

Also lost in the digital shuffle is the album cover. It was bad enough when the 12 by 12-inch LP cover was replaced by the half-sized CD jewel box. Downloading a record often took the cover art out of the equation altogether. This is a travesty. I believe a lot is said about the music by way of its cover art.

I think back on how I never would have heard some of my favorite records had the LP art not gotten my attention. Albums like *Bitches Brew* from Miles Davis or *Romantic Warrior* from Return to Forever had me transfixed before I ever heard the first note. The "moon in sun" crests from King Crimson's album *Larks Tongues in Aspic* resonated so deeply, I had it tattooed onto my left arm. Eventually, I will have the Celtic knot from the *Discipline* album artistically rendered on my right arm. (5)

Within the confines of the iPod, a record's cover art measures some two by two inches, hardly the best way to put across such an important artistic expression. That is, assuming the cover art makes it to the mp3 player in the first place! Sometimes, the cover art does not transfer to the player at all. Instead, the photographic or artistic expression of an album title is reduced to a generic pair of eighth notes. Not exactly an awe-inspiring expression.

Over time, Apple must have heard the wailing and moaning of art junkies like me, because they began to offer digital downloads of the album's cover art and liner notes. They were offered in a CD-sized rendering for those who wanted to take the time to print them off and create their own CD booklets. Thanks, but no thanks. It's just not the same.

Over time, the second major issue with downloading became apparent. The mp3 player is fine for what I call "up close" listening. That is to say, the iPod into ear buds is fine for a trip to the gym or doing the housework. It even translated fairly well into small speakers connected to my computer. But when the time came to connect it to my main stereo system, I found the sound to be lacking. (6) Heard causally, the sound of the mp3 through the stereo is adequate. But I began to notice some details were missing. I couldn't tweak the EQ quite the way I wanted. Today's music is quite bass-heavy, and these players are designed to convey the modern sound. As such, the top end, or treble, is greatly compressed. True sound balance – the sound heard by the musicians in the studio – is rarely audible via mp3.

I'm fully aware not everyone is as picky as I am where sound quality is concerned. I realize there is only so much I can do in the car or at the gym. But I simply cannot function that way when I listen to music at home. I want to hear what the band played, what the producer designed, and what the engineer spent all that time tweaking those knobs for. That's why I'm still using the same three-foot tall, 14 inch wide, 12-inch deep, 280-watt Cerwin-Vega speakers I have been blasting music through for nearly 20 years. They get me where I want to go, often to the disdain of my family, who can feel the rumble from upstairs.

***

The digital age has made it possible not only to download music via the Internet; it is possible to "stream" the music via various digital Internet "radio stations." Like many others, I jumped at the opportunity to bring the music I loved into my office without worrying about carrying a bunch of CDs, or remembering to bring my iPod to work.

Downloading and streaming are frequently viewed as the same thing, but the concepts are quite different. A download is physically manifested on the buyer's personal hard drive. It can be burned on to a CD, made into a playlist, or used in any other way the buyer sees fit. Streams, on the other hand, are played and controlled by companies like Pandora or Spotify. The songs can be enjoyed anywhere, but cannot be downloaded or copied.

My vehicle of choice was Pandora. The concept was irresistible: simply type an artist or genre of music into the search engine, and out came the chosen artist and music sharing similarities with the original choice. My personal favorite was my XTC channel, which brought forth intelligent pop, ska, and new wave music from the '80s. It was the best parts of the left side of the FM dial all over again. My second favorite channel was geared around progressive rock band Gordian Knot. I was taken through all manner of prog, mostly from Europe. King Crimson would pop up now and then, as would Rush. I also discovered a few new bands in the process.

I was a happy music junkie. But then it hit me: I wasn't paying for Pandora. The cost of admission was enduring a 30-second ad every few minutes. That was a small price to pay, given the lack of musical variety and endless stream of commercials found on FM radio. Still, I couldn't imagine a 30-second ad on Pandora cost enough to fund the royalties due the artists.

Given my own efforts to start and maintain a band – to say nothing of recording and producing a CD – I understood how hard it was to make a buck as a musician. This would be even more difficult for an independent artist whose record had little to no hope of ever generating "gold" or "platinum" sales. How on earth were the musicians I loved and admired being paid for their efforts? I found it hard to believe there was a lot of money in streaming. The truth, I learned, was far worse than I had imagined.

The deal most musicians got from record companies for CD sales was bad enough. A four-man band might have to split a dollar per CD sold, despite the $15 retail price. It was a bucket of ice water to the face to learn a million-selling CD might net the individual musician about $62,000 after taxes, legal and management fees, recording costs, and the other incidentals. The artists with the most potential might be given a big-time advance from the record company, which was awarded against future album sales. If the artist wasn't careful – and he frequently wasn't – he could find himself in serious debt, with no realistic hope of escape. (7) In any case, a musician hoping to grow rich on CD sales alone was in for a long and disappointing wait.

Streaming makes a bad situation worse. Artists do not make pennies on the dollar per stream of their songs. They make *fractions* of pennies. Even the Taylor Swifts of the world find themselves earning four-figure payments for millions of streams of their hits. With that in mind, imagine what Adrian Belew must be making. The thought makes me queasy.

Once again, I am fully aware many people do not give a damn. They have the music, which they paid x dollars per month to obtain, if anything at all. Any lack of financial gain is on the artist and the deal he was foolish enough to sign. I'm fascinated by this callous view toward musicians. After all, who among us wants to work for free? I've been doing the same job for 20 years. I love it, but I'll raise holy hell if my paycheck isn't deposited properly every other Friday.

Songwriting can be an arduous process. From the original seed of an idea to the last tweak on the final mix, countless man-hours are spent on the perfection of a song. When all is said and done, the artist (and his or her label) agrees to sell said song for 99 cents on iTunes. A buck? Seriously? I shudder to think of just how much a hit song is worth per hour, in relation to the minimum wage. Things get slightly better should the consumer decide to purchase an entire album, which usually goes for $9.99, but that's still not very much given how many directions that 10 bucks has to go.

Contrast that, however, with the $0.005 per play that streaming service Spotify pays the artist, according to well-respected (and highly knowledgeable) music journalist Anil Prasad. In order to achieve *one hour* of the United States federally mandated minimum wage of $7.25, a song must be streamed 1,450 times. That comes out to 58,000 plays for one 40-hour "work week" worth of streams.

I rarely find myself sympathizing with an artist like pop sensation Lady Gaga. But even I have to shake my head at the notion that one million streams of one of her hit songs netted her a grand total of $167. Based on her deal, it would take 4,053,110 streams per month to obtain the equivalent of minimum wage, according to Prasad. If Lady Gaga is bringing home $167, how much is an "unknown" artist like Rob Fetters getting? Starving artists, indeed.

Contrast those numbers with this one: in 2011, Spotify made $266 million. And the numbers are only going up. "Streaming is a great thing for the streaming companies, their (record) label partners, and consumers," Prasad said. "But it is horrifically unfair to the artists. Until this is corrected, listeners need to understand that they are fundamentally harming the artists they love by using these services."

I was horrified to learn of these modern musical economics. Even so, there could be no denying the entertainment value I got as I sat at my desk and worked cases. So, I made a pact: I would write down the artists and tunes I liked, then go to the record store and buy the CD. My knowledge of the rip-off at hand would be assuaged by my support of the artists with a hard copy of their efforts. But even *that* idea was leaden with land mines.

I've spent a lot of years in a lot of record stores. So, I know more often than not, I would have to special order the obscure music I liked. No big deal. What I frequently discovered, however, is a great deal of the music I was streaming was out of print in the United States. I could order the CDs from Europe or Japan, but many of the titles ran between $30 and $50 each! In the pre-family days of disposable income, I might be able to take a flyer on something like that. These days, it is much harder to do. So, I was back to ripping off the artists. With that, my Pandora listening all but ground to a halt.

Not everyone views streaming as a post-apocalyptic digital nightmare. Andre Cholmondely has been a professional in the music business for nearly two decades. Not only is he a guitarist (rising to prominence with the Frank Zappa tribute band Project/Object), he also spends a great deal of time serving as a guitar or bass technician, tour manager, booking agent, and production manager. I met him while her served as Adrian Belew's guitar tech in the fall of '14. He views streaming as little more than the Next Thing in the music industry.

"It's a complex issue," he told me via Facebook chat. "Ponder this: we've been told since 1976 or so that home taping is *killing* music. Then it was CDs, since we could make perfect copies from them. Then it was this, that or the other. Yet more bands are touring, recording and releasing music than *ever* before! I see packed and sold out shows everywhere, in every market, across genres, if the show is awesome and promoted properly.

"Think about how many things compete with the average person's attention and disposable income," Cholmondeley continued. "There are now lots and lots of things people choose to fill their free time with besides music. With things like fantasy football, X-Box, Hulu or Netflix, 500 channels of cable TV, and so on, they all contribute to the fact that when someone has $30 to spend, it's not guaranteed to be on music like it was in previous eras. Not everyone lives for music the way we do."

Cholmondeley doesn't share the physical connection with music I do. He has embraced the modern convenience. "We order food and get plane tickets online with no complaints," he said. "Hotel bookings, ordering shoes ... how many people use Zappos and don't go into shoe stores? Thousands of shoe stores have closed! Yet we are all DELIGHTED with this convenience! But it shouldn't apply to music retail?

"Do you watch movies online? Is that fair to the theater industry, with its shrinking sales in many markets? How about all the drive-ins that closed due to non-attendance? Is it fair that we all enjoy FREE and dirt-cheap access to virtually every movie in history? Of course it is! Yet we still want to walk into a store, sift through discs, and pay $15 – a dollar of which goes to the artist we keep saying is the reason we are there? We want that model to last forever?"

I understand where Andre is coming from. When all is said and done, people like Anil and I want the artists to be properly compensated for their work, regardless of how the consumer obtains it. Music may be an expression of passion and a pursuit of art, but it is also a *job*! And the people making the music we enjoy deserve to be able to make a living.

Even as I write this, I realize how funny it sounds. But the artist seems to be better off with the revenue from downloads. Apple keeps about 30 percent of the artist's revenue from use of its library. So out of a dollar, the artist keeps 70 cents. So for a million downloads of one song, the artist grosses a little less than $700,000. But now we're back to the old formula of taxes, management and agent fees, legal representation, studio costs, and so forth. It won't take long for that 700 grand to look more like 50. And what are the odds of getting a million downloads in the first place?

***

So what is the answer? How do we ensure musicians get what they have earned for their efforts? Many artists have found the answer to their financial woes is to eliminate the middleman, also known as the record label, and release the music themselves. This affords the artist a much larger piece of the pie.

Take Aimee Mann, for example. In the year 2000, Mann was set to release an album called *Bachelor No. 2*, her third studio album. It is, without question, one of the finest albums I have ever heard. I don't hesitate for a second when I call it a pop music masterpiece. *Bachelor No. 2* is loaded, front to back, with highly intelligent, deeply meaningful, and melodic songs. If asked what it takes to write a successful pop song, Mann's album is one of the first I point to.

Alas, her label at the time, Interscope, did not see it that way. In fact, they decided not to release the album at all! The reason? Interscope did not feel the record had significant commercial appeal. Mann was forced to buy her own record back from her label – to the tune of six figures – in order to release it herself.

Mann got the last laugh. She sold 25,000 copies of *Bachelor No. 2* via her web site, a staggering number for the time. As word of the record's quality spread, she was offered a distribution deal, which enabled her to sell another 200,000 copies in record stores. With Interscope out of the equation, Mann was able to reap a much larger financial reward. It's a triumphant tale, but it shouldn't have been necessary to begin with.

In an interview with *Guitar Player* magazine, King Crimson's Robert Fripp discussed the benefits of releasing his music independently. Specifically, he found that he made the same money selling 30,000 copies of his latest record via his web site that he made selling 300,000 copies via a traditional label. Fripp's record company, DGM Live, also sells downloads of select concerts from throughout King Crimson's history. While more commercial releases are made available via iTunes, Fripp reaps the maximum benefit from "official bootleg" sales by keeping the product in house. Other artists make their concerts available for download almost immediately after they take place.

That being said, Fripp has been involved in almost endless protracted legal battles with record labels over royalties that should have been paid based on record sales, downloads, and samples. His battle with the Universal Music Group raged for more than half a decade. Fripp's frustration ultimately led him to retire from active music making until the suit was settled. He returned to the music scene with a new King Crimson in 2014.

***

What is music worth? World-renowned artists Radiohead decided to find out in '07. The band's contract with major record label EMI had just ended, and they were now on their own. They decided to make their new album, *In Rainbows,* available online. Here was the wrinkle: fans were allowed to determine just how much they were willing to pay for it. That price could be as much or as little as the consumer liked, including nothing at all. Once the fan determined his price, the album was available for download.

The experiment was a great success. Radiohead not only sold millions of download copies of *In Rainbows*, but millions more purchased the physical CD when it was made available a few months later. Some even purchased a deluxe box set of the album, which contained B-sides and other goodies. There was also a mild, unexpected backlash. Despite being available for free on the band's website, some fans still sought out pirated downloads from illegitimate sources. Old habits die hard, I guess.

I participated in the Great Experiment, as well. I paid 5 pounds sterling (about $11) for the download. I loved the album, but I loved it even more when I could get a physical copy of the CD, which I also paid for. All told, I paid about $26 for two copies of the same record. I don't regret it for a second. *In Rainbows* is easily in the top three of my favorite Radiohead albums.

***

By the time the Great Purge of '06 ended, I had sold off about 75 percent of my CD collection. This included special editions, imports (mostly titles I bought in Japan), and rarities. I held on to absolute favorites, autographed CDs, local artists, and the releases of personal friends. Yes, I still had the music. But it wasn't the same. No "sunlight CD rainbows," no cover art, no liner notes … music was being reduced to this simple, cold, lifeless entity.

Musicians like Adrian Belew eschew listening to other people's music, because they believe it hinders their creative process. Adrian fashions himself as quite the mimic (he's not wrong about that), and other people's music has a way of creeping in to his own writing process. I am the opposite. "Passive listening," as I came to call it, served as a springboard for compositional ideas when I wrote for my band, the Sheltering Sky. (8) I would not copy other people's ideas, but I would hear a sound or rhythm that sparked something within me, frequently leading me down a path I may not have thought of before. Granted, I have heard my music called "the sum of [my] influences," but I always saw that more as a compliment. There's a big difference between that and, "Hey! You just totally ripped off So-and-So!"

I've been listening to music avidly since I was six. Now it was losing its meaning. Something was terribly wrong here. It didn't take long to determine selling most of my music collection was a horrible mistake. And so, over time, I began to reacquire what I had given up.

There have been a couple of up sides to "Operation: Reacquisition." For one thing, I realize that I don't need every single note released by certain bands. I cut down my total number of King Crimson titles by about a third, since some of the CDs I had were rarely played. The recordings were sub-standard, the live set lists were redundant, or the music just wasn't that interesting. Miles Davis and Frank Zappa got the same treatment. With the essentials back on my CD shelf, and the remainder still in the digital realm, I struck a happy medium.

Much of the music I gave up was being given a sonic facelift. Record companies were re-issuing classic titles with new mixes (particularly 5.1 surround) or re-masters. (9) These "new" CDs contained bonus tracks, B-sides, and rarities. The difference in sound quality could be as stark as night and day.

I'm not sure who was responsible for re-mastering the Miles Davis catalog from the '60s, but he deserves a medal. The re-masters of *Kind of Blue, Miles Smiles, In a Silent Way,* and *Bitches Brew* are nothing short of stunning. Considering the way much of the music was recorded – with just a few microphones spread throughout the room – the clarity is absolutely incredible. Admittedly, I was a little annoyed, because some of Miles's chatter toward his band and producer Teo Macero was edited out of *Miles Smiles.* But the music that remains more than makes up for it.

Even more remarkable is the re-mastering job George Martin did with the Beatles catalog. My *God!* Songs put on tape half a century before sound like they were recorded last Tuesday. This is particularly true of Paul McCartney's bass and Ringo Starr's drums. My favorite moment comes during *The Beatles* (aka *the White Album*), and a song called "Everybody's Got Something to Hide (Except for Me and My Monkey)." There is a break toward the end of the song, where the band stops, and Ringo's percussion rings out on its own. And then McCartney's bass drops back in. I laughed aloud, saying out to nobody, "What the hell was *that*?!?" I played that song at least four times before I was able to move on. It was pure bliss.

Even a sonically brutal record like Smashing Pumpkins *Siamese Dream* benefited greatly from a re-mastering. As it was, Billy Corgan and company peeled wallpaper off the wall from a half-mile radius. But now the record did so with added detail. The guitars shrieked and howled, the bass thundered and the drums hammered away, and Corgan ... well, was Billy Corgan.

My music collection is returning to what it was before the Purge. I've gotten a lot of the essential stuff back. Some of it is proving hard to find, or expensive to re-acquire. But my interest in music has come roaring back.

The lesson has been learned.

(1)   My music is stored alphabetically by group name or artists last name. If I have more than one release by an artist, then the records are stored chronologically. Otherwise, I would never be able to find anything!

(2)   I've sold and traded more than a few CDs as well. Had I kept everything I ever bought, I would probably have between 2,500 and 3,000 CDs on my shelves.

(3)   Why is that, I wonder? People change their minds all the time. The ability to add and remove songs from an iPod would have been an incredibly useful feature. I guess the good people at Apple didn't think so. Too bad.

(4)   Producer Rick Rubin alone has seriously altered the course of my music collection. I have always respected Johnny Cash, but the work he did with Rubin toward the end of Cash's life shot that level of respect into the stratosphere. Cash no doubt owed the resurgence of his career to the production talents of Rick Rubin.

(5)   I swore I would get that second tattoo within a year or so. That was 15 years ago.

(6)   Yes, I still have a home stereo system, and that will not change any time soon. While I have great ambitions for assembling a quality seven-channel speaker system for my movies and video games, noting will ever take the place of high quality stereo speakers, left and right. I am more than happy with a high-quality, high-output two-channel music speaker system. My LPs sound better that way.

(7)   See "Hammer, MC," "Braxton, Toni," "Tyler, Steven," and who-knows how many others that appeared to have "made it" in the music business.

(8)   I came to call listening to music by my band as "active listening." Just a personal quirk.

(9)   I am largely indifferent about "surround" mixes. I prefer to see myself as in front of the band, as opposed to being in the middle of them. A solid stereo mix is more than enough for me.

Markus Reuter is a master at making genre-defying music.

Track 21
Ced Music: Indefinable

"So, what kind of music do you like?"

On the surface, it seems like an innocent question. For most people, I suppose it is. But for a die-hard music fanatic like me, it's not that simple. In fact, I find it rather maddening, considering how things usually go from there.

"I love music," I reply. "I hate labels."

The inquisitor is baffled. "Do you like jazz? Blues? Rock? Country? Hip-hop? What kind of music do you like?"

"Yes," I answer with a smirk. "And then some."

"You don't have to be difficult!" they snap. "It's a simple question! You play guitar, right?"

"Yes, I do."

"So, what do you like to play on guitar?"

I sigh and bring forth what has become my stock reply over the last 15 or so years. "My biggest influences are Miles Davis, Frank Zappa, and King Crimson," I tell them. "I also love bands like Radiohead, Tool, Tortoise, and Umphrey's McGee. I love Rush every bit as much as I love James Brown. Aimee Mann is one of my songwriting heroes, along with Stevie Wonder in the early '70s. I also dig Bach, Mozart, and Beethoven. Once in a while, I enjoy a little opera. So you tell me: what kind of music do I listen to?"

The inquisitor's blank expression brings it all home. "Wow ..." they say, unable to come up with anything else.

I just shrug and repeat my original statement. "I love music."

It's not that I intend to be a pain. I just detest labels. To my mind, nothing squelches the potential of music or a musician quite like a label. Placing an artist in a particular category may be helpful in a record store. But it can lead to a personal form of segregation causing someone to miss out on something really special.

I'm not a fan of country music. I don't go out of my way to listen to anything playing on my local country radio stations. But I am a *huge* fan of Johnny Cash. I have enormous respect for the guitar playing abilities of Buck Owens and Roy Clark, whom I saw blaze away on the syndicated TV show *Hee Haw* in the '70s and '80s. These days, I hold Brad Paisley's guitar slinging ability in the same high regard. That dude flat-out *smokes*! I dug what Ray Charles did on *Modern Sounds in Country and Western Music.* I don't own it (yet), but I respect it. I love an instrumental record from three Nashville pickers who called themselves the Hellecasters. I respect the abilities of Willie Nelson, Waylon Jennings, and Hank Williams, Jr.

But I'm not a country fan.

***

The best music and musicians transcend labels.

I worry about anyone willing to dismiss a particular style of music out of hand, based on a label. I would hope they would be willing to let the music be what it is. But it doesn't happen nearly as often as I would like.

When I try to introduce a friend to a new piece of music, I do my best not to stick a label on it. If I do, the potential listener has often formed an opinion about the music before hearing so much as a single note, which pretty much defeats the purpose. I fell into this trap while attempting to turn a friend on to the music of Steven Wilson. His album *The Raven that Refused to Sing (and Other Stories)* ranks among my favorite albums of all time. "So what kind of music is it?" my friend asked.

"Well, I guess it has kind of a progressive bent to it …" I started. Sadly, I never got to finish.

"Oh, never mind," was my friend's quick reply. "I don't like progressive rock. It's too self-indulgent."

"Seriously? You're gonna blow it off, just like that? How much progressive rock have you heard?"

"I heard a Yes album a few years back," my friend said. "Didn't really care for it. Nah ... you can have that music."

Given the time, I would have said the music has a progressive bent to it, but it really covers a much larger spectrum. That particular album is far too big to be saddled with a single label. But I never got the chance. The door of musical exploration was slammed shut, with my friend content to remain on the outside. Sadly, I've had this conversation more times than I care to count.

Labeling music kills the art. I believe there are just two kinds of music on this planet: good and bad. What's the difference between the two? Well, that is entirely up to the listener.

A lot of the music I love defies categorization. Not that this has stopped music critics from trying. I've heard simple names like "jam" or "indie," and more complicated concepts like "post-rock" or "shoe-gaze." The latter amuses me the most, since it implies the musicians simply stare down at their feet while they play. Sometimes, it's even true. Still, some people might be turned off by that description, and never give the music a fair shake. It is, without a doubt, their loss.

As I type these words, my head is bobbing to the grooves of a John Scofield album called *Uberjam* (released in 2002). Scofield made his name in jazz, playing for Miles Davis in the '80s, and embarking on a remarkable solo career since then. (1) And while Scofield's playing certainly has a jazzy lilt to it, his band is using electronic percussion, samples, and elements of hip-hop for this album. The music rocks and is also funky as hell. Is this jazz? Not in the strictest sense. Yet I don't doubt an entire subsection of music fans will dismiss this album out of hand, because they don't care for jazz.

Chicago-based band Tortoise faces a similar problem. Theirs is music that I have said must not be merely heard. It must be experienced. What does that mean? To me, it means put the music on the player, press "play," and let whatever is going to happen, happen.

Tortoise is generally lumped into a category called "post-rock." Near as I can figure, this is a genre that finds its foundation in the "indie," or independent, rock category. From there, unexpected elements – such as jazz, dub, trip-hop –are added to the music, giving it a distinct sound quality. To be certain, there are few bands around who sound like Tortoise. They deserve to stand on their own.

Tortoise releases its records on a Chicago-based label called Thrill Jockey. They are, without question, my favorite independent music company. I've often said Thrill Jockey was the only label I would have tried to market the Sheltering Sky to, had we been given the opportunity. The label's bands are also mostly Chicago-based, and many of the musicians play in more than one group. I love the music made by bands like Isotope 217, Chicago Underground, Trans Am, and the Sea and Cake. But Tortoise stands out above the rest.

The details of how Tortoise entered my musical life are blurry at best. This is unusual for me. Tortoise is the guest who wandered into my musical dinner party – unexpected and uninvited – by way of the back door. Once there, they not only proved to be charming, but the life of the party. Now I never want them to leave.

Some of my friends have had trouble digesting Tortoise's music, because they feel it requires some form of additional action beyond simply listening to it. "What am I supposed to *do* with this?" they implore. My response only baffles them more: what makes you think you're supposed to do *anything*? Some music makes you want to dance. Some music makes you want to sing along. That's not what the music of Tortoise is for. My recommendation is do nothing and take it from there.

Tortoise makes great foreground/background music. It can be treated as the center of one's personal musical planet, or as something orbiting that planet. If I were the smoker of a leaf other than tobacco, this is the music I would most enthusiastically smoke to. The bass-laden grooves, atmospheric synthesizers, and head-bobbing percussion take little effort to put the listener in a very cool place.

I understand why the casual listener has trouble with bands like Tortoise. Things don't get any easier when I bring up Icelandic band Sigur Ros. Not only is their music not danceable, its lyrics are not sung in any known language! The words heard are not English, nor are they Icelandic. If anything, the members of the band refer to their language as "Hopelandic." I think this speaks to the relative irrelevance of those lyrics. Sigur Ros (loosely translated to mean "Victory Rose') creates spacey soundscapes via keyboards and drums, overlaps them with simple but groovy bass lines and guitar riffs frequently brought forth from the strings being bowed like a violin, topped off by the nonsensical lyrics. It's not easily absorbed. But once the sound got into my system, I was unable to get it out. Not that I wanted to do that, anyway.

Not only does Sigur Ros eschew the need for translatable lyrics, on my favorite album, titled simply "( )," they did away with song titles as well. The music – lovely and ethereal – is left to stand on its own merit. The final track (which can be found on YouTube as "Untitled #8") ranks as some of the most moving music I've ever heard. The song starts with a simple guitar riff, accompanied by an open-ended bass line, and drums played with brushes. Soon enough, the keyboards, bowed guitars, and layered vocals join the mix. The song builds with intensity over the course of 11 minutes, climaxing with a crescendo that never fails to get my head bobbing. There's a reason Sigur Ros often uses this tune as its finale during live performances.

Bands like Tortoise and Sigur Ros are found in the "Rock" sections in record stores. But the music is so far removed from rock, it's not even funny. I suppose "Trippy Atmospheric" wouldn't be an ideal label, either. That being said, why try to label the music at all? It's just fine being what it is.

Bands like Explosions in the Sky and This Will Destroy You also fit into this musical non-category. The primary difference between these bands and groups like Tortoise and Sigur Ros is that the former two root their sound in guitars rather than synthesizers or bass. Tender, clean guitar tones help establish the song's grooves and moods. The guitarists stepping on their distortion pedals create the emotional crescendos. Music like this is often used in movie soundtracks, to great emotional effect. I remember watching the film *Friday Night Lights*, and thinking how the music made a great backdrop. I made an effort to check the music credits at the end. Sure enough, the music came from Explosions in the Sky.

It's a small world, even from a musical standpoint.

***

I have never been a huge fan of the Grateful Dead. I don't have anything against them. I just haven't gotten around to exploring them in depth. I have only recently begun to introduce myself to their music. So, no one will ever confuse me with a traditional "Deadhead."

But if not for the Dead, bands like Umphrey's McGee, Widespread Panic, and Phish – dubbed "jam bands" by the music press – might never have achieved their level of popularity. And so, I tip my hat to the Grateful Dead, and pay them the respect they have earned.

Jam bands bring a jazz mentality to rock-based music. The band plays a song in traditional rock style, making it recognizable to fans. But somewhere along the way, the band veers off and begins to improvise, often at length. This may not be advised for every band playing these days, but for jam bands, it adds a fun-filled and exciting dimension to material that could easily become stagnant.

More than a few people have come down on the Dave Matthews Band in recent years. Somewhere along the way, it became fashionable to hate the group. (2) But in the mid to late '90s, the group provided me with some of my earliest jam band experience. They took songs I already loved, like "Two Step," and turned them into almost completely new compositions. The song I knew, already some seven minutes long on the *Crash* CD, was stretched out even further, giving each musician the opportunity to make the most of the rock-solid country shuffle being provided by the rhythm section.

Not every jam-oriented experience works. Bassist extraordinaire Les Claypool made the jam ideal work with his Fearless Flying Frog Brigade. Their two-volume live CD (released as individual sets) is essential listening. But when Les tried to take those ideals to Primus, the band that made him a name in the industry, the results were mixed, at best. I went to one of their shows, which showcased their classic album, *Sailing the Seas of Cheese.* The songs themselves were just fine. But on more than a couple of occasions, the group's attempts at jamming came off as so much aimless noodling. I appreciated the effort, but at times I was ready to yell, "Get on with it, already!" at the stage. But as Pat Mastelotto pointed out, "Sometimes when you go for it, you don't get there."

***

I live to tell my friends about new music. Recently, I decided to introduce my pal Abbi Telander to a band called Snarky Puppy. Their sound is a nice hybrid of jazz, fusion, and post-rock. I introduced Abbi to Tortoise years before, so I figured she might dig this sound as well. I was right. But it was what she said about the music that got my attention. "Had I discovered this independently," she said to me via text, "I would've said, 'This is Ced music.'" Naturally, I was intrigued by this. After all, I've never had anyone name a music genre after me.

I asked her what she meant, and would she consider writing out a definition. She agreed. A couple of weeks later, I sent her a couple of links to songs by a band called Bent Knee, who rapidly became a favorite. Their sound contains elements of pop, jazz, prog, indie, and who knows what else. Yet it doesn't rest comfortably in any of those areas. Independent of the links, I sent another note, which said, "It's genre-defying, no?"

Her quick reply was, "Genre-defying is the bedrock of Ced music." I couldn't help but laugh.

I decided to see if I could guess how she defined this new musical genre. "Ced music is genre-defying, ethnicity-obliterating, and time-signature eluding," I said. "Am I warm?"

"Yes," Abbi replied, and then extended the definition. "Ced music is well thought out. Sometimes it's complex. Sometimes it's simple. But it's *never* simplistic. It's authentic, never fake. Auto-tuners need not apply. The love of music, the *need* to make music, and the need to make *this particular music* transcends everything else."

I was blown away. Abbi managed to define the very things I look for in a musician and the music he produces. I had just never taken the time to articulate it. There was nothing I could add. All I could do was be flattered, and proudly accept the label.

***

Music journalist Anil Prasad turned me on to Bent Knee in mid-2015. Their music, he told me, was unlike anything he'd ever heard. That's saying something, given the sheer volume of music Anil has absorbed over the years. Even with that in mind, I felt like he could give me a basis for the band's sound. He declined to do so, no doubt with a little glee. Anil also understands how my musical mind works and has a good idea what I'll like before even I do. All he would say was "Buy it. Buy all of it."

The band had two full-length records and an EP available on the Bandcamp web site. I decided to try their latest release, *Shiny Eyed Babies*, first. The album opened with the title track, a simple piano and vocal piece about a woman who recently had an abortion. (3) I was struck by the power of vocalist Courtney Swain's voice. It was full-throated, sober, and direct. This woman had something to say.

Surprisingly, the song stopped almost as soon as it started, giving way to a robotic 4/4 drumbeat lasting four bars. Without warning, two mighty power chords are unleashed by guitarist Ben Levin and bassist Jessica Kion, with the downbeats emphasized by drummer Gavin Wallace-Ailsworth. Swain's voice returns, marking the lyrical beginning of the album's second track, "Way Too Long." Like nearly every other track on the album, the song was an emotional roller coaster.

As I listened to the rest of *Shiny Eyed Babies*, I found myself asking aloud, "What's going on here?" The music rose and fell, tilted and lilted, caressed and blistered. It was full of gentle beauty and raw aggression. It was, as Anil pointed out, unlike anything I had ever heard. I struggled mightily to come up with a band to compare Bent Knee to, as a frame of reference. I came up empty.

I couldn't define Bent Knee's music, but I soon became obsessed with it. It resonated in ways that few others did. There was so much information contained in each song. But the music never sounded cluttered or overwhelming. The phrase "complex simplicity" comes to mind, should I be forced to describe the style I was hearing. Swain's voice became one of my favorite sounds. When harmonizing with Kion on songs like "Battle Creek," it sounds even better. *This*, I determined, was the music that should be all over the radio. *This* music should be taking home Grammy after Grammy. Bent Knee was a band with a truly original sound. They write high-caliber, meaningful songs. Nothing about their music is disposable or trendy. They are who they are and deserve all the credit in the world for it. Of course, I know better.

The band's sound not only stretches across musical genres, but age brackets as well. I played the album for my then 13-year-old daughter, gambling that she might find something in Bent Knee's music that could get her away from the teeny-bop, disposable boy bands she loved. I figured she'd listen for about ten seconds and dismiss her dad's goofy music. Not only did my child not leave right away, she sat down and absorbed every note. When she heard the lyrics to a song called "Being Human," my daughter quipped, "(Swain) is either an incredible songwriter, or she's deeply disturbed, mentally." From the mouths of babes …

In May of '16, the band released *Say So*, which was every bit as good as the last album. In many ways, the band achieved the next musical level, however that may be defined. The simplest way to put it is they took what they did on *Shiny Eyed Babies*, and built on it. The musical structure holds up wonderfully.

Of course, the very thing that makes Bent Knee great could also lead to its undoing, if they want to be popular. (4) The band uses elements of many musical styles, including avant-garde, prog, classical, jazz, rock, and pop, rendering it almost unpalatable for modern radio. The music's lack of definition makes it impossible to place them in any one commercial format, save for Alternative. But even *that* may not work in today's radio, because the "Alternative" sounds more and more like the Top 40 mainstream. That music is catchy, danceable, and disposable. Bent Knee doesn't fit that bill. Casual music fans don't have the patience to check out a band whose music isn't spelled out to them in obvious fashion. I know, because I've tried.

I thought I created a new fan one day, having introduced her to three Bent Knee songs. She complimented Swain on her singing voice and admired the instrumental abilities of the rest of the band. I felt myself getting excited, but then the other shoe dropped. "I don't really like them all that much," she said. "Their music just isn't my style." I protested that she had only just been introduced, and music like this took a while to absorb. But she had already moved on. Bent Knee was not for her.

It's her loss.

It's also the loss of many others who've chosen to ignore the clips of that band, and others like them, I've posted to my Facebook page and Twitter feed. The musical world is so much bigger than commercial radio would have us believe. But it seems as though the majority of alleged music "fans" are interested either in what they already know, or that which can be absorbed with little to no thought. Genre-defying music runs directly in the face of that.

***

I get that not everyone listens to music the same way I do. But that doesn't prevent me from being baffled. Why does music that defies categorization have such a difficult time reaching an audience? Does the question answer itself? Where I see a potential opportunity for something new and exciting, others only seem to find inconvenience, not worthy of the time and effort needed to bring something new into their lives.

Commercial radio has no idea what to do with the likes of Ben Harper, Ani DiFranco, or Aimee Mann. Bon Iver can't get the time of day on the radio, much like Snarky Puppy, Spectrum Road, or Umphrey's McGee. Yet I believe with every fiber of my being the average radio listener is infinitely smarter than he is given credit for. Given the opportunity, commercial radio could be a glorious place full of wonderment and discovery.

This is the part when some radio programmer interjects with something along the lines of, "But if we expand our playlists to include unknowns, we could lose listeners. If we lose listeners, our ratings go down. If *that* happens, we lose advertising dollars. We prefer to give the people what they want."

Is that really what the radio programmers are doing? Are they giving the people what they want? Or is it that the people *want what they know*? Especially when said familiar music is shoved down their throats by way of repeated plays from the "heavy rotation" section of the radio station's playlist?

While I appreciate their convenience, the mp3 format is another culprit in the public's loss of musical attention span. The previous musical formats – be they reel-to-reel tape, LP, 8-track, cassette tape, or CD – were all geared around the album. Before CDs, it was a challenge to simply cue up one's favorite moments on album. With the advent of downloading and streaming, fans no longer need to bother with an entire album. They can simply pull the songs they want away from the primary source and keep moving. Everything else gets lost in the shuffle.

I am just as guilty of this as anybody else, even if my rut lands on more esoteric ground. There are times when I get locked in to the sounds of King Crimson, Frank Zappa, or Steven Wilson. I have an iPod with nearly 22,000 songs and 2,000 albums on it. Yet there are times when I listen to the same dozen artists. I have to remind myself to shake things up now and then. Usually, the "shuffle" function does the trick. It's only a matter of time before I hear myself say, "Man, I'd forgotten about that band." And just like that, the musical flood gates open again.

Bandcamp has also helped me to shake any particular ruts. While the music on that app is divided into genres, there are also sub-genres. And even *those* sub-genres have sub-genres. The deeper I go, the more difficult it becomes to define what I'm hearing. And that may be the point.

Like many others, I've spent more than my fair share of time complaining that there was nothing new or exciting going on in music these days. But the truth of the matter is, there is plenty of exciting music out there. A great deal of it is not easily defined.

I just have to look for it.

(1)   Many would argue Miles wasn't playing jazz in the '80s, either. It would be hard to dispute that.

(2)   Admittedly, I haven't bought a Dave Matthews CD in quite a while. My musical tastes went in a different direction, and the group got lost in the shuffle. I'll get back around to them sooner or later.

(3)   I'm making no political statements here. How you feel about the abortion issue is your business, not mine.

(4)   It's possible I don't need to worry at all. When I listen to Bent Knee, I hear a band striving to be great, not popular. I hope it stays that way.

Nobody is surprised when I proclaim my love for jazz. I can't buck trends all the time.

Track 22
Well Of Course He Listens to That!

I must confess: I enjoy being a musical contrarian.

When the conversation turns to music, I like surprising people who believe they have me figured out. How many people look across the room at a 50-year-old black man and say, "There is a dedicated Radiohead fan?" Or, "I bet that guy knows King Crimson's music inside and out." Yet I am that guy. Is that so odd?

Based on my concert attendances, it is.

I want to believe I live in a perfect musical world, where sounds have reached the ears of any and everyone interested in hearing them. I want to believe talented musicians from all walks of life are properly exposed and promoted. But that simply isn't the case. So more often than not, I find myself one of a handful of members representing my demographic at concerts.

It's not uncommon for my friend Trey and I to play our favorite game at rock-oriented concerts, which we call "Count the Brothers Who Don't Work Here." At a King Crimson show, for example, Trey and I will scan the room to see if we can find more than three African-Americans in attendance. The record number of finds (at a Nine Inch Nails show, in a room of about 12,000 people) was six. Usually, we rarely find more than a couple.

Sometimes, demographic has nothing to do with it. I just enjoy discovering music from off the beaten path. Why sit around and "discover" what tens of millions of people already know about? That's boring, and a serious musical non-starter. That's not to say that I hate everything that makes its way onto a Billboard chart. I am simply wary of what the powers-that-be, via commercial radio or magazine, thrust forward as the "Next Big Thing." Because more often than not, it isn't.

One of the toughest things in the world for me is going through my music collection in an attempt to find enough music to make good background noise at a party. It's the classic challenge of trying to give the people what they want, as the mass entertainers would say. Well, here's what I've discovered: the people don't know what they want; *they want what they know.* And they don't know very much about the music I enjoy.

Whether I like it or not, Radiohead does not provide the kind of ambient background vibe that keeps a party going. Neither does King Crimson. Frank Zappa as social gathering music? Forget it. Sometimes, I have to come back to the fold, if only a little.

***

I always got a kick out of the befuddled looks from my Air Force roommate as he entered our door room to the sound of something he had never heard. Sometimes, his confused looks would lead him to ask, "What are you listening to?" Once in a while, my strange tastes would rub off, and I'd find them listening to it when I came home. Most days, all I got was a strange look. When a friend of his came by to see him, the friend might motion my way, asking what the deal was with my music. More often than not, my roommate would blow it off as a case of Ced being Ced, and they would move on.

Rare was the day when someone would hear what was coming out of my speakers, look at me, and think, "Yeah … well, that makes sense." Even the jazz I loved was considered to be a bit too "old" for a man in his mid-20s to go on about. After all, it didn't exactly have a beat you could dance to.

There are times when I wonder whether I have purposely gone out of my way to avoid popular music. I suppose it's possible. To my ears, so much of it was positively horrible. It would strike me as simple and sophomoric. The artist and producers were clearly pandering to the audience, ensuring the song was a hit above all else.

I don't like being talked down to, either verbally or through my music. I'm a bright guy. Just play the music, and I'll figure it out. The artists I enjoy do just that. They do what they do and leave it up to the listeners to sort out the details. That suits me just fine.

***

Likewise, I don't listen to any particular type of music simply because the artist and I share the same ethnic background. If an artist playing the music I enjoy also happens to be black, well that's just an added bonus. It befuddles me, then, when friends look at my CD collection and border on being offended when they see the number of white artists represented. Suddenly, I'm the guy that doesn't appreciate "our" music, and I am looked upon like I should be ashamed of myself for my choices. This puts me in that place where I have to start pondering what constitutes "Black" music again, even though I know it doesn't make one damned bit of difference.

Now that I'm 50, I am bothered less and less (if at all) by those who consider my musical tastes weird. As far as I'm concerned, it's their loss if they can't relate to the likes of Steven Wilson, Tortoise, or This Will Destroy You. But there are more than a few "That Makes Sense" selections within the confines of my collection. I'm sure they bring those who peruse through my CD collection a little relief.

My parent's love of '70s soul had an effect on me. Saturday night was usually when I heard Mom and Dad play those songs, usually when there was company over. I was supposed to be playing in my room. Chances are, I was doing that *and* nodding my head along with what was on the record player.

I have an undying love for the music of Al Green, Marvin Gaye, Barry White, Curtis Mayfield, and Isaac Hayes. I've even bought albums like Green's *Let's Stay Together* and *Call Me* on LP to maintain the same vibe I felt in my parent's house.

Mom loved the ladies of soul, like Roberta Flack, Aretha Franklin, and Gladys Knight. They got my attention too. Then there was the party music from Parlliament/Funkadelic, The Ohio Players, Kool & the Gang, and KC and the Sunshine Band. Once upon a time, I played the grooves off a 45 r.p.m. single of "I'm Your Boogie Man." There can be no denying the power of the horn section during that particular song. Groovy stuff!

The '70s also produced the greatest period of music from Stevie Wonder. I can't get enough of *Talking Book, Music of My Mind, Innervisions, Fulfillingness First Finale,* and *Songs in the Key of Life.* Stevie was positively *on fire* when he made those records. He could do no wrong. I'm glad I was there to hear it all. And it now resides in my collection.

There was so much great music produced by black artists between 1960 and '80. For every artist I think of, I'm sure there are two more I am leaving off. Smokey Robinson, The Jackson 5, The O'Jays, The Spinners, The Temptations, Ike and Tina Turner ... the list goes on and on. Playing those records these days elicits nothing more than a smile and complimentary nod from my friends, who love to point out how "old school" I am. And they're right. Modern R&B – save for the neo-soul like Jill Scott, D'Angelo, and Erykah Badu – is lost on me. I don't know what these modern cats are talking about. I only know I want no part of it.

The '80s didn't do much for me, where "Urban Contemporary," as it came to be called, was concerned. I had entered my "Rock is everything" phase, so everything else got filtered out. Still, there was no ignoring the power of Michael Jackson's *Thriller*. Song for song, it's hard to name a better record from that time.

When Prince released *Purple Rain* in '84, I tried hard to ignore it. But it seeped into my consciousness, anyway. "When Doves Cry" was just too good. For the longest time, I couldn't figure out what was so unique about that song, because that was what had my attention. Eventually, I realized the song lacked a bass line, making it a one-of-a-kind type composition.

Still, Prince was not the kind of artist a Genesis-worshipping, King Crimson loving, soon to be Zappa fanatic should be listening to, I decided. And while, "America," a single from his *Around the World in a Day* album never failed to get my body moving, I remained a closeted Prince fan until '88. That year, my friend Ed Wehrenberg sat me down to show me the concert video from *Sign O' the Times*. I don't recall whether or not I told him that I wasn't that big of a Prince fan. I probably did. Still, our friendship was new, and it wouldn't kill me, I determined, to check out this video. By the time "Housequake," the third song on the video, was over, I was hooked. The band (which featured well-respected percussionist Shelia E.) was positively amazing! Ed and I played that video (and a cassette copy he made) over and over and over again. I've been a proud Prince fan ever since.

I dabbled in hip-hop during the late '80s and early '90s. In the grand musical scheme, it was a short dalliance. But a couple of lifelong connections were made. I liked the early sounds of Grand Master Flash. KRS-One, Eric B and Rakhim, and Big Daddy Kane also got my attention (the latter two for much less time than the former). As much as I understood the need for party music, I preferred my rap with a little social consciousness thrown into the mix. Perhaps that's why I'm a lifelong fan of Public Enemy.

My friend Jimmy Griffin once called P.E. "the Led Zeppelin of hip-hop." I loved that from the minute he said it. They were groundbreaking, one of a kind, and all groups after them would be influenced in one way or another by their sound. Chuck D wrote and rapped lyrics that made me rethink more than one position I held during the late '80s and early '90s. Even if I didn't always agree with him, I had to respect his opinions, as they were so eloquently stated. Say what you will about Flava-Flav, but the hype man knew what he was doing, and understood his role within the group. Terminator X was my favorite DJ for quite some time. Okay, he was one of the few DJs I knew. But still ... the dude was dope. *It Takes a Nation of Millions to Hold Us Back, Fear of a Black Planet,* and *Apocalypse '91: The Enemy Strikes Black* are essential parts of any respectable hip-hop collection.

I have a healthy respect for the early '90s works of NWA, Ice T, and Ice Cube. This was the beginning of the "Gangsta Rap" era, which started as an incredible social movement before coming off the rails in a sea of hyperbole and sensationalism. Once again, I didn't always agree with what was being said. But I had nothing but respect for the way it was being said. Ice-T's *OG: Original Gangster*, along with Ice Cube's *Amerikkka's Most Wanted* and *The Predator* still ring powerfully in my head.

There were other rap groups that held my attention for varied periods of time. I have a healthy respect for The Beastie Boys, who are far more innovative than those in my particular musical realm will give them credit for. I also enjoyed Missy Elliott and Jurassic 5. But the only hip-hop act I still actively seek out is The Roots. I had always respected their abilities within the hip-hop genre. Drummer Ahmir "Questlove" Thompson has one of the best pockets *anywhere* in modern music. And I love the vocal style of Tariq "Black Thought" Trotter. He is a top-notch free-stylist.

What really appeals to me about the band is their versatility. These cats can play *anything*, as evidenced by their late-night stints with Jimmy Fallon, both on *Late Night* and *The*

Tonight Show. Music fans owe it to themselves to watch any time Fallon breaks out a bit called "Free-Stylin' with the Roots," where the host goes into the audience and picks out a random fan. That fan offers up a few facts about himself, Fallon suggests a musical style, like disco or reggae, and the band plays a song based on that information, right then and there! It is a sight to see, and something that can only be pulled off by true musicians. I applaud every time.

There are other acts I enjoy who would fail to elicit a lot of surprise. I enjoy the sound of the Fugees and Lauryn Hill, and I love Me'Shell N'Degeocello. Other artists pop up here and there. It's just a question of catching me in the right mood with the proper level of musical ability.

***

My love of jazz makes perfect sense to people now, even if I tend to focus on the artists from the '50s and '60s. Telling someone that I love Miles Davis nowadays elicits little more than, "Well, of course you do." Not that it matters. Miles, John Coltrane, Herbie Hancock, Wayne Shorter, Art Blakey, Max Roach, Jimmy Smith, Wynton Kelly, Tony Williams, and Charles Mingus see time on my CD player. Their music never fails to soothe my soul or light a fire in my belly.

Even my fanaticism toward the Beatles seems utterly normal to my friends. Sometimes they don't quite grasp what I'm saying when I tell them that just about all music released after 1967 owes something, however small, to the Beatles. But they are able to endure it all the same. The exception might be my daughter – and nearly everyone else her age – who dismisses the Beatles (and pretty much everything else I enjoy) as "old people" music. Well, she'll come around one of these days.

Some of my favorite college music came above ground and made its way on to commercial radio stations. Some of the bands became the biggest names in music. There was a time when next to no one knew about U2. Now they are virtually inescapable. R.E.M., 10,000 Maniacs, The Cure, Depeche Mode, and the B-52s were firmly entrenched on the left side of the radio dial in the early '80s. Suddenly, they were everywhere. People would find it only slightly odd that I dug these acts. What threw them for a loop was when I talked about their early years, before they were popular.

Like many others, I may "discover" a band near the peak of its popularity. But here's where I differ from the masses: my brain is often quick to dismiss the latest work from this popular act, only to embrace something they did several years before. The Black Keys are a prime example.

I heard several singles from this band over the years, like "Lonely Boy." I liked the song, but I couldn't decide whether or not I liked it enough to buy it. I stayed on this particular fence for a very long time. The radio kept churning out singles, and I kept liking them just enough to listen. The songs were hook-laden, and plenty catchy. For most people, that's enough to send them to the record store. But what I've learned over the years is that "catchy" fades. Frequently, it turns into buyer's remorse. Today's awesome hook soon becomes "What the hell was I thinking?" Next thing I know, I'm off-loading that CD at the same store, usually for pennies on the dollar.

I asked more than a couple of people who knew me musically whether or not the Black Keys were worth my time and money. For the longest time, I couldn't get a satisfactory, straightforward answer. The results were decidedly mixed. Finally, a friend of mine put me on the right path. "You'd have no interest in the newer material, like *Turn Blue*," he told me. "It's too slick and sounds overproduced. What you'd like is the stuff they did around 2000, like *The Big Come Up*. That's the sound you're hearing that stays in the back of your mind. It's a bluesy, lo-fi sound. You'll like that a lot." Nothing more needed to be said, and I took a copy of *The Big Come Up* home with me.

Bingo! My friend had me pegged. I love that record. It had what I like to call a "gutbucket" sound. Cheap instruments played through inexpensive amps and microphones in what was no doubt a claustrophobic room. The sound was right on top of me. It was just what I was looking for.

I have made my peace with the Black Keys. They are a big enough act to play hockey arenas now. I won't be there. But I will listen to *The Big Come Up, Brothers, El Camino,* and *Rubber Factory* with great enthusiasm. I get the sound I want, and they can focus on becoming millionaires.

I went through the same issue with Jack White. I was never a fan of the White Stripes. Call me snobbish, but the drumming of Meg White is positively *unlistenable* when your personal drum standard starts with the likes of Bill Bruford and Tony Williams. Still, there was something about Jack's guitar sound. It was lo-fi and guttural, the antithesis of the precise, effects rack-leaden guitarists that I had come to idolize. It was a simpler sound, and it was honest. I finally gave in and bought

Icky Thump, the White Stripes' last album. I liked it quite a bit. It turned into somewhat of a guilty pleasure.

Jack must have been feeling constricted within the confines of the White Stripes, because he began to branch out into other side projects, which I found to be infinitely more enjoyable. The Dead Weather is the ultimate lo-fi group. They have an intense, in-your-face sound that kicks down the door, and dares you to ignore it. It can't be done. They've got you, and they're not letting go. *Sea of Cowards* is a great record for clearing out my musical palate and heading in a unique direction. I also find enjoyment in Jack's solo albums, *Bluderbuss* and *Lazaretto.*

I don't know if playing those records qualifies as "conformity," but they are a good time all the same.

***

Alas, my moments of musical conformity are usually short-lived. Just when my friends think they have me pegged, I've gone back to Tortoise, Mike Keneally, and MasticA. As much as I may enjoy a few popular acts, in the end I've got to be me.

There are those who have accused me of making my musical choices out of some desperate attempt to look cool, because it helps me stand out. That couldn't be further from the truth. Any King Crimson fan will confess that the band almost shoves you into an "uncool" – dare I say "nerdy" place. I couldn't give less of a damn about reality television, yet the masses seem to eat it up. To each his own.

"Paul Simon once said that your musical personality is determined by the time you're 18 or 19," Jim Sullivan, my friend from the F.Y.E. record store, told me one day. "After that, your course is pretty much set." I took a little time to think about that. Naturally, I wondered about when I was introduced to King Crimson, the band that fundamentally changed how I viewed music. It turns out I was 18. It looks like Jim and Paul are on to something.

I'm drawn to music from off the beaten path for one simple reason: it appeals to me. There's nothing wrong with a little musical conformity. It's nice to be able to share something with a large number of people, or to just blindly shake your hips to a catchy tune. But music means more to me than that. And that's where I differ from the masses. I demand more out of music, because I'm listening harder.

Track 23
It's About the Music

In the winter of 2014, I bumped into a former co-worker, who now patrols on the opposite shift. We hadn't shared the same space in quite some time, so we took a few minutes to catch up.

I mentioned I was writing a book about my musical explorations over the past four decades. He told me he just finished a book about something similar. Naturally, I was curious. The next day, my friend handed me a copy of *There Goes Gravity: a Life in Rock and Roll* by Lisa Robinson.

The author is a freelance writer who had been around the music scene since 1969. She spent time with giants like Led Zeppelin, the Rolling Stones, John Lennon, U2, the Clash, the Ramones, and Michael Jackson. Her writing made its way into *Creem* magazine and the New York *Post*. These days, Robinson is a contributing editor at *Vanity Fair*. I thanked my friend for the book, and planned to read it as soon as I had the time. That time finally came in late spring of the following year.

Robinson spent a great deal of time in the presence of the giants of the modern rock industry. She recorded hours and hours of interviews with them, spending time on the road with more than a few. She described in vivid detail backstage goings-on with David Bowie, Iggy Pop, and Patti Smith. As I read, I realized two things: First, Lisa Robinson led a fascinating life; Secondly, I never want to do what she has done. Not in a million years.

***

Some 200 pages into the 350-page book, I saw a pattern in Robinson's work. She was telling me all kinds of things about the scene, but almost nothing about the music itself. Wait a minute, I thought as I read. You spent all that time with the Rolling Stones, and you can't tell me how a song like "Wild Horses" came together? You spent all that time on Led Zeppelin's private jet, but you have nothing to tell me about how an album like *Houses of the Holy* was created? What the hell were you doing all that time?

I should have seen it coming. Robinson admitted she was not a rock critic. Instead, she wrote "gossipy" columns geared more toward publicity. And therein lay the fundamental difference between Lisa Robinson and me: I couldn't care less about "the scene." I have always been about the music, and little else.

Robinson spent days, sometimes weeks, with the artists she covered. The interviews I conducted for these pages rarely took more than 60-90 minutes. Yet I got much more out of my interviews than she got out of hers, because my interests were strictly musical. It was much easier to satisfy my curiosity.

I've never had the desire to spend an extended amount of time with the musicians I admire. If Adrian Belew were to invite me out for dinner and drinks one evening, I'd gladly accept. After all, that very nearly happened. Once the evening was over, that would be all I ever need. I don't want to follow him around on the road, making myself a constant presence in his personal space. I find that notion invasive and distasteful. I like the idea of a barrier separating me from my favorite musicians. I would rather give the artist his space.

If I were allowed to enter the artist's inner sanctum, it would have to be strictly from a creative standpoint. I would be happy to watch the artist work, but I wouldn't have the nerve to interfere with the process.

My friends and I have talked about where we would like to go if we could travel back in time. I have said I would love to hang with the Rat Pack, which is as close as I would come to the Lisa Robinson way of doing things. But I wouldn't want to do it as a writer. I would want to be one of the gang.

I also said I would love to hang with Miles Davis in the late '50s and early '60s. But I wouldn't want to sit around his apartment or anything like that. No, I would want to be in the Columbia Records studios during the two days he spent recording *Kind of Blue*. Or I would love to sit in the control room and watch Miles's second great quintet record *Miles Smiles*. When they were done, it would be cool to ask questions about how the songs came about, and the approach each musician used to achieve his sound. I don't really need to know anything else.

Someone from Columbia records must have heard me. In late 2016, they released *Freedom Jazz Dance*, the fifth volume of the *Miles Davis Bootleg Series*. The three-CD set chronicles the making of *Miles Smiles*, from unedited session reels to the ultimate master takes of each song. The set is everything I could want without being able to see what's going on. Miles, Herbie Hancock, Wayne Shorter, Ron Carter, and Tony Williams work their way through each song, starting with the title track. They start, stop, and start again until things come together, and they find what they're looking for. I never thought about the laughter going on behind the scenes in a jazz environment. But there it is. Miles and Company are unfiltered, unedited, and at times hysterical. The collection is a musicologist's dream.

It would have been awesome to sit next to George Martin while he and the Beatles assembled *Sgt. Pepper*, or to witness the process of Radiohead bringing *OK Computer* to life. How cool would it be to watch Brian Wilson assemble the instrumental tracks that ultimately make up *Pet Sounds*? The notion of being able to watch genius at work sends a shiver down my spine.

Thanks to the Internet, we know a lot more about musicians and their lives than ever before. We probably know more than we should. Artists are using Facebook, Twitter, Instagram, and other social media platforms to reveal what they want us to see. That is more than enough for me. I don't need to get into the gossipy aspect of a musician's life. If the artist wants to tell me about a new recording, and how things are progressing, fine. But I am not going to dig any deeper than that.

Lisa Robinson loved to write about who was on the scene when the band took the stage. Andy Warhol was there. So were Robert DeNiro and Carrie Fischer. That's super. But how was the gig? Unfortunately, she often doesn't say. I know down to the smallest detail what Mick Jagger was wearing in the early '70s, but I have next to no idea what the Rolling Stones played once they took the stage. That seems like a huge waste to me. Yet I'm certain there's a vast audience out there lapping up this kind of information. I guess that's what separates me from the Lisa Robinsons of the world. It's a question of style versus substance. Robinson is all about style.

My head nearly exploded when I read the following sentences: "To me, the mark of a very good bass player is to wear the instrument low; it's much sexier. Paul McCartney, without question, wears it too high."

Say *what*, now?

Am I to understand a music journalist has determined the physical location of an instrument is the sole determining factor when judging the quality of the player? How about how well he actually *plays* the bloody thing? Am I to discount Geddy

Lee, Tony Levin, and Stanley Clarke because they don't sling their basses low to the ground? Spare me!

Robinson is a big fan of the '70s punk movement, which is the basic antithesis of the progressive movement I prefer. She and I will have to agree to disagree on many things, where the actual music is concerned.

***

Perhaps it is merely a matter of personal preference. I consider myself to be a rather private person. There are certain aspects of my life I will never make public. That's just the way I am. I would imagine the musicians I admire share the same personal traits.

I know Adrian Belew has five children, but I can't name more than three of them. I'm reasonably sure Rob Fetters is married. I couldn't say for certain whether Vernon Reid, Mike Keneally, or Deborah Holland have a spouse. And you know what? That's just fine with me. I don't need to know that information. Anything a musician wants to tell me about his personal life will more often than not reveal itself in a song.

For example, I know Adrian went through a tough divorce because he wrote a song about it called "The War in the Gulf between Us." I know he has at least one daughter, because she sang on a song of his called "Oh Daddy." I know he likes Mexican food, because he told us about a restaurant he frequents near his home in Nashville. When I spoke to him, I didn't feel the need to pry for any additional personal information, because it doesn't have anything to do with my enjoyment of his music.

I think I surprised Deborah Holland, because my line of questioning during our interview stayed strictly along musical lines. I couldn't see her face, but something tells me she was waiting for me to ask something more probing, or personal. But I simply didn't deem it necessary. She was even taken aback when I didn't ask a lot of questions about the band that brought her to my attention in the first place. "Wait a minute," she said as I wrapped things up. "No more questions about Animal Logic? Really?"

"You've been asked those questions a million times," I said. "And I've already read your answers. I didn't see the point of walking that path again."

I could hear the sigh of relief. "I suppose you're right," she said.

There was more than one instance when a musician told me something I didn't really want to know. I would hear this little tidbit, and it would be all I could do not to yell, "Whoa, buddy! Too much information! I don't need to know about that! Stick to the music, pal." Instead, I simply listened, and data dumped what I just heard from my brain.

There are more than a few people who would love to hear about things like that. I'm not one of them. Lisa Robinson may be comfortable talking about those things, but I'm not.

***

I'm not naïve. I know that some musicians like to partake in the occasional "recreational activity." That's the nature of the business. It's not something I care to be a part of. One, because my day job simply will not allow it. More importantly, it's because it simply doesn't interest me.

From time to time, I might hang out with some of my musician friends. It's always a riot to hear them introduce me to some a fellow musician who might partake in a little "something-something" now and then. The introduction almost always sounds like this: "Hey, this is my friend Ced. He's a guitar player. He's really cool, and he's a cop."

Once the ashen look comes off their faces, I tell them all the same thing: "I'm not working. Do whatever you want. Just don't do it around me." From there on, all is fine with the world. I can't love music and take a hardline stance on drugs. Hell, isn't the cliché "sex, drugs, and rock and roll?" Based on that statement, it's hard to have one without at least one of the others.

Maybe that's one of the reasons I'm drawn to the more "progressive" side of rock music. The songs are so complex, requiring split-second timing and high levels of manual dexterity. The idea of playing a song that changes time signatures four times over 12 bars while loaded is nothing short of absurd. My friend and musician Jimmy Griffin once teased me by saying my walking backstage to find the members of King Crimson mainlining heroin would absolutely tear my world asunder. And while I laughed hysterically at the idea, I knew he was right. There are some areas of my music collection that have no place for drug abuse.

I'm sure there are more than a few places within my collection where drug use was or is prevalent. Comedian Bill Hicks once opined anyone feeling drugs had no place in music should take their record collection outside and burn it. "Because the artists that made many of those fantastic records were *rrrrrrrrrrrrrrreally high on drugs!*"

Jimi Hendrix is a major musical influence. His battles with drug abuse are well documented, and no doubt contributed to his death. Many would argue the Beatles got more interesting once they came off the road, and "expanded their minds" via drug use. It would be hard for me to dispute. Does "Lucy in the Sky with Diamonds" really mean what many think it does? Only John Lennon knew for sure. Miles Davis was a heroin addict in the '50s (a habit he says he kicked cold turkey), and allegedly abused cocaine until the mid '80s. I wasn't there, so I don't know. But it wouldn't surprise me. In fact, heroin was the drug of choice among jazz musicians in the '50s and '60s, after marijuana. Stevie Ray Vaughan suffered from major substance abuse issues in the early stages of his career. His talent was such that I couldn't tell. That is, not until I heard him play sober toward the end of his life. The difference was night and day. Don't believe me? Seek out the *Live in Austin, Texas* DVD. The show features Vaughan's two *Austin City Limits* performances: '83 (loaded) and '89 (sober). It won't take long to see (and hear) the difference.

Sometimes, the abuse of drugs or alcohol can seem almost funny. Whenever I listen to George Thorogood, a notorious drinker, I can almost smell the booze coming through the stereo speakers. His performance during the studio version of "One Bourbon, One Scotch, One Beer" led me to ask a friend just how many rounds of each he had before they pushed the "record" button.

My career as a police officer has positioned me much closer to the drug culture than I would be otherwise. It has enabled me to see things that I missed the first time I saw them. It doesn't take a rocket scientist to see Kurt Cobain was battling some serious demons while fronting Nirvana. The first time I saw Alice in Chains vocalist Layne Staley on MTV's *Unplugged*, I assumed he was trying to look cool as he wore his sunglasses indoors and sang from beside the microphone, rather than behind it. When I saw the performance a couple of years after I got my badge, I sat bolt upright and pointed to the TV. "Holy shit!" I exclaimed. "He's nodding out on stage! He's a heroin addict!" Not long after, Staley died from an overdose.

I didn't discuss drug use with my interview subjects, because it had nothing to do with what I was writing about. Lisa Robinson put the subject into my brain, so I have decided to deal with it. But I have no desire to go back and ask anyone about drugs. For one thing, I'm reasonably sure I know the answer for just about everyone I talked to. One subject surprised me by admitting he dropped LSD several years ago. Still, all I did was shrug and move forward with our conversation.

My sober friends are always quick to declare they have no idea why people would want to do such damage to themselves via drugs. After all, what part of "If you shoot this into your arm, you're going to die!" do addicts not grasp? My thought was process was similar until I spoke to a musician friend about it. (1) He tried heroin once and said that he knew right away he never wanted to do it again. Why, I asked him? "Because that dope gave me a feeling I wanted to maintain for the rest of my life," he told me with the most serious expression I've ever seen. "That's where the habit comes from. Addicts spend the rest of their lives chasing that first high, that cherry high. When the feeling fades, they'll do anything – and I mean *anything* – to get it back. The problem is, they never do get that feeling again. And it almost always kills them in the process."

That was the tutorial I needed. And while I still don't condone the use of heroin or any other hard drug, I do have a better understanding of why people do it.

Society is evolving to the point where marijuana use is becoming more and more accepted. It wouldn't surprise me to see it completely legalized within the next decade. That's fine with me. My rationale is based on two decades of law enforcement experience. I lost count of the number of people I arrested due to alcohol misuse long, long ago. There's something about booze that makes people flat-out stupid, especially when they're dealing with a police officer. And alcohol is legal. On the other hand, I can count the number of serious issues I've had with "potheads" on two fingers. One of those wouldn't have been a big deal if the suspect in question and his friend hadn't been driving around with a large garbage bag full of weed in the back seat of their car.

I've been asked more than once if I would smoke marijuana if it were legalized. The answer is no. Once again, it simply doesn't interest me. (2) But legalization certainly would make concert attendance a lot more enjoyable.

More than once, I've had to shoo away some guy smoking a jumbo-sized joint at a concert, because he was puffing away in front of me. For a few moments, I have to transition from music fan back to cop. I'm pretty sure one young man pissed his pants when he saw my badge after I tapped him on the shoulder at a Gov't Mule gig. The shocked and frightened look on his face was absolutely priceless. "Calm down," I said with reassurance. "Look, you may not have to pass a random drug test, but I do. Go over there, and we'll both be fine." The young man thanked me profusely, and then made his way to the corner of the club I was pointing to. Problem solved.

The bottom line, where I'm concerned, is this: the legalization of marijuana gives me one less thing to worry about and saves me a ton of useless paperwork.

***

I'm not saying Lisa Robinson did anything wrong. She covers music from the angle that fascinates her the most. Good for her. My personal eye rolls aside, her book made for interesting reading. She likes being part of the inner circle. She likes being "in the know." She likes hobnobbing with the "who's who" of the music industry. It's a small wonder all her name-dropping didn't register on the Richter scale. My approach is just … different.

I wonder if a journalist really gets to know the artists they cover, even after spending day after day on the road with them? In my mind, being the subject of an interview is like going on an endless series of first dates. I will only reveal what I want the readers to believe that I am. Even Robinson pointed this out, when she noted Michael Jackson had two voices: the high-pitched, boyish voice the fans loved, and his "real" voice, which was lower and more authoritative. It was *that* Michael who was in charge of the business. When I read that, I was reminded of what comedian Chris Rock said about dating. "When you first start dating someone, you're not meeting them," Rock said. "You're meeting their representative." I have no doubt musicians put up the same front, especially after being asked the same question for the ten thousandth time.

Perhaps that's why I prefer to keep any conversations I'm fortunate enough to have on a musical level. Normally, the artist loves to talk about his craft. It is there you will attain the greatest level of honesty and earnestness.

Or maybe I'm just being naïve.

(1)   It is not in my nature to write blind quotes. But in this case, I deemed it necessary. My friend never told me our conversation was in confidence. But why open Pandora's box when it isn't necessary? I will simply ask that you take my word for it. This conversation did take

place. Besides, I couldn't have made that quote up if my life depended upon it.

(2)   My personal smoking experience is limited to about half a dozen cigars. One of them made me horribly sick. I bought three cigars to celebrate my 20th anniversary on the police department. I gave one away, and basically chewed on the second because I couldn't bring myself to light it. The third remains unwrapped. It will probably stay that way.

Track 24
I'm Not Really Alone

It happens at least once a week.

I'll be sitting in my den or driving my car as the music pours over me. My eardrums will be vibrating gloriously to the sounds of Jacob Garchik, Julie Slick, or the National. I'll smile knowingly as a familiar bass line thunders against my chest. I'll make a feeble attempt to sing along to a clever lyric. I'll burst into an unrestrained fit of air guitar. And once the moment has passed, I will remember I could open every window in my house or turn my car stereo up to the point where it could be heard by everyone within a ten-block radius. Still, chances are I will be the only person familiar with the music. And that's when the question arises, aloud or internally, but *never* without an overwhelming sense of bewilderment:

"HOW AM I THE ONLY PERSON WHO KNOWS ABOUT THIS MUSIC?!? I CAN'T POSSIBLY BE THE ONLY ONE HEARING THIS!!!"

But that's how it feels.

I realize, of course, that's not the case. There are other King Crimson fans out there. Someone besides me is familiar with Ozric Tentacles. Tortoise doesn't base its career moves around whether or not they can sell me a record. There are more than a few "niche" music fans out there. Trouble is, they're not always the easiest people to spot.

I can't say that I've ever seen someone wearing an Aimee Mann t-shirt. If I ever heard Mike Keneally playing over the speakers in the local record store, I'd probably pass out. The Internet is not ablaze with people looking for the latest information on We Lost the Sea. But those music lovers are out there. They do exist. I know because I've met more than a few of them over the years.

Funny thing about fans of obscure music: we tend to run in the same small packs. Concerts are more like reunions. At a Bruce Springsteen show, I'm likely to be surrounded by 20,000 screaming strangers in a hockey arena. At an Adrian Belew gig, I'm going to share space in a 200-seat club with the same people I saw and spoke to at a Robert Fripp or Tony Levin performance, or the *last* Adrian Belew gig. And even though I haven't seen these people in months, it's like we never parted. Our conversation picks up right where it left off before the start of the last show: usually talking about the other gigs we've been to.

The truth of the matter is, I've never really been alone. My fellow music nuts are out there. These days, thanks to the Internet, they're a little easier to find.

***

Another funny thing about this music club, particularly in the beginning: membership usually comes by accident.

There was a time when a trip to the record store wasn't just about the pursuit of new music. It was a social occasion. This was particularly true for fans of more obscure music. Two people reaching for a Michael Jackson record in the mid '80s was no big deal. Hell, *everybody* had a Michael Jackson record somewhere! But, two people reaching for a Peter Gabriel-era Genesis or Emerson, Lake, and Palmer record? Now *that* was cause for conversation!

The chats were rarely short, and almost always took place within the confines of the obscure band's section of the record bins. They almost always had the same cadence: "Oh, you like this album? Well, I'll bet you'd *love* this one! My favorite albums? Oh, definitely this one, that one, and this one! You mean you don't know about so-and-so's *other* band? Oh, buddy ... you are missing out!" Some 30 to 45 minutes later, we might remember to introduce ourselves.

Before e-mail, the newfound friendship was usually a temporary one. It existed within the confines of that small section in the record store. I can't say I had a lot of musical pen pals in the '80s. Instead, we went our separate ways and continued doing what we did best: trying like hell to get our regular friends into our music.

I learned I wasn't musically isolated by way of a knowing smile from a stranger in a crowded room. A group of eight or nine might be chatting away in the kitchen during a party. The topic would turn to music. Invariably, someone would blather on about whatever was in the top ten that week. I would be asked whether or not I was familiar with that artist. "Yeah," I'd say. "But they don't hold a candle to someone like Frank Zappa." My statement almost always elicited the same reaction: stone silence. Except for that one guy, whose face would light up and he unleashed a sly grin. He knew what I was talking about, and I had a new (temporary) Friend for Life. The two of us would spend the rest of the evening bonding over the artist who brought us together, and nobody else existed.

In the '80s, I could actually get a request played on college radio. The DJ would be beside himself with glee that someone besides him knew about the music he was playing. More than once, I found myself talking to the DJ for nearly half an hour. He would put me on hold when he had to introduce a new record. I was told more than once I would have made a great DJ, and it was too bad I couldn't share the air with the jock I was talking to. (1) That opportunity finally did present itself one midnight shift in 1998 or '99, when I spent three hours on 88.1, KDHX, St. Louis' independent radio station. I don't know whether I was heard by six people or 6,000, but I had a blast introducing records from Radiohead, Reeves Gabrels, and Bruford Levin Upper Extremities.

Now and then, one of my niche artists might appear in a small paragraph or two in a magazine like *Rolling Stone* or *Spin*. But these moments were few and far between. The emergence of Michael Jackson and Madonna changed the face of *Rolling Stone*, and the magazine and I parted ways. *Spin* stayed on the cutting edge for as long as it could, but soon followed suit. I was more likely to find an article on a musician or band I admired in one of the guitar magazines I loved. But my favorite periodical of all was a now-defunct magazine called *Musician*. Over the course of 100 or so pages every month, this amazing magazine had the utter temerity to focus on … wait for it … actual MUSICIANS! It was normal to read an article on Adrian Belew, Jeff Beck, or Terry Bozzio. And the articles had substance! They weren't mere P.R. department lip service. Naturally, since I loved this magazine, nobody else did. Like my niche bands, *Musician*'s following was loyal, but small. The magazine folded in '99, but not before publishing a lengthy article on how commercial radio really worked. Thanks to that read, my war with popular music came to an end. I learned it was a fight I could never win, and it was a complete waste of effort to try. All evidence to the contrary, I really have backed away from the fight.

I was still able to share common bonds with the musicians who wandered into the record stores and guitar shops I frequented. That seemed like enough to sustain me.

But the Internet taught me otherwise.

***

I was ensnared in the worldwide web in the fall of 1997. A new world of information was opened to me by way of technology that seems downright quaint just 20 years after the fact. Thoughts of that antique personal computer with its gigantic monitor, limited memory, slow processor, and dial-up modem never fail to bring a smile to my face. But it was all cutting edge back then, right down to the whirs and static telling me my phone line was about to bring more than casual conversations with friends.

Like anyone else discovering the Internet, I was most interested in sending and receiving email and finding articles about what interested me. Naturally, I gravitated toward music. Specifically, I wanted to know if there were people out there interested in the same obscure artists I was. And indeed, there were.

It only seemed logical to begin my quest for knowledge by learning all I could about my hero, Adrian Belew. I didn't expect much. Fortunately, I was wrong.

I found more than a few articles written about my guru in recent years. My search led to a couple of very important places. The first was a web site dedicated to Adrian himself. It was not the easiest site to locate. These days, one can find just about anyone or anything on the Internet by using that person or subject's name. Today, locating Adrian Belew is as simple as typing www.adrianbelew.net into a search browser. (2) In '97, finding Adrian Belew meant typing in http://web.dbtech.net/"rhino. That doesn't exactly dance off the fingertips. Still, the web site was a thing of beauty.

A man named Rob Murphree, who lives in Alabama, was running the web site. It contained what seemed like up-to-the-minute updates on Adrian and his musical activities. Rob's dedication to Adrian and the site cannot be understated. So detailed and accurate was the information, Adrian once joked in an interview that he checked the web page, "to see what I'm doing today." Apparently, Rob was doing something right.

Rob's web site included a detailed biography on Adrian, complete with an equally detailed discography, charting not only Adrian's band and solo releases, but his guest/session appearances as well. I thought I knew Adrian Belew. Rob Murphree showed me there was someone in the world more fanatical than I was. I didn't believe that was possible! Rob also included audio and video clips, many of which were quite the revelation in the days before YouTube.

I was captivated. It felt as though I was part of Adrian's production team as he worked on one project or another. I had gone from being completely surprised by any new Belew-oriented release, to knowing what song he was recording that day. At times, I was so familiar with Adrian's movements, I thought I was just this side of a restraining order.

I also came across a site called *Innerviews*. A San Francisco-area music journalist named Anil Prasad ran it. Like me, Anil had a taste for music from off the beaten path. But what separated him from me was Anil had spoken with many of the musicians I admired. Naturally, I started with his Adrian Belew interview, conducted some five years before. Before I knew it, I was spending hours on end reading nearly every word spoken by those amazing musicians.

Innerviews would be one of the key elements to aiding my musical development in the 21st century. But I'll get back to that.

***

The Internet ushered in a great era for musicians, as opposed to rock stars. While the megastars of the music industry relied on their publicists and record labels to spread the word on their latest musical doings, more obscure musicians were all but eliminating the middle man and reaching out directly to the fans.

While Adrian had the help of a fan to inform people of his activities, other musicians – like Tony Levin – took the proverbial bull by the horns and did it themselves. Levin – whom I knew best from his bass playing in King Crimson and with Peter Gabriel – created an independent music label, called Papa Bear Records. There he was able to showcase his talents in less mainstream-oriented projects. Best of all, he made his efforts available on CD, sold directly from his web site.

I was able to track down web pages from many of my favorite "niche" artists. Those who didn't have sites made their music available through smaller, independent record labels like RoadRunner and MagnaCarta. With just a few clicks of a mouse, non-commercial music was delivered directly to my doorstep.

It was easy to find a network of people who enjoyed the same music I did. Message boards and forums for bands were all over the place. One of my favorites was a King Crimson-oriented forum called *Elephant Talk* (named after one of my favorite Crimson songs). There, people from all over the world mused poetically about our favorite band, its assorted lineups, albums, and songs. I soon found myself engaged in conversations with people from England, Canada, Germany, Italy, France, and Argentina. Logging on to *Elephant Talk* felt like walking into a clubhouse. All were welcome, but you had best know what you were talking about! If not, you would most definitely get called on it.

The musicians had their eye on these forums, as well. More than once, I caught a contribution from the likes of Trey Gunn, Pat Mastelotto, or even Robert Fripp himself. The King Crimson founder is not known for being the most engaging person. So, any contribution he made was viewed as a rare treat.

Lord only knows how many hours I spent on *ET* chatting away about life-altering subjects such as "Chapman Stick vs. Warr Guitar," the ideal King Crimson lineup, or just how much "soul" was in Robert Fripp's guitar playing. My girlfriend was flummoxed by how I chose to spend my computer time (which also kept her from getting on the telephone). But I was in hog heaven. What an ego boost it was to see a conversation I started turn into a lengthy, protracted discussion with people from all over the world. I couldn't have a conversation like this with more than two people in a record store. Now I was chatting with a guy from Spain and another from New York City at the same time.

It wasn't all sunshine and rainbows. Every now and then, someone would have to say something ignorant, either to get a rise out of the regulars, or just to draw attention. The term "troll" had not come into being yet, but that's precisely what we were dealing with. The war of words could get protracted and ugly very quickly. To make matters worse, the artist in question might chime in to try and defend himself. This rarely went well. More often than not in an Internet chat room, the inmates are running the asylum, and attempts at civility were futile gestures at best. (3)

For the most part, the message boards were all good, clean fun. Some of those people are still my friends to this very day, despite the fact we've never been in the same room at the same time.

***

Music journalist Sid Smith **(Photo courtesy of Sid Smith)**

I liked the music I liked, whether it was commercially viable or not. An artist I admired making his way up the charts meant little or nothing to me. That being said, it was still nice to see a lengthy article in a magazine about an artist I admire. That validated my association with the music more than any *Billboard* chart ever could. Needless to say, I was not finding these articles in magazines like *Rolling Stone*. It was far more likely I was reading *Musician, Guitar Player, Bass Player, Modern Drummer, Mojo,* or *Prog* when I stumbled across a cool article on Trey Gunn, Terry Bozzio, or Bill Bruford. One of the happiest days of my life came from a magazine that declared its love for "The Outsiders" of music. There on the cover was the Double Trio version of King Crimson! There was also a lengthy article on Frank Zappa in that issue. Now *there* was something you didn't see every day! I held on to that magazine for quite a while.

Over time, I realized I was seeing familiar names attached to the articles I was reading. One of those names was Sid Smith, a freelance journalist from Whitley Bay, England. Like me, Sid seemed to have a thing for progressive rock in general, and King Crimson in particular. In fact, his love of Crimson ran much deeper than mine, and that was saying something!

Smith has been a music fan since the '60s. His biggest influence, hey says, is his older sister, whom he described as, "the coolest person, with the hippest record collection. I assimilated my love of music through her." Sid's sister saw the Beatles perform live twice, and it wasn't long before Little Brother was emulating her tastes, taking ownership of his own copy of *Sgt. Pepper's Lonely Hearts Club Band* not long after she got one. Smith's passion for music grew from there. Best of all, Smith's sister worked a job enabling her to take her little brother to more than a few concerts. Among the artists he got to see was King Crimson, whom Smith saw for the first time in 1971 (a decade and a half before I made my way to the party).

Smith became a fixture in the music scene during what he calls a "Golden Age" of music, which seemed to hit one of its peaks in '73. "It was subjectively and objectively a great time for music," he told me. There were so many bands on the scene, and they were all doing something new. That year, I was probably going to six gigs a month." Smith dug through his archives and sent me an abbreviated list of the shows he attended that year, and the price for a ticket, where he could remember it. The list read like this (4):

Jan 7 DAVID BOWIE 50p - £1.00p

Jan 9 FOCUS 60p - £1.00

Jan 19 URIAH HEEP 60p - £1.10

Feb 22 GENESIS 70p

Feb 23 Caravan + Hatfield & The North NCL University

Feb 25 MOTT THE HOOPLE 50p

Feb 26 CAN 60p - 80p

Feb 27 DEEP PURPLE 50p - £1.25

March 6 GROUNDHOGS 60p - £1.00

March 2nd The Sensational Alex Harvey Band + J.S.D. Band + Glencoe

March 21 KING CRIMSON 60p - £1.00

March 22 STRAWBS 60p - £1.00p

March 23rd Daryl Way's Wolf + Jackson Heights

March 29 ROXY MUSIC 60p - £1.10p

April 24 WEST BRUCE AND LAING 75p - £1.50

April 28 CAPTAIN BEEFHEART 75p - £1.50p

April 27th Soft Machine

May 4th The Sensational Alex Harvey Band + Kingdom Come with Arthur Brown

May 10th Ten Years After

May 11th Curved Air + Gary Moore Band

May 25th Groundhogs + Backdoor

June 1st Barclay James Harvest + Longdancer +Bridget St. John

June 17 Gong + Faust

June 19 JOHN McLAUGHLIN/MAHAVISHNU ORCH. 50p - 90p

July 27th Medicine Head + Tir Na Nog

Sept 26 ARGENT 60p - £1.10p

Sept 30 LOU REED 80p - £1.65
Oct 15 MEDICINE HEAD 50p - £1.00
Oct 26 GENESIS £1.00 - £1.65
Nov 4 ROXY MUSIC 80p - £1.50p
NOV 16 GONG [with Hatfield and the North] NCL University
Dec 9 YES 75p - £2.00
Dec 11 HAWKWIND 75p - £1.50

And those were the just the big gigs he could remember!

During the '70s, Smith began to do some freelance writing about the music he was experiencing. By late in the decade, he was helping to edit a fanzine that was distributed after copies were made via mimeograph. As it was for me, music was a constant for Smith. "It was always a part of my life," he said. "I had jobs around the arts. I played in bands. Music was always there."

In the early '80s, Smith took a government job and held it for 20 years. But while the job paid well, Smith saw the profession as "soul destroying." He saw music journalism as his means of escape, even though he was not completely sure how to go about doing it. "I had a great enthusiasm for music," he said. "I wanted to share that enthusiasm with others." Still, it was a good thing he held that job for as long as he did, for he failed to make any money writing about music for the first couple of years he tried. But the motivation was definitely there, even if he struggled to bring it to life.

"There was no grand plan for me," Smith said. "I don't find writing easy. I struggle with it sometimes. I'm not one for whom the words just pour out." Still, Smith did the best he could with what he had to work with. And what he had to work with was plentiful. Eventually, it got him attention from the right places and people.

Among the many places Smith waxed poetic about his musical passions was *Elephant Talk*. His words caught the attention of a member of the King Crimson team named Hugh O'Donnel. He, in turn, informed none other than Robert Fripp about Smith's postings. By the time Smith stood before Fripp, at a CD signing in London in '96, the cat was out of the bag. "(Fripp) picked me up on a couple of things I got wrong," Smith said with a wry smile. "But he seemed to respect what I had to say."

Smith's words resonated more deeply than he thought. The following year, when Fripp took ProjeKct 4 on tour in the United States, he needed someone to man the merchandise table.

The Fripp team reached out to Smith. Initially, Smith declined. He did, after all, have a day job. But the writer eventually gave in and went on the tour. While they were on the road, Fripp suggested to Smith that he keep a road diary, documenting the happenings of the band and crew during its jaunt across the western United States. The words Smith wrote ultimately became the liner notes to P4's CD release.

After the tour, Smith said he heard from Fripp every now and again. The journalist found his words making their way to more and more King Crimson-oriented releases. I, for one, felt like I was seeing his words at every turn. It began to feel like a ritual: order a Crimson Collectors Club release, crack the seal, read Sid Smith's words, and enjoy the music. Of course, this point of view is mildly exaggerated. King Crimson's music and Sid Smith's words did not automatically go hand-in-hand. Nobody understood that better than Smith. "I don't automatically assume it will be me writing the liner notes," he said. "I certainly don't regard it as a right. In the case of one of Robert's 'Frippertronics' releases, the liner notes were written by a man who knew everything there was to know about that setup. He was infinitely more qualified to write those liner notes than I was. So, I was certainly fine with that."

As the 20th century drew to a close, Smith put his extensive knowledge of King Crimson – and the confidence of the band's founder, Fripp – to good use by writing the definitive history of the band, titled *In the Court of King Crimson*. The book traced the band's origins back to the earliest days of Fripp's experience as a professional musician, marching with painstaking care through the very first incarnation of Crimson in 1969, and each subsequent band until the year 2000 (5). Since my intimate knowledge of King Crimson was rooted in the '80s forward, Smith's book did an amazing job of filling in the gaps where I lacked information about the band between '69 and '74. Nearly every member of the band contributed an interview or two for the project, and none of them appeared to pull any punches. I've read *In the Court of King Crimson* cover-to-cover three times, and I'm sure I'll do it again one of these days. Fripp's endorsement of the book (found on the front cover) pretty much says it all: "Sid Smith's opinions," it reads, "are worthy of consideration." As Fripp is not always known for doling out affection toward journalists, these words constitute praise in the highest order.

How Smith managed to endear himself to Fripp remains a mystery, particularly to the author himself. "You'd have to ask Robert," Smith said when I asked him about it. "I have no idea."

I was surprised to learn while Smith is a great admirer of King Crimson and other progressive rock acts, he does not really consider himself to be a progressive rock fan, above all other forms of music. "There is an assumption that I'm a huge prog fan, but I'm not," he said. "I don't regard myself as a prog fan, or a jazz fan. I'm a *music* fan!" This is certainly a standpoint I can relate to.

Smith is lucky enough to be in a position where he can write about pretty much any band he wants, be it for *Prog* magazine or another publication. He attributes this to the latitude he is given by those who monitor his work. "A good 'Reviews' editor understands his writers," Smith said. "Grant Moon, my current editor at *Prog*, gives me good assignments. I have large piles of stuff coming to me in the mail every day. Grant usually asks me little more than, 'What's on your desk right now?' I tell him what I'm writing about, and nine times out of 10 it's approved. The most he might do is saying something like, 'Well, we need your column by the end of the week.' From there, I'm on my own."

Smith's mailbox receives a wide variety of music, and he listens to as much as he can. "It's not just about writing about certain bands that I already know," he told me. The music he listens to must make an immediate impact to maintain his attention. "I'm sent a lot of stuff, and I'm able to play just a bit of it. There's so much music out there. I try to have a listen to as much as I can. But it has to speak to me. I want to get enthused about it. That makes me want to write about it. Ultimately, it's about my ability to engage with the music." Smith is also careful to give every band he hears a fair shake. "I won't slag off albums just because they aren't normally on my radar," he says. "I try to judge an album on its own merit."

Smith doesn't have a bona fide methodology for writing. There is one way to describe his *modus operandi*: productive procrastination. "I spend a great deal of time *not* writing," he said. "I spend that time listening to the music, and hold off from writing about it until the very last minute. I want to know the story behind the music. I'll spend the weekend listening to the material, and then write about it on Monday. If I get stuck, I just go back to the music."

Smith is like many artists in that he cannot make himself revisit the past. Once his work is complete, he moves on. He all but refuses to read something he's already finished. "It's just too painful," he said with a laugh. "I'm never tempted to go back, even off a nice compliment. People will say to me, 'Oh I love your article in this month's *Prog*,' or something like that. I'll have no idea what they're talking about, because I've written so much other stuff since then." He also has a sure-fire way to makes sure his writing is up to snuff. "When I read a sentence I've written and think it's great, I take it out immediately," he said. "Because I'm sure it's a shit sentence." I can relate to this man on so many levels.

If there is a downside to his work, Smith points to the remarkable amount of music he doesn't get to hear, because he doesn't have the time. People are constantly sending him unsolicited music samples, usually via internet links, with the hope the journalist will help make the band famous. But those people are in for a disappointment. "I'll usually send them a reply, saying something like, 'Thanks for the link. I'll have a listen as time allows.' But I already have a big pile of stuff I *have* to listen to, because it's for work. The pile of stuff I'd *like* to listen to is positively massive! It's not that I'm trying to be difficult. It would be nice to hear it all, but there just isn't time."

I was surprised to learn how little time Smith spends with the artists he interviews. He also isn't as close to the musicians as I thought he was. "I don't get to do a lot of interviews in person," he says matter-of-factly. "That's difficult to do, because I'm not London-based. I usually just chat with them on the phone.

"Now and again, I'll get off the phone with someone and think, 'Now there's someone I'd like to spend some time with.' Some of the artists stay in touch, and that's quite nice. But I usually get most of my material from the musician's public relations company."

Perhaps it was the apparent closeness to Robert Fripp that led to my distorted vision of Sid Smith's relationship with musicians. No matter. It doesn't stop his work from being anything short of top-notch. If I want to know whether or not a record is good, I need look no further than the words of Sid Smith. The only thing better is when both Smith and Anil Prasad agree on the quality (or lack thereof) of a musician. Prasad, however, seems to come at music from a slightly different angle.

***

Music journalist Anil Prasad **(Photo courtesy of Anil Prasad)**

Anil Prasad will never be confused with the average run-of-the-mill music journalist. One need only spend a few minutes perusing *Innerviews* to drive this point home.

Canadian-born Prasad makes his home in the San Francisco Bay Area, a hotbed for music of all kinds. That's a good thing, because there is very little music he doesn't cover. If it's relatively obscure, musician-driven, and playing in California, chances are Prasad is there.

Like any other fan, Prasad found his love for music via the radio. His exploration into the more non-traditional material came via Genesis, whose *Abacab* album caught his attention when he was 12. "Of course, I heard the radio stuff first," he said. "I would find out soon enough that I really needed to hear the whole album." Before long, like me, Prasad found himself hanging out in record stores. There, he was introduced to the likes of Brand X, Brian Eno, and Peter Gabriel, as well as international sounds. "The tentacles of a group can reach all around the world," he told me, and he is absolutely right.

Prasad's entry into the world of music journalism was unconventional, to say the least. It was also quite heartwarming. In 1989, at the age of 19, Prasad was determined to ride to the rescue of his friend Paul, who was depressed to the point of contemplating suicide. "The one thing that kept him going was is devotion to and fascination with Rik Emmett, a highly devoted Canadian guitarist and vocalist who had just quit the then-popular rock group Triumph," he wrote in an article dubbed *How to Scam Your Way into Music Journalism,* which is available online. Making use of information he obtained from a Canadian rock tabloid called *Rock Express*, Prasad figured out how to contact Emmett's record label and arrange for an interview with his friend's favorite musician.

Upon learning of the interview, Paul was beside himself with excitement. There was just one problem: the two of them had no idea how to conduct an interview. "We knew as much about music journalism and how to act like a music journalist as we did about working in a coal mine," Prasad wrote. Undaunted, the two of them worked out a series of questions and prepared to document the moment on a $25 Radio Shack cassette recorder. It was the perfect crime, until Paul dropped and broke the recorder.

The duo was panic-stricken. "We called our friends and family. No-one had a recorder," Prasad wrote. "We soon realized Paul's 'ghetto blaster' – a big-ass, piece-of-crap straight out of a Kurtis Blow video – also possessed a built-in mic." And that is what the two of them took to a trailer at the Molson Canadian Light Hot Air Balloon Fiesta in London, Ontario, Canada. Fortunately, Emmett was amused by what was taking place before him and went along with it. "We're pretty sure he knew we were full of it, but he treated us well and entertained our every question, no matter how ridiculous," Prasad wrote. "Astoundingly, he gave us backstage passes. We proceeded to cavort at the side of the stage for the rest of the evening as the vastly important people we surely were." And just like that, the seeds were sown for a lifetime of music journalism.

The interview went so well, Prasad turned it into an article, which he got published in a local newspaper. From there, he was asked, "What else you got?" by his editors. He offered up the idea of an interview with Adrian Belew. The editors went for it, and the wheels were set in motion for a lifetime of more than 500 interviews.

Where Smith's appearance comes across as cherubic and congenial, Prasad's first impression might be that of someone much more driven and intense. Prasad is definitely an intellectual, and anyone choosing to engage in a battle of wits with him had better come heavily armed. To me, what comes off as intensity is really deep-seated musical passion. This man *loves* music. He loves it in a way many of the most ardent fans simply cannot fathom. More importantly, Prasad loves *musicians*, who are often a forgotten component in the entertainment equation. I have frequently said Anil Prasad has *forgotten* more about music than I will ever know. I'm only slightly exaggerating.

Once again, I point to *Innerviews* as proof. I've read countless interviews with countless musicians conducted by countless journalists. None of them can hold a candle to the way Prasad goes about his business. Prasad doesn't ask cookie-cutter questions. He does not lob softballs at the artists. If a musician is preparing for an interview with Anil Prasad, I would offer only one piece of advice: wear your thinking cap.

The average journalist will ask a musician things like, "Who are your influences? What's it like working with (famous person)? What kind of gear do you use?" Prasad isn't letting anybody off that easy. Where most music interviews can be handled with one- or two- word answers, a bit more effort is required during an *Innerview*.

"There is no methodology," Prasad said when I asked him how he comes up with his questions. "I was simply influenced by *Musician* magazine, which always asked substantial questions. My goal is to ask the questions not typically asked by other magazines. The musicians realize this interview will not consist of the standard construct presented by others."

Prasad has mastered the art of the open-ended question. He understands that the best way to get the most out of a musician is to let the musician talk, and to not interfere with that process as it unfolds. He does not ask "yes" or "no" questions. From the get-go, the interview subject is obligated to talk at length. Anything else might leave the musician looking a bit foolish.

In early 2016, Prasad interviewed keyboardist Adam Holzman, who had been working with Steven Wilson (one of my current favorites). He was also the music director for Miles Davis (a past favorite) in the '80s. At the time of the interview, Holzman was on the verge of releasing a new album. It would be easy to ask what the new record is called, or who's playing on it. Prasad's first interview question wasn't even a question. It almost seemed like a demand. "Provide some insight into the idea behind *Deform Variations*," he asked of Holzman. And just like that, the keyboardist was talking, at length.

Of Yes vocalist Jon Anderson, he put forth the following: "I understand you feel your best work is ahead of you as you enter your sixties and seventies. Tell me about that philosophy."

Prasad opened his '14 interview with Mike Keneally like this: "*You Must Be This Tall* (Keneally's latest release at the time) is drawn from material generated across many different periods. Describe how it all came together into a cohesive whole." In '15, he asked '80s icon Howard Jones, "What are the keys to remaining relevant to a broader audience when you're (in your sixties)?"

"My site is not-for-profit, so I don't have to worry about appealing to the lowest common denominator," Prasad said. "I say, 'Let's talk about the deeper elements of your music.' No-one asks these questions (in conventional publications) because it's not marketable.

"A lot of it has to do with being a fan of the artist I'm interviewing," he continued. "I'm not merely assigned to interview the artist. I only talk to who I really want to talk to. So, I ask about things that not only interest me, but the artist himself."

Prasad got serious about the *Innerviews* web site, and put things into motion in 1994, when he officially launched the site. Even then, he knew it wasn't going to be about making money. And from that standpoint, things haven't gotten any better. "It's comical to call music journalism a profession these days," he said. "That's been gone since the late '90s." But the absence of money does not equate to the absence of meaning, where his encounters are concerned. "I have salient memories of each interview," he told me. "I tend to remember things about the recording, if it means something to me."

By '96, *Innerviews* began meaning something in the music community as well. His was the first true online music magazine, and the industry began to take notice. "People were beginning to approach me, and (the site) was getting a lot of attention," Prasad said. "People were willing to meet me on my terms."

Of all the interviews I conducted for this work, I was most nervous about talking to Prasad. Why? I didn't want to sound like an idiot. After all, how does one go about interviewing the man who has perfected the craft? As it turned out, I needn't have worried. While my questions were far from Innerviews-esque, Prasad could sense my sincerity and desire to get it right. He had no problem guiding me where I was already dying to go.

Prasad is a man confident in his musical convictions. It was he who helped me cement my position on streaming, downloading, and the adverse effect they had on the musician's bottom line. His passion on the subject manifests itself on multiple levels, like the complete and utter contempt he holds for record labels and streaming companies that horde all the revenue generated by the artists, who are paid fractions of pennies for countless hours of work. "There is massive corruption in the music industry," he said. "There are a lot of complete idiots involved. It's shocking to see once you get in to it. But I don't care about the machinery. I only care about the artists."

He is equally frustrated by the oblivious and apathetic fans who do little or nothing to force the industry to change its business model. He's also unafraid to call the musicians themselves on the carpet, particularly those who simply accept the business methods of the modern industry because they are unwilling to push for anything better. Spend a little time on Prasad's Facebook page, and it doesn't take long to realize that Anil's Bad Side is NOT a good place to visit, even for a short period. There are those who may feel by not talking to Prasad, they are striking some kind of personal blow for music and musicians. But the man could not care less. "I'm not interested in talking to anybody who isn't interested in talking to me," he said flatly.

This is the intensity I see in his photos. This is what makes him seem just a bit intimidating. But once again, it's really all about his passion for music and musicians. He wants the best music possible to be heard on as many platforms as possible, as often as possible. And he wants the artists that generated those sounds to be paid for their efforts.

Like Smith, Prasad is flooded with a deluge of new music almost daily. In addition to receiving a dozen or more pieces of new music daily, Prasad spends anywhere from 35-40 hours on each interview he conducts. Add to this the time spent traveling to and from various concerts in his immediate area, almost nightly. His is not a life filled with spare moments.

Of all the interviews Prasad has conducted, there are a few that stand out. He has fond memories of conversations with the Kronos Quartet, Mike Oldfield, and with Mike Rutherford of Genesis. And there are still interviews he longs to do. "I would still love to interview Peter Gabriel," he said with a little longing. "But the machinery I'd have to go through to get to him … I don't have the stomach for it."

In a fair and just world, Anil Prasad would be he president of the recording industry, because he would make things the way they should be. But if that happened, he may not have time to assemble the kick-ass interviews I live to read.

One might think a journalist like Prasad would see himself as above the music industry, or as an essential cog that keeps the wheels turning. But that couldn't be further from the truth. Prasad's humility is summed up succinctly when he said to me, "My entire body of work is not worth one note of music."

I beg to differ.

***

Rhea Frankel with Yes lead vocalist Jon Anderson
(Photo courtesy of Rhea Frankel)

Spend enough time at certain concerts, and you start to see familiar faces. The first couple of times I saw Adrian Belew in person, I was wrapped up in being within close proximity of my idol. But I've seen Adrian in person several times now as a solo artist, with the Bears, and with King Crimson. Before long, I was starting to see not just my hero, but the people who came to see him as well. And more often than not, they were the same people.

For whatever reason, there aren't a lot of women at progressive-oriented rock shows. Perhaps it's because it's not easy to dance in 11/8 time. So, when I started to see the same woman over and over at gig after gig, it got my attention. It got to the point where I started to look for her at the shows. I don't think she ever disappointed me.

I remember going to a Bears gig with a friend, who caught me scanning the room we were in prior to the show. "What are you looking for?" my friend asked.

"There's a woman," I replied. "She's bound to be here. She's at every show where Adrian is involved. I find it hard to believe she wouldn't ... *there* she is!" And then I started to laugh. I had found my concert mate, even though we had never met.

The first time we informally met was very nearly an unpleasant encounter. It was during a King Crimson concert in 2000. My concert mate was standing in front of me, along with her boyfriend or husband (a man who bore a *striking* resemblance to Adrian Belew, I might add). At the end of the

413

show, the band came to the front of the stage to take a bow. Pat Mastelotto tossed his drum sticks into the crowd, as was his habit. One of the sticks flew in between me and my concert mate, leading us to reach for it at the same time. In my mind, we each caught part of the stick simultaneously, which led to a brief struggle over its possession. In my mind, I heard my mother's voice, insisting that I be a gentleman at all times. So, I let go of the stick, relinquishing it to the lady.

In her mind, things were a bit different.

I saw my concert mate at another Adrian-oriented gig a couple of years later. Once again, we found ourselves close to one another. I mentioned that we had been in contact before, at the Crimson gig. Her eyes lit up with instant recognition. "*You tried to take my drumstick!*" she exclaimed, a triumphant smile coming across her face. That's not the way I saw it, and I guess I should've been mad. But all I could do was laugh. From there, a conversation ensued.

Still, it was at least another concert or two before I learned my concert mate's name was Rhea Frankel. I arrived at yet another Adrian Belew solo gig mega-early. I figured I would be first on line. Actually, I was second. Rhea was there before me. When I saw her, I couldn't help but smile. "Well, you're here, so now it's officially a gig," I said, and she laughed. We talked until the doors opened.

I would learn Rhea was originally from Philadelphia (which, in my mind, explained the toughness and determination that came with grabbing that drumstick). Her favorite music group was Yes, whom she had seen more than 90(!) times in person. That number makes up just short one-fifth of the total number of concerts she has attended.

Rhea's love for music started early. She recalled hearing things like the soundtrack from the Broadway musical *Annie* and Debbie Boone's "You Light Up My Life" in the '70s. But the pivotal moment came at age 12, when her family got cable television, and she discovered MTV. The "hair metal" of the day caught her attention initially, culminating with Heart becoming her first concert experience. "There was so much music out there. I just wanted to hear it all," she told me. "I saw Jimmy Page on his *Outrider* tour, the Moody Blues, David Bowie's *Sound and Vision* tour (where Adrian Belew was his guitar player), and Paul McCartney."

Rhea's musical aesthetic was shifted shortly after high school, when she was introduced to King Crimson via their debut, *In the Court of the Crimson King*. Not long after that, she found herself working at her college radio station, WXPN, based at the University of Pennsylvania. It was here she was introduced to new wave music and bands like the '80s King Crimson (which featured Belew) and Talking Heads. "I also saw Adrian on his *Here* tour, which would have been in '93 or '94," she said. "That was also around the same time I was introduced to the internet, which opened up an entire new world of music for me."

Given our connection through all things Belew, I was more than a little surprised to hear Rhea name Yes as her favorite act. But the issue was never in doubt. "They got my attention in around 1989 through the *Anderson, Bruford, Wakeman, and Howe* album," she said. "I just loved the sound of Jon Anderson's voice, and then (Rick Wakeman's) keyboards. I went to a concert from that tour, and then to all three Philly shows of the *Union* tour a year or two later."

I'm a Yes fan, too. But Rhea is on a different level. She obsesses over them the way I obsess over King Crimson. What was it about Yes that kept her so involved? "I really like the variety of sounds, and all the different timbres," she said in a way that left me feeling like I should have been paying closer attention. "The sound could be really heavy, but very clean at the same time. I loved it. Plus, I've found myself becoming very song-oriented. Melody is very important to me. I appreciate the instrumental passages, but I enjoy the singing even more." Even Bruford, who played drums with both Yes and King Crimson, has pointed out that the former band is more song-based and cheery compared to the dark, minor key nastiness of the latter group. Clearly, Rhea was on to something.

Progressive rock-oriented bands traditionally fail to draw a large female crowd. It was the elephant in the room I felt compelled to discuss with Rhea. Her take on the topic had a very "it is what it is" tone, which tickled me to no end. "My best friend is a drummer, and we went to see Rush together," she said. "It didn't strike me as that big of a deal. Two girls, heavy show, no problem!" Still, Rhea noticed she was hearing music a little differently from her other female friends. "For the most part, they were looking for something that could just be played in the background. Or, I could get them to go to one show with me, but I had trouble finding someone to go to every show."

Rhea was ahead of me in that she learned early on it's better to go to a concert alone, rather than waste time trying to find someone to go with. "I saw my first show by myself at 16, when I couldn't find anyone to go to the second of two Yes shows with me," she stated. "In college, I got a lot of free tickets to concerts via the radio station, but a lot of the time, it wasn't convenient for my friends. So I went alone. When it's a prog-oriented band, I have a certain group of friends I can go with. But a lot of the time, I just don't bother asking people anymore." Once, she noticed she was one of only two women in the room for a Mike Keneally show. "Of course, we knew each other," she recounted with a laugh.

Rhea is a fan that doesn't let something trivial like having to travel to get to a gig bother her. Being from Philly, she had a built-in conduit to concerts all over town, as well as in New York City and New Jersey, both short train rides away. She met her husband, Roy (Adrian's clone), while traveling to one of her many Yes gigs. Because of him, she found herself moving to St. Louis. Rhea and Roy routinely took trips to Kansas City, Chicago, Nashville, or anywhere else there was a concert they wanted to see. Rhea leads the musical life I would have led had I not had a child. Family has a way of making disposable income disappear quickly, leaving considerably less room for musical exploration.

It didn't take long to determine that Rhea's musical knowledge was not to be trifled with. I saw more than one alleged know-it-all get destroyed after incorrectly rattling off a piece of King Crimson- or Adrian Belew-related trivia. It was like having a ticket to a very one-sided MMA match, only more fun.

Every time I bumped into Rhea at a show, our conversations got a little longer. To me, our talks were part of the overall concert experience, nearly as important as the meet-and-greet session with the artist after the show. But like so many good things, my in-concert chats with Rhea have come to an end, as she and Roy moved back to Philadelphia. She pops up in my social media feed every now and then. Of course, she's almost always headed to a show. I'll miss bumping into my friend at concerts. But even more, I'll miss being able to talk to a woman who "gets it."

***

Abbi Telander with Josh Ritter **(Photo courtesy of Abbi Telander)**

When people say they love music, more often than not what they really mean is they love certain *songs*. Usually, those songs are whatever is being spat forth from the local Top 40 station. They usually can't distinguish one of these songs from the other. Sometimes, this love of "music" will spread all the way out into a single genre, like country or pop. My chats with "music" lovers frequently end in disappointment and frustration.

But there are exceptions to this rule. And those exceptions are a joy to behold. Abbi Telander is one of those exceptions.

When I got married and found myself with three nearly-grown step-children, I did not expect one of those children to have a friend who would make her way into my musical circle. But musically inclined people tend to recognize each other across any and all barriers. One true music fan recognizes another. That's what I found in Abbi. Here, I thought, was someone I could teach, since she is younger than me. That is, after I realized she had the musical open mind I appreciated.

That open mind was discovered quite by accident. Abbi's husband is a very computer-savvy young man named Mike Toohey. I needed Mike to help me with a problem on my ancient PC one day, so he came by to do just that. Abbi came with him.

The three of us already had a common connection through our mutual love of *Star Trek*. But on this particular day, the television was off, and the CD player was running. I was playing a CD from the band Tortoise, called *Millions Now Living Will Never Die*. The music caught Abbi's attention. I could tell by the quizzical look on her face. So, while Mike and I looked into my computer problem, I restarted the disc for Abbi, who sat on my couch and absorbed the sounds. I knew I was on to something when she walked toward me with a faraway look on her face. She then uttered a single word: "Whoa ..." Just like that, I had a protégé.

Abbi and I would talk from time to time about what was going on in music. *Our* music, that is. The stuff located far away from the charts. I even got her to go to an Adrian Belew gig. I'm not sure how much Mike liked the show, but I knew I hooked Abbi.

I taught Abbi about Tortoise and Adrian, and she told me about groups like Mumford and Sons and the Avett Brothers. Thanks to Abbi, I learned I had a folksy side I paid little to no attention to.

Our chats were sporadic, but enjoyable. But family life has a way of interfering with musical exploration. I became a father and got busier than ever. Not long after, Abbi became a mother, and walked a similar path. Before long, our only way to talk about music was to trade links to music videos via Facebook. It was better than nothing, but not quite the same. When I finally got to sit down and talk to Abbi about our mutual passion, it was the first time we'd been able to do so in years. Literally.

"I've been a music fan my whole life," Abbi told me. "I don't understand people who don't appreciate music. When people tell me that, I want to look at them and ask, 'Who are you? Can we actually be friends?' If you don't have music, then how do you cope? What do you do in the car?'" We both laughed hysterically at this. If I didn't know already I had a kindred spirit, I certainly knew it then.

Abbi and I are similar in that we've allowed music to become an integral part of our emotional well-being. Certain songs trigger certain feelings or are more appropriate in certain situations. When things are not going quite right, Abbi is one of those people who can find a certain song or band to help things. "Sometimes, the only answer is to turn it up loud and absorb it," she said. I know exactly what she means. Those are usually my Nine Inch Nails or Tool days.

Abbi grew up in Little Falls, Minnesota. The town, she says, is located almost literally in the middle of the state, between St. Cloud and Brainerd. She had the good fortune of having a music teacher for a mother and a music lover for a father, meaning music was a constant in her home for as long as she can recall. "I can still remember my parents getting a stereo system from Montgomery Ward in 1984 or '85," she said. "It was quite a big deal! The system came with a record player, and I was in awe of it. Of course, my parents made me deathly afraid to touch it!"

Abbi strikes me as having a musical soul about 10 or 15 older than she actually is (around 35). Her approach to music is relatively "old school," in that she is still very album-oriented, preferring the physical medium of records and CDs, when most people her age have given in to the digital playlist. "I prefer the physical media, because picking out a record is a very deliberate act, and I'm more connected to it that way," she told me. "Streaming tends to relegate the music to background noise. Most times, a playlist just doesn't cut it." That being said, she does understand and appreciate the benefits of digital music. "I don't have a lot of disposable income," said the married mother of a five-year-old daughter. "So it's nice to know I can listen to an entire album before I decide whether or not to buy it. But I do understand the economics, where the artist is concerned. And if I like the music, I definitely buy a copy!"

Like me, Abbi is baffled by the current generation of music consumers, who seem to believe they are entitled to what they're listening to, with compensating the artist a mere afterthought. She told me about a conversation she had with one of the 20-something co-workers in her office. "She was steaming a new record I was planning to look into, which I pointed out to her," Abbi told me. "I told her that I hadn't heard it all yet, but I was planning on buying it soon. She looked at me with the strangest face and said, 'What? You still *buy* music?'" We shared a collective look of befuddlement.

Kids today. Sheesh.

Abbi's old soul reared its head again when I asked her about her first album purchase. I just knew it would be something from the '90s, when her generation came into its own, musically. So imagine my surprise when she quickly informed me it was Simon & Garfunkel's *Parsley, Sage, Rosemary, and Thyme*. "It's not what you'd expect someone born in 1982 to pick," she said with a grin.

But her generation's music was just not cutting it. "I was not a consumer of pop music in elementary school, middle school, or high school," she told me. "I thought it was inane and ridiculous. I saw myself having the musical journey of someone 20 years older, and my parents were really good about letting me pick my own musical path." Nevertheless, Abbi briefly felt the need to explore what her friends were listening to, to see if she was missing anything. She wasn't. "In the '90s, it was boy bands, Hootie and the Blowfish, and country music," she said. "One day, I was determined to listen to the pop music radio station for a day. In the end, I found myself asking, 'Do they always play the same eight songs over and over?'" Her tale of musical woe struck me as incredibly funny, if only because it sounded incredibly familiar.

Abbi decided she was better off following her old musical soul. "I wasn't finding any kind of connection to what my friends were listening to," she said flatly. "I really like lyrics, and they were much better back then."

Not that the pop music of the time didn't do its best to permeate her soul, particularly while she was in college. It seems on her dormitory floor, there was a radio in the community bathroom, perpetually set to the local Top 40 station. And that radio was *never* turned off. Any attempts to do so resulted in feeling the wrath of the floor's residents. But while Abbi later gained appreciation for a couple of the radio station's regulars, she spent most of her musical time off the beaten path.

One thing Abbi did embrace (albeit with a tinge of guilt) during this period was the file sharing service Napster. It was there she found an entire new musical experience, which would influence many of her future purchases. "It offered great access to music I might never have heard otherwise," she said. "It was great to be able to hear alternate and live mixes of songs I already knew, along with all the other things."

Abbi came to the live music scene late, as her parents were not overly fond of her going to concert venues in her teen years, and Abbi described herself as a "very law-abiding child." Her first concert experience was Maroon 5 and John Mayer in '04. But whom she saw wasn't nearly as impressive to me as where she saw them. The concert was at Red Rocks Amphitheater, the legendary venue outside Denver, Colorado. That, to my mind, is one hell of a first impression. From there, until the birth of her daughter, Erin, Abbi found herself at 10 to 12 major concerts a year.

Like Rhea and me, Abbi occasionally struggled to find someone to go to concerts with. Mike enjoys music, but not going to shows. "So, I would kind of invite myself to shows with friends, or just drag them along," she said with a laugh. "I'd find out they had a copy of the band's CD or something, and say something like, 'Oh, I see you've got a copy of so-and-so's CD in your bag there. They're playing the Pageant next week. You wanna go?'" When she says this, her native Minnesota reveals itself in a huge way, inducing an accent straight out of the movie *Fargo*. Even she finds this hilarious. When all else fails, she goes to shows alone, book in hand for the time between sets. The solo trips are worth it, she says, "Because it's great to hear the songs re-interpreted for the stage."

Abbi points to one concert experience above all others. She saw singer/songwriter Josh Ritter at Off-Broadway, a rough-around-the-edges club in south St. Louis. "It was July, and about 105 degrees outside," she recalls. "The place is packed ... and then the air conditioning goes out! But nobody left! We stayed in there, together, absolutely soaked in sweat. And the show was magical. It was the kind of experience you can't possibly get while sitting on your couch. I wouldn't trade that night for anything."

My friend is also what I'd call the ultimate concert attendee, in that she makes a concentrated effort to see the entire show. "I always show up for the opening band, and I give them my full attention, even if they suck," Abbi said. "I'll buy a CD from that band I may never play again. But at least they'll know I gave them 10 bucks toward their efforts."

Abbi is doing her best to pass her love of music on to her daughter. Still, it can be an uphill battle that's only getting more challenging. "When she was a baby, I could do Mom and Erin and Oatmeal Breakfasts," Abbi said. "Erin would sit in her high chair, and I could play albums from Miles Davis like *Birth of the Cool* or *Kind of Blue*. But as she got older, some of my music got harder to play. I would put on something from the Doors or the Rolling Stones, and Erin would say something like, 'No. This is too loud!' Or another time, I was trying to play *El Camino* from the Black Keys. I was having a good time, but Erin declared she wanted to listen to (children's show) *Veggie Tales*. I tried to say no, but Erin would say, 'Mom, Daniel Tiger says we share.' So we'd wind up listening to *Veggie Tales*. Curse you, Daniel Tiger!"

As a man with a teenage daughter, I can certainly relate to this struggle. It is said that children should never inherit the musical tastes of their parents. I don't entirely agree with this. Children can certainly be influenced by their parents, even if they don't walk the identical musical path. Did I get into jazz the same way my father did? No. But I did show up to the party. Without my mom, I suspect there would be no love for classical music or David Bowie. There's nothing wrong with finding one's own musical path by way of the parents. Call it variation on a theme.

My friend Abbi Telander is a musical "lifer." Music is a part of her DNA. There is no removing it. Nor should there be. As long as there are fans like her out there, I feel like the future of music is secure.

***

Loving obscure music is a double-edged sword. On one hand, it feels like being a member in a very exclusive club. People in the know can trade knowing smiles and nods of recognition when a favorite – but relatively unknown – artist or song surfaces. Concert venues are small, and tickets are usually both cheap and relatively easy to obtain. There's even an above-average chance fans will be able to interact with the musicians they came to see.

The downside usually involves the struggle to acquire the artist's music through conventional means, like record stores. A special order of some kind is almost always required. Most people have no idea who the fan is referring to in conversation, so blank stares in the middle of spirited musical discussions are common. Small concert venues mean fewer tickets for sale, which can lead to quick sell-outs. Or, even worse, a concert comes and goes without the fan's knowledge, due to the lack of a publicity machine behind the artist.

In the end, I think it's worth it. The musicians I admire operate, for the most part, outside the music industry. Because of this, they are free to follow their personal Muse wherever it leads. The "Outside" musician knows his fans will be there for him, no matter what.

In the early '90s, being a fan of obscure music could seem like more trouble than it's worth. But in the internet era, the musical world is much smaller, and the communities are both tightly knit and easier to locate. There's no way I can really feel alone.

(1)   I've been complimented more than once on the distinct quality of my speaking voice. While I find the remarks flattering, I also live with myself. Therefore, I have no idea what's so damned special about it. I did try out for and was accepted to Broadcast Center – a small St. Louis school for aspiring radio personalities – in '93 or '94. I very nearly went. But their idea of "guaranteed job placement" was a spot on some low-wattage AM station in the middle of nowhere for 12 grand a year. The police

department, it seemed, held a great deal more potential. Twenty-plus years later, I'm still a cop. I guess I made the right call.

(2)   Even simpler, one can just go to Facebook and punch in Adrian's name. There, the fan will find a page updated constantly by the man himself.

(3)   Adrian once became involved in a protracted debate on *Elephant Talk*, where a troll asked whether or not AB belonged in King Crimson to begin with, since the troll preferred the voice of '70s singer John Wetton, or whomever. Adrian's lengthy, thoughtful response to the troll only made things worse, to the point where an exasperated Belew threw up his hands and declared *ET* "a turd" to Robert Fripp, who quoted him in Fripp's online diary. It was hard to argue Ade's feelings in this instance. On the other hand, the encounter also spurred Adrian to pen the words for the KC song "ProzaKc Blues," which leads off the *ConstruKction of Light* album.

(4)   As of this writing, one-pound sterling was the equivalent of $1.40 American. Considering how expensive concerts can be in this day and age, many of these shows were a bargain at *twice* the price!

(5)   As I write this, rumors abound that *In the Court of King Crimson* is due for an update, since the band went through four more lineups between the end of the original book and 2016. When I asked Sid if the update was at hand, he would neither confirm nor deny its existence.

The accidental rediscovery of Supertramp
opened the floodgates to my musical past.
A lot of the music was better than I remembered.

Track 25
Going Forward by Looking Back

One pleasant fall day in 2012, I found myself in a friend's living room. There was a glass of scotch in my hand, a football game on the TV, and music playing in the background. This was a good day.

My friend and I were chatting about whatever it is forty-somethings chat about when they're too old for college girls and too young to retire. I had no control over the music's volume, and it was a little low. But there was something familiar about the bass line, and the vocal I thought I was hearing. It wasn't long before my friend's voice receded into the background, and the music moved forward.

I was busted quickly. "Have you heard a word I said?" my friend asked. That snapped me back. Not that it mattered. So, I just went with it.

"Is this ... Supertramp?"

My friend gave me an exaggerated eye roll. "Man, it really *is* all about music with you, isn't it? Yeah, it's Supertramp. I'm pretty sure this tune is…"

"Child of Vision," I interjected without missing a beat. "It's the last track from *Breakfast in America*. Came out in '79."

Another head shake from my friend. "Why am I not surprised you knew that? I take it you're familiar with this record?"

"I had this record when I was a kid. I remember going to Peaches with my dad and buying a copy with my allowance. God, I loved this record! I haven't heard it in years."

"If you enjoyed it so much, why didn't you play it more?"

I told my friend about the summer of '85, the discovery of King Crimson, and how nothing was the same after that. Supertramp was one of those bands that fell through the cracks. They were collateral damage during my discovery of a new musical world. I dumped a lot of crappy music after that summer. Unfortunately, I dumped some pretty good stuff, too.

My friend could see a bit of sadness behind my eyes, and he took a little pity on me. "You want me to start this one over, and turn it up?"

I grinned. "Yes. Yes, I do."

As I listened to the opening keyboard chords of "Gone Hollywood," the song that opens *Breakfast in America*, I found myself transported back to my bedroom at age 13. The memories flowed over me like a waterfall. I couldn't see it then, but I realized quickly that Supertramp was one of the bands who made it possible for me to absorb the progressive rock of King Crimson. Sure, the band had charming little hits on the album, like "The Logical Song" and the title track. But Supertramp was better than the average pop band. These guys had chops! Rodger Hodgson was more than his pleasant alto voice. He had keyboard and guitar skills, as well. His vocal counterpart, Rick Davies, was also a skilled keyboardist and an excellent songwriter. Hodgson and Davies could almost be seen as the progressive rock version of Lennon and McCartney.

For the moment, I was still that captivated seventh grader, who just *had* to have more of this band's music and begged his father to take him back to the record store the following weekend to see what else they had to offer. As it turned out, the band had quite the impressive back catalog. But better still, the year after *Breakfast in America* was released, Supertramp issued a live album, called *Paris*. That double LP became a mainstay on my turntable. I remember living for side four, when the band launched into the 10-minute "Fool's Overture." Even after that LP obtained a scratch or two, I kept playing it, to the point where I integrated the pops and scratches into my mental interpretation of the music. As far as I was concerned, the scratches were just part of the overall sound.

Sitting on my friend's couch, I made the mistake of doing math in my head. I was quite certain I hadn't played anything from Supertramp since 1988, at the earliest. How had I not allowed myself to listen to this band for 24 years? It was absolutely unreal.

I wanted to blame my refusal to play older music on Miles Davis, who was well known for his "Don't look back" philosophy and approach to making music. But it was pointed out to me that Miles may not have played music from his past, but he looked back all the time. A musician *has* to look back! Otherwise, he won't know where he's been. And that is what determines where he wants to go. Even within the confines of my listening, I looked back constantly. The jazz I collected was of my dad's era. The soul music I preferred was from the '70s. Only classic rock that had gotten the boot from my mindset. That, I finally realized, was a huge mistake. And in my mind, the floodgates finally opened.

A voice went off in my head. "It's all right," the voice said. "You can go back now." That was all the impetus I needed to head back to the record store.

***

I was destined to be on my friend's couch that fall afternoon. I had been griping more and more frequently that year that modern music completely sucked, and there was nothing new or exciting holding my attention, save for a precious few acts like Steven Wilson. My new music purchases had nearly ground to a halt. My usual favorites, like King Crimson and Adrian Belew, had greatly slowed or halted their production of new music. Jazz had become rather stagnant, nothing was happening in R&B, and even post rock artists seemed to have faded into the background. I was bored. Supertramp re-emerged at precisely the right time. I wouldn't have been able to hear them a couple of years before. I could hear them perfectly now.

Time magazine published an article about people who used social media to reconnect with boy- and girlfriends past. The magazine called these people "retrosexuals," which I thought was hilarious. But now I was developing a fetish for the music of my youth. I wonder what *Time* would have called that?

Luckily, my record store was more than ready to accommodate my retro-musical needs. So were the bands I was trying to reconnect with. A&M records, for example, had recently re-mastered and re-released Supertramp's catalog. Because of this, I was able to obtain pristine sounding copies of *Breakfast in America, Even in the Quietest Moments, Crisis? What Crisis?* and *Crime of the Century.* The only thing I couldn't get my hands on, to my great disappointment, was *Paris.* Luckily (I guess), Amazon had a digital version available for download. That was better than nothing. But I'll find that CD yet.

It was great hearing that old music again. It made me nostalgic for a simpler time, when my biggest worries were doing my homework and getting the trash to the curb on Mondays and Thursdays. And in what may be the least surprising development in the history of mankind, I began to wonder what else I had cast aside, and would be willing to hear again? The answers came pretty quickly.

While I maintained Jeff Lynne's *Armchair Theater* as one of my favorite records of all time, I had cast aside the band that made him famous, the Electric Light Orchestra. It wasn't long before I was in possession of yet another copy of *Face the Music* (which featured the blistering instrumental "Fire on High") and the album that brought me to the band in the first place, *Out of the Blue.* I still remember playing that double LP for my dad, back in the earliest days of our music sharing experiences. He seemed amused by Lynne and company as they took rock music (which Dad was never a huge fan of) to a different plane of existence, adding violins and cellos to the standard guitar-based sound of '70s rock. I don't think Dad was a Beatles fan, but even he probably heard the clear connection between the Fab Four and the music of Jeff Lynne.

The music industry knows Lynne as an extraordinary producer, so it was a short walk to re-acquiring two gems he helmed in George Harrison's *Cloud Nine* and Tom Petty's *Full Moon Fever.* Granted, they were both released well after the summer of '85, but they fell by the wayside all the same, and shame on me for that. They are both extraordinary albums, as is the first album from the Traveling Wilburys, which featured Lynne, Petty, Harrison, Roy Orbison, and Bob Dylan. I wore that record out when it was released and then just stopped playing it. Why did I do that?

Thanks to a couple of my high school friends, I had heard nearly every note played by Bob Seger, the Eagles and ZZ Top. I've still had my fill of Seger, whose songs never did a ton for me to begin with. But the sentimental tug of that trio of hombres from Texas was getting too strong to ignore. We wore out our cassette copy of ZZ Top's *Eliminator* (made famous on MTV for the hit songs "Sharp Dressed Man" and "Legs"), and the band released some killer tunes in the '70s. This more than justified the purchase of their greatest hits CD. Oddly, that release left me feeling a little empty, as greatest hits packages are known to do. There's always something missing that should have been there, and something there that had no business being on the CD in the first place. One day, I'll dig deeper into that catalog again.

"Hotel California" from the Eagles ranks among my favorite songs of all time. The guitar exchange between Joe Walsh and Don Felder at the end is one of the reasons I took up the instrument myself, even if I never came close to learning how to play the song.

Still, I heard the *Hotel California* album so often, I didn't feel the need to walk that path again. But the Showtime network documentary on the Eagles softened my point a view, and eventually a re-mastered copy found its way back into my collection.

And then there was The Boss.

Like everyone else, I got swept up in the mid-'80s mania that was Bruce Springsteen. I can't begin to calculate how many times I heard *Born in the U.S.A.*, but I know it was a lot. Naturally, this led to the exploration of the rest of his back catalog, of which *Born to Run* and *Nebraska* rank amongst my favorites. I have nothing but the utmost respect for Springsteen's abilities as a songwriter. But after a while, the themes behind his songs started to run together in my head. I mean, how many times could the man take Janie down by the river in his muscle car after getting laid off from his union job, leading him to try to pay his bills by committing a crime? By the early '90s, I checked out. But recently, I came back. I picked up a copy of *Wrecking Ball*, released in '12, pretty much on a whim. I was going back to everyone else, so why not Springsteen? I was positively stunned by how much I enjoyed that record. When I learned Tom Morello, the guitarist from Rage Against the Machine, would play a large role on *High Hopes*, the album Springsteen released two years later, I was all over it. The duo didn't let me down. The Boss was back in the fold, culminating with his *Live 1975-85* masterpiece he recorded with the E Street Band. I don't play the CDs often, but when I do, the volume goes way up.

These days, my trips to the record store are little more than an effort to recapture my past. One distinct advantage to all this retro-active shopping is I know ahead of time which albums are essential, and which can remain on the store's shelves. I don't like Steely Dan enough to invest in everything they did, but having a copy of *Aja* makes perfect sense. Eventually, I will re-purchase Fleetwood Mac's *Rumors*, their best record with Lindsey Buckingham, Stevie Nicks, and Christine McVie. The rest would be, in my collection, mere filler.

As much as I love the Beatles, I was relatively slow to collect the solo works of John, George, and Ringo. Only Paul McCartney captured my interest consistently. The man had a fine sense for pop music. I stuck with him all the way through both Wings and the albums he released under his own name. But somewhere around *Flowers in the Dirt*, I checked out and moved on to other things. I have been walking that back in the recent past. Like many others, his records have been re-mastered and augmented with bonus tracks, making the purchases seem brand new. What fun it was to hear *Wings over America* again for the first time since the early '80s, even if it didn't quite hold up the way I thought it would. Teenage Me and Middle-Age Me hear things a bit differently. I can remember wearing out my three-LP version of that release under my headphones in the comfort of my teenage bedroom. Attempts to play the record out loud were almost always met with a *"Turn that damn thing DOWN!"* from my mother. That may be because my speakers were against the wall that connected to our upstairs family room. Oh, well. These days, my ears are a little more critical, and the band doesn't always sound perfectly in sync with one another. Well, it's still a pretty good gig. It probably would have been even better to be there.

I was still listening to Genesis on a fairly regular basis, but my tolerance for the solo works of Phil Collins remained bottomed out. The man's name had become an underserved punch line in contemporary music. Even Trey Parker and Matt Stone took a good swipe at him in one of my favorite episodes of *South Park*. For me, things came of the rails musically around the time of ... *But Seriously* (released in 1990), which I bought more out of a sense of personal obligation than actual musical interest. I had grown completely fried on *No Jacket Required*, the album that made Phil a household name. If I heard

"Sussudio" one more time, I was pretty sure I would run screaming madly into the night.

Still, I've always enjoyed Collins's first two solo records, called *Face Value* and *Hello, I Must Be Going*. The former had been immortalized by its opening track, "In the Air Tonight," which found its way into commercials and movies, most memorably being appreciated by former heavyweight boxer Mike Tyson during a hilarious scene in the comedy *The Hangover*. The latter featured one of my favorite Collins songs, "I Don't Care Any More," immortalized by its hammering drum riff. These records deserved a return to my collection, I decided, and I began a casual search for them. As it happens, I found them both on LP in the same shop. Sixteen dollars later, they were on their way home with me. In '15, the Collins solo catalog received the re-master/bonus track treatment on CD, and I picked up those first two titles once again. I don't need to hear them every day, but it's nice to know they're around.

I re-purchased a "greatest hits" collection from Kansas. The first two albums from Boston came home with me. Two classic albums from Steve Winwood – *Arc of a Diver* and *Back in the High Life* – returned to my musical fold. Sure, some of the music was a little dated, but it was fun to hear songs like "While You See a Chance" and "Higher Love" again. I didn't realize how much I'd missed those songs.

I have nothing but the highest regard for the guitar playing abilities of Eric Clapton and Carlos Santana. But their careers had taken turns that I was no longer able to follow. I've often joked that no one has done more with the pentatonic blues scale than Clapton. But he wasn't doing anything revolutionary with it any more. His records sounded a little stale. But skill is skill, and it must be recognized. So I allowed myself to go back and collect re-mastered versions of *Slowhand, 461 Ocean Boulevard,* and *Behind the Sun*, among other titles. It's nice to be able to go back to that sound every now and then. Of course, the rediscovery of those solo albums led me directly to the music of Cream and Derek and the Dominoes. No music collection is complete without the music of these classic bands.

Few guitarists pour their heart and soul into a note like Carlos Santana. But when he left Columbia records for Arista, mega-producer Clive Owen did his best to turn Santana into a pop superstar, pairing him up with the hottest Top 40 acts like Robb Thomas from Matchbox 20, among others. I had no stomach for what was produced. I'm sure Carlos cried all the way to the bank over my absence. But over time, I softened my position on the music Santana and Clapton were making during the twilight of their careers. It finally dawned on me that these two had been on the road for the better part of five decades. By now they had earned the right to play whatever the hell they felt like playing, regardless of what snobs like me thought. There was no law saying I had to buy the new stuff. I could focus on the older Santana albums I loved like *Abraxas* and *Moonflower*.

It surprises more than a few people to learn I am a fan of the band Chicago. More than likely, this is because they equate the band with the syrupy sweet love ballads they've been producing since the mid '80s. Good God, how many times was "You're the Inspiration" dedicated on the radio and at high school dances during that time? Well, I hated that version of the band (even though I must confess to once owning copies of *Chicago 16* and *Chicago 17*, both produced by pop-magnate David Foster). So, when I say I am a Chicago fan, I am referring to the band's first ten albums. They all have one thing in common that the vast majority of the remaining records do not: guitarist Terry Kath.

The early Chicago (originally known as Chicago Transit Authority) was an air-tight, hard rockin', chops layin', funky-assed outfit that had the ability and the will to release double albums on each of its first three efforts. There was a ballad or two here and there ("Color My World," anybody?), but for the most part, these guys were practically a jazz act. Chicago had a major fan in none other than Jimi Hendrix, who felt the horn section of Lee Loughnane (trumpet), James Pankow (trombone) and Walter Parazaider (saxophone) sounded as though they were breathing through a single set of lungs, and that Kath was a better guitarist than he was. Hendrix's horn theory is evident throughout Chicago's early work, but it's "Sing a Mean Tune Kid," from *Chicago III*, that shows the trio at the peak of its prowess. At the risk of sounding crude, Kath was the band's balls. The sound could never get too soft with his Gibson SGs and Fender Stratocasters on the scene. An accidental gunshot wound killed Kath in 1976, and the band was never the same. Bassist/vocalist Peter Cetera stepped forward to lead the band, and the sound changed almost overnight. It was a direction I couldn't handle.

Still, I find great musical joy in the early works of Chicago. When I'm feeling nostalgic, that's where I turn.

It has shocked more than a couple of people to learn I was a Billy Joel fan. His catchy pop tunes and super-sweet ballads have made him a mainstay on MOR radio. But the Billy Joel I loved had an edge. It was songs like "Big Shot," "You May Be Right," and "It's Still Rock 'n' Roll to Me," that made their way into my collection of 45s. I caught myself leafing through his section in the record store one day. And while opportunities to reunite with albums like *The Stranger*, *Glass Houses*, and *The Nylon Curtain* were available, I couldn't bring myself to pull the trigger on those purchases. There was, however, one record I re-welcomed with open arms.

In 1981, Joel released a live album called *Songs in the Attic*. This record was unique, because it didn't represent the Billy Joel people had come to know and love in the previous three years. Instead, this album featured songs from the earliest days of his career, spanning records like *Cold Spring Harbor*, which was released in '71, and *Piano Man*, from which only the title track achieved notoriety. While songs like "Say Goodbye to Hollywood" and "She's Got a Way" were released as singles, the songs I loved on *Songs in the Attic* were "Miami 2017 (Seen the Lights Go Out on Broadway," "Captain Jack," and "The Ballad of Billy the Kid," which were epic in their own right. The arenas where these songs were recorded could barely contain the power of Joel and his band, which played at full throttle and took no mercy on the fan's eardrums. I've seen Joel in concert twice (including a sonically challenged gig at the concrete echo chamber known as the Tokyo Dome), but he has never come close to playing any of those three songs, much to my great disappointment.

For the longest, I couldn't get my hands on a CD of *Songs in the Attic*. I did see it on vinyl at my store, and very nearly picked it up. But something told me to wait. Once again, the little voice was right. A few months later, there the CD sat, waiting for me. Four bucks later, it was on its way home.

I was a huge fan of Sting in the mid-'80s. His early solo works, while certainly not to be confused with the Police (one of my favorite bands of all time), were musically intriguing. This was primarily due to his backing band, which featured prominent jazz musicians like saxophonist Branford Marsalis, pianist Kenny Kirkland, bassist Darryl Jones, and drummer Omar Hakim. One of my greatest memories remains catching Sting at Tokyo's famed Nippon Budokon Arena in '92. The earliest of Sting's solo albums, *The Dream of the Blue Turtles*, *Bring on the*

Night, ... Nothing Like the Sun, and *The Soul Cages* were rock solid. But as time went on, my priorities shifted, and Sting was left in the dust. It didn't help that his songs were now the background music in television commercials. I was done. But now that I was able to re-visit the musical past, these records regained their relevance. I even added '93's *Ten Summoner's Tales* to the mix after Rob Fetters mentioned it to me, declaring it a nearly perfect album. He was right, by the way.

But there was one place I refused to go for the longest, even though they were the first band I ever became obsessed with. I can still remember telling friends that I owned 18 LPs, and literally half of them were from Styx, one of the official Corporate Rock poster bands of the '70s. *Pieces of Eight* was the first LP I ever bought, and the first CD I ever bought. But when I closed the door on Styx, I closed it hard. I wanted nothing more to do with them after the cold light of objectivity (and the musical chops of King Crimson) showed me what I initially loved rang hollow to my maturing ears. There was no need to re-visit that area again. Until there was a need to revisit it.

Thanks to cable television, I discovered a network called AXS. One of the things they specialized in was concert videos of bands past and present, with heavy emphasis on the past. I caught gigs from Yes, Cheap Trick, Fleetwood Mac, Heart, Aerosmith, and others with mild fascination. One day, the network aired a concert from Styx. I was all set to change the channel and catch something on ESPN. But something wouldn't let me do it.

Styx was playing a gig in Las Vegas, recorded sometime around 2013. It wasn't even remotely the same band I grew up with. Keyboardist/vocalist Dennis DeYoung had long since departed (or been fired, depending on whose version one chose to believe), bassist Chuck Panozzo had retired and, sadly, his twin brother and drummer John had passed away. The only remaining original members were the guitarists/vocalists, James "J.Y." Young, and Tommy Shaw. (1) That alone made me want to change the channel again. Alas, that little voice told me to maintain my current position. So, I did. And you know what? That hour of television was a lot of fun!

Styx broke out all the old rockin' hits I remembered, like "Blue Collar Man," "Renegade," and "Come Sail Away." Better still, they eliminated the saccharine-laced ballads DeYoung insisted on, like "Babe." This was a gig I would have enjoyed seeing a live. These guys could still put on a show! And just like that, another doorway opened, which allowed me to re-introduce Styx to my collection. This time, however, I limited my additions to *Pieces of Eight* and *The Grand Illusion.* That was more than enough. They're still fun albums, and I only occasionally find myself shaking my head at them. (2)

While my top musical priority remains the exploration of today's new and undiscovered music, I have found joy in going back to the past. It's not something I do often, but it's nice to remember what led me down this 40-plus year path to begin with.

(1)   Yeah, yeah, yeah! I *know* Tommy Shaw was *not* an original member of Styx. He replaced John Curulewski in 1976, after the band had already released four albums on RCA and its first on A&M. But the band didn't begin to achieve popularity until Shaw joined, and they recorded *Crystal Ball.* So, for the sake of argument, just let me have this one, ok?

(2)   Seriously: what the hell was "Aku-Aku" about? Anyone who can tell me is welcome to drop me a line.

Bassist Julie Slick gives me hope for the future of music.

Track 26
BONUS TRACK: What's Next?

One of the nicest compliments I've ever received came from a friend named Staci Olsen. In the mid '80s and early '90s, I spent a great deal of time hanging out with Staci, her husband Dave, and other friends at the Olsen home. This is what happens when you become the first of your peers to buy a house: single friends just show up, and never seem to leave.

We would sit in the living room, enjoy a drink or two, and chat amiably about whatever was on the mind of young 20-somethings back then. There would always be music in the background. Often, I was the one providing it.

One day, Staci and I were sitting and listening to something I brought with me. I don't recall precisely what it was. No doubt, it was from the coming "Alternative" movement, which hadn't completely gained its footing in St. Louis. I remember having my eyes closed as I listened and we chatted. At some point, I realized Staci had stopped talking. I opened my eyes to find her staring at me as the next song on the CD started playing. Needless to say, I was a bit befuddled.

"What?" I asked.

Staci grinned at me. "How do you do it?"

"How do I do what?"

"You always seem to be two steps ahead of everyone else when it comes to music," she said. "It's been like that since I've known you. How do you do it?"

I must admit, I could feel immense pride (and perhaps a touch of cockiness) growing inside me. I did my best to tramp it back down. I simply shrugged. "I don't know. I guess I just listen a little more intensely than most people." I don't know if she bought that answer or not. I supposed it didn't matter. She was already absorbed in the new song.

There is something cool about being ahead of the curve. There was a time when my friends would come to me and tell me about the "new" bands they were hearing, like R.E.M., U2, and the Cure. I would nod and smile, and then I would tell them about the records released before the ones they were showing me. I tried to do it without displaying a "been there, done that" attitude. Still, I'm sure there may have been just a tiny bit of smugness in my comments now and then. I couldn't help myself. I was a musical "hipster" before anyone knew what that was.

But there was no great secret to my discoveries. I heard most of the bands now being exposed on mainstream radio on college stations two or three years before. It just took commercial radio a little more time to catch up. Once it did, the game was pretty much up.

When "Alternative" radio entrenched itself on the right side of the radio dial, the musical gap between my friends and me was greatly reduced. Now, sometimes we were hearing new bands at almost the same time. Before long, my friends and I were running neck and neck. It stayed that way for years.

But now, the industry has passed me by.

Well … I don't know if that's accurate. What I probably should say is, I've lost interest in what the industry has to offer.

The Alternative station sounds more and more mainstream to my ears. I liked the Alternative movement because it put me on the edge of musical possibilities. Now, the movement appears to have entrenched itself in the middle, embracing artists and sounds that are just as comfortable on a Top 40 station, the bane of my musical existence.

I understand musical trends are cyclical. Guitar music of the '70s was replaced by electronic sounds in the '80s. In the '90s, the guitars made a slow, but steady comeback until the turn of the century, when electronics started to creep back in to the sound again. As I write these words, commercial music has taken on an updated '80s tone. I'm not overly fond of it.

The platform of musical delivery has also evolved, even if I have been painfully slow to embrace it. All but gone are the days when I walked into a record store and heard something I liked over the blaring speakers. This would almost always lead me to head straight to the counter, where I would ask Rock Guy or Soul Brother behind the register what was playing. Or I could just look at the display near the register, usually a hand-made sign with bold letters declaring, "Now Playing," with a copy of the album in question underneath. When I walk into a store these days, what I hear 90 percent of the time registers as just so much noise. Or it's a band or artist I'm already familiar with. Less and less new and exciting music was reaching my ears.

Commercial record stores are struggling to stay relevant in the modern entertainment era, to the point where the emphasis is being taken off music in these stores and being placed on merchandising and other forms of entertainment. In 2015, there were new archive releases from both Frank Zappa and Miles Davis. While neither was ever the most "mainstream" of artists, their music was still easily located in a record store. But that was not the case this time. In the cases of Zappa's *Dance Me This* and Davis's *Live at Newport*, I would find that not only were the CDs not in the store, they were not scheduled to arrive. *Ever.* The corporate offices were de-emphasizing the stocking of new music, especially if it came from someone who had been dead for more than two decades. But there were plenty of DVDs, t-shirts, and movie merchandise items to choose from. (1) If it is possible to be stunned without being the least bit surprised, that's precisely how I felt.

Even my favorite smaller shops, who specialized in music from obscure artists, were becoming more and more unreliable. Once again, the music I sought wasn't there, and there were no plans for its arrival. The employees, once the lifeblood of my musical discovery, seemed completely clueless. I was telling them about new releases, and they seemed stunned by my discoveries. The tables had completely turned. I spent years going to record stores to learn. Now I was spending most of my time teaching. What a drag.

A lot of my dilemma had to do with the new economics of the music industry. Record deals, once the most prominent way for an artist to make himself heard, were becoming a thing of the past. The industry had been slowly eating itself for years, trying to force a '60s era business model to work in the 21st century. But the Internet was changing everything. Artists were able to eliminate the middleman, as it were, and get their product directly to the consumer themselves, without the help of major record labels. Assuming the material hadn't already been pirated and uploaded on to the web, where many fans found ways to get hold of the music for free.

Streaming services were becoming the new way for the industry to expose music fans to new artists, as well as established ones. But the pittance paid to the artists for their work turned me away from sites like Spotify and Pandora. I may be in the minority on this, but I think it's essential the artist be properly compensated for his efforts. I'm well aware of how much work and expense goes into putting a record together.

American music magazines like *Rolling Stone* and *Spin* have long since lost their purpose in my existence. When music magazines focus more on style than music, what's the point? I did find salvation, however, in two magazines from England. *Mojo* was the magazine I wanted *Rolling Stone* to be. Page after page of news and features geared toward … wait for it … MUSIC! What a concept! And the magazine came with a sample CD featuring the artists in the magazine that month, or a variation on that theme. It was glorious. Equally exciting was *Prog*, the magazine geared around one of the music forms I hold most dear. It was awesome to read new articles on bands like King Crimson, Yes, Genesis, Rush, and Steven Wilson. And once again, I got a sampler CD. (2)

Of course, there was a catch. Since *Mojo* and *Prog* are European magazines, the best place to find and explore most of the music featured is – naturally – Europe. American stores stocked precious few of the CDs I was reading about. Oh sure, I could special order some them. And after waiting anywhere from a couple of weeks to several months, I could fork over $30 to $60 for a single disc. Assuming the store was able to track down the CDs in the first place.

In the end, I have been all but forced to join the 21st century ways of obtaining new music. I have come to embrace more artist-friendly streaming web sites like Bandcamp and Soundcloud. Admittedly, my transition has been slow. But once I got into them, the musical OCD has kicked in, and I've become addicted.

Many of my favorite modern artists, like Julie Slick, Markus Reuter, and Pat Mastelotto had already been posting tracks on Bandcamp. Not only were they posting new albums, but the occasional demo of material they were still working on. What an exciting way to explore music!

In addition to catching up with known favorites, I was finding new music as well. These days, I've fallen in love with the music of Snarky Puppy, toe, and We Lost the Sea. Spending a couple of hours on a site like Bandcamp bears a striking resemblance to spending a similar amount of time in record stores.

Logging on to the site is like opening the front doors to my favorite store in its prime. I am greeted by link after link of artists eager for my attention (and ultimately, my money). The sensation can be almost overwhelming at times. I remember feeling the same way when I walked into the store. I may have had an agenda before I got to the door, but once inside – faced with a virtual avalanche of musical possibility – any organized plan of attack pretty much went right out the window.

With that in mind, I employed a strategy online very much like what I did in the stores: I gravitated toward something I knew about. That would give me the time to focus and settle in before it was time to branch out. Robert Fripp had an axiom for becoming a better musician. "Start with the familiar," he suggested, "and then move gradually toward the unfamiliar." This also seemed to work for streaming. Once I found an artist I knew about, I could settle in on the musical style that held my interest. Before long, it was time to branch out.

Bandcamp acts like the record store employees of yore in that it acknowledges my musical selection, and then recommends artists and styles based on that choice. The only thing the app needs is a laid-back voice saying to me, "Dude, if you like that band, then you're gonna LOVE these guys!" The major difference between the real and the virtual clerk is that the latter offers up a LOT more alternatives. Sometimes, it's enough to make even the most seasoned music fan's head spin.

It may not be the most scientific way to explore music, but it works for me. When in doubt about which record to choose from, I often took the one with the most interesting cover art. Was I judging a book by its cover? Maybe I was. After all, that method has worked in the past. I never would have shown interest in Return to Forever if not for the cover art on the *Romantic Warrior* album. It didn't take long to realize the music was every bit as good as the art.

I was already familiar with the Japanese band toe. They had a sound and groove that reminded me of one of my favorite post-rock bands, Tortoise. After listening to a few cuts, I started browsing the available titles for something to experiment with. Before long, I came across a rather interesting cover, depicting the takeoff of a tiny space shuttle against a much larger land and seascape. The name of the band was We Lost the Sea. The album was called *Departure Songs*. I'm a huge fan of the space program, so this seemed like a good place to stop and check out the tunes.

The album opens with an atmospheric piece called "A Gallant Gentleman." A single guitar, devoid of overdrive but drenched in reverb and delay, plays a sparse double-stop pattern for several moments. The guitar manages to sound up close and far away at the same time. The pattern is being used to build emotional tension, and it was working! I could almost feel the rest of the band champing at the bit to get into the mix. But they held out for a little while longer. A keyboard enters the fray, followed closely by the downbeat and crash of the drum kit. This signal was the equivalent of opening the cage, as the rest of the band (two more guitars and bass) cuts loose with riffs more suited for a metal record than post rock. It was a remarkable – and completely unexpected – beginning. And it only got better.

The second track, called "Bogatyri," is a song I never saw coming. It comes in on a gentle breeze, and then strikes with the force of an F5 level tornado. The song begins with a relatively simple and guitar pattern evolves from gentle, groove-oriented post-rock into riffs that would be perfectly at home on a Tool record. But the song is more than mere metal. The song builds, and builds, and builds, putting layer on top of layer without ever sounding cluttered. The listener is pulled into a sonic vortex full of emotion, with notes cascading from all sides by the time the song reaches its emotional crescendo. By the time "Bogatyri" ended, I was emotionally drained, and damn near in tears. And I was completely hooked on a new band.

If bands like We Lost the Sea were the future of music, and that future would reveal itself mostly on apps like Bandcamp, then I was all in.

***

As I've said, I'm all for supporting artists, and compensating them for their musical efforts. So I wasn't offended in the least when the Bandcamp app prompted me to allow We Lost the Sea to email me with information on how to purchase their work. After a certain point, the listener runs out of free streams. I, for one, wore out "Bogatyri." Eventually, the app wouldn't allow me to play the song any more until I bought it. And you know what? That's completely fair. The app asks the listener to "reach into your heart/wallet," and the prices they seek are more than reasonable. Ten Australian dollars later (about $7.65 American), I had my own copy of *Departure Songs*, which I sent directly to my iPod.

Eventually, I will also buy a physical copy of the album. This is another great feature of Bandcamp: not only can the listener get a physical copy of what he's been listening to, that purchase also comes with an automatic download. I will always favor CDs and LPs to MP3s, but it's nice to know I can play the new music at the gym or in the car whenever I like.

It is a cruel irony that the download generation is – at the time of this writing – devoid of its major platform for potential playback. Not long after I purchased my 160-gigabyte iPod, Apple announced they would no longer be manufacturing and selling them. This makes no sense to me. The compact disc, according to many industry moguls, is a dying platform. The LP is more boutique option than true means of musical distribution. The MP3 was the way of the new musical world. Why eliminate the primary means of listening to them? It boggles the mind.

Apparently, Apple was banking on the probability that most music fans aren't quite as obsessive as I am, and therefore would not require the larger platform players to store and play their music. Instead, Apple figured most people would be using their iPhones and iPads. Any additional storage could be handled by their MacBooks. Apple was right.

Less than a decade after purchasing my first iPod, the device seems quaint to the modern-day music fan. Once again, I am slow to evolve with the rest of the music-listening world. Forgive me if I want to keep my musical and communication platforms separate. (3) Something tells me that one day soon, I will be scouring places like eBay, on an endless quest to find a backup for my current iPod, should it meet some untimely demise. In the meantime, I am highly selective about where my current player goes, and very careful about the way I store it.

Since downloading appears to be the way of the future, I have also started plotting to replace my aging stereo equipment. I don't ever want to be caught in a position where I can't play my CDs and LPs. That's a fate worse than death. The days of being able to casually stroll into an electronics store to purchase home stereo equipment are also rapidly ending. Stereo gear only seems to be available at high end shops specializing in home theater. While I am all for creating an ideal, customized seven-channel sound system to house my movies and video games, I would much rather hear my music in good old-fashioned two-channel stereo. Chances are, I will have to make a few adjustments.

***

Even if I do locate the perfect musical output platforms, one question still remains: will there be anything worth playing? As I've said, modern "Alternative" radio is sounding less and less like my kind of music and more and more like my teenage daughter's. I suppose this makes sense, since she is much closer to the sought-after demographic age than I am. Aging fans like me are being relegated to the classic rock stations, or tossed into the Bin of Obscurity altogether, never to be seen or heard from again. But I won't go down without a fight!

Based on what I had been hearing, I was growing rather pessimistic about the future state of music. But Julie Slick did not share my doom and gloom outlook. Aside from her own musical efforts (which are quite remarkable), the young bassist pointed out a few other bands worthy of attention in the days ahead. We are both Radiohead fans (even though they are slowly becoming part of the old guard). She also pointed to the music of groups like Massive Attack, Animals as Leaders, Battles, and Bent Knee. Every group she mentioned has a distinct sound, rooted in different genres of music. And every group is rock solid.

I wondered what made her name those particular groups off the top of her head. "All of those bands are doing something which I find to be unique, rather than just recycling music from the past and creating another derivative project," she told me. "There are only so many permutations of note combinations, but these groups find a way to be original in a sea of 'blah,' creating excitement for the listener, rather than just background noise to be 'shuffled' on after hearing the hook."

To me, that speaks to the heart of album making. In my mind, that is becoming a lost art. Now that people are able to download songs one at a time, an artist may not put the time and effort into making eight to 10 high quality songs. The goal seems to be to make the most out of one song via endless radio airplay and concert performance. To me, only artists like Steven Wilson continue to strive to make the best possible work, from beginning to end, album after album. Not everyone agrees with my assessment, but I'm hard pressed to name the modern-day *Sgt. Pepper* or *Pet Sounds.*

* * *

The musical idols of my youth are not getting any younger. Adrian Belew is in his mid-60s, along with most of the rest of King Crimson. Jeff Beck, Herbie Hancock, Wayne Shorter, and Eric Clapton are even older. David Bowie became a virtual musical recluse before he passed away. B.B. King and Chris Squire (the influential bass player from Yes) passed away in 2015. David Gilmour's latest record, however well intended, pretty much put me to sleep. And this is the guy that played the guitar solo in Pink Floyd's "Comfortably Numb," a seminal moment in rock history! King Crimson's latest incarnation has yet to fully convince me it's the real deal. Rush recently completed what they say is their last major tour. Bill Bruford, my favorite drummer, has retired from recording and touring. Father Time remains undefeated.

I keep looking for that somebody new. I'm finding a few gems here and there. But while they are making marvelous "fringe" music, I don't see any of the new artists I enjoy having the major breakthrough that will keep their name on the tongues of music fans for years to come. But there may be one exception.

I have become enamored with the music of Steven Wilson over the past few years. I have often joked that he is my new Adrian Belew, since he seems to show up in musical projects all over the place. I first heard Wilson when he was fronting his progressive rock band, Porcupine Tree. I was captivated by his songwriting ability, and the playing chops displayed by Wilson and the rest of the band (particularly guitarist John Wesley and drummer Gavin Harrison). The band sounded like the offspring of King Crimson and Tool, mixed perfectly. It was heavy, open-ended, and melodic at the same time. It was very exciting music, indeed.

The first Porcupine Tree album I heard was called *Deadwing.* (4) Aside from the killer opening title track, the band also beguiled me with heavy riffing songs like "Open Car," a tender ballad called "Lazarus," and a prog epic called "Arriving Somewhere, But Not Here," which remains among my favorites songs of all time. I had definitely stumbled across something special in this band!

In true musical OCD fashion, I set out to hear everything created by this band. Turns out they had been around for close to a decade before I arrived to the party. Like Trent Reznor was

Nine Inch Nails in the studio, Wilson essentially was Porcupine Tree at the beginning. But as time went on, he brought more and more musicians into the fold to help shape his sound, to great effect. The album previous to *Deadwing*, called *In Absentia*, lays the groundwork nicely for the record I was taken with. *Fear of a Blank Planet*, which followed *Deadwing*, takes the concept album to the highest level. By the time the band recorded *The Incident*, they seemed to be at critical musical mass. Perhaps Wilson felt this, too, because he was already off on his next musical adventures.

In addition to participating in collaborative projects with others, like No-Man and Blackfield, Wilson had embarked on a remarkable solo career. His debut, *Insurgentes*, sounds like an extension of Porcupine Tree. That's not necessarily a bad thing. The songs are, without a doubt, solid. But Wilson starts to stretch with his second release, the two-disc *Grace for Drowning*. With this album, Wilson employs more musicians from outside Porcupine Tree, including King Crimson alums Tony Levin and Pat Mastelotto. In addition, Wilson was putting together a top-flight touring band, featuring keyboardist Adam Holzman (who played with Miles Davis), guitarist Niko Tsonev, bassist Nick Beggs, saxophonist Theo Travis, and drummer Marco Minneman. The band was taking quality studio tracks and kicking them up a notch once they hit the concert stage. They were a sight and sound to behold, as evidenced in the CD/DVD set, *Get All That You Deserve*.

Apart from Porcupine Tree, Wilson was able to express the other sides of his musical personality, which incorporated the sounds of pop and jazz into his arsenal. There was more than enough prog to keep PT fans happy, but it was clear Wilson was striving for something else. With his next solo record, he found it.

The Raven That Refused to Sing (and Other Tales) is hands-down my favorite album of 2013. It is as close to a perfect record as anything I have ever heard, on par with *Pet Sounds* and *Kind of Blue*. Regardless of the listener's angle of approach – be it compositional, instrumental, vocal, or production – it is impossible to find a flaw in this album. The opening track, a 12-minute opus called "Luminol," lays the groundwork for what is to come. And what comes is positively stunning. If I needed another reason to despise the Grammy awards (and I don't), it stems from the complete exclusion of *The Raven ...* from so much as a sniff at Album of the Year or Best Rock Album of 2014. (5)

I didn't think Wilson would be able to top himself. And while I may be subjectively correct in that assessment, I will say that his follow-up to *The Raven*, called *Hand. Cannot. Erase.* (released in '15) is every bit as ambitious, and every bit as remarkable. Wilson relied a bit more on his pop instincts for this album, scaling back on the jazz. The results are glorious, with Wilson creating a concept album around the story of a woman who died three years before, but her death passed by completely unnoticed. Not exactly a topic Taylor Swift would cover.

I'm sure this album will go ignored by Grammy voters as well. It's a good thing I don't rely on them to tell me what's good in music.

Wilson also has one of the sharpest ears in the music industry, based on the amazing remixes he has done on several classic albums by Yes, XTC, Jethro Tull, and King Crimson. His services as a re-mixer are being widely coveted throughout music, and with good reason. I thought I had heard everything there was to hear during my dozens of plays of King Crimson's *Larks Tongues in Aspic*. But Wilson proved me wrong; as his re-examination and new approach to the tracks led me to believe I was hearing an entirely new album! The comparison of his work to the original mix (which was pretty damned good) is night and day. Steven Wilson is a man with a gift, and he intends to make the most of it. He has no wife or children. Music is his life, and if he has anything to say about it, it will remain that way. Good for us, I say.

There have been rumors swirling about that Wilson is thinking of taking up the Porcupine Tree mantle once again, putting the band back into action in 2017 or '18. I've never been so torn about a musical possibility. As much as I appreciate PT, I'm just as eager to see and hear where Wilson will go next as a solo artist. I suppose it doesn't matter. If it has Steven Wilson's name on it, I'm buying it.

***

Steven Wilson aside, my outlook for the future of music (based on what is actually getting airplay) was pretty grim. There just doesn't seem to be a lot out there. Fortunately, apps like Bandcamp and Soundcloud are proving me wrong. There is a metric ton of new and exciting music out there, just waiting to be found. I just have to take the radio out of the equation.

I'm hoping radio consultants and programmers finally wake up and realize 1) exposing people to more music is never a bad thing; and 2) there is nothing wrong with letting a DJ be a DJ, as opposed to a CD programmer. I'm hoping quality musicians like Adrian Belew, Aimee Mann, Mike Keneally, Rob Fetters, and Deborah Holland are able to reap the rewards for their immense talents long before they are too old to appreciate and enjoy them.

I'm hoping people continue to flock to clubs to support bands on the rise, rather than waiting for them to appear at the latest corporate whore-atorium. I'm hoping record stores experience a renaissance, leading them to return to making music the top priority. I'm hoping people continue to get past the artificial ethnic borders put up long ago by people who no longer matter and keep enjoying whatever music they like. I'm hoping for a new generation of "Intelli-Pop" artists to blow the doors of the modern-day drivel disguising itself as quality music.

I'm hoping the next generations of guitar shop owners and employees continue to inspire potential musicians the way the guys at J Gravity Strings inspired me. I'm hoping musicians like Tory Z Starbuck continue to emerge, thumbing their noses at the conventional musical wisdom of the day. I'm hoping streaming services finally come to their senses and reward hard-working musicians with their fair share of the pie.

I'm hoping the need to play guitar in a band overwhelms me again, and I don't stop playing until the day I drop. I'm hoping more people than me have a musical Holy Trinity and have massive music collections to reflect their love for those artists, and others like them. I'm hoping the next wave of original musicians is waiting around the corner, poised to strike, and destined to blow the minds of anyone who sees fit to give them a listen. I'm hoping to be on the front line of that revival.

I can't wait for the next musical revolution. If all goes well, I won't be the only one hearing it.

(1)   I confess: I have bought more than a little of this merchandise. There are more than a few movie action figures adorning my den. And I'm sure there will be more.

(2)   Sadly, bookstores that stock these magazines are becoming a thing of the past. I subscribe to *Prog* and *Mojo* electronically these days and read it on my iPad.

(3) Full disclosure: my iPhone contains the Bandcamp, Soundcloud, and *Flux by Adrian Belew* apps. I rarely use them, but I want them there, should I find myself stuck somewhere with no other entertainment options.

(4) Ironically, I gave this band a shot because Adrian Belew made a pair of guest appearances on the album. Once I stopped focusing on Ade's playing alone, I was able to hear how awesome the band was, even without my hero playing with them.

(5) The winners that year? Daft Punk and Led Zeppeliin, respectively. Now I love Led Zeppelin, but can we be serious here? A Grammy for a live record containing no new material? Please.

THANK YOU, AND GOOD NIGHT!!!

Author Bio

Regardless of what he's doing, Cedric Hendrix is always listening. He doesn't want to miss the next great riff, chord change, or solo which could come from anywhere. For more than 45 years, music has been the one constant in his life. Hendrix resides in St. Louis, Missouri, but is rapidly becoming an unofficial resident of Chicago, Memphis, and Nashville where he loves to attend concerts in intimate venues and visit record stores. During rare non-musical moments, Hendrix can be found at the movies, on the golf course, or watching his beloved St. Louis Cardinals play baseball.

Made in the USA
Lexington, KY
23 June 2018